# VOICE & VOTE

## CELEBRATING 100 YEARS OF VOTES FOR WOMEN

Edited by Mari Takayanagi,
Melanie Unwin and Paul Seaward

VOTE100

Printed in England by Gavin Martin Colournet Limited
on 150gsm Essential Silk. This paper has been independently
certified according to the standards of the Forest Stewardship
Council® (FSC)®.

A catalogue record if this publication is available
from the British Library.

ISBN: 978-1-906670-56-6

*Front cover and page 4*
Nancy Astor, Viscountess Astor (1879–1964), campaigning
during the 1919 by-election at Plymouth Sutton.
© Universal History Archive/UIG via Getty Images

# INTRODUCTION

The Representation of the People Act 1918 marked a crucial milestone in the struggle of women in the UK for the right to vote. The Act finally enabled a majority of women over 30 years old to vote in parliamentary elections. It had been more than half a century since the first attempt to get Parliament to change the law, over 50 years of brave, inventive and determined campaigning by both women and men at all social levels, through many setbacks and despite sometimes intense divisions over strategy and tactics. In the same year the Parliament (Qualification of Women) Act was also passed, ensuring that women were not only able to vote for Members of Parliament, but to become Members themselves.

This book, which accompanies a major exhibition in Westminster Hall to mark the 2018 suffrage and parliamentary equalities anniversaries, tells the story of women's involvement in politics and in Parliament, and of their struggle for equal representation. It deals with the often forgotten part women played in politics before the middle of the nineteenth century, and the pioneers of women's suffrage; with the long campaign for the vote, and with the experience and achievements of female parliamentarians since winning it.

The book, like the exhibition, is arranged around the spaces with which women were associated within Parliament: the Ventilator, in the attic above the House of Commons chamber before 1834, from where women, out of sight and out of mind, watched and analysed the proceedings; the 'Cage', the nickname for the Ladies' Gallery, where women spectators were isolated safely hidden behind grilles in the new chamber after 1850; the 'Tomb', the small 'Lady Members' Room' prepared for the convenience of the women Members who arrived in the years after 1918; and the Chamber, marking the final arrival of women in the late twentieth century in the very highest offices of state, and presiding over proceedings in the Speaker's Chair in the House of Commons, and the Woolsack in the House of Lords.

The two 1918 Acts were not the culmination of women's struggle, for it would be another ten years before women's voting rights were made equal to men's; it took four decades before women were able to become members of the House of Lords; and, although in the last twenty years many more women have been elected to the Commons, they still make up only a third of the House. Much more remains to be done, but this book records and celebrates what has been done: the huge achievement both of those who worked to achieve the representation of women, and of the women who have worked to represent the rights and interests of others.

# CONTENTS

**CHAPTER ONE**
**THE VENTILATOR: BEFORE 1834**                           8
The galleries and the ventilator                          10
Women and elections                                       13
Campaigning women                                         21
Women in politics                                         26
Women working in Parliament                               31

**CHAPTER TWO**
**MAKING THE CAGE, 1834–97**                              34
Women in early Victorian public life                      36
Working-class women and protest                           45
The campaign for women's suffrage, 1866–97                47
Women in local government and campaigning                 49
The matchwomen and the Bow strike, 1888                   52
Tensions and splits                                       54

**CHAPTER THREE**
**ESCAPING THE CAGE, 1897–1918**                          56
The suffragists: the NUWSS                                58
The suffragettes: the WSPU                                61
The Liberal government and
    the suffragettes, 1906–11                             62
Conciliation: 1910–13                                     69
Cat and Mouse and the Great Pilgrimage                    70
A "sex war"?                                              72
The First World War                                       74
The Representation of the People Act                      76

**CHAPTER FOUR**
**THE TOMB, 1918–63**                                     80
The first female MPs                                      82
The 1930s                                                 86
The impact of the war                                     90
The 1945 election and after                               95
Women in the House of Lords                               98

**CHAPTER FIVE**
**THE CHAMBER: 1963 AND AFTER**                           104
Selection committees, quotas and
    winnable seats, 1963–2015                             106
Women and the culture of Parliament                       109
Women at the top                                          113
Challenging Westminster culture
    from the 1990s                                        117
Women in the House of Lords
    from 1963 to the present                              121

**CHAPTER SIX**
**BNY MELLON**                                            126
Original thinkers                                         128
Exceptional people                                        132
Investing in the future                                   136

**CHAPTER SEVEN**
**CULTURE AND MEDIA**                                     140
Department for Digital, Culture, Media & Sport            142
Pinch Point Communications                                145
The British Fashion Council                               146
WPP                                                       147
City Football Group                                       148
brookscomm                                                149
All3Media                                                 150
Oystercatchers                                            152
Propellernet                                              153
The Institute of Practitioners in Advertising            154
Arts Council of Wales                                     155
Image Source                                              156
Zaboura Communications                                    157

**CHAPTER EIGHT**
**SOCIETY**                                               158
Home Office                                               160

Ministry of Defence 162
Ministry of Justice 164
Government Equalities Office 166
Ministry of Housing, Communities
    and Local Government 168
Department for Transport 170
Foreign and Commonwealth Office 172
Switchboard 175
Royal Navy 176
CMS 180
The Nutrition Society 182
Karma Nirvana 184
Francis House Family Trust 185
Hodge Jones & Allen 186
Cambridgeshire Constabulary 188
The Inner City Trust 189
Essex Police 190
Zoological Society of London 191
Kent Police 192
Durham Constabulary 194
Duchenne UK 195
Sussex Police 196
The Royal Association for Deaf people 198
Devon and Cornwall Police 199
Strength With In Me (SWIM) Foundation 200
Stirling Council 201
British Sociological Association 202
The GEO Group 203
ELM group 204
Police Service of Northern Ireland 205
Anglican Mainstream 206
Laurence Simons 207

Swansea University 214
Thornton College 216
Tormead School 217
Mount House School 218
The University of Sunderland 220
Merton Court Preparatory School 221
Royal Veterinary College 222
Devonport High School for Girls 224
King's High Warwick 225
York St John University 226
Altrincham Grammar School for Girls 228
The Centre of Excellence 229
University of Central Lancashire 230
London College of Fashion 232
NASUWT 233
The University of York's Department
    of Chemistry 234
West Thames College 236
St James Senior Girls' School 237
University of Exeter 238
Pearson 239
TeachBeyond 240
VTCT 241

**CHAPTER NINE**
# EDUCATION

EDUCATION 208
Department for Education 210
The Brier School 213

**CHAPTER TEN**
# BANKING AND FINANCE

BANKING AND FINANCE 242
HM Treasury 244
Queen's Award For Enterprise 246
Women in Banking and Finance 249
Schroders 250
KPMG 252
Prudential plc 254
Goldman Sachs 256
Invesco Perpetual 258
M&G Investments 260
TSB 262
Thomson Reuters 264

MV Credit 266
Kite Lake Capital Management 267
Western Union 268
PIMFA 270
Hannay Investments 271
Addidi 272
Development Partners International 274
Allied Irish Bank 275

———————

**CHAPTER ELEVEN**
## HEALTH 276
Department of Health and Social Care 278
Children's Heart Surgery Fund 280
Rethink Mental Illness 281
RB (Reckitt Benckiser) 282
Home Instead Senior Care 284
NHS Slough Clinical Commissioning Group 286
Bradford District Care NHS Foundation Trust 288
Bury Hospice 289
NHS Eastern Cheshire Clinical
   Commissioning Group 290
Richmond Fellowship 292
St Margaret of Scotland Hospice 293
PJ Care 294
Camden & Islington NHS Foundation Trust 295

———————

**CHAPTER TWELVE**
## INDUSTRY AND COMMERCE 296
Department for Business, Energy
   and Industrial Strategy 298
William Hill 300
Cisco 302
Yoox Net-a-Porter Group 305
Royal Mail 304
Korn Ferry 308
Which? 310

Archco Developments 312
Lookers 314
Brightstar 316
Wates 318
Arm 320
Opus Energy 322
JK7 324
CGI 326
Ford 328
Procorre 330
Estelon 332
Carl Zeiss Vision UK 334
Kohinoor 336
ThoughtWorks 338
Elurra Gold 339
Crest Nicholson 340
UBM plc 342
Aster Group 343
Tesco 344
glh Hotels 346
Qudini 347
Cox Automotive 348
Ruby Cup 350
Ofgem 351
Edina 352
Worldwide Fruit 353
E.ON UK 354
Panalpina 355
NTT Data 356

———————

**APPENDICES**
Illustrations 357
Acknowledgements 359
Contributors 360
Credits 361
About the publisher 362
Index 364

June 185... &... -Sketch of

# THE VENTILATOR: BEFORE 1834

Before the later 19th century, women – unless they were monarchs – were excluded from virtually all formal positions of political power. However, this did not mean that they had no political views or played no part in public campaigns. Women were highly visible throughout political life – in elections, in campaigns, in the salons that operated in the background of politics, and as the staff who made parliament work. At times in the 18th century their presence in the chambers themselves was very conspicuous, as visitors in the galleries of both Houses. But after 1778, women were largely barred from the gallery in the Commons.

*Elaine Chalus*
*Amy Galvin-Elliott*
*Elizabeth Hallam Smith*
*Sarah Richardson*
*Anne Stott*

*Previous pages*
Sketch of Ventilator,
House of Commons, by
Frances Rickman, 1834.
The artist, a frequent
visitor to the Ventilator,
captures the architecture
of the space as well as
figures of women listening
to the debates below in
the Commons chamber

*Above*
"Roof of St Stephens,
Listening to the Debates
thro' the Ventilator", by
unknown artist, 1833

### THE GALLERIES AND THE VENTILATOR

Instead, they had to watch proceedings from the obscurity, and heat, of the attic above the chamber, looking down at the Members' feet and the tops of their heads through a strange contraption designed to let out air, the ventilator. The move resulted from the efforts of several Members to exclude the public from the House in order to prevent the newspapers from reporting Parliament's proceedings, and came after an incident in which the Speaker had attempted to clear the gallery, but female observers had resisted. *The Times* described the resulting fracas as "a state of most extraordinary ferment and commotion" as "officers found their duty of turning out the fair intruders no easy work; a violent and determined resistance was offered to them." Afterwards men were able to return to the galleries, but women were not, as "the good sense of the country was opposed to making the ladies of England into political partisans." Unable to view the debates in the conventional way, women discovered the space of the ventilator.

The 18th century House of Commons chamber was the medieval St Stephen's Chapel, part of the old Palace of Westminster. In the 17th century a false ceiling had been built, to cover the high vault. A chandelier hung from the ceiling, and above it a ventilation shaft was built to take heat and fetid air from the chamber. It also provided a view of the feet and the tops of the heads of the leading politicians below. Conditions were less than ideal: there was only enough space for a small number of people (one source says 14), and it was hot and uncomfortable. Nevertheless, the ventilator became a popular space for women to engage with politics. Not much is known about how it was used. The little evidence we have – from private letters – suggests that the spectators present were largely middle and upper class, though maids and attendants were also there, and others may have been present. As it was not an officially recognised parliamentary space, there is an absence of official records as to who was present. Presumably it was used until the fire of 1834 destroyed the original House of Commons chamber.

The Lords had been even more reluctant than had the Commons to allow visitors into its chamber, though as with the Commons, the presence of non-Members was often connived at. The peers decided to build a gallery (for the use of its Members) in 1704, but removed it in 1711. After another quarter of a century they decided to reinstate it; but in 1739 an incident foreshadowing that in the Commons nearly 40 years later may have encouraged them to take it down again. An attempt to keep spectators out of the gallery met spirited resistance from a group of highly-placed women including the Duchess of Queensberry. The House

*Right*
The Ventilator,
House of Commons,
by Lady Georgiana
Chatterton, 1821

*Below*
View of the Interior of the
House of Commons during
the Sessions 1821–23, by
James Scott, 1836. Above
the chandelier is the grille
that covered the Ventilator

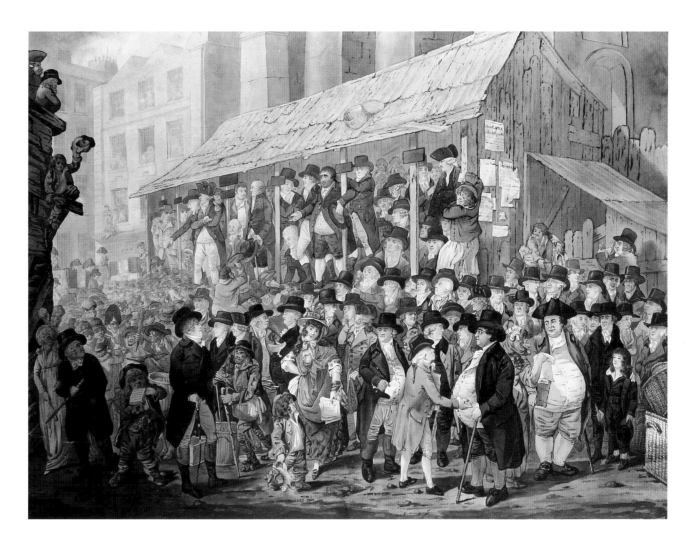

*Above*

The Westminster Election, 1796, by Robert Dighton. Women of all classes are present in the crowd

only brought galleries back when it had moved to a larger chamber, and when it needed additional space for the "trial" of Queen Caroline in 1820. At first this was a temporary structure; only in 1831 did it finally decide to create a proper gallery, when a small part of the gallery was made available for women – ironically only a few years before the chamber was destroyed in the fire of 1834.

### WOMEN AND ELECTIONS

While women were not directly involved in the debates in Parliament they were, therefore, very much a presence at Westminster. And similarly, while women may not have been able to vote, they were far from absent from electoral politics. An election campaign in pre-reform Britain was a celebratory, ritual and often disorderly occasion in which voters and non-voters – men, women and children – were involved. They carried banners, marched in processions, lined the streets and gathered in the windows, expressing their allegiance to one or other candidate physically, visually and vocally. The presence and approval of that "more delightful portion of the creation" was frequently commented upon by contemporary reporters. But it would be vastly underplaying women's electoral involvement if we assumed that it stopped – at any

level of society – at providing incidental colour or political window dressing.

Women in the late 17th and 18th centuries participated in election processions and treats; they sewed banners and made cockades; they served copious amounts of bread, cheese, beer and cider to voters and non-voters alike (some of which was likely to have been produced by women); and they capitalised on the influx of business that the election brought to their taverns and lodging-houses. Voters' wives were also often more directly involved, especially during contested elections. They were frequently canvassed by candidates and their agents, as they were presumed to have – and often did have – influence over their husbands' votes. Coaxed, cajoled and oft-times kissed, they might also be offered small amounts of cash or douceurs. Offers of drink, dresses (possibly in the candidate's colours) and the payment of debts were not uncommon; neither were hints of (or threats to) future patronage. While some women were flattered, persuaded or cowed into agreement, others took open pleasure in resisting all blandishments, proudly proclaiming their personal or familial political independence. Lady Susan Keck, canvassing on behalf of one of the candidates in the 1754 Oxfordshire election, grumbled at being obstructed by just such a "Viper", who "told me she

CANVASSING for VOTES. Plate II.

To His Excellency Sr. Charles Hanbury Williams Embassador to the Court of RUSSIA. This Plate is most humbly Inscribed By his most Obedient humble Servant Will. Hogarth.

*Above*

"Canvassing for votes: Plate II (Four Prints of an Election)", by William Hogarth, 1757. One of four prints produced by Hogarth as a criticism of election corruption. The presence of women suggests they were active players in the process

always was of the high party", whereas Lord Townshend, canvassing in Tamworth in 1765, noted several such wives ruefully in his notebook: "Wife governs, against us"; and then again, "wished us well, but his wife governed". The most formidable of voters' wives might even use the election to settle old personal scores with the local men who canvassed, or pointedly make formal complaints of bribery and corruption against canvassers whom they felt had been disrespectful.

Local women could also be part of the country's formal election machinery. Women, especially older women, can be found serving as witnesses during the process of the election, drawing upon their personal knowledge of people and places to challenge or confirm individuals' rights to vote. Sometimes they accompanied "tallies" – groups of voters – to the hustings to oversee the process of voting. When the result of an election was disputed, and the case was argued out in Parliament, women who often are otherwise completely missing from the historical record – female servants, tavern-keepers, laundresses, chimney sweeps' wives, and the like – joined local men, at candidates' expense, to testify. Ironically, the depositions of these women, who did not vote themselves, served to shape parliamentary decisions and determine election outcomes.

For the women of the political elite, participation in electoral politics varied according to personal circumstances, individual character and commitment, but was generally an extension of the family's larger

involvement in the local community. Politics was a family business and some degree of women's involvement was largely accepted and even expected by contemporaries. It could even be demanded by male family members. Their activities became problematic only when they appeared to cross class boundaries, particularly between elite women and working men (such as when the duchess of Devonshire was alleged to have kissed a butcher during the 1784 Westminster election), or when the women proved to be such charismatic political figures or successful canvassers that they emerged as political figures in their own right and implicitly challenged the established gender order, as Lady Susan Keck did in the Oxfordshire election of 1754.

Whether men or women, 18th-century electoral politics was not for the faint-hearted. The most successful female campaigners needed to be thick-skinned and self-confident, able to shrug off sexual slander and crass satire. Lady Susan Keck (a daughter of the duke of Hamilton and a former lady of the bedchamber to George II's daughters) was ideally suited to the fray: she combined quick wit, a forthright tongue, a ready pen and a well-developed sense of the absurd with hard-headed political pragmatism. Despite declining health, she relished the challenge of the election and was so actively involved in treating, organising and canvassing in support of the ultimately victorious side in the Oxfordshire election of 1754 that she became the target of many execrable ballads and satires. Criticised by the opposition's hacks for

*Below*

"Wit's last stake or The Cobling Voters and Abject Canvassers", by Thomas Rowlandson, 1784. Georgiana Cavendish, Duchess of Devonshire, is shown canvassing with Charles Fox in the 1784 election, ostensibly paying the cobbler's wife for her shoe repair, but suggesting bribery, as well as indicating the cobbler's wife may have influence over her husband's vote

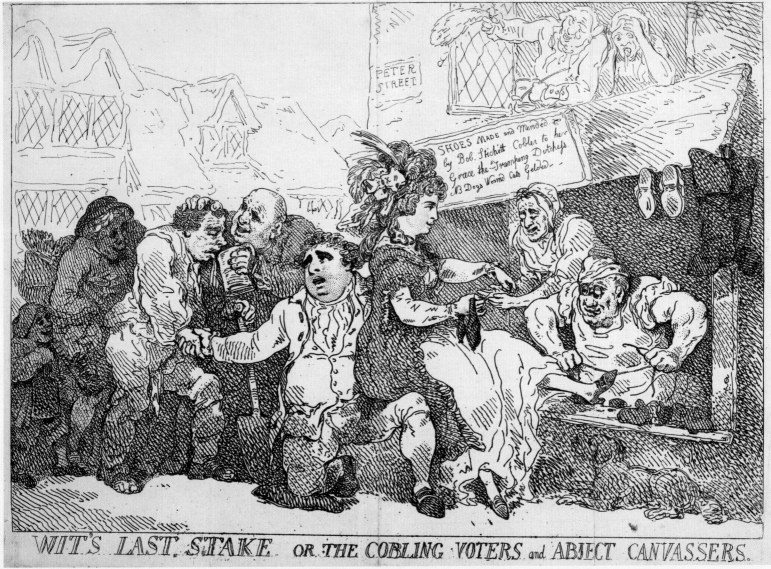

WIT'S LAST STAKE OR THE COBLING VOTERS and ABJECT CANVASSERS.

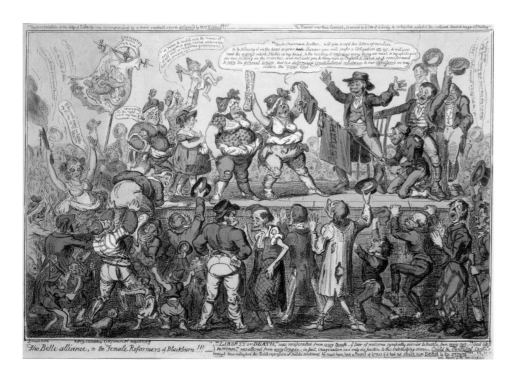

The Belle-alliance, or the Female Reformers of Blackburn!!!

her looks, her hair, and her age, the gusto with which she embraced canvassing led her to be accused of unsexing herself – of becoming "my Lord Lady Sue". Adeptly, and with humour, she and the hacks on her own side neatly turned the argument on its head, undermining the masculinity of the opposition by pointing out that Lady Susan, while a woman, was the best "man" for the job. Her primary goal in the election was to energise the electors and to get out the vote – and she did both successfully.

What neither Lady Susan nor other 18th-century women did, however, was vote. While there are a couple of known cases of women voting in parliamentary elections in the 17th century, and a ruling in the courts in 1739 confirmed that women could vote for and hold minor parish offices, there is no evidence that women voted in parliamentary elections in the 18th century. That said, variations in the franchise and in customary practice meant that there were always some women who had recognised electoral privileges. Women had, in theory anyway, a legitimate interest in elections in around two thirds of all boroughs before the Great Reform Act of 1832. In some towns where the right to vote lay in the freemen, widows or daughters of freemen frequently had the right to make their husbands into voters. In others, the franchise was linked to the ownership of specific properties (burgages), and women who were the owners of burgages were at least technically entitled to vote until 1832. In Horsham in Sussex, for example, more than a fifth of the burgages were held by women in 1764. By custom their husbands would exercise the right to vote on their behalf; single and widowed women holding burgages would appoint proxies to exercise their votes. Many of these were undoubtedly male relatives, but the avidity with which these women were canvassed during hotly contested

elections (and burgage boroughs often saw repeated contests), and the amounts of money that women might be offered for their proxies or their property, shows their electoral importance.

Many elite families used the ownership of burgages to establish or secure their political control over, or at least some influence, or "interest", in the constituency. Lady Andover included her burgages and control over one seat at Castle Rising in her daughter's dowry. Lady Irwin, who inherited control over both seats at Horsham on her husband's death, fought repeated elections against the duke of Norfolk between 1778 and 1807. She managed to retain control of the borough and bequeath it and her political interest to her daughter. Other elite women managed burgage boroughs for absent husbands or underage sons. Even Sir James Lowther, a notorious "boroughmonger" – someone who collected boroughs for their own aggrandisement – owed a debt to his widowed mother Katherine, who purchased twenty-seven burgages in Appleby between 1751 and 1754, while he was still a minor, in order to ensure that the family retained control of one of the two seats. She similarly battled with Lord Egremont to buy up burgages in the borough of Cockermouth in 1756.

The importance of politically active widows controlling family interests should not be underestimated. Aristocratic families often experienced periods when the head of the family inherited when not old enough to take control of his own financial and political interests. It was common for the wife of the deceased to take over their management. The women who did so operated in much the same way as their male counterparts. They worked together with stewards and committees to plan strategy and canvassing, used tenancies to their electoral advantage and directed votes. They held "treats" for

*Above*

Elizabeth Coke of
Derbyshire (1676–1739),
by Mary Beale, c.1690.
Coke was political agent
for her brother Thomas in
Grampound, Derbyshire,
in 1710

freeholders, flattered local gentry with entertainments
and public days and canvassed their peers in person
and by letter. They drew upon their female as well as
their male networks to achieve results.

There was always therefore a small group of
women who managed or controlled seats in Parliament
and whose political influence was recognised in the
locality and by the politicians managing elections in
London. The Dowager Lady Orford's control of both
seats at Callington and one seat at Ashburton was noted
in the 1750s and 1760s, as was Harriot Pitt's control of
one seat at Pontefract between 1756 and her death in
1763. There were other women, such as Lady Downing
who battled unsuccessfully for control of Dunwich in
Suffolk between 1764 and her death in 1778, who were
known political figures at the time but are less well
remembered now. The same is true of the many women
and men who possessed sufficient estates to give them
some local political significance, even if it did not go so
far as control of a whole borough.

Records of election campaigns underline how
for the elite at the time politics was a family affair.
Sisters, mothers, wives and widows might step in as
family representatives to cover for absent, ineffective
or underage men, or work in conjunction with male
family members to run election committees, organise
canvassers and direct campaigns. Elizabeth Coke,
seemingly out of frustration, took over her absent
brother's ill-organised campaign for Derbyshire in 1710.
She led the committee, planned strategy, oversaw
canvassing, tracked votes and used her social skills to
try and win over neighbours who had been annoyed
by her brother's politics, and wrote to chide him on his
non-appearance in the borough. After the election, she
stepped back seamlessly into her family role. Georgiana,
Countess Spencer, similarly managed elections at
St Albans for decades for her husband and son, while
they were preoccupied with campaigns in other family
boroughs. Despite being a political woman to her
fingertips, she exemplified the tensions some women
felt in electioneering. While she often grumbled about
politics, she embraced campaigning and clearly enjoyed
planning strategy and directing canvassing with her
committee. She remained very concerned, however,
about protecting her reputation and preserving her
physical and social distance from the electorate itself.
When canvassing in Northampton in 1774 along with
the candidate's wife, she spoke to voters from the safe
refuge of her carriage, putting "a little spirit into our
people" – which was the reason that her husband
had advised her to go – while also ensuring that they
did not threaten the social divide or their reputations.
Her daughters, Georgiana, Duchess of Devonshire,
and Henrietta, Countess of Bessborough, took a very
different tack ten years later in the vituperative 1784
Westminster election. As the most high-profile and
arguably most successful of at least 25 women who

# "I have been in the midst of action – I have seen parties rise and fall"

Georgiana, Duchess of Devonshire

*Left*
Georgiana, Duchess of Devonshire (1757–1806) by Francesco Bartolozzi, after Lady Diana Beauclerk (née Spencer), 1779. As an elite woman, Georgiana Duchess of Devonshire had the opportunity to see politics from the inside

*Left*
Hannah More (1745–1833),
writer and philanthropist,
by Henry William
Pickersgill, 1822

traditions and expectations, and specific election circumstances. The biggest changes after the Reform Act of 1832 would come for the women of the middle classes. It is they who would begin to attend political meetings; they who would sign anti-Corn Law petitions in the tens of thousands; and they whose teas and bazaars would defray the costs of voter registration and election expenses.

## CAMPAIGNING WOMEN

Women's direct involvement in campaigning politics of this kind was not new in the early 19th century. Women were often at the forefront of protests in the 17th and 18th centuries, especially food riots, such as the raid near Oxford in 1766 during which sacks of flour were seized from a mill and distributed free. A common and established – almost ritual – form of protest, the food riot went beyond mere criminality. Women's prominence in them is easy to understand: they were the ones who suffered most if prices rose or grain was hoarded, and the legal position of married women could mean that it was their husbands, not they, who were held responsible for their actions.

From the Civil War of the mid-17th century we can see women participating more directly in the political arena. In February 1642, in the tense lead-up to the war, a group of women petitioning Parliament made the bold claim that because they were "sharers in the common calamities that accompany both church and commonwealth", they too had a role in public life. In August 1643, a year into the war, women launched their great peace petition. Hundreds wearing white silk ribbons in their hats massed outside the doors of Parliament calling for peace and the return of the King to London. They blockaded the House of Lords, and when soldiers turned up to disperse them, they tore their colours out of their hats. After two noisy hours, they were finally dispersed by a troop of horses.

The collapse of many of the institutions of the government and the church during the Civil War gave women new means of expression. Many were active in the separatist Protestant congregations that thrived as the authority of the established church fell away.

canvassed in this election, they became notorious for canvassing tradesmen on foot. The duchess was attacked in the press for exchanging kisses for votes in an attempt to drive them from the campaign with a barrage of sexual slurs. It almost worked.

Women did not retreat quietly into the confines of the domestic sphere as a result of either the nastiness of the 1784 election or concerns about gender and politics that were encouraged by the French Revolution. The Reform Act of 1832 made women's exclusion from elections explicit by defining voters as "male persons", and women lost their only remaining electoral privileges with municipal corporation reform in 1835. But they did not lose their personal influence or their involvement in local elections. Moreover, they were not immune to Radical politics and would come to play an increasingly visible part in the campaigning movements from the 1790s onwards. At the top of society, elite women's electoral involvement remained largely unchanged. It continued to be based upon factors including character, ability and experience, strength of political beliefs, family

*Opposite*
Mary Wollstonecraft
(1759–1797), author
of the *Vindication of the
Rights of Woman*, by John
Williamson, 1791

Some of them even preached in public, though this was widely condemned. The loosening of press censorship during the war meant that women found it possible to write and publish about controversial religious matters. One woman, Katherine Chidley, moved from religious polemics to political activism. During the 1620s she and her husband had been members of an illegal separatist congregation, or conventicle. Shortly after the Long Parliament met in November 1640, beginning the political crisis that would lead to Civil War, she published *The Justification of the Independent Churches of Christ*, a defence of congregational church government and wifely autonomy, in opposition to a book written by Thomas Edwards, a fierce opponent of the separatist congregations. In further pamphlets, she argued that the defence of separatism was "a task most befitting a woman", appealed for the release of imprisoned separatists and offered to debate with her opponents on church doctrine. In 1647, she and her son founded a separatist church in Bury St Edmunds.

Chidley's religious campaigning took her into politics, and the radical Leveller movement. She became prominent among female Levellers in London, and in April 1649, with hundreds of other Leveller women, she besieged Parliament demanding the release of their imprisoned leaders. When one of them, John Lilburne, was again on trial in 1653, she organised a petition to Parliament with, it was claimed, 6,000 signatures. When they delivered it, two MPs came out to tell them that "they being women and many of them wives... the Law took no notice of them". The women replied that they were not all wives and that those who were had husbands to protect them and to defend the liberties of the people. Nothing more is known about Chidley, who may have died shortly afterwards.

Chidley's turbulent career was made possible by the revolutionary times in which she lived. The reassertion of political and religious authority in the 1650s and afterwards again restricted the opportunities for women to involve themselves so directly in political campaigning. But the French Revolution a century and a half later, and the widespread enthusiasm for the religious and political freedom it engendered, encouraged more women to seek to make a contribution. The plea for liberty for religious dissenters was taken up at the end of the 18th century by the poet and educationalist, Anna Letitia Barbauld. In *An Address to the Opposers of the Repeal of the Corporation and Test Acts*, written in 1790, she attacked the Church of England and claimed full civil and political rights for religious dissenters, who were barred from holding civil office. The tract was written during the early phase of the French Revolution, in the wake of the fall of the Bastille and the Declaration of the Rights of Man, and she believed she was witnessing the dawning of a new and better age, a time of equality, rationality, and peace. This millenarian optimism was echoed later in the year in Mary Wollstonecraft's *Vindication of the Rights of Men*, a spirited riposte to Edmund Burke's deeply conservative *Reflections on the Revolution in France*. Like Barbauld she saw the Revolution as "a glorious chance... now given to human nature of attaining... happiness and virtue".

In 1792 Wollstonecraft took female campaigning to a new level when she produced her most famous work, *A Vindication of the Rights of Woman*. This was a hugely ambitious call for a radical restructuring of the relationship of the sexes, nothing less than "a revolution in female manners" so that women could "labour by reforming themselves to reform the world". Her "wild wish" was "to see the distinction of sex confounded in

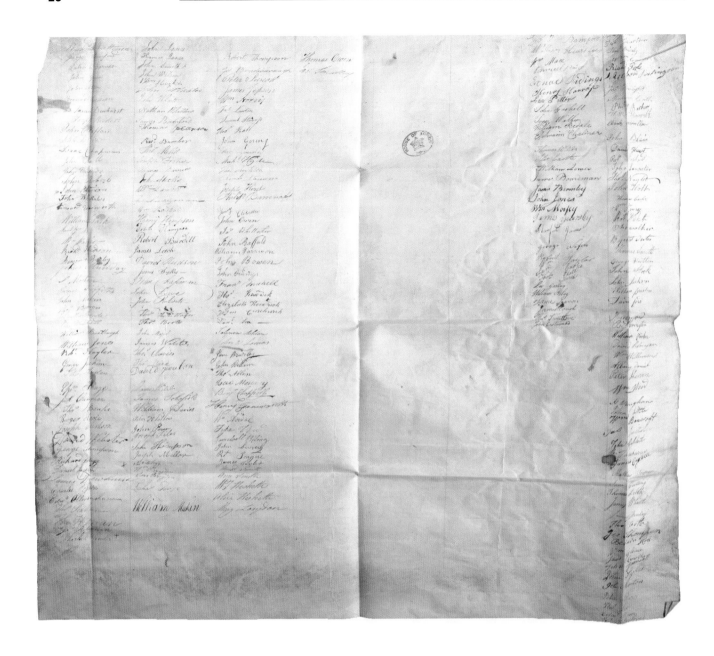

*Opposite and above*
Petition from the
inhabitants of Manchester
in support of the Foreign
Slave Trade Abolition Bill,
1806. This anti-slave
trade petition is more than
5 metres long and includes
more than 2,000 names,
including some women

society", as "it is vain to expect virtue [she meant
intellectual and moral qualities] from women till they
are, in some degree, independent of men". Though she
made a plea for women to have "a direct share... in the
deliberations of government", this was not the main
thrust of her argument. Instead she focused on the
skills they might acquire and the professions that should
be open to them if society were more rationally
organised. Women might "study the art of healing
and be physicians as well as nurses". They could study
politics through wide reading. "Businesses of various
kinds they might likewise pursue." Through hard work
and independence women could become worthy
of a public role. Despising the empty courtesies
and flatteries offered them by men, they should rise
"with the calm dignity of reason above opinion" and
dare "to be proud of the privileges inherent in man".
These novel arguments met with a predictable
backlash. Horace Walpole spoke for many when
he called Wollstonecraft "a hyena in petticoats".

Barbauld and Wollstonecraft were not the only
campaigning women in the troubled 1790s. Anti-
revolutionary women also entered the political debate.
Hannah More's *Village Politics*, completed at the end
of 1792, was a skilful distillation of Burke's counter-
revolutionary arguments for a popular readership.
The plight of the French émigrés, the refugees from
the revolution, opened up another avenue for female
campaigning. In 1793 a Ladies' Society was set up to
raise subscriptions for the émigré clergy and Hannah
More and the novelist Fanny Burney, who had married
an émigré, published fund-raising pamphlets.
Short-lived though it was, the campaign introduced
many women to the previously masculine tasks of
fund-raising and committee work.

Above all it was the cause of anti-slavery that
drew women into campaigns. In 1787 the all-male
Committee for the Abolition of the Slave Trade had
been set up, and the following year saw a flood of
abolitionist literature, much of it written by women,

to coincide with the opening of the parliamentary debate. The campaign's most famous member, William Wilberforce, was drawn into it partly through his friend, the Prime Minister, William Pitt, but also through Margaret Middleton, the wife of the MP and naval officer Sir Charles Middleton, whose home at Teston, Kent, became a centre for the abolitionist cause. Lady Middleton's friend, Hannah More, contributed a poem, "Slavery", to the cause, while the radical Helen Maria Williams argued for abolition in her *Letters on the French Revolution*. In 1791 Barbauld published her poem, "A Letter to William Wilberforce". If writing was one campaigning method open to women, the consumer boycott was another, and was particularly suited to their roles as purchasers and homemakers. From 1792 some women were refusing to buy West Indian sugar, and when sugar from the East Indies later became available they bought that instead. The abolitionist campaign crossed religious and political barriers, bringing together Anglicans and Dissenters, radical and conservative women. Many women joined in the petitioning campaign against the slave trade: several women, for example, can be identified among the more than 2,000 people from Manchester who signed a petition against the trade presented to the House of Lords in 1806.

After a campaign lasting 20 years, the slave trade was abolished in 1807 and, for a while, the abolitionists believed that slavery itself would die a natural death. When this hope proved illusory the Anti-Slavery Society was set up in 1823. Cautious emancipators like Wilberforce soon found themselves outflanked by radical women campaigners. In 1825 the first Ladies' Anti-Slavery Society was set up at the home of Lucy Townsend, the wife of a Birmingham clergyman. A network of other ladies' anti-slavery societies followed, which set up nationwide committees, collected subscriptions from women, and arranged quarterly meetings. One of the most innovative and persistent of the campaigners was the Quaker Elizabeth Heyrick,

leader of the Leicester Ladies' Anti-Slavery Society. She had already taken on the male establishment in 1824 when she published anonymously her pamphlet, *Immediate, not Gradual Abolition*, an argument she developed in two succeeding pamphlets. She was the first white British campaigner to voice the argument that black slaves were already making – that they were not prepared to wait for gradual emancipation or the slow amelioration of their condition. Her call was taken up by other ladies' societies until in 1831 her stance was finally adopted by the national Anti-Slavery Society. A woman campaigner, backed by a network of thousands of other women throughout the country, had brought about a major change in policy.

Contributions to the growing readership of newspapers, magazines and cheap pamphlets and books was an obvious means by which women, denied the opportunity for office, could intervene in public debate. In this way Harriet Martineau – historian, journalist, and social commentator – became one of the most noted intellectuals of the 19th century. Her fame, and particular attitude to the existence of God, caused a contemporary to quip, "There is no god, and Harriet Martineau is his prophet." Born in 1802 into a family of Unitarian manufacturers in Norwich, Martineau was forced by the failure of her father's business to earn her own living. Her breakthrough came in 1831 when she began work on *Illustrations of Political Economy*, a series of stories published monthly from February 1832, written to explain the principles of the free-market capitalism espoused by Thomas Malthus and James Mill. The tales gave her an entrée into London intellectual circles, where the ear trumpet she carried with her to counter her deafness made her an instantly recognisable figure. Between 1852 and 1866 Martineau contributed more than 1600 articles and leaders to the liberal *Daily News*. She espoused three causes in particular: anti-slavery, feminism, and the positivist movement in philosophy. The common thread running through them all was

*Opposite*
Harriet Martineau
(1802–1876), writer and
journalist, by Richard Evans,
exhibited 1834

# "Women, like men, can obtain whatever they show themselves fit for"

Harriet Martineau

her belief in self-improvement. On her tour of the United States between 1834 and 1836 and in her *Society in America*, published in 1837, she expressed her "horror and loathing" of slavery, but also argued that true emancipation must come from the slaves themselves. The true heroes of anti-slavery, she believed, were the runaway slaves rather than the white abolitionists. The same principle applied to women. She believed that they must work for their emancipation: they should earn the franchise by becoming intelligent and responsible citizens – a position very close to Wollstonecraft's.

Martineau's actions and writings were dominated by her twin passions for justice and self-improvement, and much the same could be said of other women campaigners between the 17th and 19th centuries. Though most would not have thought of themselves as feminists, they made bold claims for women. Denied the right to vote or to sit in Parliament, they refused to stay silent. Through their polemical writings, consumer campaigns, fund-raising, and committee-work, they asserted their rights to be citizens and sharers in the public realm along with men.

## WOMEN IN POLITICS

Women were often subjects of political debate – as well as being subject to the laws of the land generally, Parliament regularly legislated on matters relating to women. They were frequently petitioners, both as part of a group and often as individuals. They could be called in to give evidence to either House, particularly when they were involved in private Acts on subjects such as naturalisation, changes of name and estates: the earliest naturalisation Act held in Parliament is for a woman. Women were of course involved in divorces, which could only be completely achieved by obtaining a special Act of Parliament until the law was changed in 1857. Most divorces were procured by men, but in 1801, Jane Campbell successfully brought the first divorce Act obtained by a woman, on grounds of her

husband Edward Addison's "incestuous adultery" with her sister Jessy. Women were, of course, barred from participating directly in parliamentary debates in the chambers of the House of Commons and the House of Lords. But in the late 18th and early 19th centuries a great deal of parliamentary politics took place outside parliament: in the masculine world of committee rooms and political clubs that proliferated in the vicinity of St James's; but also in the female-managed arenas of drawing rooms, salons, dinners and garden parties. The "social queens", or political hostesses, who presided over them played a significant part in the political life of the nation.

By the early 19th century, as politics was slowly becoming less aristocratic and marginally more socially inclusive, a wide variety of political salons, "at homes", dinners and parties dominated the social landscape. They included the exclusive "pink" parties of the leading aristocratic hostesses such as Lady Londonderry or the Duchess of Devonshire; the intellectual and literary "blue" gatherings which were descended from the famous bluestocking salons of Elizabeth Montagu, Hannah More, Elizabeth Carter and Hester Piozzi from the 1760s; and the more modest provincial social evenings of the urban middle class which were important in shaping civic political culture. In an era before formal party organisation, political salons, assemblies and soirées, and their enduring popularity were arenas for developing networks, bestowing patronage, and sharing news. The very informality of political life created spaces where women with the right connections and political motivations could thrive. These were mixed-sex, often cross-class, groupings where the female organisers could seek to influence the fortunes of governments, make or break the career of an aspiring politician, shape ministerial policies, and determine the outcome of elections.

The most influential and famed political hostesses were the aristocratic women who played a key role in managing party politics in the last quarter of the 18th

*Above*

Addison/Campbell Divorce
Act and associated
papers, 1801

century and the first quarter of the 19th. The Duchesses of Gordon, Sutherland and Devonshire and Ladies Palmerston, Holland, Waldegrave and Jersey were amongst the most prominent. Many of these women became politicians in their own right, rather than just supporters of their husbands' interests. After Georgiana, Duchess of Devonshire, had been publicly shamed for openly canvassing for votes for Charles James Fox in the 1784 Westminster election, she transferred her energies to nurturing alliances behind the scenes and was a significant player in the formation of the "Ministry of all the Talents" coalition in 1806. Not all political hostesses acted independently from their husbands: many male politicians owed their success to the efforts of their wives. Elizabeth Lamb used her dinners and parties to raise the profile of her husband, Lord

Melbourne, the future Prime Minister, who was created a peer in 1770 and promoted to a Viscount in 1781. She managed her husband's electoral interests in Bedford and worked hard to counter Melbourne's reputation as a philanderer and rake.

The Conservative premier Benjamin Disraeli, a regular attendee at the parties, soirées, dinners and salons of Mayfair, lampooned the figure of the political hostess in his novel *Endymion* (1880), basing his character Zenobia on the flamboyant society figure Lady Jersey, who acted as a key political confidante for the Whigs before changing sides and championing Wellington and Peel during the discussions on parliamentary reform in the 1830s. She was, he wrote: "the queen of London, of fashion, and of the Tory party... To be her invited guest under such circumstances proved at once that you had entered the highest circle of the social Paradise".

Social events in London usually took place in a town house close to Westminster. Lady Palmerston entertained at Carlton House Terrace and Cambridge House; Lady Waldegrave at Carlton Gardens; Lady Melbourne at Sackville Street and Piccadilly; and Lady Jersey at Berkeley Square. These were particularly important during the re-building of parliament after the fire of 1834. There were often two or three parties per evening and visitors would go from one to the next. The leading political hostesses would often confer so their parties did not clash. Such events played an important part in the lives of leading male politicians. George Canning during his first 16 months as an MP between 1793 and 1795 went to Mrs Crewe's suppers

and salons 47 times and Lady Payne's soirées ten times; he dined at Lady Charlotte Greville's nine times, Lady Malmesbury's 34 times and with the Countess of Sutherland 36 times.

A good deal of back-room politics took place at these social events. Patronage could be bestowed or removed, talented young politicians might find a safe parliamentary seat or a place in cabinet, alliances could be forged or dismantled and ministries could be formed. The *"salonnières"* often played a key role in smoothing political disputes by hosting parties attended by those of all shades of the political spectrum. Lady Stanley of Alderley, described by Palmerston as the co-whip (with her husband) of the Whig party, held a popular salon at her home in Dover Street. Realising his importance to the Whigs, she was the first aristocratic hostess to invite Daniel O'Connell, the

*Left*
Dinner at Haddo House, 1884, by Alfred Edward Emslie, 1884. The campaigner and philanthropist Ishbel Maria-Gordon, Countess of Aberdeen, presides over a dinner with the prime minister, William Gladstone, to her right, and the future prime minister, the Earl of Rosebery, to her left

*Above*
Trial of Queen Caroline in House of Lords 1820, by J. G. Murry, after James Stephanoff. Queen Caroline, the only woman present, is shown seated surrounded by male Peers and others

controversial leader of the Irish MPs, to her drawing room. She gave a banquet in his honour, followed by a reception for politicians to meet him. The evening was described as the most important social and political event of the season. Lady Palmerston also invited a broad spectrum of political opinion to her receptions. In 1852 following the collapse of Lord John Russell's Liberal ministry, over three hundred people attended including three members of Lord Derby's newly formed Conservative cabinet and over 40 backbench MPs.

These very public social occasions contrasted with the more intimate roles these powerful women could play. Harriett Arbuthnot for instance acted as a political sounding board for the senior Tory politicians Lord Castlereagh and the Duke of Wellington. Castlereagh visited her nearly every day at breakfast between 1820 and his suicide in 1822, in her words, "to take his orders". Later, Wellington forewarned her of every major initiative of the Tory ministries including George IV's divorce from Queen Caroline, Catholic Emancipation and Parliamentary reform. He showed her confidential letters from the King and foreign courts and often consulted with her before he referred matters to his cabinet. Harriett was thus soon regarded by politicians and foreign diplomats as the conduit for access to the highest echelons of the Tory administrations.

In the 19th century, the aristocracy's dominance over parliamentary politics began to be challenged by a new group of middle-class politicians. The established hostesses incorporated these men into their parties and suppers but new salons sprang up frequented by men and women who met on equal terms. These assemblies often had a more intellectual character

than the traditional gatherings, with topics such as current affairs, art, philosophy, religion and literature regularly on the agenda. Political economy was an immensely fashionable topic in the so-called "blue" salons (to distinguish them from the aristocratic "pink" parties) of the early 19th century. Drawing rooms and dinner parties were buzzing with discussions on the currency question, the value of labour and the classical principles of political economy. The novelist Maria Edgeworth wrote in 1822 that: "It has now become high fashion with blue ladies to talk political economy. Meantime fine ladies now require that their daughters' governesses should teach political economy." Women such as Harriet Martineau and Jane Marcet regularly challenged politicians and economists at these gatherings, influencing the development of economic policy.

Although London continued to be the centre of such activities for aristocratic and middle-class hostesses, salons also developed in the towns and cities of the rapidly industrialising nation. Susannah Taylor held a regular influential gathering in Norwich during the French wars. It was here Harriet Martineau obtained her political education, joined by other women destined to play a significant part in early 19th-century politics, including Amelia Opie and Sarah Austin. The women of the Darwin-Wedgwood clan were also active in organising salons at their homes in London and the Midlands, and even abroad: Jessie Sismondi, sister-in-law to Elizabeth Wedgwood, held a regular "Thursday evening" party at her home in Geneva. These networks proved crucial for the circulation and exchange of news on domestic and foreign affairs.

St Stephen's Chapel & Speaker's House.
from Westminster Bridge

---

And beyond the world of salons and polite networks, women were – as they always had been – involved in organising, supporting in, and engaging in, protest and radical politics, the great movement for political reform in the early part of the 19th century that would eventually result in the achievement of the Reform Act of 1832. Women were present at the great meeting in 1819 in Manchester that resulted in the Peterloo massacre: many were injured and some died. The campaigns for reform demanded the removal of corruption and aristocratic influence in the constitution, and the proper representation of newly industrialised and urban areas; they did not encompass yet a demand that women be given the right to vote. But women were starting to use the arguments of reformers to push for change, even if they could expect little serious consideration. A petition was presented on 3 August 1832 from an individual, Mary Smith of Stanmore in the County of Yorkshire, by the radical MP Henry Hunt, who had been at the centre of the Peterloo rally in 1819. The petitioner stated that: "she paid taxes, and therefore did not see why she should not have a share in the election of a Representative; she also stated that women were liable to all the punishments of the law, not excepting death, and ought to have a voice in the making of them." Her petition was laughed out of the House.

## WOMEN WORKING IN PARLIAMENT

From the fruit sellers of Westminster Hall to the servants, wives and children in grace and favour houses, women were a constant if generally unobtrusive background presence in the old Palace of Westminster. Before much of the original Palace of Westminster was burnt down in the devastating fire of 1834, beautiful gardens stretched down to the Thames where today the Commons terrace

stands. In the mid-19th century Anne Rickman, the Clerk Assistant's daughter, recalled playing there in her youth with the children of the Teller of the Exchequer, Samuel Wilde, trailing their hands into the water at high tide from Mrs Wilde's drawing room window.

The lot of many of the women workers at Westminster was altogether less idyllic. They emerge in low-status jobs, alongside men, in remarkably detailed inventories of maintenance work at the Palace. One such was the anonymous woman paid 9d in 1644 for "keeping clean the seats of the House of Commons", another, a "necessary woman" who in 1725-6 was allocated almost £6 for taking care of its stool rooms – the lavatories. In the Lords, the Gentleman Usher of the Black Rod employed a necessary woman, Mary Phillips, in 1761; and a female Fire Maker, Sarah Matthews, in 1768. In the 1770s Martha Harrison received about £3 a year for night work and emptying the privies of both Houses, and Elizabeth Mills, hallkeeper, £2 2s for the more supervisory role of opening and shutting doors for workmen. A few women exercised trusted, responsible and well-remunerated roles, essential to the running and upkeep of the ancient and patched-up buildings and to the functioning of parliamentary business. One was Peternelle Vernatty, a wealthy gentlewoman, who between 1717 and 1731 was paid more than £200 per parliamentary session for "setting up, lighting, maintaining and repairing the lamps in Westminster Hall and other places for the accommodation of both Houses of Parliament". She had inherited her lucrative business from her father, descendant of swashbuckling Dutch entrepreneurs and the holder of a patent for candle lamps; on her death, her business passed to her husband.

Although women occupied a significant place in the capital's commercial life at this time, Vernatty was unusual in running her own business while married. More typical of women entrepreneurs was Deborah Reding, a widow who from 1708-29 continued her husband's scavenging and maintenance operations, including clearing rubbish, drains and gutters for Parliament and "looking after the flap at the King's Bridge to prevent the tide overflowing". Similarly, from 1706–24 widow Anne Brown ran her late husband's business as a slater, repairing the roofs of the records room, the Lord Chancellor's apartments and the "bog house", all near Westminster Hall.

The vast majority of Parliament's salaried posts, though, were occupied exclusively by men until the late 20th century. The housekeepers of the House of Commons and the House of Lords were however an exception. The Lords' housekeeper was a grand and significant appointment made by the Lord Chamberlain on the crown's behalf. Established in 1509 and by 1700 paid some £130 a year, the duties of the housekeeper were to ensure the safety and security of the House. Its perquisites included the right to occupy or to let several rooms near the Lords' chamber. From 1573 to 1690 a succession of male Wynyards held this role, but on the death of John Wynyard in 1690 his daughter Anne succeeded as Lords' Housekeeper, occupying the role jointly with her husband John Incledon. In 1705, they described their apartments as comprising four rooms, some in a ramshackle state, cellars, washhouses and a garden: a 1718 plan reveals that the housekeepers occupied a substantial suite near to the House of Lords, somewhat larger than the adjoining room occupied by the Lord Chancellor. Anne died in 1705, her burial plaque at St Margaret's Westminster conventionally describing her as "a woman of modesty, integrity, prudence and singular piety". Thereafter, the office of Lords Housekeeper was occupied by several women, initially the Incledons' female descendants. The last pre-fire holder of the position, Frances Brandish, was an absentee, delegating her job to others. On the night of 16 October 1834, her duties were being undertaken by Elizabeth Wright, mother-in-law of her deputy. She was a prime suspect in allowing the fire to rage unchecked through the Palace.

The duties of the House of Commons Housekeeper were altogether more workaday, as were its incumbents. Reporting to the Serjeant-at-Arms, the Housekeeper was responsible for looking after the Commons chamber and committee meetings. Established in 1660 for Thomas Hughes, and subsequently held by his daughter Anne from 1692 to 1703, the office's allowance of £10 was raised to £30 in 1697. Anne's son and successor Thomas Smith was in 1716 awarded the additional duties of keeping clean the "house of office" (again, the lavatories) for the Commons, supervising the pumping of water and the flushing and cleansing of the vaults where the effluent was stored, all for a daily fee of 12d. On Thomas's death in 1722 these unattractive duties were retained by his widow, Sarah Smith – although the principal Housekeeper role passed to Thomas Ward with a doubling of his salary to £60. Fortunately for Sarah, the "bog house" was located to the south-west of the House's lobby and well away from her room, seemingly in the attic storey above the chamber. From here, she was additionally required to supervise the ventilation system for the Commons, devised by the eccentric inventor Dr Theophilus Desaguliers. This never worked properly, not least because, as Desaguliers later recalled, Mrs Smith: "did all she could to defeat the operation of these machines", vehemently refusing to light the fires required to get the air circulating, as they made her room too hot.

After Sarah's death in 1741, other women, Anne Hollingshead and Anne Stephens, at times exercised Sarah's cleansing and attendance duties, but this time jointly with their husbands. By 1811, when John Bellamy and his wife Maria became deputy Housekeepers, this role was much expanded. It brought in £429 a year, John's father having established a lucrative catering business, Bellamy's, selling coffee, wine and his famous mutton pies to MPs. One of Parliament's most celebrated institutions, in the 1830s Bellamy's was supervised by "Jane", eternally-youthful, flirtatious, clad all in black, whose leading characteristic was, Charles Dickens tells us in a satirical Boz sketch, to show "a thorough contempt for the great majority of her visitors".

*Below*

The Destruction of the Houses of Lords
and Commons by Fire on the 16th Oct
1834, by William Heath, 1834. In 1834
a huge fire swept through the old Palace
of Westminster. Westminster Hall was
saved but the House of Commons and the
Ventilator were destroyed

# MAKING THE CAGE, 1834–97

In 1834 most of the Houses of Parliament was destroyed in a great fire. The Commons' and Lords' chambers were burnt down, and the ventilator went along with them. It provided an opportunity to re-think accommodation for women, and a Select Committee considered the issue in 1835 in relation to the House of Commons. It was eventually agreed that a separate Ladies' Gallery should be constructed, set apart from the men at the north end of the House, and "screened in front by an open trellis work".

*Simon Morgan*

*Louise Raw*

*Kathryn Rix*

*Jane Robinson*

*Previous pages*
Ladies' Gallery, House
of Commons, 1870.
Unknown artist, published
by *Illustrated London News*

From the beginning, women using the new Ladies' Gallery complained of the defective ventilation that made the space hot, stuffy and smelly. It was too small and cramped, nearby facilities were limited, and its position high above the Speaker's Chair meant the angle to view debates was very steep. The metal grilles, placed over the windows to place women outside the chamber and to prevent men being able to see the women watching then, made it dark and very difficult to see. The campaigner Millicent Fawcett, who had to spend many hours watching debates on behalf of her blind MP husband, wrote: "One great discomfort of the grille was that the interstices of the heavy brasswork were not large enough to allow the victims who sat behind it to focus… it was like using a gigantic pair of spectacles which did not fit, and made the Ladies' Gallery a grand place for getting headaches." The grilles became both a physical and metaphorical symbol of women's exclusion from Parliament, and later a target of suffragette agitation.

## WOMEN IN EARLY VICTORIAN PUBLIC LIFE

Industrialisation, the growth of towns and cities and the expansion of the newspaper press contributed to the rapid extension of the public sphere from the early 19th century. The reform of municipal government in 1835 prompted the development of new forms of civic pride, reflected in prestigious buildings such as town halls and corn exchanges, but also in the proliferation of voluntary and charitable organisations. On the face of it, this was a world from which women were excluded. Evangelical religious movements fostered the idea that women moved in a "separate sphere" to men. Women's moral and spiritual authority was idealised, but their physical and intellectual capabilities downplayed. Theoretically, at least, women tended to be restricted to the domestic sphere. The "public sphere" of work, politics and voluntary organisation was held to be the domain of men. In practice, the

division was hard to achieve for many. Working-class women often had no choice but to work, either in domestic service or in industries such as textiles, ceramics and some of the metal trades.

Even for middle-class women, however, the boundaries were never rigidly fixed, and many talented women were able to push well beyond them. Indeed, the social, economic and cultural changes of the era opened up a surprising range of opportunities for women to contribute to public life. Evangelicalism, while it helped to restrict women's participation in public life, also encouraged women to take an active role in their communities as dispensers of charity and spiritual succour. Many women would become resourceful and energetic organisers of efforts for the relief of the poor. In 1817, the Quaker Elizabeth Fry set up a prison visiting society at Newgate, initially to look after the spiritual and physical needs of female inmates. In 1858 Louisa Twining set up the Workhouse Visiting Society for a similar purpose. Both women turned individual philanthropic activities into national movements. By the 1860s, "ladies' committees" were ubiquitous in prisons, workhouses and hospitals. Initially resented by male governors, their work became accepted as extensions of women's domestic roles as household managers and providers of emotional and spiritual comfort. But increasingly women like Fry and Twining built on their knowledge and experience to claim influence in growing areas of public policy.

Other women who followed this route to recognition and influence included the journalist and author Harriet Martineau, whose fictionalised tracts established her as a populariser of political economy in the 1830s and 1840s; Mary Carpenter, who worked for the reform of juvenile delinquents; and, most famously, Florence Nightingale. Nightingale achieved fame as the "lady with the lamp", tending to the wounded during the Crimean War (1854-56), but it was her analytical mind and capacity for hard work that underpinned her

*Right*
Suffragist campaigner
Millicent Garrett Fawcett
(1847–1929), who spent
many hours watching
debates from the Ladies'
Gallery, c. 1870

*Right*
The House of Commons
in 1858, by Joseph Nash.
The Ladies' Gallery is behind
the stone screen high above
the Speaker's Chair

*Above*
Prison reform campaigner
and Quaker minister
Elizabeth Fry (1780–1845),
by Samuel Drummond, 1815

achievements in promoting hospital reform and the establishment of professional nursing. Pioneers such as temperance lecturers Anne Carlile and Clara Lucas Balfour, or the black American anti-slavery campaigner Sarah Parker Remond (who was active in Britain), leveraged their expertise to open the public platform to women. In 1857, experience gained locally through workhouse visiting, charitable work, and the promotion of sanitary advice to the poor was given a national platform with the foundation of the National Association for the Promotion of Social Science. This organisation encouraged women's participation from the start, providing opportunities to give formal papers on subjects of national concern to influential audiences.

As well as expertise and "woman-power", women made a key contribution to civil society through fundraising to support voluntary organisations. Nineteenth-century voluntary organisations were primarily funded by annual subscription. This was essentially a masculine system: subscription lists were published to encourage the wealthier residents of the town to contribute according to their means, and those who subscribed most exercised a disproportionate influence on the committee. Women of independent means could subscribe, but were barred from executive committees. As a minority, they exercised little collective influence. However, the reverse was true in women's and children's hospitals, or the

so-called "Magdalen Asylums" aimed at reforming prostitutes. In these "feminine" institutions women made up the overwhelming majority of subscribers and established women's committees that were vital to their continued operation. As subscribers to medical institutions, they could also exercise a degree of influence by voting on the election of medical staff.

Women developed distinctively feminine modes of fundraising. Door-to-door card collections were pioneered by women's auxiliary missionary societies, established from the 1820s onwards, which provided vital financial support to Christian missions overseas and in the backstreets of Britain's teeming cities. However, the most distinctive method was the bazaar, or ladies' sale, ranging from small affairs in support of a local charity, to elaborate festivals taking place over several days. They allowed women to contribute financially to campaigns and institutions that were not necessarily feminine in character. Their effectiveness brought female organisers a degree of public respect and acknowledgement. One of the most spectacular was held at Covent Garden Theatre in May 1845, raising £25,000 for the formidable electoral machinery of the Anti-Corn Law League. The league, which campaigned to abolish tariffs on imported food, blamed the Corn Laws for the prevailing poverty of the time. Women's involvement in a controversial campaign of domestic reform was a new departure, albeit based on the

A Corner in the Ladies' Gallery

# "A grand place for getting headaches"

Millicent Fawcett

precedent of women's anti-slavery activity, and seen as an extension of their charitable work and of their interest in cheap provisions as household managers. In later years, several veterans of the women's movement credited involvement in the Anti-Corn Law League as a key moment in their political education.

s    All this activity gave women experience of organisation beyond the purely domestic, while the gendered nature of the public sphere and their usually subordinate place within it helped foster a sense of collective identity. Some translated this into a desire to improve women's position. An important moment came with the 1851 census, which revealed for the first time the true extent of women's economic activity, along with a marked imbalance in the numbers of women over men, challenging the notion that women's economic needs were looked after by male relatives. In 1854, Barbara Leigh Smith (later Bodichon) published her *Brief Summary... of the Most Important Laws of England Concerning Women*, showing in particular how married women were disadvantaged by the law. Along with Bessie Rayner Parkes, she founded the *English Woman's Journal* in 1857, which campaigned for women's higher education, access to professions such as medicine, and reform of the marriage laws. The journal was closely associated with the Society for Promoting the Employment of Women, while the Social Science Association provided an important platform for their ideas.

Women had some successes before 1870 in amending the grossly unequal marriage laws. After a long and personal campaign by the author Caroline

Norton, the Infant Custody Act of 1839 allowed children of separated parents under the age of seven to reside with their mothers (previously custody had automatically gone to the father). The Matrimonial Causes Act of 1857 made divorce slightly more affordable, and granted divorced women some control over their property. The marriage laws were further amended in 1870 to allow married women the right to their own earnings. Women also maintained a toehold in local politics. Although municipal and poor law reform eroded its political significance, female ratepayers were often allowed to vote at parish vestry meetings according to custom, and in 1851, there were 865 women serving as church officials in England and Wales. After the reform of the Poor Law in 1834 women ratepayers could still vote for poor law officials, but were excluded from sitting as Poor Law Guardians until 1870, though the slow progress of the reforms meant that a landowner like Anna Maria Tempest could be elected overseer of the poor for the parish of Ackworth as late as 1849.

Some women were propelled into a more direct involvement in national politics by the Contagious Diseases (CD) Acts of 1864 and 1866. These Acts, provoked by a political panic about the spread of venereal disease in the army and navy, introduced compulsory health checks for women suspected of prostitution in port and garrison towns. The checks included invasive internal examination by speculum; but, as men were not subject to checking as well, the exercise was futile. The Acts provoked fury by placing responsibility for the contagion on women, and by

*Right*

Caroline Norton (1807–77),
by Frank Stone

*Above*

Josephine Butler (1828–
1906), campaigner against
the Contagious Diseases
Acts, c. 1885

attempting to ensure a supply of "clean" prostitutes for soldiers and sailors. The emphasis on suspicion rather than proof meant that any woman could be harassed by police and forced to undergo the examination. Many of the women were vulnerable and had no idea of their legal rights. A determined repeal campaign was led by feminist campaigner Josephine Butler, who successfully overturned taboos against women speaking in public on matters relating to sex. Butler argued that the state was effectively supporting immorality and encouraging sexual exploitation of working-class girls by middle-class men, threatening the sanctity of the middle-class home. On the one hand the campaign reinforced the notion that women's interests were primarily domestic; but on the other, it challenged the claim that women's political interests were identical with those of men and showed that political decisions in the "public" domain could have direct effects on the "private" sphere of the home. The laws were repealed in 1886.

Women therefore exercised a profound, if often indirect, influence on public life before 1867. There was no consistent route from philanthropy to feminism. Some prominent women, including Nightingale, later opposed women's enfranchisement; others, such as Norton, expressed no interest in the subject. However, the experience many gained working on committees for charitable purposes, setting up educational institutions or raising and managing funds provided compelling arguments for the opening of local elected positions to women in the succeeding decades, and provided an important springboard to the vote itself.

It appears from the Handbills issued by MR. CHILDERS
this morning, that
# HE IS AFRAID TO MEET US,
And answer our questions on the Contagious Diseases Acts.

THEREFORE

# M<sub>RS.</sub> BUTLER

REQUESTS THE

# WOMEN OF PONTEFRACT

TO MEET HER AT THE

# LARGE ROOM, IN SOUTHGATE,

(USED BY MR. JOHNSON AS A SPINNING ROOM),

## THIS EVENING AT SEVEN O'CLOCK.

MRS. BUTLER will shew that the Bill of which MR. CHILDERS
says he is now a supporter, while pretending to Repeal the " Contagious
Diseases Acts " is an extension of their principle to the whole country.
MRS. BUTLER will shew that MR. CHILDERS belongs to a
Government which has extended these Acts not only to this Country
but to the Colonies and Dependencies of the British Empire.
JOSEPHINE E. BUTLER, Hon. Sec. of the Ladies' National Association.

*Above*

Josephine Butler
addresses the women
of Pontefract, 1872

## WORKING-CLASS WOMEN AND PROTEST

Industrialisation in the 19th century radically altered perceptions of female labour. Women had worked since records began but, in agrarian societies, they were more likely to do so in family groups or small workshops, and to be paid in kind rather than currency. As the population shifted to burgeoning towns and cities, many women sought work beyond the home. Victorian commentators predicted disaster. They variously opined that women's wages were too low and would drive them "onto the streets", or were too high and would lure them to vice via the gin palace and music hall. The term "working girl" became a euphemism for "prostitute". Drunkenness amongst men, high mortality rates among working-class children, even the degeneration of the British race were all laid at the door of the very women who had helped to make industrialisation possible. In reality, the separation of home and workplace made working women's lives exponentially harder as they struggled to balance work and family. Their low earnings, around half the average male wage even for identical work, were justified by the myth of the "family wage" of the male breadwinner, and made them easy to replace. A survey of lives of the London poor in 1882 noted of women engaging in dangerous work at minimal wages: "Why do not the women refuse? Because they would be discharged… The struggle for bread is too fierce for the fighters to shrink from any torture in its attainment". Women without union strike pay needed great courage – or desperation – to take action. If arrested, they could be sentenced to hard labour. If not defeated legally, they were often simply "hungered back" to work.

Despite this, female workers fought against exploitation. The first all-female union on record was formed by Leicester hand-spinners in 1788. It was 18,500 strong, and notably militant. Strikes amongst women cotton workers were recorded in 1808 and 1818: during the latter, strike-breakers were dunked under water-pumps. Male and female spinners fought side by side for equal pay in Glasgow in 1833 and both sexes united in the struggle for parliamentary reform in the same decade. The all-inclusive Grand National Consolidated Trades Union, established in 1833, had a considerable female membership and self-organised women's branches.

Women were active and influential too in the Chartist movement, and were in the forefront of local campaigns against the Poor Law, the much-resented system for workhouse-based poor relief introduced in 1834. Chartism's explicit list of demands insisted only on universal male suffrage, and many (though far from all) Chartists, were either dismissive of the idea that women should also receive the vote, or regarded it as an impractical goal. Nevertheless, from 1838 onwards, as Chartism became a powerful national movement, many female associations were formed, some of them (such as the Birmingham Female Political Union) growing to thousands of members, though most were small local bodies. They were largely viewed by the men of the movement as having a valuable, but subordinate part to play in the campaign; and many men regarded women's

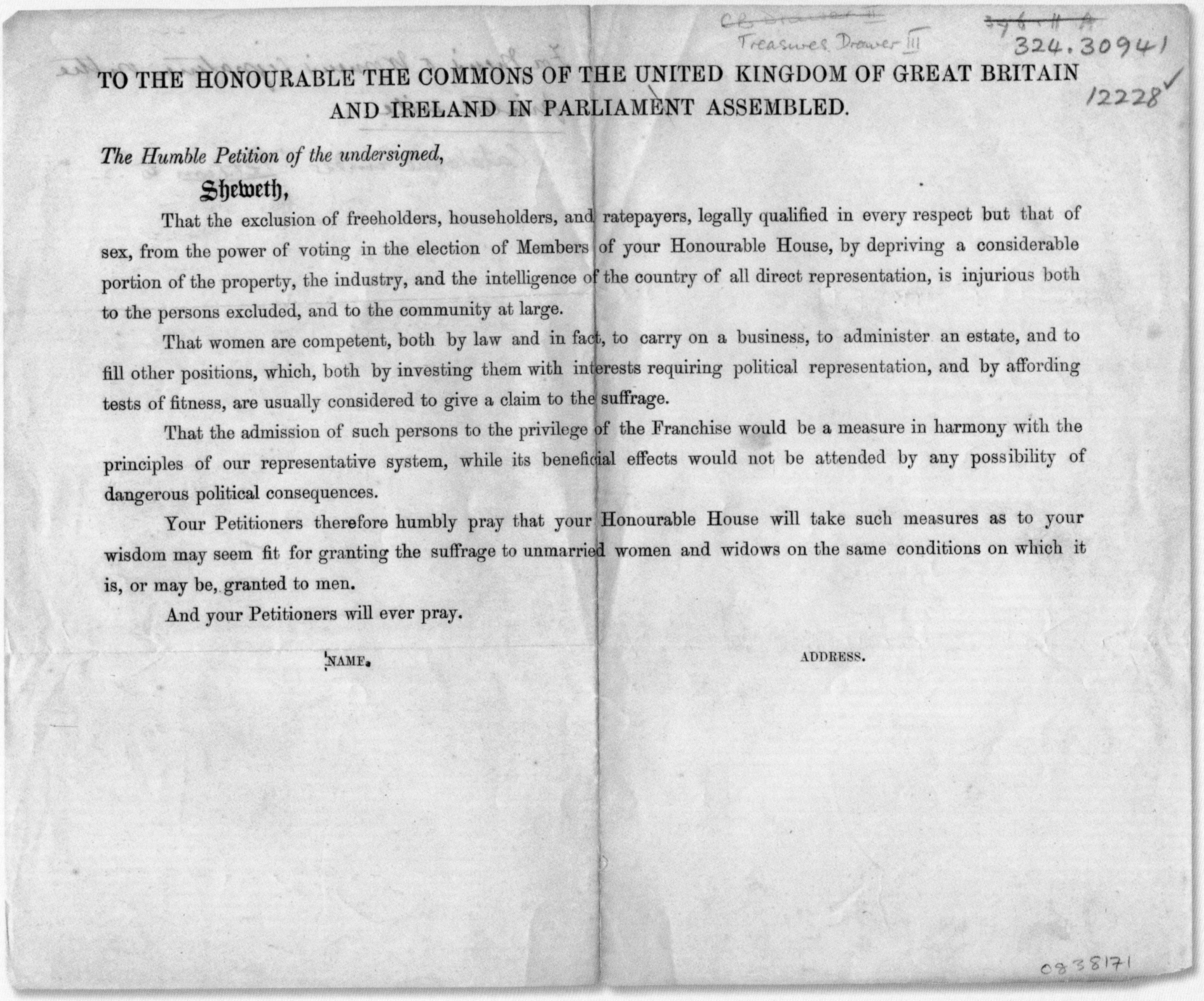

# TO THE HONOURABLE THE COMMONS OF THE UNITED KINGDOM OF GREAT BRITAIN AND IRELAND IN PARLIAMENT ASSEMBLED.

*The Humble Petition of the undersigned,*

**Sheweth,**

That the exclusion of freeholders, householders, and ratepayers, legally qualified in every respect but that of sex, from the power of voting in the election of Members of your Honourable House, by depriving a considerable portion of the property, the industry, and the intelligence of the country of all direct representation, is injurious both to the persons excluded, and to the community at large.

That women are competent, both by law and in fact, to carry on a business, to administer an estate, and to fill other positions, which, both by investing them with interests requiring political representation, and by affording tests of fitness, are usually considered to give a claim to the suffrage.

That the admission of such persons to the privilege of the Franchise would be a measure in harmony with the principles of our representative system, while its beneficial effects would not be attended by any possibility of dangerous political consequences.

Your Petitioners therefore humbly pray that your Honourable House will take such measures as to your wisdom may seem fit for granting the suffrage to unmarried women and widows on the same conditions on which it is, or may be, granted to men.

And your Petitioners will ever pray.

NAME.                                    ADDRESS.

*Above*

Petition circulated by the
Women's Suffrage Petition
Committee, 1866. This
document marks the start of
the organised mass suffrage
movement in the UK

*Above*
John Stuart Mill (1806–73),
philosopher and politician,
by P A Rajon after G F Watts

factions. With the decline of Chartism, the British labour movement would effectively turn its back on women for the next three decades. In 1875, Henry Broadhurst of the Trades Union Congress declared that its aim should be to "bring about a condition... where wives and daughters (are) in their proper sphere at home, instead of being dragged into competition for livelihood against the great and strong men of the world". He was sceptical when middle-class women began to appear at the annual TUC Congress to voice the concerns of working women, announcing that he "doubted... the wisdom of sending women to these congresses. Under the influence of emotion they might vote for things they would regret in cooler moments". Even after the founding of the Social Democratic Federation (SDF) and the Independent Labour Party, female equality remained largely an issue for women alone. The SDF leader Ernest Belfort Bax, touted as the "philosopher of the movement", was an avowed misogynist, and the author of *The Fraud of Feminism* (1913). Not until 1888 would spontaneous industrial action by those excluded from the labour movement force it to pay serious attention to women as a force to be reckoned with.

### THE CAMPAIGN FOR WOMEN'S SUFFRAGE, 1866–97

In June 1866, John Stuart Mill, Liberal MP for Westminster, presented the first mass women's suffrage petition to the House of Commons. Signed by 1,521 women, it originated from debate at the Kensington Society, a discussion group for women, and was organised by a small informal committee. The leading figures behind it included Barbara Leigh Smith Bodichon, Bessie Rayner Parkes, Emily Davies and Elizabeth Garrett (later Anderson). Davies and Garrett brought the petition to Westminster Hall, and Davies later told the story of hiding it under the stall of an old woman fruit seller while they waited for Mill. Their support of women's suffrage was part of their wider advocacy of women's rights, campaigning on issues such as married women's property rights and female education and employment. Helen Taylor, whose mother Harriet Taylor had married Mill in 1851, described the women's demand for the vote in 1866 as "the first humble beginnings of an agitation". The next three decades saw sustained organisation and lobbying of Parliament by women to promote their cause, laying important foundations for the women's suffrage campaign after 1897.

role as to evoke sympathy by playing the victims of a harsh and repressive system. Yet the women were key to the organisation of Chartism, especially at a local level: women participated in meetings, demonstrations, riots, and the petitioning that was at the heart of the movement. They also developed interests and an importance beyond the wider movement. The influential secretary of the London Female Democratic Association, Elizabeth Neesom, called in 1839 for women to "shake off that apathy and timidity which too generally pervades among our sex", and asserted the rights of women "as free women (or women determined to be free) to rule ourselves". In the case of Neesom, activism was channelled into campaigning for women's education. There were many other causes, particularly temperance, that were given a fair wind through the networks and initiation provided by Chartism.

Chartism peaked as a movement in the late 1830s. Thereafter it went into a slow decline, increasingly neutralised by the elite's response to some popular grievances (including the repeal of the Corn Laws in 1846), the lack of effective leadership and the movement's tendency to divide into personality-based

Further women's suffrage petitions were presented by Mill and others as the Commons debated the 1867 Reform Act, which extended the franchise to a significant proportion of working-class men in borough constituencies. On 20 May 1867, Mill moved that the word "person" be substituted for

*Above, left*
Priscilla Bright McLaren
(1815–1906), Scottish
campaigner for
women's rights

*Above, right*
Jacob Bright (1821–99),
politician, campaigner
and younger brother of
Priscilla Bright McLaren,
photographed in 1883

"man" in one of this Act's clauses, but was defeated by 196 votes to 75. The MPs who voted with Mill were largely Liberals, but included a dozen Conservatives. Despite its defeat, Mill's amendment had successfully put women's suffrage on the parliamentary agenda.

This activity coincided with the beginnings of an organised women's suffrage movement. Following earlier efforts in the city by Elizabeth Wolstenholme Elmy, the Manchester National Society for Women's Suffrage held its first meeting in January 1867. Lydia Becker became its secretary and Richard Pankhurst (future husband of Emmeline) was among its earliest supporters. Also founded in 1867 were the London National Society for Women's Suffrage, whose first executive committee included Millicent Garrett Fawcett, and the Edinburgh National Society for Women's Suffrage. These regional bodies formed a loose federation, the National Society for Women's Suffrage (NSWS), in November 1867, which was joined by organisations from other towns, including Bristol and Birmingham. Local campaigners held meetings, wrote articles for the press, distributed literature and lobbied potential supporters. Between February and June 1868, 75 petitions with almost 50,000 signatures were sent to the Commons. In 1870, the *Women's Suffrage Journal* began publication with Lydia Becker as editor, continuing until her death in 1890.

In 1867, Lily Maxwell, a Manchester shopkeeper, became the first woman known to cast a parliamentary vote in modern times. Having accidentally been put on the electoral register, she voted for the victorious Liberal, Jacob Bright, at a by-election that November.

Lydia Becker subsequently co-ordinated a campaign to register other women who possessed the required property qualification, since under an 1850 act, legislation applying to men was also held to include women. Thousands of women across the country lodged claims, but most were rejected by the local courts which oversaw the registers. In November 1868, judges in the Chorlton v. Lings case ruled that the 1867 Reform Act did not include women. This did not prevent a small number of them from voting at the general election later that month, but struck a decisive blow against future claims.

After Mill lost his seat in 1868, other sympathetic MPs promoted the women's suffrage cause in the Commons. Jacob Bright, the Liberal MP for Manchester and brother of the leading Radical John Bright, was one of the most prominent, bolstered by his sister, Priscilla Bright McLaren, and his wife, Ursula Mellor Bright, both very active campaigners. In 1870, Bright introduced the first women's suffrage bill, to enfranchise female householders on the same basis as men. His speech on the second reading of the bill, which was carried by 124 votes to 91, summarised several key arguments for female enfranchisement. He considered it unjust for women to pay tax, yet be denied representation, and for propertied and intelligent women to be excluded from the franchise while men of inferior position and character possessed it. Women, he argued, had been entrusted with the local government vote without adverse effects, and were already engaged in parliamentary politics, through petitioning or following debates from the Ladies' Gallery. Bright contended

*Above*

Suffragist leader Lydia Becker (1827–90)

that: "to tell me that women should not be political is to tell me that they should have no care for the future of their children, no interest in the greatness and progress of their country". Despite his initial success, opponents subsequently rallied to defeat his bill.

Petitioning by women's suffrage organisations expanded during the 1870s, when petitions with over 2,200,000 signatures were presented. There was only one year in the decade when women's suffrage was not debated in the Commons, although no other bill progressed as far as in 1870. Press reports and public meetings generated publicity and support for the women's cause. But the campaign was disadvantaged by relying on private members' bills to press their claims, since backbench legislative efforts stood less chance of success than government-endorsed reforms. The introduction of a reform bill by William Gladstone's Liberal ministry in 1884 provided an opportunity to attach female suffrage to a broader, and government-

backed, measure. William Woodall, Liberal MP for Stoke-on-Trent, moved an amendment to the bill in June. But it was rejected by 271 votes to 135: the opposition of Prime Minister William Gladstone, who argued that including this divisive issue would give the Lords an excuse to block franchise reform altogether, prompted some pro-suffrage Liberal MPs to put party loyalty first and vote against Woodall's amendment. The disappointment was added to by the large increase in the male electorate under the 1884-5 Reform Act, enfranchising groups such as agricultural labourers, and reinforcing the suffragists' sense of injustice at women's political exclusion.

### WOMEN IN LOCAL GOVERNMENT AND CAMPAIGNING

Despite their exclusion from parliamentary elections, women were nevertheless able to participate as voters – and, in some cases, candidates – for local government. In 1869, thanks to an amendment to the Municipal

# "Shake off that apathy and timidity"

Elizabeth Neesom

Franchise Act proposed by Jacob Bright, women in England and Wales who were ratepayers were enabled to vote in municipal council elections. (Women in Scotland and Ireland had to wait until 1882 and 1898 respectively.) Following doubts about whether married women could qualify, an 1872 judgement restricted the franchise to single and widowed women. This reflected the fact that married women's property rights were subsumed in those of their husbands. From 1870 women with the relevant property qualification were allowed to vote for and be elected to School Boards, which oversaw the local administration of education. The small number of women elected to School Boards in 1870 included Lydia Becker in Manchester and Elizabeth Garrett and Emily Davies in London. Wales's first female School Board member was Rose Crawshay (Merthyr, 1871) and Scotland's was Jane Arthur (Paisley, 1873). In 1875, Martha Merrington in Kensington was the first woman elected to a Board of Guardians, which supervised administration of the poor law. By 1885 there were 50 female poor law guardians, mostly in urban areas.

Women could also vote for the new county councils created in 1888, but following legal objections to the election of two women, Jane Cobden and Margaret Sandhurst, to the first London County Council in 1889, they were not allowed to stand as candidates until 1907. Women received further opportunities under the 1894 Local Government Act. This allowed them to vote for and stand for election to rural and urban district councils and parish councils, and made it easier for them to stand as poor law guardians, by removing the high property qualification. Most significantly, it allowed married women to become local government electors, provided they did not register for the same property as their husbands. By the late 1890s there were 729,000 female voters in England and Wales, comprising 13.7 per cent of the municipal electorate. In 1895 there were 128 female School Board members and 893 female poor law guardians. While it could be argued that the

responsibilities of local bodies – for education, the poor and health – were an extension of women's traditional domestic role, the local government arena was significant in giving women experience as voters and office-holders.

Although female involvement in parliamentary elections was not new, women acquired a far more significant role after the 1883 Corrupt Practices Act. This measure limited election spending by candidates and restricted the number of paid election workers. Candidates had to rely instead on voluntary help from supporters, which became increasingly necessary after the electorate was enlarged in 1884. Through extended party organisations in the constituencies, women (and men) were enlisted to perform essential electioneering tasks such as clerical work and canvassing voters. In 1883, the Primrose League was founded to support the Conservative cause, and became the largest mass political organisation of its day, encompassing men, women and children. By 1891 it had 500,000 female members and these "Primrose Dames" were praised by Conservative candidates for their electioneering efforts.

While the Primrose League did not take an official position on women's suffrage, the main Conservative organisation, the National Union of Conservative and Constitutional Associations, passed resolutions backing female enfranchisement in 1887, 1889, 1891 and 1894, and the party's leader, Lord Salisbury, spoke favourably on women's suffrage in 1888. It was generally felt that if women were enfranchised on the same basis as men – giving the vote largely to propertied middle-class women – this would be to the Conservatives' advantage. It was not only Liberal backbenchers who brought forward women's suffrage bills, but also Conservatives, such as William Forsyth in 1874 and Sir Albert Rollit in 1892. Generally speaking, though, the Conservative leadership was more sympathetic towards women's suffrage than were the party's rank-and-file MPs. The reverse was true of the Liberals.

*To the Right Honourable the Lords Spiritual and Temporal of Great Britain and Ireland in Parliament assembled.*

*The humble Petition of the undersigned the Head Mistress & Assistant Mistresses of the Dulwich High School*

*Sheweth.*

That a measure is now before Parliament for extending the Franchise to all men householders in the United Kingdom.

That by this Bill two millions of the least educated section of the Community will be added to the electorate; while educated and intelligent women, who are heads of households, are excluded from the operation of the Bill, although they contribute equally with men to the taxation of the Country.

That among the persons so excluded are women landowners, who form one seventh of the land proprietors of the country; women of means and position living on their own property, schoolmistresses and other Teachers, women farmers, merchants manufacturers and shopkeepers, besides large numbers of self supporting women engaged in other occupations. They believe that the claim of these householders for admission within the pale of the Constitution is as reasonable as that of the County Householders, and that they would be at least equal in general and political intelligence to the great body of agricultural and other labourers who are to be enfranchised by the Government Bill.

That the injustice of excluding women householders from representation would be greatly intensified by the operation of the new service franchise, under which the servants of a Lady, living in houses for which she paid rent and taxes, would have the vote in right of the occupation of those houses while she herself though the head of the household would have no vote.

*Wherefore your Petitioners* humbly pray that in any measure which may be submitted to your Right Honourable House, for amending the Laws relating to the Representation of the People, your Lordships will make such provision as shall seem expedient for the exercise of the Franchise by duly qualified women.

*And your Petitioners will ever pray &c.*

*Right*
Petition from the Mistresses of Dulwich High School, 1884. This rare surviving original women's suffrage petition to Parliament was presented to the House of Lords during the passage of the Third Reform Bill

*Above*

Primrose League badge

The Liberals too sought to harness female support, although women's suffrage proved a divisive issue for Liberal party organisation. Founded in 1887 as a federation of 63 local women's Liberal associations, by 1895 the Women's Liberal Federation (which favoured women's suffrage) had 448 branches with 82,000 members. However, opponents of women's suffrage had split off to found the Women's National Liberal Association in 1892. Although their electioneering assistance offered women potential leverage over candidates, in 1896, the Women's Liberal Federation declined to make women's suffrage a test question, leaving it to local branches to decide whether to campaign for candidates who failed to endorse it. Not until December 1897 – with Gladstone no longer party leader – did the General Committee of the main party organisation, the National Liberal Federation, endorse women's suffrage.

Although trade unions were often heavily influenced by the demands of male breadwinners, relegating women to domestic roles, women did participate in the trade union movement, both in women-only bodies, such as the Leeds Tailoresses Union (1889), and in mixed organisations, such as the Northern Counties Amalgamated Association of Cotton Weavers, two-thirds of whose membership was female by the 1890s. However, organisations such as the Women's Trade Union Association, founded in 1889

by Clementina Black, struggled to sustain support from low-paid female workers. The Social Democratic Federation, founded in 1884, and the Independent Labour Party, established in 1893, both admitted women as members on an equal basis with men. The Independent Labour Party's 1895 conference passed a resolution in support of extending electoral rights for both men and women. However, for the burgeoning labour movement, wider socialist objectives had a higher priority than parliamentary reform.

### THE MATCHWOMEN AND THE BOW STRIKE, 1888
Against all the odds, working women still came together to fight their exploitation in the workplace. A major turning-point came with the Bryant & May strike of 1888 in Bow, in the heart of London's East End. Bow's respectable residents already felt they had a good deal to put up with from Bryant & May's matchwomen, who liked to travel arm-in-arm in noisy female gangs, "cheeking" passers-by and using distinctly unladylike language. They personified the new and alarming figure of the "factory girl", often presented in middle-class accounts as a tough, belligerent virago who struck fear into the hearts of the "respectable", whilst also possessing a dark sexual allure.

The Bow matchwomen's walkout from their factory in the summer of 1888 was sparked by a dispute over their appalling working conditions. They had no union,

no resources, and no status. When Fabian journalist Annie Besant exposed the horrors of their work, including the industrial disease phosphorus necrosis (the dreaded "phossy jaw" to the matchwomen themselves), the firm reacted furiously, demanding all workers sign a paper stating the claims were false. Despite knowing that they faced immediate dismissal, they refused to sign. Bryant & May then made a serious miscalculation, sacking one young matchwoman in an attempt to intimidate the others. Instead, her workmates simply downed tools and followed her. Outside the factory gates, they organised themselves into a committee, and began picketing the factory.

Soon a 1,400-strong strike force was parading the streets, singing unflattering songs about their employers, and collecting funds from passers-by, who threw coins which the women deftly caught in their white work-aprons. The secret of their unexpected victory lay in solidarity, sisterhood – and hats. Their unwritten code insisted first and foremost upon loyalty among workmates. If a woman was sacked or ill, her workmates would put up a collection to help her. Occasional disagreements were settled outside the factory, with quick but decisive fist fights: local police declined to interfere. The women took a defiant pride in their appearance, developing their own styles and fashions – always topped off with huge and colourful feathered hats, which they shared, paying into a "feather club" to buy them. These things helped foster a strong sense of identity, and signalled a refusal to be either unseen or unheard.

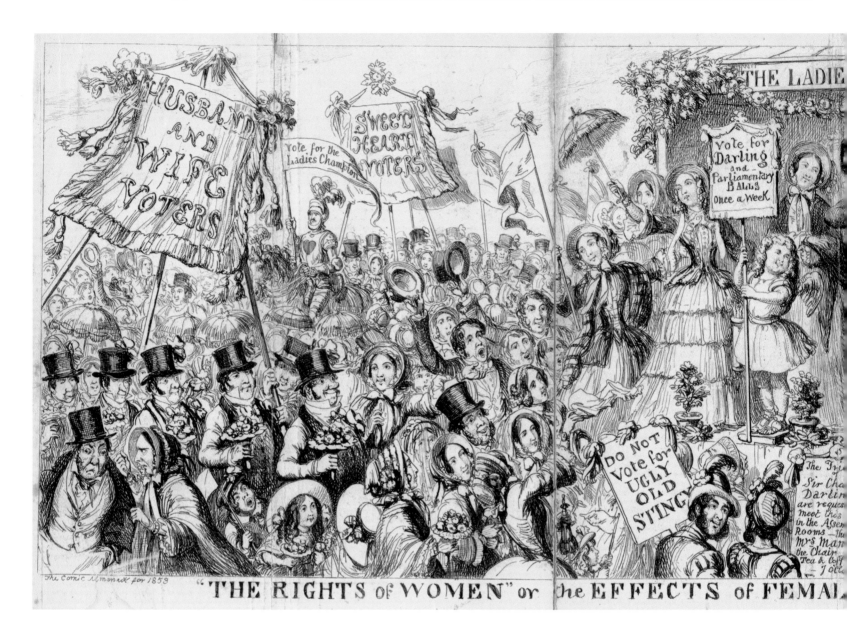

*Above*

The Rights of Women
or the Effects of Female
Enfranchisement, by George
Cruikshank (1852). This
satirical scene of an election
husting highlights concerns
surrounding women's
suffrage in the mid-19th
century, including women
being swayed by physically
attractive candidates and
influencing their husband's
political activities

Local papers initially sided with the "gentlemen" employers, but the women turned the tide with astonishing speed. Marching to Parliament, they told their story to MPs, and an independent report proved conditions at the factory to be even worse than Besant's exposé had suggested. Share prices began to tumble, and the employers were forced to give in to the women's demands for better pay and conditions, and the right to form the largest union of women and girls in the country. The extraordinary victory by the poorest women workers marked a turning point in Britain's industrial history. Other similarly-exploited workers followed suit, using strike action to demand the right to unionise. They spread the message to other women, holding meetings for workers in nearby jam factories and confectionery works.

**TENSIONS AND SPLITS**

Despite the success of the matchwomen, frustration at the failure to make progress on suffrage – particularly after the 1884-5 Reform Act broadened

the franchise for men but again failed to include women – led to growing tensions within the women's suffrage movement. Several issues caused divisions among campaigners during this period, some more serious than others. The National Society for Women's Suffrage (NSWS) split in the early 1870s over the relationship between the suffrage campaign and Josephine Butler's Ladies' National Association for the Repeal of the Contagious Diseases Acts. Some feared that the involvement of prominent suffragists with the campaign against the Acts might undermine the respectability of the suffrage cause. This, and tensions with the Manchester suffragists, prompted the London National Society for Women's Suffrage to decline to join a new Central Committee of the NSWS in 1872, although it did eventually do so in 1877. In 1888, there were divisions over proposed changes to the NSWS's rules to allow women's Liberal associations to affiliate. While most members endorsed this, some, including Millicent Fawcett and Lydia Becker, objected to

While the early suffrage campaign largely involved middle-class women, the 1890s saw efforts to attract wider support. Spurred by the progress of a women's suffrage bill in 1892 – when the majority against its second reading was just 23 votes – the various women's suffrage bodies united to organise a "Special Appeal". Particular efforts were made to circulate it to working-class women, including through the Women's Co-operative Guild. Esther Roper, secretary of the Manchester Society for Women's Suffrage, collected signatures from local textile workers by holding meetings at factory gates during dinner breaks. It became the largest Parliamentary petition since the 1840s, with over 250,000 signatures, and was displayed in Westminster Hall in May 1896 to show MPs the weight of support for women's suffrage.

In February 1897, a women's suffrage bill introduced by the Conservative Ferdinand Faithfull Begg received loud cheers in the Commons when it passed its second reading by 228 votes to 157. The number of MPs voting for women's suffrage was more than three times what it had been in 1867, demonstrating the progress made in building up support. But Begg's bill progressed no further: greater efforts were required if a women's suffrage bill was to pass through Parliament. However, a new phase in the campaign for votes for women was about to begin with the establishment of the National Union of Women's Suffrage Societies.

In another way, though, women were already becoming more visible in the Palace of Westminster, increasingly working as secretaries to MPs. In 1895 the House of Commons decided to establish an in-house typing service, and the firm of Ashworth & Co won the contract to provide it. It was run by May Ashworth, who had set up her own business down the road in Victoria Street in 1888. The Serjeant-at-Arms gave permission for Ashworth to keep in the typewriting room at the House of Commons as many machines as she thought necessary, and to place a sufficient staff of skilled operators also qualified to write shorthand at the disposal of MPs. She would go on to expand and run the service through marriage, divorce and wartime to her death in 1928, and Ashworth & Co continued to work in Parliament until after the Second World War. In 1897 Ashworth described how "an MP rushes into our room and begins at once to dictate something or another", and MPs often expressed "wonderment at the great speed obtained by the girls". Yet despite Westminster becoming increasingly dependent on women, it would take two further decades of campaigning before they obtained the vote.

abandoning the society's non-party stance, prompting a split into two rival bodies.

Another thorny question was whether to seek the vote for married women (who under the principle of "coverture" had no separate legal identity from their husbands) or for single and widowed women only. The women's suffrage bills brought forward from the 1870s took varying approaches. One compromise solution was to enfranchise women on the same basis as men, which would exclude married women while the franchise was property-based, but kept open the possibility of future enfranchisement. Some suffragists, however, wanted a clear commitment to enfranchising married women, as well as spinsters and widows, notably Elizabeth Wolstenholme Elmy, who founded the Women's Franchise League in 1889. Alongside internal divisions, suffragists faced the emergence of female anti-suffrage efforts, such as the 1889 "Appeal against the Extension of the Parliamentary Franchise to Women", signed by 104 prominent women led by Mary, Mrs Humphry Ward.

# ESCAPING THE CAGE, 1897–1918

Although by the beginning of the 20th century some progress had been made, success was still frustratingly far away. Other issues, notably the Irish question, convulsed the political world, and the increasing control of the political parties, with their own agendas, over Parliament limited the opportunities for individual MPs to push for change. Yet by the time the 19th century drew to a close, the suffragists (which at this stage meant all those who supported the "Votes for Women" campaign) shared a common hope that victory was in sight. Women were now more prominent in public life and party politics than they had been 30 years before, and the now fairly broad enjoyment of the franchise by working men made it even more difficult to argue that women's continued exclusion was justifiable.

*Krista Cowman*
*Jane Robinson*
*Mari Takayanagi*

*Previous pages*
Christabel Pankhurst in
Trafalgar Square urging
the public to join the
WSPU "rush" on the House
of Commons in 1908.
Postcard published by
Sandle Brothers, London

## THE SUFFRAGISTS: THE NUWSS

There were already differences of objective and tactics
which would bedevil the movement for women's suffrage.
Different groups had different interpretations of what
victory might mean: a vote for unmarried women on the
same terms as it was already granted to men; a vote
including married women, or a universal vote for men
and women over 21 (or 30, or 35). What mattered to
everyone, however, was breaking that most intransigent
of barriers: any Parliamentary vote for any woman at all.

In October 1896, representatives of women's
suffrage committees and societies across the British Isles
came together in Birmingham to discuss their strategy
before the final push. Regional groups had done all they
could since 1866 to further the campaign for the vote,
but were stymied by a lack of funds and coordination.
A year later, the National Union of Women's Suffrage
Societies (NUWSS) was born; a nationwide, non-militant,
non-party body of activists both male and female (but
mostly the latter) which at its height numbered 600
branches and over 100,000 members. They are the
people we now remember as suffragists, as opposed to
their more militant sisters, the suffragettes. Officers of
the NUWSS at national and regional level were seasoned
in public service through work as Poor-Law Guardians,
School Board members and town council electors.
At their head was Millicent Fawcett (1847–1929).

Fawcett was the younger sister of Elizabeth Garrett
Anderson, the first woman to qualify and practice as a
doctor in Britain. She was brought up in a Liberal Suffolk
household and educated at an "Academy for the
Daughters of Gentlemen" in London, leaving at the age
of 15. Introduced to the Victorian women's movement
by her elder sisters, in 1867 she married Cambridge
professor and eminent Liberal MP Henry Fawcett, 14
years her senior, and blind. Millicent Fawcett flourished
as a political and academic amanuensis to her husband,
a campaigner for higher education for women and
increasingly an activist for women's political rights.
Full of common sense and enthusiasm, she was also an
indomitable optimist – an essential quality for coping

with the repeated disappointments of the suffrage
campaign. Those were gifts; she worked hard to
acquire complementary accomplishments to help her
develop into an excellent administrator and public
speaker, firstly to aid her husband, and secondly to
arm herself in the fight for the vote.

Mrs Fawcett developed a strategy of lobbying
sympathetic Parliamentary members and candidates,
garnering all-party support for constitutional change
and educating public opinion about the campaign and
its significance to individuals and their communities.
This the NUWSS did through disseminating literature
via regional branches, publishing a national journal *The
Common Cause*, and encouraging members to hold
meetings in towns and on tours of rural areas. Within a
few years, however, a division began to emerge about
how best to undertake the fight, with the foundation
of Emmeline Pankhurst's Women's Social and Political
Union (WSPU) in 1903. The WSPU would become
frustrated with what was seen as the complacency and
lack of proactivity within the ranks of the NUWSS,
though it was only when a journalist from the *Daily Mail*
coined the term "suffragette" in 1906 that a distinction
began to emerge between militant and non-militant
activists, or the suffragettes of the WSPU and the
suffragists of the NUWSS. Very broadly speaking, the
WSPU became more involved in protest while the
NUWSS concentrated on demonstration.

Mrs Fawcett was at first supportive of Emmeline
Pankhurst and her suffragettes, hosting a banquet at
the Savoy for ten recently-released WSPU members
imprisoned for attempting to storm the Palace of
Westminster in 1906. "Far from having injured the
movement," Mrs Fawcett insisted, "they have done more
during the last twelve months to bring it within the
realms of practical politics than we have been able to
accomplish in the same number of years." But as the
militancy of the WSPU increased in intensity over the
next years, suffragists began to distance themselves
from direct action, feeling uncomfortable with (though
not always unsympathetic to) the suffragettes' tactics

*Right*
Emmeline Pankhurst
(1858–1928), by John
H F Bacon, c.1908

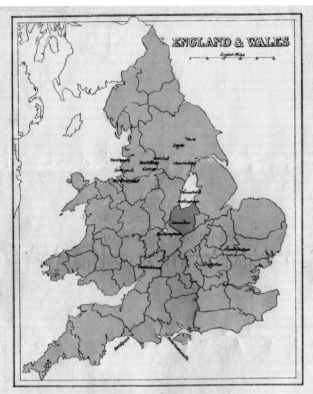

AREAS of the various Societies.

■ = North of England Society for Women's Suffrage. Secretary: Miss Roper, 5, John Dalton Street, Manchester.

■ = Central and East of England Society for Women's Suffrage. Secretary: Miss Palliser, 10, Great College Street, London, S.W.

■ = Central and Western Society for Women's Suffrage. Secretary: Mrs. Charles Baxter, 39, Victoria Street, London, S.W.

■ = Bristol and West of England Society for Women's Suffrage. Office: 69, Park Street, Bristol.

■ = Leicester Society.

□ Nottinghamshire   Nottingham and Mansfield Societies.

○ Birmingham and the district for 20 miles round Birmingham Society.

The Societies in Leeds, York, Halifax, Liverpool, Birkenhead and Wirral, Southport, Rochdale, Gorton, Cambridge, Luton, Bridport, Cheltenham, Bournemouth, and Barnsley, undertake the work in their own districts, but are in connection with the main Society in whose area they are situated.

The London constituencies are divided between the Central and East of England Society and the Central and Western Society for Women's Suffrage.

## National Union of Women's Suffrage Societies.

WITH a view to the more systematic and combined organisation of the work throughout the country, a National Union of Women's Suffrage Societies has been formed on the lines of the scheme adopted at the Birmingham Conference of 1896, by which England was divided for organising purposes into four large territorial areas, one of which was allotted to each of the four chief Societies.

Since the close of 1895 there has been in existence a representative Committee, consisting of delegates at first from the two Women's Suffrage Societies whose offices are in London, and from the Manchester Society, and at a later date from Edinburgh, Bristol, and other Societies. This Committee was found to be of considerable practical utility in facilitating combined action for Parliamentary work, and in other ways, and it has now taken a more definite and permanent form in the National Union.

The geographical division of work, which forms the basis of the present Union, has led to the modification of the names of several of its constituent Societies, whose titles will in future indicate their special sphere of work. Thus the Central Committee of the National Society for Women's Suffrage becomes "The Central and East of England Society," the Central National Society becomes the "Central and Western," and the Manchester National becomes the "North of England Society."

It is hoped that this Union will shortly become completely representative of every active non-party Suffrage Society in the United Kingdom.

It will easily be seen that organisation on so extensive a scale must involve extended work in each area, and therefore increased expenditure, and the Committee of the Central and Western Society earnestly hope that the friends of the movement will give them that liberal support which alone can enable them to carry out such an enterprise successfully in the large district which they have undertaken.

M. M. RUSSELL COOKE, *Treasurer.*
MARIE LOUISE BAXTER, *Secretary.*

CENTRAL AND WESTERN SOCIETY
FOR WOMEN'S SUFFRAGE,
39, VICTORIA STREET, WESTMINSTER, S.W.

*Nov., 1897.*

*Above*
Notice of the formation
of the National Union
of Women's Suffrage
Societies, November 1897.
The map shows the national
coverage of the NUWSS
from its earliest days

*Right*
NUWSS lapel pin. The union
was keen to make clear
its independence from
political parties and
constitutional approach

# "We are here, not because we are law-breakers; we are here in our efforts to become law-makers"

Emmeline Pankhurst

and with the vitriol they attracted in the press. Suffragists tried to counter the popular image of mentally chaotic womanhood by campaigning in a demonstrably responsible fashion. However passionate they felt about the cause, they were aware that such passion was all too easily dismissed as hysteria. Suffragists were highly skilled at salvaging advantage whenever they could until they had accumulated success. They did not storm any citadels, nor did Mrs Fawcett lead her followers into battle. Instead she tried to persuade the opposition to work cooperatively. For her, women's suffrage was not a matter for fiery revolution but an evolutionary certainty.

## THE SUFFRAGETTES: THE WSPU

The WSPU had its origins in Manchester and in Labour politics. It was set up in October 1903 at the initiative of Mrs Emmeline Pankhurst and some women members of the Manchester Independent Labour Party (ILP). Pankhurst (1858–1928), like Fawcett, had had various connections to the Victorian feminist movement, and had married a socialist and campaigner for women's suffrage who was considerably older than her. Emmeline's leading role in suffrage politics came after the death of her husband in 1898. Her small union spent much of its first two years campaigning for the vote in and around Manchester. Although it attracted little national publicity at first, its methods were quite different from those of the older, more sedate suffrage societies, and borrowed heavily from the street politics of the ILP. WSPU women speakers stood on chairs to address impromptu gatherings, boldly challenging hecklers in a way that many contemporary observers found shocking. The organisation came to national attention in October 1905. Emmeline's daughter Christabel and Annie Kenney, a young working-class woman, attended a Liberal party meeting at

Manchester's Free Trade Hall. During question time they persistently demanded an answer from the senior politician Sir Edward Grey on whether a Liberal government would give votes to women. They were thrown out of the hall and arrested on the pavement outside when they attempted to address the growing crowd. At Manchester Police Court they refused to pay a fine, and were sent to Strangeways Prison for a week.

The event made national headlines. The WSPU had become news and was determined to capitalise on its new status. Suffragettes pursued leading cabinet ministers throughout the North West, disrupting election meetings with questions, leaflets and handbells. Recognising that maintaining a high-profile campaign would require continued proximity to key political figures, the union moved its headquarters to London. Parliament – where the election had produced a huge Liberal majority – became a key focus for its activities. In February 1906 Annie Kenney organised the WSPU's first large London demonstration, coinciding with the King's speech at the opening of Parliament. Over 3,000 women, many of them carrying babies, attended a meeting at Caxton Hall in Westminster where Emmeline Pankhurst urged them to abandon the old constitutional methods of campaigning and follow her to the House of Commons. The women walked in small groups to comply with an Act of 1817 that prevented open-air meetings within the immediate vicinity of Parliament. The event passed peacefully, but the following October saw a shift in the WSPU's attitude to Parliamentary protests. A large number of women, many from outside London, gathered in St Stephen's Hall and Central Lobby in the Houses of Parliament on the day of the King's speech. Mary Gawthorpe, the WSPU's Lancashire organiser, climbed behind the statue of Stafford Northcote, the Earl of Iddesleigh, to lead the cries of "votes for women", which were audible in the chamber

government following a pact with Labour, which included some of the women's strongest allies, including the party's leader, James Keir Hardie, and George Lansbury. But while a majority in both parties were sympathetic in principle to women's suffrage, and there were plenty of Conservative MPs who supported it, the obstacles continued to be formidable. Some Conservatives would accept the enfranchisement of better-off and propertied women; but a majority of the Labour party balked at accepting partial enfranchisement of women on the basis of property qualification, insisting on the franchise for all adults, regardless of their property. The Liberals were committed to further electoral reform, but they too were divided about its nature. The issue was complicated by continuing arguments surrounding Irish Home Rule (devolution) – a subject which had split the party in the 1890s – and quickly obscured by the government's increasing difficulties with the House of Lords. Compared to their other difficulties, to the principal Liberal politicians, votes for women seemed a minor issue; and while many senior figures in the party, including the prime minister, Sir Henry Campbell-Bannerman, were supportive, others were actively hostile.

One of the hostile Liberals was Herbert Asquith, who in 1908 replaced Campbell-Bannerman as prime minister. He made it clear that he had no intention of legislating for women's suffrage, nor of helping on its way a private members' bill, despite the support of other Liberals. All he would concede was that when the government was ready to legislate on further electoral reform, if ordinary members wanted to bring in an amendment to the bill that would allow women to vote, it would not oppose it. However it was clear that no such bill was likely to be brought forward soon, and the government soon became embroiled in other disputes, notably the bitter confrontation with the House of Lords over the 1909 budget of Chancellor of the Exchequer David Lloyd George, and the subsequent two elections of 1910.

Throughout, the WSPU sought to maintain its pressure on the government and bring its cause to the attention of the public. Its demonstration in December 1906 would set a pattern for a decade of suffragette engagement with Parliament. From February 1907 the WSPU organised a series of "Women's Parliaments"; highly symbolic affairs, designed to emphasise the entirely male membership of the Westminster Parliament.

of the House of Commons itself. Twelve women were arrested. In December 1906 the union attempted to repeat their protest, but this time the police response was more immediate and they were only able to get as far as Old Palace Yard before they were removed. There were five further arrests.

### THE LIBERAL GOVERNMENT AND THE SUFFRAGETTES, 1906–11

The pressure that women placed on Parliament from 1906 onwards was partly the result of disappointed expectations. Many women had believed that the resignation of the Conservatives in 1905 and the subsequent election, by a landslide majority, of a Liberal government, would be likely to lead relatively quickly to enfranchisement. The Liberal party had been historically (though far from universally) more sympathetic to the cause than had the Conservatives who had been in power since 1895; and in 1906 they arrived in

*Right*
Keir Hardie (1856–1915),
by Cosmo Rowe, c.1907.
A friend of the Pankhurst
family and an active
supporter of their cause,
he spoke regularly in the
Commons on suffrage issues

with every good wish
for 1907 and all the
coming years

J. Keir Hardie

*Below*
Emmeline and Christabel Pankhurst together with Mrs Drummond were prosecuted for the "rush" and subsequently imprisoned. This medal awarded to Mrs Pankhurst on her release from Holloway prison identifies the location of her cell, H (Hospital block), Floor 2, cell 4

MISS C. PANKHURST AT TRAFALGAR SQUARE INVITING THE AUDIENCE TO "RUSH"
THE HOUSE OF COMMONS ON OCTOBER 13.
The National Women's Social and Political Union,
4, Clements Inn, W.C.

MRS. PANKHURST AT TRAFALGAR SQUARE INVITING THE AUDIENCE TO "RUSH"
THE HOUSE OF COMMONS ON OCTOBER 13.
The National Women's Social and Political Union.

MRS. DRUMMOND AT TRAFALGAR SQUARE INVITING THE AUDIENCE TO "RUSH"
THE HOUSE OF COMMONS ON OCTOBER 13.
The National Women's Social and Political Union,
4, Clements Inn, W.C.

ARREST OF MRS. PANKHURST, MISS PANKHURST, AND MRS. DRUMMOND,
MR. JARVIS READING THE WARRANT AT CLEMENT'S INN, OCTOBER 13, 1908.
The National Women's Social and Political Union, 4, Clements Inn, W.C.

*Above*

The WSPU arranged for postcards to be issued publicising the "rush" campaign. One shows the Pankhursts and Mrs Drummond being arrested. Postcards published by Sandle Brothers, London

WSPU branches from all over the country sent delegates. Branch collections covered delegates' train fares, something that led to accusations in the press that they were paid agitators. Women's Parliaments would meet in Caxton Hall, close to the Palace of Westminster, at a time designed to coincide with a specific event such as the state opening of Parliament, the King's speech or a women's suffrage debate. They ended by endorsing a resolution that would then be taken to Parliament by small groups of delegates. Large numbers of police would be deployed to keep women out of the building. There were always high numbers of arrests. Occasionally deputations breached police lines. In one ruse, at the third Women's Parliament in February 1908 the WSPU hired two furniture removal vans, which disgorged twenty-one women at the entrance.

Women's Parliaments attracted much publicity. The sight of large numbers of women, well-dressed wealthy ladies and Northern factory workers in shawls and clogs, brawling with the police in Palace Yard, fascinated the photo journalists who worked for popular titles such as the *Daily Mirror*. The arrests drew attention to the spread of support for the WSPU's demands; after the Women's Parliament of February 1908, the *Daily Mail* noted the presence of women from Bradford, Bury,

Leeds, Halifax, Preston, Stoke-on-Trent, Liverpool, Hanley, Glasgow, Chester, Manchester and Rochdale. Women's Parliaments were not exclusively WSPU events. Members of the Women's Freedom League (WFL), the militant suffrage organisation led by Charlotte Despard, Teresa Billington-Greig and Edith How-Martyn that split off from the WSPU in November 1907, joined in and also organised their own Parliamentary protests. A number of other suffrage societies that supported direct militant actions, including the Actresses' Franchise League and the Church League for Women's Suffrage, were represented at the ten Women's Parliaments held between February 1907 and November 1911. In 1908 the WSPU adopted the colours purple, green and white. Used in processions and merchandise, the branding proved enormously successful. Other suffrage societies devised their own colour schemes: the NUWSS was red, green and white; the WFL was green, white and gold.

One of the largest demonstrations came in October 1908. To attract wider support for the fifth Women's Parliament in October 1908, the WSPU printed a handbill that invited the public to "Help the Suffragettes to Rush the House of Commons". Emmeline and Christabel Pankhurst and Flora Drummond were arrested and gaoled for producing the leaflet, and were

# "Help the Suffragettes to Rush the House of Commons"

*Right*
Plaque marking Emily
Wilding Davison's overnight
stay in Parliament on
census night 1911, placed
in the Chapel of St Mary
Undercroft cupboard by
Tony Benn MP in 1988

IN LOVING MEMORY OF
**EMILY WILDING DAVISON**

IN THIS BROOM CUPBOARD EMILY WILDING DAVISON HID HERSELF, ILLEGALLY, DURING THE NIGHT OF THE 1911 CENSUS.
SHE WAS A BRAVE SUFFRAGETTE CAMPAIGNING FOR VOTES FOR WOMEN AT A TIME WHEN PARLIAMENT DENIED THEM THAT RIGHT.
IN THIS WAY SHE WAS ABLE TO RECORD HER ADDRESS, ON THE NIGHT OF THAT CENSUS, AS BEING "THE HOUSE OF COMMONS", THUS MAKING HER CLAIM TO THE SAME POLITICAL RIGHTS AS MEN.
EMILY WILDING DAVISON DIED IN JUNE 1913 FROM INJURIES SUSTAINED WHEN SHE THREW HERSELF UNDER THE KING'S HORSE AT THE DERBY TO DRAW PUBLIC ATTENTION TO THE INJUSTICE SUFFERED BY WOMEN. BY SUCH MEANS WAS DEMOCRACY WON FOR THE PEOPLE OF BRITAIN.

Notice placed here by Tony Benn MP

"I must tell you, Mr. Speaker, that I am going to put a plaque in the House, I shall have it made myself and screwed on the door of the broom cupboard in the Crypt."

*Caption:*
Right
Plaque marking Emily Wilding Davison's overnight stay in Parliament on census night 1911, placed in the Chapel of St Mary Undercroft cupboard by Tony Benn MP in 1988

thus unable to participate in determined but unsuccessful attempts to penetrate the police cordon outside Parliament on the day chosen, 13 October 1908. Nevertheless, Margaret Travers Symons, a member of the WSPU, managed to get onto the floor of the House while MPs were debating the Children's Bill. As Keir Hardie's secretary she was able to watch proceedings through a "peephole" in the door to the Chamber, and ran inside. Her words, "Leave off discussing the children and attend to women first! Votes for women!" were widely reported at home and abroad, and officially recorded in Hansard. Two weeks later, on 28 October, the Women's Freedom League again attempted a large-scale protest inside and outside Parliament. Dorothy Molony climbed the base of the statue of Richard I in Old Palace Yard and addressed a large crowd of women, while male supporters protested in the Strangers' Gallery, women protested in St Stephen's Hall, and inside the Ladies' Gallery, two other Women's Freedom League members, Helen Fox and Muriel Matters, padlocked themselves to the grille that kept women out of sight of MPs in the chamber. While attendants struggled to remove them (eventually having to remove the actual grille) Violet Tillard was able to drop a banner into the debating chamber and deliver a lengthy speech that drew attention to their inferior status behind the "insulting grille" and their continued exclusion from Parliament and its processes. Others continued the protest in the yard.

Following the grille incident, the Parliamentary authorities purchased a pair of bolt-clippers. In April 1909 four WSPU suffragettes chained themselves to statues in St Stephen's Hall. Margery Hume chained herself to the statue of Viscount Falkland; the police report recorded that the clippers proved most satisfactory, although the damage caused to the Falkland's spurs can still be seen today. Another smaller-scale but successful breach of Parliamentary security was carried out by Emily Wilding Davison on census night in April 1911. Suffragettes had urged women to boycott the census, arguing that as they did not "count" enough to have a vote, then "neither shall they be counted". Some women spoiled their census forms with suffrage slogans while others spent the night in large groups and refused to fill in returns. Emily Davison chose to pass the night hiding in a broom cupboard in the House of Commons, and was duly recorded by the Clerk of Works as having been "found hiding in the crypt of Westminster Hall". Davison is known to have hidden or demonstrated in the Palace of Westminster on at least five other occasions, and had even been banned by the Speaker. Two years later,

## PROCLAMATION.

**Whereas** the Nation depends for its progress and existence upon the work and services of women as well as of men;

**Whereas** the State is organised for the mutual protection and co-operation of all its citizens, women as well as men;

**Whereas** the Government conducts the national business by means of taxes levied upon women as well as men;

**Whereas** the women of the Nation have made clear their need for political rights, and their desire to possess the Parliamentary Vote;

**ereas** working women, and women in the home, are in especial need of the protection of the Vote since legislation is interfering more and more with their interests;

the

## N'S FREEDOM LEAGUE

calls upon the Government to remove the sex-disability which deprives qualified women of their just right of voting in the Parliamentary elections, and

## DEMANDS

the immediate extension of the Franchise to Women on the same terms as it is, or may be enjoyed by men.

The Nation can never be free until the law recognises and establishes

## VOTES FOR WOMEN

THE DEMAND IS JUST.          THE REFORM INEVITABLE.

DELAY IS UNWISE AND UNJUST.

**Therefore** in the Name of Liberty and Humanity the Women's Freedom League claims the Vote

## THIS SESSION.

W. CONQUEST & Co., PRINTERS, TOTTENHAM.

*Below, left*
Proclamation banner and police report:
This Women's Freedom League banner
was unfurled in the House of Commons
on 28 October 1908 during the grille protest.
The police report of the incident names
Miss Helen Fox and Miss Muriel Matters
as responsible

6

28th October 1908

I have to report for information of the Sergt at Arms that at 8·30 pm a Demonstration took place in the Ladies Gallery and St Stephens Hall also the Members Gallery simultaneously by Members of the Womens Freedom League.

The following had been taken to the Ladies Gallery at about 5·30 pm by Mr Stephen Collins M.P

Miss Helen Fox ⎫ 1 Robert St
Muriel Matters ⎭ Adelphi WC

Both chained themselves to the ironwork of the grill and were brought out with the ironwork and the locks were filed off in a Committee Room The following were ejected from St Stephens Hall

Miss Henderson
„ E. Bremner

*Opposite, top*

These Porter's "Easy" Bolt Clippers No. 2, c.1908–9 were bought by the Parliamentary authorities to release chained suffrage protestors from the building. They were used in April 1909 to remove WSPU suffragettes chained to statues in St Stephen's Hall

*Opposite, bottom*

This restraining belt is reputed to have been used in the Women's Freedom League protest in the Ladies' Gallery on 28 October 1908

*Above*

Rosa Mary Billinghurst, known as the "Cripple Suffragette"

Davison died following her protest at the Derby, becoming the suffragette martyr.

### CONCILIATION: 1910–13

By the time of the 1910 and 1911 protests, the most significant attempt to break the deadlock had been underway for some time. Supporters of women's suffrage in the Commons set up an all-party "conciliation committee" in February 1910, headed by Lord Lytton and the journalist HN Brailsford, in an attempt to bring pro-suffrage MPs from all parties together to draft a women's suffrage bill that could be accepted by both Conservatives and Liberals. The resulting "Conciliation Bill" fell short of the WSPU's demand for votes for women on the same terms as they were given to men, but proposed using the municipal franchise qualification to enfranchise around one million women. Their bill passed a second reading and the government even agreed to allow it time to be further debated: but then the death of Edward VII and the clash with the Lords prevented further progress and resulted in the dissolution of Parliament and the second election of the year.

Suffragettes responded with a large demonstration to Parliament on the day of the dissolution, 18 November 1910 – "Black Friday". Large numbers of police were drafted into the area, and the demonstration was met with higher levels of violence than usual. Among the demonstrators was Rosa May Billinghurst, an active suffragette and wheelchair user, who was thrown from her adapted tricycle by the police. Several women were seriously injured. Winston Churchill, as Home Secretary, rejected calls for a public inquiry and was reluctant to answer questions on the matter in the House of Commons, fuelling speculation that the police brutality had been endorsed by the government.

Following the election of December 1910, which resulted in a Liberal government dependent on Labour and especially Irish nationalist support, a second

Conciliation Bill was brought in with revised terms more satisfactory to all suffrage campaigners. Given a second reading by a large margin, the government promised to provide time for it to be debated in the following session in 1912. The terms of the bill, though, were still controversial, particularly within the Liberal party, where it was seen as favourable to the Conservatives. Then in November 1911, Asquith unexpectedly announced the government's intention to introduce a Manhood Suffrage Bill that would not include women – though it could be amended to give them the vote.

Campaigners reacted with outrage. A large demonstration was called at Parliament, but, fearing a repeat of the violence of Black Friday, suffragettes simultaneously initiated a mass window-smashing campaign against government offices and commercial properties in London's West End: it was better, they said, to break windows than to break women's bodies as had happened on Black Friday. The protest was repeated in March 1912 when the Conciliation Bill was defeated – with many Liberal MPs now preferring to wait for the promised Suffrage Bill. The protests resulted in the arrests on conspiracy charges of Mrs Pankhurst and her close collaborators, Emmeline and Frederick Pethick Lawrence. Mrs Pankhurst's daughter, Christabel, evaded arrest and escaped to Paris.

The government introduced its Franchise and Registration Bill in June, placing as many obstacles in the way of the supporters of women's suffrage as they could. Their task was already difficult enough as a result of the simultaneous battle over Irish Home Rule. Tension increased further as the opportunity to amend the bill approached. In January 1913 Sir Edward Grey and David Lloyd George agreed to meet a small deputation of working women organised by Flora Drummond on behalf of the WSPU to discuss suffrage amendments to the current Reform Bill. The deputation was well-received, leaving the women feeling confident. But very shortly afterwards the Speaker's sensational

ruling that it was not consistent with the House's procedures to add women's suffrage to an existing bill, and that if the amendments were passed the bill would have to be withdrawn and begin again, caused fury. When Flora Drummond's request for another meeting with Lloyd George was refused, suffragettes responded with a large demonstration to Parliament that resulted in several arrests; there were also more violent protests, among them the attempt to destroy the house being built for Lloyd George in Surrey.

## CAT AND MOUSE AND THE GREAT PILGRIMAGE

The defeat of the Conciliation Bill and the mass window-smashing of 1911 and 1912 had already marked a shift in WSPU tactics. Whereas previously the union had celebrated large numbers of arrests during deputations to Parliament, it now shifted to acts of clandestine militancy, including arson. Disruption to normal patterns of life was the main aim. Women carrying out these actions were supposed to evade arrest. Women who were arrested for obstruction received only a few weeks or a month in prison, often as a result of refusing to pay a fine. But those who were arrested for arson or similarly serious forms of criminal damage faced higher sentences, often with hard labour. Many women who were imprisoned responded with hunger strikes. Prison authorities used forcible feeding, but by 1913 this was becoming problematic. A number of high-profile cases, including those of Lord Lytton's sister Lady Constance, forcibly fed when disguised as a working-class suffragette despite her weak heart, and Lilian Lenton, a young WSPU member who developed pleurisy when food was poured into her lung rather than her stomach, suggested that forcible feeding was not medically safe nor carefully monitored.

Fearing the impact of a suffragette death in prison, the Home Secretary Reginald McKenna approved a different course of action. The Prisoners' Temporary Discharge for Ill-Health Act, passed in April 1913, allowed prison authorities to release hunger-striking suffragettes when their health became a concern. Women would be released on licence, and re-arrested

as soon as they were well enough to go back to gaol. The Act was known as the "Cat and Mouse Act" as it replicated the way a hunting cat would play with a mouse prior to the final kill. The Government anticipated (correctly as it turned out) that hunger-strikers would be less than keen to return to prison once they were deemed fit. Suffragettes on licence were clandestinely photographed, tailed and monitored by police. Despite this a number managed to evade re-arrest through a network of safe houses run by suffrage supporters.

From 1912 onwards, the NUWSS and its affiliated suffragist societies abandoned their non-party stance and allied themselves to Labour candidates, believing the Liberal and Tory administrations to have squandered their chances to enfranchise women. Though a Liberal herself, Mrs Fawcett developed the Election Fighting Fund (EFF) specifically to support Labour candidates at general and by-elections. She sent countless deputations to politicians; wrote them letters; pleaded with them to admit that women were "people" in legal terms and must therefore be eligible to vote under any "Representation of the People" Bill.

In contrast to the WSPU, the NUWSS responded to the increasing frustration with a new series of peaceful demonstrations. Its committee member Mrs Katherine Harley proposed a grand gesture to break the deadlock and to rehabilitate the image of the campaign: a peaceful crusade, a march to end all marches, involving thousands of suffragists across the British Isles, culminating in a massed rally in Hyde Park. Such a spectacular event, she argued, could not fail to capture the public's imagination and convince the government that votes for women were not only desirable but inevitable. Called "the Great Pilgrimage", after just two months of frenzied organisation, the first Suffragist pilgrims set off in the summer of 1913.

Aristocrats marched shoulder-to-shoulder with colliery girls, academics with housewives, the young with the old and men with the vast majority of women: the Great Pilgrimage was about solidarity and mutual support. Wearing the suffragist colours of red, white and green, they traced major routes across the

*Above*

Alice Hawkins was a machinist at the Equity shoe factory in Leicester. A socialist and trade unionist, she believed women's suffrage was essential for working women's rights to be taken seriously. The mother of six children, it was possible for Alice to be an active WSPU campaigner because her husband was also a supporter. She was imprisoned five times for her role in WSPU protests. The Alice Hawkins collection, still held by her family, documents her involvement. It includes her WSPU hunger strike medal, her scrapbook, which includes a bail warrant following her arrest outside Parliament, and her extensive suffrage postcard collection

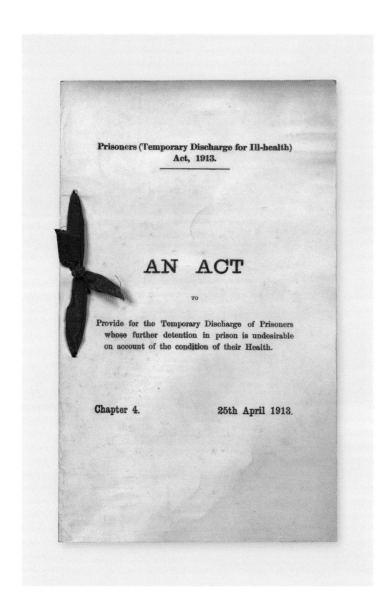

Prisoners (Temporary Discharge for Ill-health)
Act, 1913.

# AN ACT

TO

Provide for the Temporary Discharge of Prisoners whose further detention in prison is undesirable on account of the condition of their Health.

Chapter 4.                    25th April 1913.

*Above*

Prisoners (Temporary Discharge for Ill-Health) Act, 1913. Aimed at hunger-striking suffragettes, it was nicknamed the "Cat and Mouse" Act

them to be arsonists and stone-throwers. To counter this, pilgrims' banners were gracefully conciliatory while still attempting to rouse support, with elaborately-embroidered slogans like "By Faith Not Force", and "Better is Wisdom than Weapons of War". When a recently-discovered banner from Keswick was unrolled for the first time, pellets of lead-shot fell from its folds, no doubt fired at the pilgrims by a furious onlooker.

The purpose of the Great Pilgrimage was to demonstrate to Parliament and the people how many "quiet, home-loving women" of Great Britain wanted the vote: that not every campaigner for women's suffrage was a rebel or a suffragette. When Mrs Fawcett and others met Prime Minister Asquith after its completion, even he had to admit that the Great Pilgrimage had proven that women did deserve to be counted as "people" after all.

## A "SEX WAR"?

Journalists often wrote about the suffrage campaign in terms of a "sex war"; women's excuse for a wholesale rebellion designed to turn the world of men upside down. Certain reactionary medical men and educationalists continued to argue that if women thought too much, their wombs would wither, imperilling the physical future of the nation. Cudgelling their brains in an attempt to cast a meaningful Parliamentary vote, given their monthly "disturbances", would not only be useless but dangerous. But even some women advanced similar arguments. The National League for Opposing Woman Suffrage (NLOWS) was founded in 1910, amalgamating major men's and women's anti-suffrage societies. Among its officers were the popular novelist Mrs Humphry Ward (former president of the women's Anti-Suffrage League) and the explorer Gertrude Bell. Both were independent, high-achieving women who devoutly believed that Parliament was no place for them. Women had enough power already, they claimed, through their influence on husbands and children. Besides, the process of voting was vulgar and unfeminine. Its views were represented by another NLOWS officer, Lord Curzon, who published "Fifteen Good Reasons Against the Grant of Female Suffrage" as a manifesto. Among the reasons was the assertion that: "Women have not, as a sex, or a class, the calmness of temperament or the balance of mind, nor have they the training necessary to qualify them to exercise a weighty judgement in political affairs."

Conversely, while the Suffragettes attempted to restrict most of their Parliamentary protests to women to emphasise the distinction between their exclusion and

country: from Newcastle and Carlisle in the north, Cromer and Yarmouth in the east, Aberystwyth in Wales and Land's End, Portsmouth, Brighton and Margate in the south. Further routes fed into these main ones like tributaries, all flowing to the capital city. Many stayed the whole course, travelling as far as 300 miles during the six weeks from the middle of June to the end of July. Most pilgrims walked. Others rode in horse-drawn caravans, on horseback, in the occasional motor-car or charabanc and on bicycles.

The pilgrims had to contend with an assumption that they were associated with the militants, rendering them liable to be kicked and trampled by crowds who assumed

*Above*
National League for
Opposing Women's
Suffrage badge, c. 1914–15

*Right*
Wooden Suffragette Doll,
c. 1912–14. This very rare
doll depicts a suffragette
as a shouting harridan

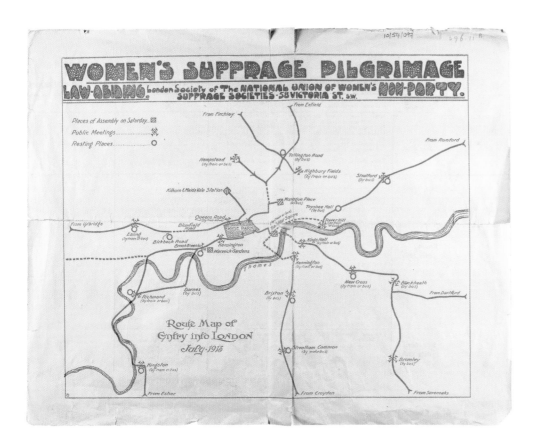

*Above, left*

The Women's Suffrage Pilgrimage, July 1913. This map shows routes taken by "pilgrims" travelling across the country to London

*Above, right*

NUWSS pin badge

men's inclusion in parliamentary processes, sympathetic men were involved. When Marion Wallace-Dunlop carried out her individual protest by stamping the phrase "it is the right of the subject to petition the King" on the wall of St Stephen's Hall in 1909, Victor Duval, a member of the Men's Political Union (male supporters of the WSPU), helped her in the attack and was charged alongside her. Members of the Men's Political Union and the Men's League for Women's Suffrage were key witnesses to the most violent response to the protests on Black Friday in November 1910.

One of the most enduring emblems of the NUWSS was a stylised tree in the suffragist colours, with a strong trunk representing the central administration and a host of flourishing branches representing not only the regional women's suffrage societies, but a myriad of affiliated organisations. They ranged from writers', artists' or actresses' suffrage societies to those of gym-teachers and short-hand typists. There were larger groups, which defied categorisation as militant or non-militant, among them the Women's Freedom League. Activists for women's suffrage usually belonged to more than one group. Some even shared their allegiance across the divide between suffragists and suffragettes. Millicent Fawcett's sister, Dr Elizabeth Garrett Anderson, was a member of both the NUWSS and the WSPU, and several prominent campaigners veered from one to the other. Sylvia Pankhurst broke away from her mother and sister to form the East London Federation of Suffragettes in 1914. Princess Sophia Duleep Singh was a member of the

WSPU but also prominent in the Women's Tax Resistance League. Kate Parry Frye, actress and daughter of a Liberal MP, marched in processions with both the NUWSS and the Actresses' Franchise League, was a member of the WSPU, and was then employed for several years as an organiser for the New Constitutional Society for Women's Suffrage.

### THE FIRST WORLD WAR

The outbreak of war in 1914 had a devastating impact on many working women. Food prices soared, male breadwinners went off to fight, and businesses collapsed in areas such as dressmaking. Some suffrage organisations shifted their focus onto relieving distress, by raising funds and setting up workshops to help unemployed women earn money. As the war continued, women began to abandon some traditional female areas of work such as domestic service, and instead took jobs previously undertaken by men in factories, offices, transport, agriculture, policing and munitions work. This was accelerated by the introduction of conscription in 1916 when many more women came into the workforce in the Home Front to free men for active service. Such work often involved long hours in dangerous working conditions, especially in munitions factories.

In itself, the war caused both the House of Commons and House of Lords to employ women in roles other than cleaning and catering for the first time. The Commons employed four "Girl Porters" from April 1917 until male staff returned from the Great War in March 1919. They were Elsie and Mabel Clark (aged

*Faked photograph of*

### SUFFRAGETTE OUTRAGE IN ST. STEPHEN'S HALL.

WOMENS DEPUTATION
JUNE 29th
BILL OF RIGHTS
It is the right of the
Subjects to petition
the king and all
commitments and
Prosecutions for
such petitioning
are illegal.

Miss Wallace Dunlop, the suffragette, reading the inscription which she stamped on the wall in St. Stephen's Hall yesterday. It took two men over two hours to ...se the violet inkstains with pumice-stone, soap and water.—("Daily Mirror" photograph.)

NATIONAL UNION OF WOMENS SUFFRAGE SOCIETIES.

UNIVERSITY WOMEN'S SOCIETIES · SCOTTISH · LONDON · MANCHESTER · NORTH WESTERN · WEST LANCs. & CHESHIRE · NT WALES · WEST MIDLANDS · WEST of ENGLAND · SOUTH WALES · SOUTH WESTERN · OXFORD. BERKS. BUCKS · SURREY. SUSSEX. HANTS · MIDLANDS EAST · NORTH EAST RIDING · WEST RIDING · NORTH EASTERN · EASTERN COUNTIES · KENT

N.U.W.S.S.

FOUNDED 1867

THE N.U.W.S.S. CONSISTS OF 449 SOCIETIES UNITED INTO 16 FEDERATIONS THE LONDON SOCIETY & UNIVERSITY WOMEN'S SOCIETIES.

16 and 14), Vera Goldsmith (age 16) and Dorothy Hart (age 18). The Serjeant-at-Arms was initially very worried by this "innovation", but by the time they left he wrote, "It is impossible for me to speak too highly of the way these girls have done their work, and their conduct has been exemplary throughout." Meanwhile, the Lords employed May Court and Mabel Waterman as clerical assistants from April 1918. Court, whose twin brother Robert had previously worked in the Lords' Accounts department before being killed in action, went on to become Accountant and head of department, retiring in 1944 after 26 years' service in the House of Lords.

All suffragette prisoners were released at the beginning of the War. Women worked on the front lines as doctors, nurses and ambulance drivers. Suffrage campaigners in these roles included Elsie Inglis, who set up the Scottish Women's Hospitals for Foreign Service; and Louisa Garrett Anderson and Flora Murray, who established military hospitals including the all-female-staffed Endell Street Military Hospital in London. Nurses included Princess Sophia Duleep Singh for the Red Cross, who tended wounded Indian soldiers in Brighton. Women served in the Women's Auxiliary Army Corps from 1916, the Women's Royal Navy from 1917, and the Women's Royal Air Force from 1918. Suffrage leaders were divided in their attitude to the Great War. Emmeline and Christabel Pankhurst suspended the WSPU's militant campaigning and put their energies into helping mobilise women for war work, motivated by strong patriotism as well as a belief that this would help women secure the vote after the war. In contrast, Sylvia Pankhurst opposed the war as a pacifist. She initially worked to alleviate the poverty of women in the East End at the outbreak of war, and later campaigned against conscription and for the peace effort. Charlotte Despard, another socialist and pacifist, also campaigned for peace even though her brother, Sir John French, was commander-in-chief of the British Expeditionary Force. Over in Australia, Adela Pankhurst became a leading speaker for the Women's Peace Army.

*Below*

Mrs Salter Khan, Princess
Sophia Duleep Singh,
Ms P Roy and Mrs Bhola
Nauth collecting funds
for soldiers during
the First World War,
19 October 1916

The leadership of the National Union of Women's Suffrage Societies split over the war. Millicent Fawcett chose to support the war effort. Others, including Catherine Marshall, Chrystal Macmillan and Kathleen Courtney, resigned in protest, believing that international peace and women's rights were interlinked. Macmillan, Courtney and Emmeline Pethick Lawrence were the only three British attendees at the Women's International Congress in The Hague in 1915; Marshall and others helped plan the event but were barred from travelling by the British government. The Congress led to the formation of the Women's International League for Peace and Freedom.

The war affected other suffrage campaigners in different ways. In 1915 former WSPU activist Margaret Haig Thomas (later Viscountess Rhondda) was returning from a business trip to the USA with her father on the *Lusitania* when it was torpedoed. She spent hours in the freezing water before being rescued. She went on to help mobilise women for the war effort in Wales and nationally, emerging as a great feminist leader after the war. The suffragist Eleanor Rathbone worked in Liverpool organising separation allowances to support wives of soldiers and sailors, which led her to develop her later thinking on family allowances.

## THE REPRESENTATION OF THE PEOPLE ACT

The suffrage campaign continued throughout the war. Breakaway groups such as the "Suffragettes of the WPSU", led by Rose Lamartine Yates, continued to advocate militant tactics after Emmeline and Christabel Pankhurst abandoned them, and the Women's Freedom League never stopped actively campaigning. It was clear that there had been a significant shift in public opinion in favour of woman's suffrage since the beginning of the war, and even Asquith accepted in August 1916 that change was inevitable. Nevertheless, the behind-the-scenes lobbying of Millicent Fawcett and Eleanor Rathbone was crucial in ensuring that votes for women were considered alongside men in the Speaker's Conference on Electoral Reform convened that year, and that the Conference recommendations were implemented.

The origins of the Speaker's Conference lay in an urgent need for technical changes to electoral registration for any election after the War; but it quickly became a vehicle for long-debated reforms, including the enfranchisement of the approximately 40 per cent of men not entitled to vote because of the residential and property qualifications required. A cross-party conference of 32 MPs and peers, chaired by James Lowther, Speaker of the House of Commons, was set up in October 1916 to discuss the extent of reform required. The conference considered franchise reform, the redistribution of seats, electoral registration and the method and cost of elections. It included some long-standing supporters of women's suffrage such as Willoughby Dickinson and Sir John Simon, as well as some dedicated opponents such as Frederick Banbury. In January 1917 the conference recommended by a majority that the vote be given to women on the local government register, or whose husbands were on it, provided they had reached a specified age "of which 30 and 35 received most favour".

The Representation of the People bill introduced later in 1917 embodied the recommendations of the Speaker's Conference. Although there was still strong residual opposition in Parliament, the crucial divisions on women's suffrage were passed decisively, with 385 votes to 55 in the Commons, and 134 votes to 71 in the Lords.

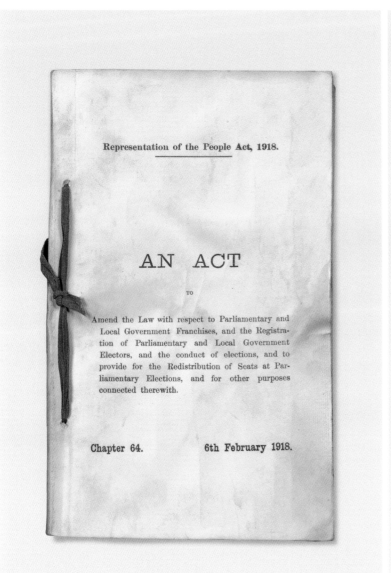

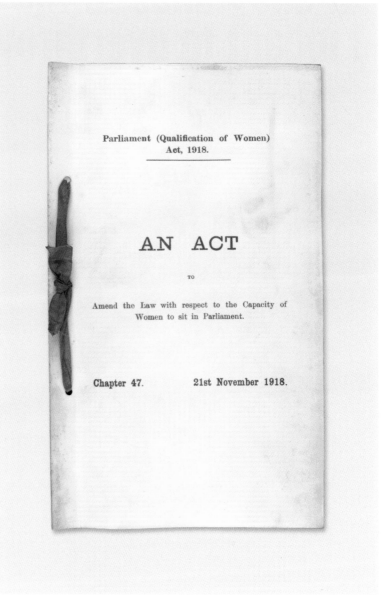

*Above, left*
Representation of the People Act, 1918,
the Act that allowed virtually all men and
the first women to vote in Parliamentary
elections for the first time

*Above, right*
Parliament (Qualification of
Women) Act, 1918, the Act
that allowed women to stand
for election to Parliament

# "I would never take an oath of allegiance to the power I meant to overthrow"

Constance Markievicz

Labour and Irish Nationalist MPs unanimously voted in favour, with significant reversals among both Liberal and Conservative MPs who had opposed before the war.

As passed, the Representation of the People Act 1918 allowed nearly 13 million men and eight and a half million women to vote. All men over the age of 21 were given the vote, apart from conscientious objectors who were disqualified for five years. Men on military or naval service connected with the current war could vote from the age of 19. The vote was given to women over the age of 30 who qualified for the local government franchise, meaning they had to occupy either a dwelling-house of any value, or land or premises of a yearly value of not less than five pounds. Women were also enabled to vote under the university franchise on the same basis as men, providing they were 30 years old. In practice, the age limit meant that no young women war workers could vote, even if they were serving in the armed forces or working in a munitions factory. The property qualification additionally disenfranchised women over 30 who lived at home with parents or other family members, or in furnished rooms or hostels, even though many such women were likely to have been supporting the war effort working in factories, shops and offices. Domestic staff living in their employer's house were also excluded.

The age and property restrictions were designed to ensure women did not form the majority of the electorate, as they would otherwise have done because of the loss of men in the war. Overall the provisos placed on the women's vote left unenfranchised approximately one third of the adult female population. Approximately one third of those excluded were over 30. Gender equality and rewarding war service were not as important principles of reform as the retention of traditional considerations of electoral eligibility, such as age, respectability, class, property and education.

Once some women had the vote, attention immediately turned to the question of whether women could become MPs. Women were barred from standing as Parliamentary candidates by common law, not statute law, which meant that it would be a matter for individual returning officers in constituencies as to whether to accept female candidates or not – a recipe for chaos. Following a test case by Nina Boyle from the Women's Freedom League, a resolution to correct the situation was brought to the House of Commons by Liberal MP Herbert Samuel in October 1918, and overwhelmingly passed. The Parliament (Qualification of Women) Act 1918 was subsequently rushed through both Houses just in time before the end of the Parliamentary session, and allowed women to stand for election to the House of Commons in the General Election of December 1918. The Act qualified women aged 21 and over to stand for Parliament – even though women under 30 were still not entitled to vote.

Seventeen women candidates stood, including former suffragette Christabel Pankhurst for the Women's Party. Constance Markievicz was the only one elected. Markievicz had been active in the cause of women's suffrage, Irish nationalism, socialism and trade unionism. A member of the Irish Republican party, Sinn Féin, she had been convicted of treason for her part in the Easter Rising in 1916. Though released from prison in an amnesty in 1917, she was imprisoned again as a result of alleged collusion with the Germans in 1918, and fought the election from a cell in Holloway Prison. Like other Sinn Féin party members who were elected, she did not take her seat in Westminster. Technically, her election may have been invalid as a result of her conviction and her marriage to a foreign national, though the objection was not made at the time. She went on to take her seat as a member of the first Irish Parliament, the Dáil Éireann, and to play a significant role in Irish politics.

*Right*
Constance Markievicz
photographed on the
S. S. Aquitania in 1922

# THE TOMB, 1918–63

In 1918, anticipating the arrival of women MPs, the Office of Works set up the first Lady Members' Room, "a gaunt room with large heavy oak tables and chairs, as forbidding as a Victorian school-marm." Nancy Astor was its first inhabitant following her election in 1919. She was joined in 1921 by Margaret Wintringham – a Liberal – and by the first Labour women in 1923. Ellen Wilkinson later described it as "Really rather like a tomb"; it was ill-ventilated, with too few desks, only one coat hook, the toilet placed at the farthest possible point from the room, and no bath.

*Paula Bartley*
*Oonagh Gay*
*Helen McCarthy*
*Duncan Sutherland*
*Jacqui Turner*

*Previous pages*

The introduction of Nancy
Astor as the first woman
Member of Parliament
in 1919, by Charles Sims.
Her supporters are David
Lloyd George, the prime
minister, to her left, and
Arthur Balfour, the former
prime minister, on her right

*Above*

"The Tomb": the first
Lady Members' Room
in Parliament, 1919

## THE FIRST FEMALE MPS

The Lady Members' Room was re-located down the hallway to a slightly larger space in 1931, but was still inadequate for the slowly growing number of women MPs. Other facilities for the early women MPs, and also their female staff and visitors, were poor. Women were restricted from various areas such as dining rooms and galleries for many years. However, the Lady Members' Room did allow for some female camaraderie to develop in some circumstances. Shirley Williams recalled one occasion following a speech where, "I retreated to the Lady Members' Room where Margaret Thatcher was ironing a dress. 'You did well,' she said. 'After all, we can't let them get the better of us'."

In her 1926 pamphlet *What The Vote Has Done*, Millicent Fawcett championed the Act that had made it "possible for a constituency to choose a woman as its representative in the House of Commons". Few women, however, stood for election throughout the 1920s, and even fewer succeeded. Despite their small number, the presence of women in the House reminded politicians of the importance of the female electorate and served as a stimulus for progressive legislation. The election of women brought political attention to their needs, and to issues related to the home and family.

The work of the first cohort of female MPs has often been overshadowed by the pre-war feminist movement and suffrage campaigns that got them there, but the contribution and significant achievements made by women both inside and outside of parliament affirms their political influence. Twenty-one female MPs trickled into parliament between 1919 and 1931. In this early period there were distinctly different types of female politician. The majority of Conservative and Liberal women MPs succeeded to their husbands' seats or were muscled into

a constituency by aristocratic or well-connected families via carefully controlled by-elections. Of the 21, seven were elected to their husbands' seats and a further three were heavily sponsored by their husbands or families. By contrast, the mostly unmarried Labour MPs had strong local government, feminist or trade union backgrounds and were elected in greater numbers at general elections.

The first female actually to sit in the chamber of House of Commons was the American divorcee, Nancy Astor. In 1919, she replaced her second husband, Waldorf Astor, as the Conservative MP for Plymouth Sutton after he inherited a peerage and became a member of the House of Lords. She won the resulting by-election with more votes than the Labour and Liberal candidates combined. Nancy's time in the Commons was initially intended to be temporary, as her husband intended to extricate himself from the Lords and return to the Commons. In fact, he never did and she remained in the Commons until 1945.

Suffrage campaigners were initially dismayed that the first woman MP to take her seat was so much a product of the political establishment. To many her proximity to her husband made her an acceptable candidate; to some it negated the work that the Votes for Women campaign had achieved. Nevertheless, Astor's introduction to the Commons was an indication of how much a challenge for the political establishment the arrival of women would be. The presence of a woman had an immediate impact on parliamentary etiquette and procedure: the Speaker, James Lowther, wondered how to address the "Gentlemen of the House" and if he should allow her to keep her hat on when speaking.

Despite her position Astor had to cope with a constant and insidious sexism that undermined

*Right*
Nancy, Viscountess
Astor (1879–1964), MP
for Plymouth 1919–45,
by Zsigmond Kisfaludi
Strobl, 1933

3, ELLIOT TERRACE,
THE HOE,
PLYMOUTH.

15th Novr. 1919.

Dear Mrs Le Cras,

I was more than touched by your
charming present last night, and thank you once more for
your splendid work which I must thank you for personally,
but we are all realizing that it is really for the country.
Again thank you so much for the beautiful flowers.

Yours Sincerely,

Nancy Astor

It has been a
fight – but for
the right.

Mrs. P.B. Le Cras,
58, Ebrington Street,
PLYMOUTH.

---

3, Elliot Terrace,
Plymouth.

*November 25th, 1922.*

Dear Madam,

I am very sorry indeed that I was not able to thank personally
all those who came forward to help me at the election.  They are so many
that it would have been impossible to see them all before I left Plymouth.
But I want to send you my most grateful thanks for your own share
in the victory.  I realise that the splendid majority obtained, is largely
due to the loyalty and hard work of those who like yourself rallied
round me during the election campaign.  I appreciate deeply this proof
of your confidence in me and I will try to do all I can to be worthy of
it, by working to the best of my ability for the welfare of Plymouth
and of our country.  I shall never forget the whole-hearted support
and the devoted service given by so many in the division.

Yours sincerely,

Nancy Astor

---

Mrs. Le Cras.
58, Ebrington Street,
Plymouth

---

N.A.
4, ST JAMES' SQUARE,
S.W.1.

LWJ.                              5th Dec., 1919.

Dear Mrs. Le Cras,

Many thanks for your letter, and for the
suggestion as to the Primrose League meeting.  You cannot
tell how much I appreciate all you are doing to help me in
my difficult task.

Yours sincerely,

Nancy Astor

58, Ebrington Street,
Plymouth.

It is a Task too –
but God Governs & we can only
pray for his will

---

**Parliamentary Borough of Plymouth.**

**SUTTON DIVISION.**

**NOVEMBER, 1919.**

Please admit Mrs. *Le Cras*
at the Counting of the Votes in the Guildhall, at
10.45 a.m., on Friday, the 28th November, 1919.

**Please Produce this Card**

*Acting Returning Officer.*

---

## THE SUTTON ELECTION.

### Lady Astor First English Woman M.P.

### BIG MAJORITY.

| | |
|---|---|
| VISCOUNTESS ASTOR | 14,495 |
| Mr. W. T. GAY | 9,292 |
| Mr. I. FOOT | 4,139 |

---

**SUTTON DIVISION PARLIAMENTARY BYE-ELECTION, 1919.**

## Lady Astor's Central Committee Room.

ELECTION AGENT.
C. G. BRIGGS.

'PHONE
PLYMOUTH 203
TELEGRAMS
UNIONIST. PLYMOUTH

17, LOCKYER STREET,
PLYMOUTH.

Nov 11/19

Dear Mrs Le Cras

The Bearer is a
friend of ours from Rugby &
is anxious to obtain some information
re Co. Op. Movement.

Will you please assist
him?

Yours faithfully,
C. G. Briggs

---

COUNTING AGENT.

TOWN CLERK'S OFFICE,
PLYMOUTH

*November, 1919.*

**PARLIAMENTARY ELECTION.**

SUTTON DIVISION.

Madam,

You having been appointed an Agent by
*The Viscountess Astor* to attend
on her behalf at the Counting of the Votes at the Guildhall,
on Friday, the 28th instant at 11 a.m., it is necessary that
you should make a Declaration of Secrecy before the com-
mencement of the Poll.

I enclose a Form of Declaration which should be made
before any Justice of the Peace for the Borough and returned
to me **before the opening of the Poll on Saturday next.**

I am, Sir,

Yours obediently,

Mrs Le Cras                       ACTING RETURNING OFFICER.

---

This is to certify that
Mrs. Le Cras was the first
lady to vote at the Grey Coat
School.

E. H. Ralph                    14/12/18.

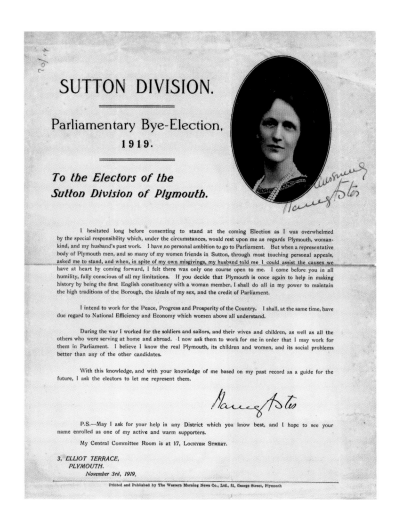

woman to be passed into law, the Intoxicating Liquor (Sale to Persons under Eighteen) Bill.

The Commons never grew to love Astor. Her enemies dubbed her "Lady Dis-Astor". She was unable, or unwilling, to cultivate a parliamentary manner, and while the many Astor anecdotes have an eccentric charm, her colleagues grew irritated by her constant interruptions and audible commentaries on others' speeches. Astor was "an unconventional MP". She admitted herself that she was more of a "nuisance" than a "force" in the Commons, in part because she lacked any political philosophy. She was however, a vociferous advocate of equal voting rights and she supported welfare reforms and access to the professions for women. She helped to spare the women's section of the Metropolitan Police from the "Geddes Axe" (the 1920s cuts in public expenditure). She encouraged other female MPs regardless of political party, including the second woman MP, Margaret Wintringham, elected in 1921 as a Liberal, replacing her husband on his death. She struck up often unlikely friendships with each new intake of women, including "Red" Ellen Wilkinson, the Labour MP for Middlesbrough East elected in 1924. Astor believed that the support of women was the reason she stayed in Parliament; but entering it had been a different matter: "Now I realise it was a jolly good thing that I was the first woman, for the first person, I knew nearly everybody in London, I knew many people in the House of Commons, I was connected with a priest, intimate friends with the editor of *The Times*, owning *The Observer*, and I really cared about social reform and I cared what I was there for and I had money enough to get good secretaries. It wasn't so much what I was but I had so much to keep me up." Ultimately, Astor was a greater success as a cause than as an individual MP. Her enduring significance was secured the moment she swore the oath.

Amongst the causes Astor was most passionate in supporting was equal franchise, giving women the vote on the same terms as men (to women under the age of 30 and without property qualifications). Women's suffrage organisations continued to campaign on this issue after 1918, and it was the subject of many private members' bills and Parliamentary questions between 1919 and 1927. The House of Commons passed a bill in favour of equal franchise as early as 1919 but the government was not willing to support it. Many Conservative MPs, including Winston Churchill, feared the effect that equal franchise would have on their party, and the *Daily Mail* whipped up a tabloid campaign against the "flapper vote". But, following personal statements in favour of equal

*Opposite*
Items relating to Nancy Astor's by-election campaign in Plymouth Sutton, 1919. They were collected by Bessie Le Cras, one of the earliest female election agents. Her work included helping manage the election campaign and assisting the party constituency organisation

*Above*
Astor's first election campaign leaflet, November 1919

her attempts to be taken seriously. She prevented comments on her clothing by adopting a uniform of dark jacket and skirt, white blouse and tricorn hat which set the style for her feminine colleagues in years to come. She took on a culture of misogyny and often outright resentment as she spent almost two years as the only woman in the House of Commons. She delivered her maiden speech on 24 February 1920 before an audience of over 500 male MPs, many of them hostile. Her speech, reflecting her abstentionist politics, was on the need for restrictions on the sale of alcohol: she commented that it took "a bit of courage to address the House on that vexed question, drink". Consistently aware that she was representing her sex as well as her constituency, she claimed: "to speak for hundreds of women and children throughout the country who cannot speak for themselves". In 1923, she was responsible for the first bill introduced by a

by an acute awareness of class-based injustice. Ellen Wilkinson wrote in the suffragette journal *The Vote* that "the woman who earns her living, whether as a wife or a wage earner... is suffering mainly from the wrongs that afflict all her class". She described herself as a "flaming socialist". Similarly, Jennie Lee, brought up by working class and socialist parents, expressed a fiery determination to change the fortunes of her class.

## THE 1930S

When in 1936 Eleanor Rathbone reflected upon the impact which women MPs had already made – and might make in the future – on British political life she played down the extent to which they were distinctive: "Those who expect women's contribution to be... utterly different from the contribution of men, will be disappointed," she wrote. "Perhaps five-sixths or nine-tenths of that contribution will be a fair sample of the whole mixed bag of parliamentary effort." Women, she argued, were formed politically in same way as men, through the "interacting forces of heredity, education, social environment, party politics, the nature of the constituency and its interests". It was fanciful to suppose that all women MPs would behave in an identical manner, favour the same causes and speak at all times with a united voice. Nevertheless, she accepted that the remainder of their contribution would be based on their unique perspective as women: "It is unquestionable that their differences in function, especially the difference between the paternal and the maternal function and all its results upon social life and occupational groupings, do bring it about that each sex tends to acquire a special kind of experience and to develop its own forms of expertise."

During the 1930s the expectation that women MPs would represent not only their constituents, but the interests of their sex, was widely held. But Rathbone's prediction that only a small portion of women's political energies would be channelled in this direction was proved correct. On occasion, women MPs forged cross-party solidarities and platforms for joint action, but most of the time they toed party lines or pursued political agendas unrelated to their shared status as women. Furthermore, women's capacity to effect change in Parliament was constrained by the fact of their being vastly outnumbered by men, and by the trivialising treatment they received from the interwar popular press.

Rathbone's own parliamentary career offers an illuminating example of what women MPs could achieve individually and the circumstances under which they could act collectively in the 1930s. An avowed feminist who disliked partisanship, Rathbone won election in 1929 as Independent Member for the Combined

franchise by Prime Minister Stanley Baldwin and his Home Secretary William Joynson Hicks, a Conservative government finally passed the Equal Franchise Act in 1928, with "just ten men" voting against it in the House of Commons. The Equal Franchise Act was one of a host of Acts passed during the 1920s affecting women's lives and gender equality. They also included the Sex Disqualification (Removal) Act 1919 that allowed women to enter certain professions for the first time including law, and legislation on property inheritance, nurses registration, marriage and divorce, equal guardianship, widows' and orphans' pensions, and adoption.

Women had been able to join the Labour party on the same terms as men since its inception and the party had put women at the heart of their 1918 manifesto. At the "Flapper Election" of 1929 following the Equal Franchise Act, of the 14 women then elected, nine were Labour. Most of this first cohort of Labour women were from working-class backgrounds, and were motivated

*Above*

Susan Lawrence leading a demonstration on equal franchise, c. 1920. Lawrence later became one of the first Labour women MPs

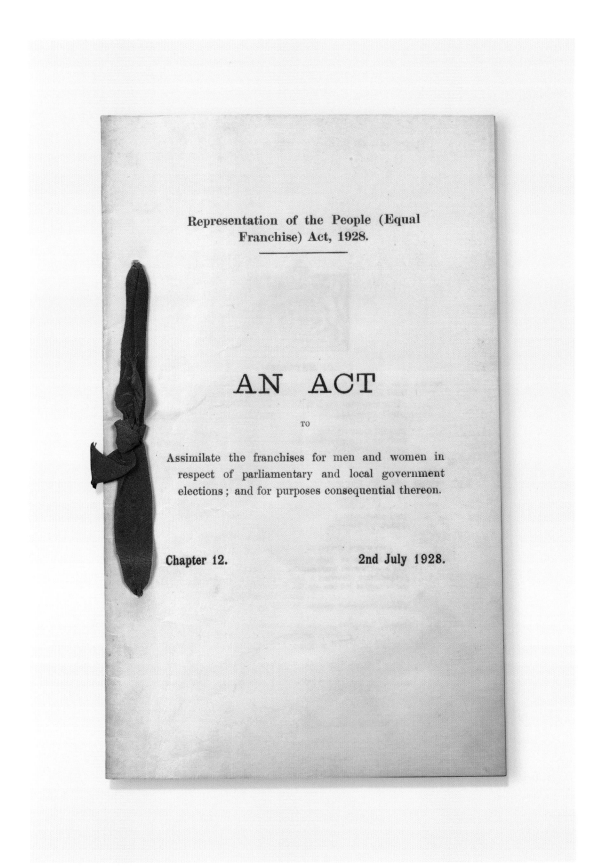

*Right*
Equal Franchise Act, 1928,
the Act that gave women
the vote on the same
terms as men, at age 21
and without any property
qualifications

English Universities, one of a small number of seats still returned by separate university electorates. She was a campaigning MP who ploughed her energies into promoting reforms which would help women, especially poorer mothers who were economically dependent on men. Rathbone's advocacy of Family Allowances, which were finally introduced in 1945, was one result. In the later 1930s, she also became a key voice in foreign-policy debates, vocally opposing the National Government's policy of appeasement and championing the cause of refugees seeking safe haven in Britain.

In her radicalism both on the domestic front and in international affairs, Rathbone found common cause with other women MPs. She helped to facilitate coordinated action in opposing the withdrawal of unemployment benefits to married women in 1931; in reforming the law which forced women to give up their nationality upon marriage to a foreign national; and in demanding equal pay for women civil servants. The first of these campaigns was unsuccessful, but the latter two demands were achieved in 1948 and 1955 respectively. As a critic of foreign policy, Rathbone forged an especially strong partnership with two other notable female parliamentarians of the decade, Labour's Ellen Wilkinson and the Conservative member for Kinross and

West Perthshire, the Duchess of Atholl. The trio made a well-publicised trip to war-torn Spain in 1937, drawing attention to the suffering of General Franco's victims and to the consequences of the British government's support for the policy of non-intervention.

In other areas, party loyalties and ideological differences could not be set aside so readily. Despite her best efforts, Nancy Astor's attempt to create a women's bloc in Parliament in 1929 foundered. Most women members chose instead to cultivate careers as faithful party supporters or as cause-driven campaigners – or to walk a tightrope in trying to balance the two. They did so from a position of numerical weakness. The pre-1945 highpoint for women's parliamentary representation was reached immediately after the 1931 election, when 15 female candidates were returned, accounting for a mere 2.4 per cent of the total number of MPs (though the election was a disaster for the female MPs of the Labour party, who all lost their seats). Nor were great strides made at ministerial level. Britain's first female Cabinet minister, Margaret Bondfield, who had been appointed Minister of Labour in 1929, lost her post with the fall of the second Labour government in the summer of 1931. There were to be no more women ministers until Florence Horsbrugh's appointment as parliamentary

*Left*
Women Labour MPs,
1929. Margaret Bondfield,
the first woman Cabinet
Minister, is centre front

*Above*

Eleanor Florence Rathbone (1872–1946), by Sir James Gunn, 1933

secretary at the Ministry of Health in late 1939. Women were thus still very much newcomers in the masculine world of Westminster. Labour's Edith Summerskill described the atmosphere in Parliament as akin to that of "a boys' school which had decided to take a few girls".

This marginal status was compounded by a tabloid press which treated women MPs as novelty items by running endless stories about their sartorial choices and personal lives – coverage of a kind rarely experienced by male politicians. Some women found ways to make this media interest serve their own purposes. Ellen Wilkinson, for example, took full advantage of the cameras and reporters who accompanied her as she marched with the unemployed men of Jarrow from north-east England to Parliament in 1936. Wilkinson

knew that the spectacle of a diminutive redhead flanked by flat-capped male workers would grab headlines and help to raise public awareness of the continuing problems of unemployment. Nonetheless, taken as a whole, women MPs struggled to convince the press to report their political views and activities seriously in the 1930s. The obsession with dress, appearance and "human interest" was an ominous foretaste of what subsequent generations of female politicians would be forced to tolerate when dealing with the media.

The 1930s was, then, a decade of limited progress for women in Parliament, notwithstanding the distinguished contributions made by individuals such as Rathbone or Wilkinson. The fullest expression of what women could achieve collectively as legislators

– that distinctive element identified by Rathbone – would have to wait until their representation in Parliament came much closer to approaching a critical mass. It was to be a long wait.

### THE IMPACT OF THE WAR

With the outbreak of the Second World War, Westminster was put on a war footing. Extraordinarily, more than 40 women worked in a munitions factory in the heart of Parliament under Central Lobby. They were mostly Parliamentary staff and wives of MPs working on

a voluntary basis, plus some paid staff. Other women participated in activities such as firewatching and Red Cross nursing. Six became auxiliaries in the Palace of Westminster Home Guard. The war saw increased employment opportunities for a few women. Kay Midwinter was appointed the first woman clerk (a senior official, organising the procedure of the House and its committees) in the House of Commons, working for the National Expenditure Committee. She went on to work for the Foreign Office and then the United Nations after the war. Two other women were employed as committee clerks on a temporary basis. Jean Winder was appointed the first permanent female Hansard reporter, fighting a long battle for equal pay before retiring in 1960.

In 1940 Edith Summerskill helped to form the Women for Westminster group to encourage more women to stand for Parliament. The group urged women party activists, whatever their political affiliation, to support female candidates. Its creation recognised the still negligible numbers of women in the Commons. At the outbreak of the Second World War there were 628 men MPs and a mere 12 women. Six of the 12 were Conservatives: Nancy Astor, Florence Horsburgh, Thelma Cazalet-Keir, Frances Davidson (Viscountess Davidson), Mavis Tate, and Irene Ward. Four were Labour: Ellen Wilkinson, Jennie Adamson, Agnes Hardie and Edith Summerskill. There was one Liberal, Megan Lloyd-George, and one Independent, Eleanor Rathbone. They were later joined by two widows, Beatrice Rathbone and Violet, Lady Apsley, who replaced husbands killed on active service. Beatrice Rathbone (whose husband was Eleanor's nephew) married again, changed her name to Mrs Wright and in 1943 became the first sitting woman MP to have a baby. Lady Apsley was the first woman MP who was a permanent wheelchair user.

This small group of women played a significant part in domestic politics. Three of them – Nancy Astor, Mavis Tate and Ellen Wilkinson – were said to have played a role in forcing the vote that toppled Neville Chamberlain as Prime Minister in May 1940. When Winston Churchill succeeded him, he appointed Wilkinson and Florence Horsburgh to ministerial posts. Both women were key figures in civil defence. Horsburgh, as a Parliamentary Secretary in the Ministry of Health, helped to organise the evacuation of one and half million women and

*Above*

Scrapbooks of Norah Runge MP, 1931–1935. Runge
was Conservative MP for Rotherhithe, east London.
Her speeches in Parliament reflect concern for the
poor in her constituency, slum clearance, and a strike
by Thames Lightermen. Her daughter Peg collected
two scrapbooks of press cuttings concerned with her
Parliamentary career

# "Jarrow has passed through a period of industrial depression without parallel in the town's history"

Ellen Wilkinson

*Opposite*
Ellen Wilkinson addressing
a crowd of Jarrow Marchers
in Hyde Park following
their march from Jarrow to
London, 1 November 1936

*Above*

House of Commons 1940, by John Worsley, 1947. Two women are visible on the government's side of the House, including Astor, clearly identifiable by her outfit

children from the major cities to safer places in the country. Later, she organised the casualty services, set up hostels for those bombed out of their homes, assumed responsibility for health and sanitation in the shelters and helped draft the post-war National Health Scheme. Ellen Wilkinson as a Parliamentary Secretary in the Home Office took charge of shelter provision, recruited women as fire-watchers and supervised changes in fire-fighting. Both exhausted themselves touring the country; both were bombed out of their homes, each on two separate occasions.

Women MPs responded vigorously to the challenge presented by wartime employment and labour policies which patently disadvantaged women workers. In 1940 Nancy Astor encouraged women backbenchers to

form a Woman Power Committee (WPC) to lobby government over a range of issues which concerned women, particularly equal pay and working conditions. There were disagreements: Ellen Wilkinson feared that the largely middle-class WPC might try to take over the role of the trade unions in representing women workers, and wrote to the Minister of Labour Ernest Bevin asking him to ensure that this did not happen. Bevin tried to circumvent the committee by establishing in March 1941 a separate Women's Consultative Committee (WCC) including trade unionists as well as women MPs. He asked them to advise him on the recruitment and organisation of women workers. However, most Labour women MPs continued to collaborate with the WPC, and the Conservative Mavis Tate formed an Equal Pay Campaign Committee, consisting of women from both bodies.

In December 1941, the committees worked together to try to obtain a guarantee of equal pay in the National Service (No. 2) Bill, which made certain groups of women liable for conscription. Though they failed, they continued to draw attention to the issue. In 1944 the Conservative MP Thelma Cazalet-Keir introduced an amendment to RA Butler's Education Bill to give women teachers the same pay as men. Although the amendment was passed, the following day Churchill demanded a reversal of the vote, angrily treating the issue as a matter of confidence in the government. The amendment was overturned, with only two women – Edith Summerskill and Agnes Hardie – voting for equal pay. It was a major defeat for the feminist MPs and a great disappointment for Cazalet-Keir, forced to vote against her own amendment.

Women MPs collaborated to challenge other discriminatory laws, including the 1939 War Injuries Act, which had set women's compensation for war-related injuries at 33 per cent less than men's. In November 1942 Mavis Tate, seconded by Edith Summerskill, moved an amendment to the Act, arguing in her speech that "this is not a party issue. It is not an issue between the sexes. It is an issue that is confined to justice". Other women backbenchers voted for Tate's amendment but the two women ministers remained loyal to the government and voted against. Tate's amendment failed but the government accepted the injustice of the 1939 Act and set up a

*Above*

Women MPs celebrating Megan Lloyd George's 20th anniversary in Parliament, 31 May 1949

Select Committee on which five women MPs served. On 7 April 1943 Parliament voted to accept its recommendations of equal compensation.

At times, parliamentary debates on these issues were characterised not so much as a clash between the parties as a clash between male and female MPs. There was wit and humour as well as seriousness. When Mrs Tate was asked by a male MP whether women ever made mistakes, she replied "I should be the last woman in the world to pretend that women do not make mistakes, when I look around and see some of the men they bring into the world."

In 1945 Ellen Wilkinson and Florence Horsburgh accompanied Clement Attlee, Anthony Eden and Lord Halifax to the San Francisco conference that established the United Nations. Following the end of the war in Europe, the Coalition government disbanded and was replaced by a Conservative caretaker government. Churchill appointed Thelma Cazalet-Keir Parliamentary Secretary in the Ministry of Education but told her not to bother with her "equal pay nonsense"; in what seemed like a gesture of compensation, however, the government passed Eleanor Rathbone's Family Allowance Act 1945.

There can be no doubt that women had been essential to the war effort, in agriculture, in industry, in civil defence, and in community welfare. Many served with the uniformed services; large numbers worked in factories; others worked as mechanics, engineers, ambulance drivers, electricians and plumbers. Some became secret agents working in occupied Europe. And a very small number were MPs who worked hard to protect women's interests even in the face of government opposition. Nevertheless,

at the end of the war, as had happened at the end of the First World War, many women were encouraged to give up paid work and return to the home to take care of their husbands and family.

### THE 1945 ELECTION AND AFTER

The July 1945 election was a watershed for many reasons. It had been ten years since the previous general election (there was no election during the war) and the war had produced huge changes in government and society and new policy challenges. The decisive result of the 1945 election, a landslide for Labour, produced the first Labour government with a secure majority and mandate to introduce a welfare state. It also produced a significant increase in the number of women in the House. They included some of the most important politicians in the post-war period.

Eighty-seven women stood as candidates, a 25 per cent increase on 1935. Twenty-four women MPs were elected, 15 of whom were new members. All but three of the 24 were Labour. There was only one Conservative (Viscountess Davidson), one Liberal (Megan Lloyd George) and one Independent (Eleanor Rathbone). The Conservative minister Florence Horsburgh lost her seat. A by-election in 1946 brought in a second Conservative woman, Priscilla, Lady Tweedsmuir. Some areas of the UK elected a woman MP for the first time, including Birmingham (Edith Wills), Liverpool (Bessie Braddock) and Leeds (Alice Bacon). But after 1945 there was little further progress in the number of women MPs: up to 1987 it did not increase beyond 29, representing under five per cent of the House.

Three of the women re-elected in 1945, Ellen Wilkinson, Edith Summerskill and Jennie Adamson, were promoted immediately. Wilkinson, as Minister of Education, became the second woman to hold Cabinet rank. She died shortly after raising the school-leaving age to 15 in April 1947. Summerskill was appointed a junior minister in the Ministry of Food, dealing with food rationing and continuing shortages. In 1949, she sponsored the Milk (Special Designation) Bill, requiring milk to be pasteurised against tuberculosis, so fulfilling a long campaign begun by Astor and Wintringham in the 1920s. As a doctor, Summerskill's parliamentary interests also extended to women's health issues, including childbirth and abortion. Adamson was

*Above*

Women MPs including Irene Ward, Barbara Castle and Dr Edith Summerskill outside the House of Commons with a petition of 80,000 signatures for equal pay, 8 March 1954

appointed a junior minister at the Ministry of Pensions, but she resigned as an MP in 1946 to become Deputy Chair of the Unemployment Assistance Board. Jennie Lee had to wait until 1964 for a substantial government post, when she became Minister for the Arts, and was charged with establishing what became known as the Open University. Megan Lloyd George, first elected in 1929, but emerging as a strong political force and radical voice in her own right following the death of her father, became Deputy Leader of the Liberal party in 1949.

Most of the new women MPs elected in 1945 had spent decades in the Labour or trades union movement, and knew each other. Some had sought selection for over a decade. They included journalist Barbara Ayrton-Gould, a former suffragette, imprisoned for window-smashing in 1912, and the barrister Freda Corbet. Nearly all, apart from Grace Colman, had been married. Most had families which had promoted political careers for daughters and wives, and many had trained as teachers. Jean Mann, a Glasgow MP with five children and a husband long unemployed, knew the realities of the poverty which she hoped the welfare state would eradicate. Many had been councillors, including Bessie Braddock, who had been prominent in local politics in Liverpool. Caroline Ganley and Mabel Ridealgh had long careers in the Co-operative Movement.

Labour women MPs were dedicated to the introduction of the welfare state and the implementation of their party manifesto, rather than pursuing an explicitly feminist agenda. They were vocal on the housing shortages, rationing and health needs of their constituents. Lucy Middleton, for example, served on the Estimates Committee and was influential on securing war damage payments. But many of the issues they pursued were of particular relevance to women. Leah Manning unsuccessfully pressed for family planning to be included within the NHS. Women continued to pursue equal pay and fought for an end to the married women's bar in the civil service and local government.

Three of the younger women MPs elected in 1945 – Barbara Castle, Alice Bacon and Margaret Herbison – would come to serve in the Labour governments of the 1960s and 1970s. In the 1945 Parliament, Castle became Parliamentary Private Secretary (PPS) to the Chancellor Stafford Cripps, an early indication of her abilities and ambition. She promoted the only successful private members' bill by a woman MP in this Parliament, the Criminal Law Amendment Bill of 1950, which gave women working as prostitutes more legal protection. As ever, the press were as ready to focus on her red hair and glamorous outfits as on her intellect. The Conservative Lady Tweedsmuir, who

*Below*
Margaret "Peggy" Herbison was Labour
MP for North Lanarkshire, 1945–70.
A collection of her papers and artefacts
were found in a Parliamentary desk in
2005, having apparently been abandoned
there in the 1950s. The papers reflect her
interests including Scotland, education,
women and the Labour Party

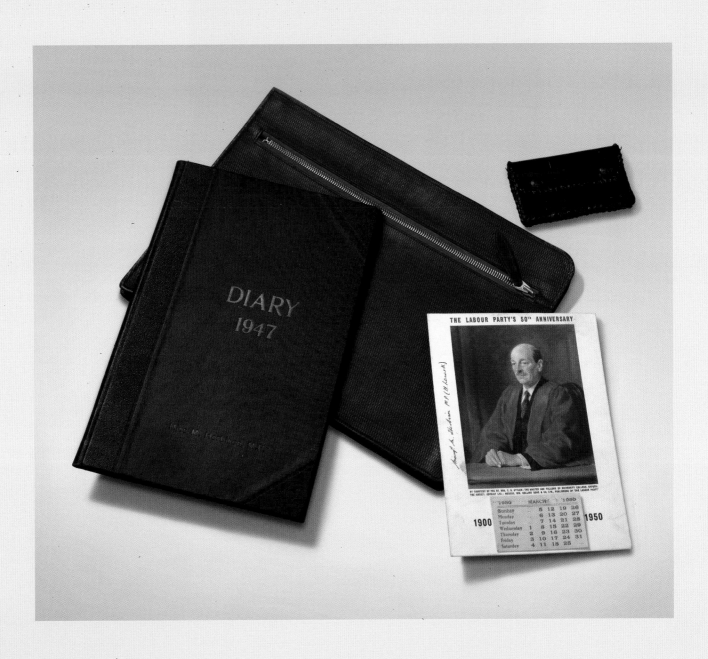

came into the House through a by-election in 1946, was – at 31 – the youngest woman MP, and attracted similar attention.

Women MPs progressed within party and parliamentary structures. Florence Paton became the first woman to join the Speaker's Panel of Members appointed to chair committees. In 1948 Viscountess Davidson became the first woman MP to be elected to the Conservative 1922 Committee Executive. In 1951, when Churchill returned as Prime Minister of a Conservative government, he appointed Florence Horsburgh – who had just regained a seat in the Commons – as Minister of Education; in 1953 he made it a Cabinet post, and Florence Horsburgh thus became the first woman to be a Conservative Cabinet Minister.

There were colourful interludes: Bessie Braddock lost a long-running libel case against the Bolton Evening News which had claimed she danced a jig on the floor of the House during the Transport Bill guillotine debates

in 1947. Braddock, a formidable presence, became in March 1952 the first woman to be named and suspended from a Commons sitting, following her protests about not being called to speak. Dame Irene Ward took an interest in developing female staff recruitment in the Commons, highlighting the lower pay offered to wartime female clerks: in 1955 she threatened to demonstrate how she was physically capable of carrying a library ladder into the Commons chamber if an advert specifying male-only librarians were not withdrawn; women had been employed in the Commons Library since 1946. Special legislation was passed in October 1945 to allow Jean Mann to retain her seat, when it emerged that her membership of a Scottish rent tribunal had inadvertently disqualified her as an MP.

And while women now held roles as senior party politicians and had national profiles, there were still cross-party friendships, promoted in part by the Lady Members' Room. In June 1949 Megan Lloyd George held a tea party for all women MPs to celebrate her 20 years in the House, and in her autobiography Leah Manning related visits with the Liberal MP to cinema matinees.

Progress had clearly been made. But the increase in the numbers of women elected to Parliament was not sustained: for 40 years after 1945 the number of women in the Commons hovered around the mid-twenties, or sometimes less, and women were still poorly represented in the Cabinet and even at junior ministerial level. It would take much more deliberate action to increase their numbers.

## WOMEN IN THE HOUSE OF LORDS

The story of women's admission to the House of Lords is less well-known than that of the campaign for votes for women, but it is a remarkable one. It was not until 1963, 45 years after winning the vote, that women sat in both

# "Probably this is the first occasion in 900 years that the voice of a woman has been heard in the deliberations of this House"

Baroness Elliot of Harwood

Houses of Parliament on equal terms with men. This is in contrast both to the House of Commons and other spheres such as the legal profession, which accepted women in the period around 1918. Indeed, for many men, it was partly these advances elsewhere which made it imperative to preserve the Lords as a male-only institution. But a more enduring obstacle than sexist attitudes was the question's entanglement with the difficult issue of overall reform of the Lords, then mainly made up of men who were there by virtue of their inherited peerage titles. The issue had been under debate since the reforms to the parliamentary franchise in the 19th century – and it remains far from completely resolved even now. After 1918 politicians debated whether women's admission to the House of Lords should precede or accompany the reform of the unelected chamber. It was the latter view that tended to prevail.

For centuries, women were able to hold peerages in certain circumstances, either by creation or by succession if there were no male heirs, although they lacked the political rights – especially the right to sit in the Lords – which usually accompanied a peerage. The status of female peers was rarely raised in the suffrage debates, partly as suffragists feared alienating moderate supporters by making additional demands. Twenty women held hereditary peerages in 1918. Their position became even more anomalous after ministers blocked efforts, made in the Commons and the Lords, to include them in the Parliament (Qualification of Women) Act.

The most politically active woman peer was former suffragette Margaret Haig Mackworth (née Thomas), Viscountess Rhondda, who inherited her father's peerage and business interests in 1918 and later founded The Six Point Group, a feminist campaigning organisation, and Time and Tide, a feminist, political and literary journal.

Viscountess Rhondda decided to seek admittance to the House of Lords, motivated by a desire mainly to establish the principle of equality rather than to sit. The 1919 Sex Disqualification (Removal) Act seemed to provide her with an opportunity. Although an amendment specifically covering the Lords had been rejected, the Act nonetheless proclaimed that persons would not be barred by sex or marriage "from the exercise of any public function", so she petitioned the Crown for a writ of summons to Parliament.

In 1922 the House of Lords' Committee for Privileges, and the Attorney General, agreed that she should receive a writ. Women celebrated this decision, but it caused concern in official quarters right up to the King: the Lords now faced the arrival of more than 20 women led by a formidable ex-suffragette. By contrast, there were still only two women MPs. No decision of the committee for privileges had been challenged since 1869; nevertheless, the Lord Chancellor, the former anti-suffragist Viscount Birkenhead, had her claim referred back to it for reconsideration. The committee was expanded with about 20 additional members, including Birkenhead. After heated debate it disallowed Rhondda's claim, concluding that the words "public function" did not include sitting in the Lords.

These manoeuvrings angered women's groups, and Lady Rhondda declared that the decision lowered the status of all women. Undeterred, she had a lawyer draft the Parliament (Qualification of Peeresses) Bill to rectify the situation. Sponsored by two supportive MPs, the bill easily passed the Commons. The real battle came in the Lords, where Viscount Astor, Nancy Astor's husband, introduced it five times between 1924 and 1929. Women peers themselves expressed varying levels of interest but Rhondda recruited a few of them to lobby members of the Lords for the bill.

THE HOPE OF HER SIDE.

*Above*

Lady Rhondda goes out to bat for women at the House of Lords, *Daily Express* cartoon, 19 May 1922

In 1925 the bill was defeated by just two votes (78 to 80) and victory seemed near. But when it was presented again a year later its opponents rallied, filling the House with "backwoodsmen", hereditary peers who rarely attended, to vote against it. The bill was defeated by 126 to 80, an exceptionally high turnout for the time, showing how seriously members regarded the threat of female encroachment. In 1930 Astor tried to get the House to support the proposal in principle with a non-binding motion, rather than introducing the bill again. This was also rejected.

Some of the speeches in these debates were sexist and derisive. Fifteen women's groups protested against the tone of the 1926 debate. The opponents of admitting women to the Lords described the admission of women into the Commons, where Nancy Astor had ruffled sensibilities, as a mistake to be avoided. They challenged the qualifications of these "privileged ladies" to sit in the Lords (although simply inheriting a peerage was sufficient qualification for men). Birkenhead referred to women as mere "conduit pipes" for transmitting peerages between male generations, noting disapprovingly that some had not produced male heirs. Baroness Ravensdale, one of the interested women peers, likened the opponents of the bill to drowsy flies in a warm room, fearing the entry of a few hornets. Lord Astor responded to them by accusing his colleagues of treating the House like a golf club, where they could blackball applicants, rather than an assembly passing laws affecting 40 million people (including an increasing amount of legislation specifically concerning women).

The issue lay dormant until 1946 when the House considered proposals for the reform of the Lords which included the creation of life peerages and the appointment of new women peers. The suggestion aroused less hostility than before but consensus remained elusive. The proposals were withdrawn without a vote. Disappointed, Rhondda and Baroness Ravensdale consulted solicitor Edward Iwi, a constitutional expert, and with Baroness Beaumont they launched a petition in 1947 to demonstrate public support. Backers included the heads of women's colleges, veteran suffragists, bishops, cultural luminaries including novelist Rebecca West and actress Sybil Thorndike, and women's societies, which helped collect 50,000 signatures. At last in 1949 the Lords voted in principle to admit hereditary women peers. But the motion – introduced by the Marquess of Reading and backed by the veteran suffrage campaigner Frederick, now Lord, Pethick Lawrence – was not binding. While peers' attitudes had softened, the Labour government, committed to a more comprehensive reform of the Lords, stated, frustratingly, that extending the hereditary principle to women would be wrong, though some ministers were uneasy with this position. The Labour government was more concerned with the House of Lords' powers than its composition and passed the 1949 Parliament Act simply reducing its ability to delay legislation, despite MP Leah Manning's impassioned plea to include a clause admitting women as members.

By the 1950s most accepted that the House should include women – the situation appeared more absurd after Elizabeth II became Queen – but still disagreed over

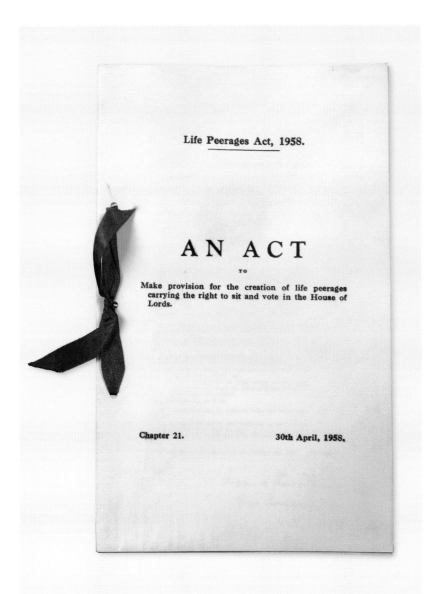

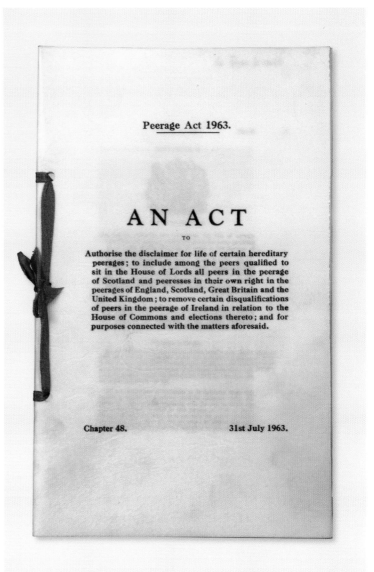

*Above, left*
Life Peerages Act 1958, the
Act that allowed women
and men to be appointed
Peers for life rather than
on a hereditary basis

*Above, right*
Peerage Act, 1963. This Act was passed
to allow Tony Benn MP to disclaim his
peerage. It also allowed hereditary women
peers to sit, therefore abolishing the final
inequality in Parliamentary membership

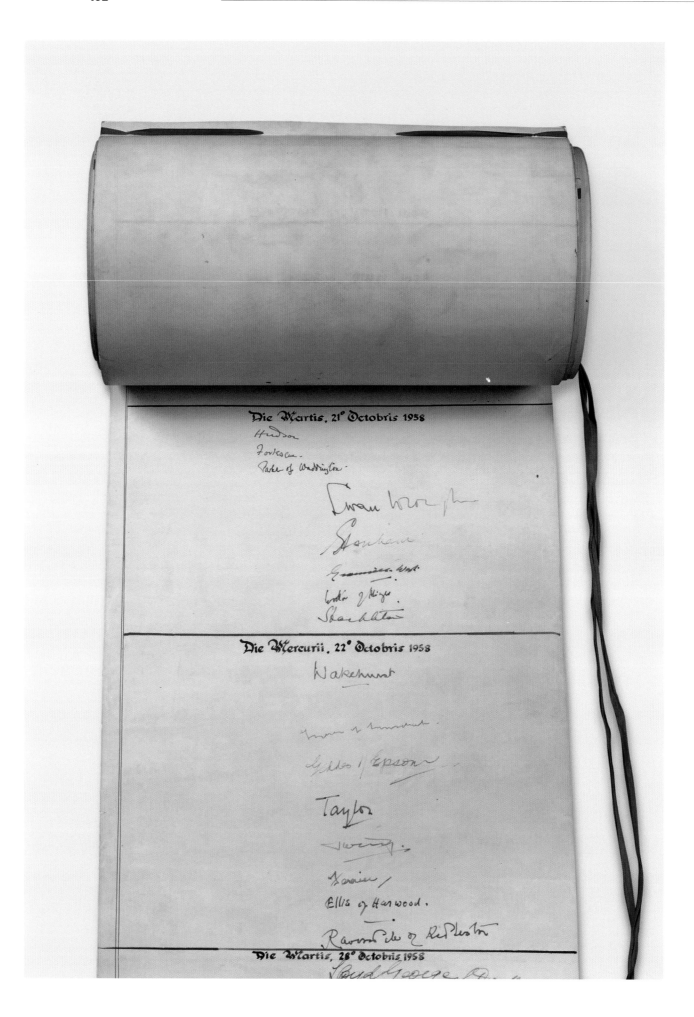

admitting them before more comprehensive reform. Ultimately it was the critical urgency of Lords reform which facilitated women's entry, though the intent was not to make it more representative but more effective. Its ability to legislate properly was crippled by an ageing membership, low attendance and serious party imbalance (Conservative hereditary peers greatly outnumbered Labour ones and Labour politicians were reluctant to accept hereditary peerages to close the gap). To recruit the new members required, the Conservative government finally adopted the idea of creating peerages that could not be inherited. The Life Peerages Act was passed in 1958. The Act ensured that women, as well as men, could become life peers, for it made no sense to continue barring half of the population if more members were needed.

A number of diehard peers continued to resist it. It was argued that the move could lead to the appointment of female ambassadors, which would be "vulgar", and that there was no room for the additional facilities that women would require; one even said that they did not want to sit with women on the benches or meet them in the library, candidly acknowledging that an underlying concern was maintaining male space. But these were now decidedly minority views. An amendment excluding women from the bill was decisively rejected. In the Commons, though, opposition to the bill came from the Labour party on the grounds that it would prevent proper reform. The Labour MP Jennie Lee unsuccessfully moved a similar amendment, unhappy with the idea that women peers might prop up what remained an undemocratic House of Lords. "The sooner it is replaced by a sensible and reformed House, the sooner we can get a decent improved constitutional arrangement," she argued. "If we cannot do that, if we have to have a second Chamber, let it be a sensible Chamber and, for goodness' sake, let us not try to drag in a number of women to camouflage it." She was opposed in the debate by Lady Tweedsmuir and Bessie Braddock.

The first 14 life peers included four women. They took their seats in October 1958, watched with interest by many women in the gallery. In common with the first women MPs, the majority had close family ties to Parliament. Three took no party affiliation. Katherine Elliot, Baroness Elliot of Harwood, was a Conservative party official, the widow of an MP, and a former United Nations delegate. Stella Isaacs, the dowager Marchioness of Reading, was recognised for having founded the Women's Royal Voluntary Services and became Baroness Swanborough. Irene Curzon, Baroness Ravensdale of Kedleston, a daughter of the staunch anti-suffragist Marquess Curzon of Kedleston, was nominated for her voluntary work, especially with youth clubs, and had been a hereditary peer since 1925. The only woman not following a male relation into parliament was social scientist Barbara, Baroness Wootton of Abinger, who "couldn't resist blitzing an all-male institution". A long-time magistrate and penal reform expert, she steered the bill abolishing capital punishment through the House in 1965 and became deputy speaker in 1967, three years before a woman attained this position in the Commons. The only discrimination she recalled was from the waitresses who suggested a women's table in the peers' dining room.

In early 1959 the Lords passed a further motion to admit the women hereditary peers but the government declined to act. They finally gained entry under the 1963 Peerage Act, which was primarily concerned with letting hereditary peers renounce their titles and stand for the Commons. The first to take her seat was Baroness Strange of Knokin, who had held her title since 1921. Some of those who entered the Lords, like Baroness Beaumont, had been waiting decades for admission. Viscountess Rhondda, though, was not among them, for she died in 1958, shortly after the first women life peers were announced. In 2011, she finally took her place in the House of Lords in another sense, when her portrait was hung in the peers' dining room to commemorate her campaign.

*Opposite*
House of Lords Test Roll, 1958. The Test Roll is signed by Peers as they take the oath. This Roll shows the signatures of the first four women to take their seats in October 1958

# THE CHAMBER: 1963 AND AFTER

By 1963 women MPs had been elected for all major parties, and from all the constituent parts of the UK (Northern Ireland had its first female MP in Patricia Ford in 1953). A number of women had had a significant role in several parties. But women were still a tiny minority in the House of Commons, and there were no more than a handful in the Lords. It would take another 40 years before women occupied many of the most prominent political positions in Parliament and government – including the role of presiding officer in either House, symbolised by the Speaker's Chair in the Commons, and the Woolsack in the Lords.

*Emma Crewe*
*Oonagh Gay*
*Emma Peplow*

## SELECTION COMMITTEES, QUOTAS AND WINNABLE SEATS, 1963–2015

There continued to be significant advances in the presence of women in the Commons. Women made a particular impact in the new and minor parties. In 1967 Winnie Ewing was only the second MP elected for the Scottish National Party (SNP). In 1969 the Irish Nationalist Bernadette Devlin made a strong impression as a 21 year old, elected for Mid-Ulster. Women who represented other minor parties include Caroline Lucas for the Greens and Naomi Long for the Alliance Party of Northern Ireland, both elected in 2010.

Diane Abbott's election in 1987 made her the first BAME (black, Asian or minority ethnic) female MP. Beatrice Wright had been the first woman to give birth as a serving MP in 1943, but the pregnancies of MPs Helene Hayman and Harriet Harman attracted much media attention in the 1970s and 1980s. As before, many women MPs had family connections with politics. Virginia Bottomley and Gwyneth Dunwoody were married to MPs at their first election. Harriet Harman's husband later became an MP. Winnie Ewing's daughter, Annabel Ewing, and daughter-in-law, Margaret Ewing, became MPs. The long-standing practice of widows taking over their husband's seat continued into the 2000s with Irene Adams and Gill Furniss.

Yet despite changes outside Westminster that increased female political activism and participation in the working world, it was not until the 1987 Parliament, when 41 female MPs were elected, that the proportion of women MPs in the Commons rose above five per cent of the whole House. It was clear the major obstacle to more women joining the Commons was the process of the selection of candidates by the political parties, and particularly selection by the major parties for "safe" or "winnable" seats. The percentage of female candidates had increased by 1992 to 18.3 per cent (up from 4.9 per

cent in 1945) but many of these women had little chance of topping the poll. Women in all major parties had difficulties in getting selected. MPs from both parties were questioned by selection committees about why they were leaving behind their husbands and families, or criticised for not knowing how to run a household if they were unmarried. Emma Nicholson was told by the Conservative Central Office that "the Conservative Party does not want women". Some Labour women felt excluded by the party's working-men's club, union-driven culture.

Things began to change in the Labour party in the late 1980s. Having avoided party politics in the 1970s, women's rights activists had joined the party in large numbers after Margaret Thatcher's election. Towards the end of the decade their interests aligned with a party leadership keen to modernise, especially after polling demonstrated that few female voters chose Labour. In 1983 the party committed itself to increasing women's involvement at all levels, and in subsequent years it adopted new rules designed to achieve it. In 1990 it set a target of women forming 40 per cent of Labour MPs by the year 2000. Shortly afterwards it introduced a policy of "all-women shortlists", designed to force local parties in half of the winnable seats to select women candidates. It was controversial amongst both men and women, and took the personal commitment of Labour leader John Smith to secure its passage. Challenged by two men who had been prevented from seeking selection by the policy, a tribunal decided in 1996 that the all-women shortlists were not lawful, ironically because of the Sex Discrimination Act 1975. By that time, though, enough women had already been selected to make a significant difference.

The number of women elected to the Commons had risen to 60 by 1992, but the biggest rise – to 120 – came as a result of Labour's all-women shortlists policy, at the general election of 1997. The increase had an immediate effect. One Liberal

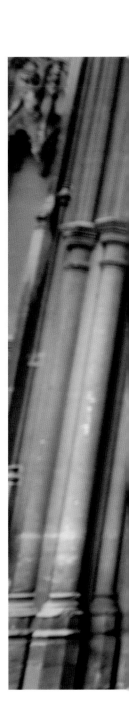

*Previous pages*
Women Members of Parliament and former Members of
Parliament now in the House of Lords, by Rolf Marriott,
2015. On 18 March 2015, shortly before the House rose
for the General Election, all women MPs and former
MPs now sitting in the House of Lords, were invited to
sit for this photograph. The numbers they are holding is
their place in the order of all women ever elected to the
House of Commons – Constance Markievicz was No. 1

*Below*
Diane Abbott MP
photographed in June
2010, during her campaign
for the leadership of the
Labour Party

Democrat MP recalled in the History of Parliament's oral history project how exciting it was to be part of this "dramatic" change. A Labour MP already in Westminster noted how the appearance of the chamber changed suddenly with women standing out in bright, colourful outfits. There were extremely high expectations. Some feminists believed that there was now a critical mass of women at Westminster, who would be able to make real changes. More women began to be elected for the other parties as well. Conservative women were elected in much greater numbers after 2005; in 2015 SNP women made a breakthrough, with 21 elected, forming over one third of their parliamentary party. From all parties, women MPs formed 29 per cent of those elected in 2015, and their substantial presence in the Commons is now taken for granted.

## WOMEN AND THE CULTURE OF PARLIAMENT

By the 1960s no one doubted that women should be involved in the political process. Yet it remained difficult for women to flourish in the overwhelmingly masculine culture and space of the Palace of Westminster. Interviews with women politicians, including for the History of Parliament's oral history project, testify to how much overt sexism remained in the 1960s and 1970s and even later. Women MPs were regularly mistaken for secretaries, employees or wives of MPs. It was frequently alleged that they were "more emotional" than their male counterparts. The Commons chamber, with its sometimes raucous, confrontational atmosphere, could be an intimidating place for outnumbered women MPs, whose sex could be used against them in personal attacks. For some it was worse: Barbara Castle wrote about a fellow cabinet member undoing

the buttons of her blouse during one vote, and more than one woman remembered being subject to groping within the chamber.

For most women politicians of this generation, this was part and parcel of working life. Many described having to "be tough" to succeed, or that it was "not as bad" as previous experiences in local government. Those who tried to change things found themselves facing more discrimination. Not all women sympathised with them, preferring instead to ignore the sexism and fit in with the men. Some rejected the idea that sexism was a problem at all, and argued that being a woman, and standing out from the men, could be a career advantage.

Westminster still had an atmosphere which many described as like a public school or a gentleman's club; women tended to refer to it more disparagingly as a "boys' club". Some women found it difficult to fit in. One, who remembered being welcomed by her male counterparts, still reflected that "men act in gangs" and "help other men out", excluding women from informal networks. Places like the Smoking Room were seen as not appropriate for women: one woman was told she was not a "nice girl" for venturing in. Yet to get things done, to keep up with the gossip and find out what was going on, women needed to enter these spaces and accept, ignore or counter the sexism they found there. Women also had problems with the press, which operated on very similar lines. Gendered press criticism, and a focus on dress, remained. Women seemed often to be "too" something – too colourful, too frumpy, too young or too old.

The timing and organisation of the Commons' sittings made things especially difficult for women with dependents, including young families. All-night or late-night sittings were common in the 1970s,

# "The beastlier people are to me, the more sure I am of my own rightness. To go down fighting with no thought of humiliation or abdication, that's life's biggest thrill"

Barbara Castle

*Right*

Barbara Castle on the
House of Commons terrace,
photographed c. 1960

*Above*

Lady Olga Maitland,
photographed in July 1984

and the conventions of the House were not designed to accommodate children. Considered "strangers", children could not be brought into the chamber or voting lobby. The Labour MP Helene Hayman (now Baroness Hayman) became well-known when she had a baby in the difficult summer of 1976. A tiny Labour majority meant that all members were required to be on call in case a vote was called at any time while the House was sitting. Heavily pregnant, she was unable to leave the House on long, hot summer nights; back just two weeks after giving birth, she was forced to bring her son with her. The press covered her story in detail, and as a consequence she received plenty of hate mail accusing her of neglecting her child, though contrary to press reports she did not breastfeed in the chamber. She was far from unusual, although not all women had quite the same perspective. Some were without families; for some, with dependents far from Westminster, in their constituencies or elsewhere, the problem was a different one.

By the 1970s women from different parties were no longer sharing a room. Janet (now Baroness) Fookes described "real friendships" created in the Conservative room and Hayman the "solidarity"

of Labour's. However, it was now less common for women of different parties to mix or to work together. Some issues did provoke female collaboration: Conservative MP Marion Roe's breakthrough bill on female genital mutilation in 1985 required cross-party support. Nearly two decades later Labour's Ann Clwyd promoted the Female Genital Mutilation Act 2003, replacing the 1985 legislation.

Women often felt a responsibility to support campaigns on what were thought of as "women's issues". Jo Richardson promoted the Domestic Violence and Matrimonial Proceedings Act 1976 to give women who suffered from domestic violence the right to apply for an injunction. The Bill was taken up by the Labour government, as the first major law to recognise domestic violence as a crime. While Clare Short's attempts to ban *The Sun* newspaper's Page 3 photos of topless women were not successful, her campaign brought her much popular support, and *The Sun* eventually discontinued the feature. But those – for example pro-NATO defence campaigner Lady Olga Maitland – with an expertise on policy areas that were particularly dominated by men, often felt that they were shut out of these debates, though they campaigned on them regardless. And the range of subjects covered by women went well beyond "women's issues", working, for example, on private members' bills on very diverse topics. Dame Irene Ward secured several including the Rights of Entry (Gas and Electricity Boards) Act 1964, the Nurses (Amendment) Act 1961 and the Penalties for Drunkenness Act 1962. In 1960 Margaret Thatcher made her maiden speech introducing the Public Bodies (Admission to Meetings) Bill. Jill Knight piloted the Design Copyright Act 1968, a response to injustices suffered by a constituent whose work was subject to unauthorised copying.

From the late 1960s, women began to be appointed to more senior staff roles in Parliament. House of Commons Hansard employed its second permanent female reporter, Margaret Pass, in 1968; the following year saw Jacqy Beston (later Sharpe) and Alda Milner-Barry become the first women clerks since the Second World War. The House of Lords followed in the 1970s, with the first clerk, Fiona

MacLeod (later Martin), arriving in 1981. Further breakthroughs came in the late 1990s with the arrival of the first "Lady Doorkeepers", Maureen Coxon in the Commons and Stella Devadason in the Lords. In 2008 Jill Pay became the first woman Serjeant-at-Arms, in charge of ceremony and security in the House of Commons. In 2018 Sarah Clarke was appointed the first female Black Rod (the counterpart of the Serjeant-at-Arms in the Commons). No women have advanced to the most senior positions of Clerk of the Parliaments or Clerk of the House.

### WOMEN AT THE TOP

It continued to be rare for women to be ministers, and it took a long time for them to be accepted in more senior positions within the major political parties. But despite the obstacles, by the 1960s and the 1970s, a few women were taking positions of real standing and power within their respective parties. The careers of three of them, Barbara Castle, Shirley Williams and Margaret Thatcher – the most prominent and famous

*Right*
Jill Pay, Assistant Serjeant at Arms, by David Partner, 2007. Jill Pay was appointed Serjeant at Arms, the Parliamentary official responsible for security of the House of Commons, in 2008, the first woman to hold the post since its establishment in 1415

of women politicians in the 20th century – illustrate how gradually women advanced into the front rank of politics.

Barbara Castle was first elected as Labour MP for Blackburn in 1945. Her ability was recognised in the first Labour government formed under Harold Wilson in 1964, when she became Minister for Overseas Development, and then Minister for Transport in 1966. She was the first woman to hold successive posts in Cabinet. At Transport, she introduced major initiatives, including the compulsory wearing of seat belts and breathalyser tests. In 1970, as Secretary of State for Employment and Productivity, she was responsible for introducing the first equal pay legislation in 1970 and for an unsuccessful attempt to reform trade unions.

As Secretary of State for Social Services in 1974–6 she was responsible for a reform of state pensions to take account of years spent in caring responsibilities at home, and fought to introduce non-means-tested child benefit payable to the mother. After standing down from Parliament in 1979, Mrs Castle continued her career as a Member of the European Parliament and then in the House of Lords from 1990 until her death in 2002.

Shirley Williams, first elected for the Labour party in 1964, entered the Cabinet as Secretary of State for Prices and Consumer Protection in 1974. Her most important contribution, though, was to oversee the expansion of the comprehensive schools programme as Secretary of State for Education from 1976 to 1979. The move to abolish grammar schools and secondary moderns had begun under Margaret Thatcher in 1970, but Williams presided over a decisive but controversial change in British education policy. Defeated in the general election of 1979 and disturbed by the drift of Labour to the left, she resigned from the party and became one of the "Gang of Four", the founder members of the new Social Democratic Party (SDP). She became its first MP in 1981, when she won a by-election at Crosby, and was elected SDP President in 1983. But she lost her seat in the 1983 general election and never returned to the Commons. The SDP would merge in 1987 with the Liberals to form the Liberal Democrat Party. Appointed a Liberal Democrat peer in 1993, Williams served as that party's leader in the Lords from 2001 to 2004, retiring from the House in 2016.

Margaret Thatcher's achievement in becoming the first woman Leader of the Opposition and the first female Prime Minister was remarkable, given how few women had been Conservative MPs. She spent nearly a decade attempting to be elected as a Conservative candidate, finally winning Finchley in 1959. She was appointed Secretary of State for Education in 1970 in Edward Heath's administration, but she stood against Heath for the leadership of the Conservative party and won, becoming the Leader of the Opposition in 1975 – at a time when there were only seven Conservative women MPs in the Commons. She built on this success by leading her party to victory at the next general election in 1979.

Mrs Thatcher held the office of Prime Minister for longer than anyone else during the 20th century.

*Right*
The Rt. Hon. Margaret
Thatcher OM, MP,
Prime Minister, by
Henry Mee, 1992

*Above*

Virginia Bottomley, Secretary of State for National Heritage, at the launch of International Jazz Day, 1996

Among the most influential of 20th-century prime ministers, she remains the most controversial. Her actions, for example, in instituting the right to buy for council tenants, going to war with Argentina over the Falkland Islands in 1982, and privatising major state-owned businesses – telecoms, gas, electricity and water – still arouse passionate support and hostility in equal measure. She lost office in 1990 when she was herself challenged successfully for leadership of the Conservative Party, after her poll tax policy proved unpopular with the electorate. Mrs Thatcher became a life peer in 1992. She died in 2013.

Mrs Thatcher did not include another woman within her Cabinet until Baroness Young became Leader of the Lords in 1982, and it was not until after John Major succeeded her as Prime Minister in 1990 that more than one woman sat in a Conservative Cabinet at a time – Virginia Bottomley and Gillian Shepherd were both in the Cabinet between 1992 and 1997. The Labour party briefly had a female leader in 1994, when Margaret Beckett became acting leader for a period after the sudden death of John Smith. Tony Blair's Cabinet in 1997 was the first to have as many as five women Cabinet Ministers at any one time. David Cameron's Cabinet had four in 2010, increasing to seven in 2015. In 2016 Theresa May became the second female Prime Minister, and

appointed eight women to the Cabinet, 35 per cent of its total membership. Since 2000, it has become normal for women to be senior ministers. They have held most of the major offices of state for the first time, including Home Secretary (Jacqui Smith, 2007), Foreign Secretary (Margaret Beckett, 2006), and Lord Chancellor (Liz Truss, 2016). The only exception remains the Chancellor of the Exchequer, a position which has never been held by a woman.

As women moved into positions of power within political parties, policy agendas began to change in response. The introduction of equal pay legislation in the 1970s is one example. The creation of a statutory minimum wage in 1998 was the biggest increase in women's pay since the Equal Pay Act 1975. Another example was domestic violence, although it was a backbencher, Jo Richardson, who piloted through the House of Commons the Domestic Violence and Matrimonial Proceedings Act 1976, the first major law to recognise domestic violence as a crime. More recently Theresa May, as Home Secretary in 2015, ensured that coercive control was included within the definition of domestic violence. Tessa Jowell, as Minister for Employment, was the prime mover behind the introduction of the right to request flexible working hours in the Employment Act 2002, and this right was eventually extended by

*Above*

Women Secretaries
of State by John Ferguson,
2010. All served in the
Labour governments of
1997–2010

the Coalition government to all employees in 2014. It was Harriet Harman, as Minister for Women and Equality, who piloted the Equality Act 2010 through the Commons, which harmonised and extended existing law affecting women's rights.

## CHALLENGING WESTMINSTER CULTURE FROM THE 1990S

Many of the women who came into Parliament for the first time in 1992 and 1997 were from a younger generation, shocked to discover Parliament still dominated by a sexist culture that was increasingly challenged in wider British society. They described "boorish" and abusive behaviour in the chamber. Young women MPs were still mistaken for staff and secretaries, and it was still assumed that their interests would be limited to "women's issues"; some felt in addition that their growing numbers induced a stronger reaction from some men. Coverage of women MPs in the press and elsewhere continued to focus on their gender and their dress. Labour women who posed for an infamous photograph surrounding the new Prime Minister were labelled "Blair's babes". At the same time, they faced criticism from many in the women's movement for not doing more for women's interests. Analysis of their voting behaviour suggested that Labour women were less

likely to rebel against the party whip than were their male counterparts, though the reasons for this are complex. Some women argued that their style of politics was less confrontational, a more collaborative and behind-the-scenes approach, which was not respected by either the press or many in Westminster. Political scientists and historians remain divided about whether such a specific style exists, or how effective it was.

Nevertheless, the 1990s saw a shift in the attitudes, culture and working practices of Westminster, starting from the top. There had been women Deputy Speakers since Betty Harvie Anderson became the first in 1970, but it was not until the election of Betty Boothroyd as Speaker in 1992 that women started to significantly influence the working practices of the House of Commons. Boothroyd became an outstanding Speaker, commanding the confidence of the House at a time when John Major's government had only a tiny majority. She dispensed with the traditional wig, and introduced a more modern style of dress, and as such came to represent a new type of speakership.

Changing the way that the House of Commons was run, though, proved frustratingly difficult. The problems of doing so were symbolised by the demands to turn the rifle range into a crèche (the

# "Elect me for what I am, and not for what I was born"

Betty Boothroyd, in the Speakership Election 1992

range survived until 2015). Even women could disagree on the nature of the changes required. The demand for "family-friendly" working hours for the Commons, for example, was of much less concern for those whose constituencies, and family homes, were well outside London, and who were unable to return to see children or partners on a free evening. Nevertheless, changes were made. Plans to modernise sitting hours had been under discussion since the early 1990s, but real progress was only made after 1997 and the establishment of the Modernisation Committee under the first woman Leader of the House of Commons, Ann Taylor. Under successive Leaders of the House, including Robin Cook, the committee became the driving force behind more "family-friendly" hours in the Commons. The time at which the House of Commons met was brought forward and time limits routinely placed on discussion on bills; the date of recesses was fixed in advance. Late-night votes and all-night sittings became much rarer, and the change fed through into changes in the culture of Parliament. Taylor had been one of the first women to become a whip, in the fraught Labour years of 1976-79, when the government's slim majority meant that every vote counted. In 1998 she became the first female Chief Whip, responsible for managing the Parliamentary Labour Party. There is some evidence that female appointments helped from the 1990s onwards to soften the traditionally aggressive approach of the whips' offices to ensuring the attendance of Members at key votes.

Women MPs began to chair select committees during the 1960s. Bessie Braddock was made chair of the Kitchen and Refreshment Rooms Select Committee in 1964/5, and Margaret Herbison chair of the Overseas Aid Select Committee in 1969/70. The establishment of the new departmental select committees in 1979 offered an alternative career to MPs. A number of women benefited, achieving prominence in the Commons and a considerable presence outside it. Renee Short was the first woman to take the chair of one of these committees (the Social Services Committee). Gwyneth Dunwoody was a formidable operator as chair of the Transport Committee, successfully defying the whips to keep her position when there was an attempt to remove her in 1992, a pivotal moment in developing the independence of the select committee system. Margaret Hodge was the first woman chair of the prestigious Public Accounts Committee in 2010. Reforms to the standing orders of the House to enhance the role of backbenchers, initiated in the wake of the disastrous expenses scandal in 2009, resulted in the creation of the Backbench Business Committee in 2010. The first chair was Natascha Engel, who was seen as effectively exploiting its powers for the benefit of the select committees and individual backbenchers.

From the viewpoint of the 2010s the House of Commons looks very different to what it did in 1963. The Conservatives and Liberal Democrats have both worked to address the lack of women in their cohorts. The SNP group elected in 2015 was 36 per cent female. A nursery was introduced in 2010, and a Women and Equalities Select Committee was established in 2015 to match the ministerial post created in 1997. The children of MPs are no longer

*Right*
The Rt. Hon. Betty
Boothroyd, by Andrew
Festing, 1994

*Above*
The Prime Minister and
Members from both Houses
gather in Central Lobby to
celebrate the centenary of the
Representation of the People
Act 1918, 6 February 2018

"strangers". It was the male half of Andrew Hames's Liberal Democrat parents, Duncan Hames and Jo Swinson, who first took him through the voting lobbies. Women MPs continue to work for a wide spectrum of policy issues through debates, questions, bills and amendments, and their achievements are no longer unusual or exceptional. Women MPs are now an essential component of today's Commons. But parity of representation remains some way off. The House of Commons has become considerably more female-friendly since 1963, but recent instances of harassment show that many inequalities persist, and it remains well short of perfect.

## WOMEN IN THE HOUSE OF LORDS FROM 1963 TO THE PRESENT

The first woman to take her seat in the House of Lords, Baroness Swanborough, described the House of Lords as "a delicious place to be in. People move so slowly. Nobody runs down passages; nobody uses used envelopes; nobody does anything for himself if he can ask a gentleman with a gold chain to do it for him". Some male peers took time to adjust to the advent of women, with several complaining that women's lavatories took up space or even that women in politics was distasteful. But gradually women's presence was accepted, and women came to occupy an increasingly important role in the chamber.

As in the Commons, numbers of women in the Lords took a long time to grow to significant numbers. There was a small leap in the mid-1960s. As before, a number of the earlier appointments were wives or widows of senior politicians (for example Anna Gaitskell, Baroness Gaitskell; Barbara Brooke, Baroness Brooke of Ystradfellte; Clementine Churchill, Baroness Spencer-Churchill), although many of them had themselves been politically active, some of them – such as Violet Bonham-Carter, Baroness Asquith of Yarnbury – at the highest level. There were others who had themselves been MPs, such as Edith Summerskill (Baroness Summerskill), Frances Davidson (Baroness Northchurch), Irene Ward (Baroness Ward of North Tyneside), Alice Bacon (Baroness Bacon) and Jennie Lee (Baroness Lee of Asheridge) – despite the latter's opposition to the Life Peerages Act. There were some who had been important backroom political operators, women such as Beatrice Serota (Baroness Serota), quickly made a minister after her elevation to the peerage in 1967, or Marcia Williams (Baroness Falkender), Harold Wilson's political secretary who was accused of exercising an undue influence over nominations to the peerage in the so-called "Lavender list" affair of 1976. There were politically-associated campaigners, such as Betty Lockwood (Baroness Lockwood), equal pay campaigner and first chair of the Equal Opportunities Commission. But a growing number were less directly associated with party politics: Lucy Faithfull, Baroness Faithfull, elevated in 1975, was a children's campaigner; Sue Ryder, Baroness Ryder of Warsaw, who accepted her peerage in 1979, had become famous for her work on relieving post-war destitution in Europe.

By the early 1980s, women constituted a little more than 5 per cent of the House. As in the Commons, it was not until the 1990s, and especially after 1997, that there was a significant change in the proportion of women, though this was as much the effect of the removal of men as the introduction of more women: the 1999 House of Lords Act evicted all but 92 hereditary peers, thereby almost doubling the proportion of women peers from 8.8 to 15.8 per cent.

Allowing a relatively small number of hereditaries to remain was a compromise reached during the passage of the Act. The 92 were chosen by election by all of the hereditary peers. During the election, women secured the most votes in two of the categories in which the vote was organised: the Countess of Mar as a Deputy Speaker and Baroness Darcy de Knayth as a Crossbencher.

Following the removal of most of the hereditary peers, the independent House of Lords Appointments Commission was established in 2000 to appoint each year a small number of non-party political or crossbench life peers. Only 23, or 36 per cent of the life peers appointed on its recommendation by 2015 were women. Attracting applications from women, rather than the selection process, seems to be the reason for this low proportion: 80 per cent of the nominations the commission received in its first round were from men. The Appointments Commission's members have said that the calibre of those women candidates who were nominated was exceptional.

Most peers still, though, are appointed as a result of nominations by the leaders of the political parties. These appointments have been even more skewed towards men: only 22 per cent of those chosen by party leaders since 1958 have been women. Party peerages continue commonly to be a reward for service in the House of Commons (one quarter of

peers appointed between 1997-2015 were former MPs), so this poor record partly reflects male dominance in the lower house.

By the summer of 2017, nearly 26 per cent of the members of the House of Lords were women. Three groups have endured as overwhelming male: hereditary peers, bishops and law lords. Of the hereditary peers, only one is a woman and since the vast majority of hereditary peerages can only be inherited by men, few of the 92 are likely to be women in the near future. The 26 seats occupied by the Bishops were all taken by men until 2015 when the Bishop of Gloucester, Rachel Treweek, sat as the first woman Bishop. Only one woman – Baroness Hale – had been one of the Law Lords, who were members of the House of Lords and operated as the final court of appeal in the legal system, before the creation of the Supreme Court in 2009 and their removal from the Lords.

Although there have been far fewer women than men in the Lords, the women have had a disproportionate impact. One reason is that they attend more often. In the 1980s 44 per cent of women as against 22 per cent of men attended half or more of the possible sitting days. With the departure of most hereditary peers, many of whom attended rarely, the difference decreased, but was still noticeable. In 2010-2014 women peers

*Left*
Leaders of the House of Lords: Baroness Ashton of Upholland, Baroness Amos & Baroness Jay of Paddington, by Desirée Pfeiffer, 2008

*Above*

Baroness Hayman,
The Lord Speaker, by
Desirée Pfeiffer, 2008

attended 70 per cent of possible sitting days while men attended only 60 per cent. Women also relatively quickly took leading roles. The Labour peer Baroness Llewellyn Davies of Hastoe was the government Chief Whip in the Lords in 1974-9; Baroness Hylton-Foster was Convenor of the Crossbench peers from 1974 to 1995; and Baroness Young was Leader of the House from 1981 to 1983. This was far earlier than similar roles had been taken by women in the Commons. The first Lord Speaker, elected in 2006 following the separation of the roles of Lord Chancellor and speaker of the House of Lords, was Baroness Hayman (Helene Hayman); the second, who followed her in 2011, was Baroness D'Souza (Frances D'Souza). Six out of the last nine Leaders of the House have been women, one of whom, Baroness Amos, was also the first black woman cabinet minister in the UK.

Women peers are currently better represented on the front-bench in the Lords than are women MPs in the Commons. In 2015 only 24 per cent of ministers in the Commons were women, compared to 37 per cent in the Lords, and both Leaders of the House of Lords were women. The first Lord Speaker, Baroness Hayman, commented that "it gives me some quiet satisfaction that, should a man break through the glass ceiling to succeed me, he will be known as the first male Lord Speaker" (as Lord Foster became in 2016).

Women thrive in the upper House. Nothing compels backbenchers to attend, aside from requests from the whips or peer pressure, so those with dependents or time-consuming responsibilities outside are less disadvantaged than in most organisations. In the Lords' debates wit,

*Left*

Debate – Human Fertilisation and
Embryology Bill: Lord MacKay of Clashfern,
Lord Jenkin of Roding, Lord Alton of
Liverpool, Baroness Tonge, Baroness Barker
and Baroness Deech, by Desirée Pfeiffer,
2008. Participants in the debates on the
bill pictured in the House of Lords library

self-deprecation and a light touch are prized above aggression. The self-regulated chamber, with no peer chairing debates, operates rather like a Quaker meeting, and this suits women well. It has been argued, though, that the self-regulation of its debates can work against women: when there is strong competition to speak the House makes a collective decision who will speak next, and that choice may be influenced by considerations related to gender. When women fail to impress as speakers sometimes it is explained by reference to their gender – they might be described as sounding as shrill as "fishwives", for example. Like the Commons, outside the chamber or committees, the Lords feels like a gentleman's club. In the corridors and bars women can feel excluded and demeaned by comments on their physical appearance or assumptions about how they operate. And different women in the Lords, and different groups of women, may have different perspectives According to estimates, there were only 20 female black and minority ethnic peers in 2016. Three lesbian peers only came out recently (the first was Conservative Baroness Stedman-Scott), a reminder that some groups of women remain especially under-represented or marginalised.

Women peers' relatively high standing partly emerges out of the relationship between the two Houses. The Lords plays a less powerful role in the British constitution than does the Commons. Its classic role is to review and revise the government's proposed bills, rather than the direct confrontation over them

expected in the House of Commons. Some members of the Lords on the government side become ministers and speak for the government, but they usually have less status than their counterparts in the Commons. Those who rise to the top of the Commons reach positions of considerable power. In the Commons politics is carried out in a series of competitive and aggressive rituals, designed to communicate the strength of one's own side and the weakness of one's opponents. In less publicly visible sites – the House of Lords chamber, committees and meetings and MPs' constituency surgeries, as examples – where politics is less concerned with competition and aggression, women parliamentarians tend to excel.

As Lord Longford claimed in a debate in 1985, "there is no side of British life where women are quite so prominent and influential as in the House of Lords". In theory, at least, all peers are equal: peers are listened to with equal respect and the impression they make on each other depends on how they perform. One expresses a typical view: "Working peers are not considered inferior, even former senior ministers are not looked up to. Dukes do not get more respect. Each peer is judged by their contribution, so internally it is a meritocracy." With just over a quarter of peers being women – 218 out of 837 in 2017 – there is clearly still far to go. But as the numbers of women have steadily grown over the last half century or so, they have become one of its most valued and powerful elements.

# BNY MELLON

Original thinkers 128

Exceptional people 132

Investing in the future 136

# ORIGINAL THINKERS

When it comes to diversity, inclusion
and gender equality, BNY Mellon draws
from its founder's radical spirit

WWW.BNYMELLON.COM

Alexander Hamilton, one of the founding fathers of the United States and the man who established the Bank of New York in 1784, said that "experience is the parent of wisdom." Almost two and half centuries later, the vision of this extraordinary man is seen in the bank's modern incarnation.

Today, BNY Mellon embraces a wide diversity of talents, perspectives and backgrounds, with more than 50,000 employees around the world harnessing their differences – those they were born with and those acquired through diverse life experiences – to make unique contributions. As of 31 March 2018, the company now has $33.5 trillion of assets under custody and/or administration, with operations in more than 100 markets across 35 countries.

For Hani Kablawi (pictured right), Chairman – Europe, Middle East and Africa (EMEA), BNY Mellon, Hamilton's legacy is embedded in the bank's ethos and how it does business today, particularly in terms of how it promotes gender equality. "Hamilton was a true visionary," says Kablawi. He was a man of ideas but also a man of implementation. As the creator of the financial system and the first Secretary of the US Treasury, he laid the groundwork for the modern global economy. He championed equal opportunity for all. This is reflected in the fact that Hamilton's face has appeared on the $10 bill (pictured, opposite) since 1928.

Hamilton was a man of firsts, founding the US Coast Guard, the US Mint and the *New York Post* newspaper. Carrying on this spirit of enterprise and entrepreneurialism, BNY Mellon is, likewise, a company of firsts. It created the first tax-exempt funds, the first commodity exchange traded funds and the first mobile securities processing application. One of BNY Mellon's most significant firsts, however, was the decision to do business with women, which dates back to the 1870s when it started encouraging

women to take control of their finances. This focus continues with services and research supporting women investors, and raising awareness among financial services companies on how to effectively serve women investors. Today, BNY Mellon believes that striving for gender equality and financial inclusion, both within and beyond its offices, is key to its success.

An unwavering commitment to diversity and inclusion is central to BNY Mellon's commitment to its people and to making talent a competitive advantage. In 2017, 42 per cent of BNY Mellon's global workforce, 41 per cent of its new hires, and 36 per cent of its vice presidents were women, while a quarter of BNY Mellon's board was female. These achievements were recognised by the firm's inclusion for the third year running in the inaugural Bloomberg Gender-Equality Index.

"Gender equality is good business," says Kablawi. "Companies that prioritise it are more successful." McKinsey & Company found that companies in the top quartile for gender diversity on their executive teams were 21 per cent more likely to experience above-average profitability than companies in the bottom quartile. Boston Consulting Group conducted a global survey, revealing a strong relationship between diversity of management teams and overall innovation. Companies reporting above-average diversity on their management teams also reported innovation – measured in terms of new products and services launched in the past three years – that accounted for 45 per cent of total revenue versus just 26 per cent for companies with below-average management diversity.

Furthermore, women's financial inclusion can increase economic growth and market returns. BNY Mellon's new report, *Powering Potential*, published

in partnership with the United Nations Foundation in March 2018, highlights the potential opportunities for financial services companies to expand women's access to financial products and services. The research found that closing the gender gap in women's access to financial products and services could unlock $330 billion in annual global revenue and transform the lives of hundreds of millions of women.

Research by Pershing LLC, a BNY Mellon company, shows women in the US control two-thirds of annual spending and will be responsible for 70 per cent of intergenerational wealth transfer over the next 40 years. Additionally, Pershing's research found that 80 per cent of women are solely responsible for household financial decisions at some point in their lives.

BNY Mellon's vision is improving lives through investing. That sense of purpose and commitment to local communities also drove the decision by Newton Investment Management, one of BNY Mellon's UK businesses, to sponsor the Women's Boat Race between the universities of Oxford and Cambridge. The men's race had received significant funding and been featured on television for many years, while the women's race was relatively underfunded and lacked similar attention. That changed in 2010 when Newton became the women's race's first sponsor. "Through sport, you can create networks of people who have had very strong team-building experiences, such as the Men's Boat Race, which lead them to employ and empower each other," says Hanneke Smits (pictured opposite), CEO of Newton Investment Management. "If their female equivalents have not had that experience, they are unable to develop those same networks."

Newton worked to help bring the women's race in 2015 from Henley, Oxfordshire, to the same stretch of the Thames in London where the men race, thereby ensuring they shared television rights, funding and exposure. The collaboration required to bring this about was boosted in 2013 when BNY Mellon took over sponsorship of the men's race.

In 2016, BNY Mellon and Newton decided to donate their title sponsorship rights to Cancer Research UK (CRUK) in order to boost the fundraising ability of this ground-breaking charity, which relies on donations for 100 per cent of its funding. The initiative was a world first.

Last year, in seeking to develop their support for the charity, BNY Mellon and Newton launched an initiative called CASCAID, which brought the investment management community together to raise funds for CRUK. Smits and a team of 60 colleagues raised £75,000 by walking across the Isle of Wight, while a BNY Mellon crew rowed 72 miles across the Irish Sea. In total, BNY Mellon and Newton, together with the CASCAID initiative have raised more than £3 million for CRUK.

In 2018, Newton and BNY Mellon joined forces with The Boat Race Company and Fulham Reach Boat Club to launch Future Blues, a charity that reaches out to underprivileged children in the London boroughs that border the Boat Race course. The charity engages these children in rowing activities and, in doing so, helps them improve their teamwork, focus and confidence.

These are just a few examples of BNY Mellon's enterprise-wide corporate social responsibility mission. Kablawi says that both the history and current practice at BNY Mellon point to the benefits of achieving and sustaining gender diversity. As he explains, "we are really focused on thinking about things from different perspectives. The more experience we can bring to the table, the more we can look at issues from different perspectives, the better the decisions we can make."

# "Gender equality is good business – companies that prioritise it are more successful"

---

Hani Kablawi, BNY Mellon

# EXCEPTIONAL PEOPLE

Financial services giant BNY Mellon knows
that its people are its greatest asset

WWW.BNYMELLON.COM

"For us, being a top employer means creating an environment where our people can succeed – to challenge and enable them to do their best work, and reward them for their achievements," says Monique R Herena, BNY Mellon's Chief Human Resources Officer and Senior Executive Vice President, Marketing and Communications.

BNY Mellon and its subsidiary companies know people are their greatest asset, and valuing people's unique perspectives and contributions will empower them to thrive. This means a commitment to building, developing and retaining exceptional and dynamic teams is a strategic focus across all business areas and levels of the organisation. "We believe our best investment is the one we make in our people," says Herena.

BNY Mellon has invested in many initiatives to recruit and retain some of the sharpest minds and most innovative professionals in the financial services industry, and develops their careers to their full potential. Its Signature Leadership Forum – a flagship diversity recruiting and retention initiative for high-performing internal and external talent – is providing critical senior management exposure to top women and minority ethnic professionals from underrepresented demographic groups who are looking to advance in their careers.

At BNY Mellon, employees with shared characteristics or experiences have formed employee and business resource groups to network, create opportunities for professional development and enhance leadership skills. These groups not only play a critical role in driving business goals, they also help expand and diversify BNY Mellon's talent pipelines. The Women's Initiatives Network (WIN) business resource group is one such example, acting as a catalyst for change in the advancement of women at BNY Mellon through skill-building workshops, enhanced visibility and greater connectivity with other employees and clients.

In March 2018, WIN EMEA (Europe, Middle East and Africa), in collaboration with BNY Mellon's Talent Acquisition team, successfully launched "Take Two". This initiative aims to broaden talent sourcing and acquisition

methods by attracting senior female talent looking to re-enter the workforce and educating hiring managers on the valuable potential of this group. Early results of the initiative are already impressive and underscore its continuing importance to BNY Mellon.

"My focus is on helping all of our people realise their full potential and, in doing so, we accelerate business transformation to unleash BNY Mellon's full potential," says Herena. In particular, BNY Mellon is determined to build on its proud history of furthering the position of women, which is reflected by the broad and deep representation of senior female talent at the company.

Michelle Neal, who has held senior positions at a number of banks and is now CEO of BNY Mellon Markets, can attest to that. Although she was acutely aware of the assertion that there was a glass ceiling in financial services that limited the promotion of women, she never found that to be the case. "It has been my experience since the earliest days of my career that applying yourself, working hard and being as good as – if not better than – the rest, has always been noticed and rewarded," she says.

In a similar sense, Herena highlights the positive role played by many male and female sponsors, who took chances on her and shared wise advice that proved instrumental in helping her advance her career. "I'd advise women starting out in a career in financial services to meet new challenges head-on," she says. "Demonstrating a willingness to tackle projects outside your comfort zone will give you a chance to prove the breadth and value of your capabilities. Courageously ask for real-time feedback on your progress, because this feedback will accelerate your career and inspire those around you to do the same."

In order to hire exceptional talent, BNY Mellon makes sure it thinks outside the box. It has attracted people with unique skills and diverse experiences who might otherwise not have chosen financial services as a career. Newton Investment Management made two successful hires that highlight the advantages of sourcing talent through non-traditional routes.

# "We believe that the best investment is the one that we make in our people"

Monique Herena, BNY Mellon

"By giving opportunities to people from a diverse society, our workplace will become more representative of society"

Hanneke Smits, Newton Investment Management

Lottie Meggitt, an investment analyst in Newton's Responsible Investment team, was attracted to a career at the firm through its sponsorship of the Women's Boat Race. "A fellow member of the squad had done an internship at Newton and had loved it and said very good things about the company – this encouraged me to apply," says Meggitt, who read classics at Cambridge.

Meggitt started at Newton in 2014 in the Investment Communications team within Marketing. She admits she was nervous before her first day at work but adds: "Because I had been so aware of the company for two years – wearing clothes bearing Newton's logo every day – it made me feel more familiar and comfortable with the firm, and more reassured it would work out."

Rosie Parfett came to Newton through The Brokerage Citylink, a charity that helps young people from London's state schools access work and increase employability and skills through partnerships with employers. She started at Newton in September 2012 as a Dividends Administrator through the vocational traineeship programme. "I was unsure of what to expect as I had not worked in an office environment before, but also nervous as this was the first company that I had worked at where I saw the possibility of a career," she says. "I remember feeling very lucky to have such a welcoming team and an extremely helpful supervisor during those first days."

Parfett says the combination of work experience and academic studies provided a more concrete understanding of the industry. "Being in a paid role also meant that I was more determined to achieve a grade that Newton and I were proud of, and to ensure that it was understood I had not taken this opportunity for granted."

Both Meggitt and Parfett found careers at Newton through non-traditional routes. "Rather than looking for people to fill certain roles," says Newton CEO Hanneke Smits, "we hire people with potential, and then shape roles around them. By giving opportunities to people

from a diverse society, our workplace will become more representative of society, and drive long-term success."

While working to ensure gender balance and diversity is essential to the continued success of BNY Mellon, one must not overlook the contribution of men towards reaching those goals. "To achieve gender parity, men need to be part of the conversation; while men still dominate the senior leadership ranks, they need to take responsibility for making change happen," says Dan Kramer, Executive Vice President responsible for client experience within the Asset Servicing division of BNY Mellon and sponsor of WIN's Male Allies Programme. The Male Allies Campaign, launched around International Women's Day in March, has already attracted 600 male employees. They will be heavily involved in the Vote 100 anniversary, hosting sessions and discussions around equality, engaging with the challenges, and working on viable actions.

Susan Revell (pictured right), Deputy Chair and General Council, EMEA and WIN EMEA Executive Sponsor, puts it this way: "WIN has a long and distinguished heritage at BNY Mellon. Its evolution has led to greater alignment with our employees, business and clients, with WIN acting as a vehicle for driving the social and business case for inclusion," she says. "This maturity enables us to leverage valuable opportunities for us to engage with a broader audience and, in particular, to enlist the support of our male allies to further our gender parity objectives."

With 60 chapters globally and close to 6,000 employees engaging as members, WIN shows the growth potential for the Male Allies Programme. "The goal is to turn passion and commitment into action," says Dan Kramer. "The tactical goal is more inclusion of males in WIN, but the strategic goal is a more inclusive culture to attract, retain and advance more talented women, and increase gender diversity of senior management at the bank. That is the ultimate prize, and having Male Allies will help us achieve that."

# INVESTING IN THE FUTURE

BNY Mellon and Newton Investment Management
are helping to educate a new generation

WWW.BNYMELLON.COM

"It was a strong theme coming down from my grandparents that education is the only gift we can give you, so you have to take advantage of it," says Hanneke Smits, CEO of Newton Investment Management. Hanneke is Dutch and her grandparents lost much of their wealth in the Netherlands in the 1930s recession and the Second World War. However, they used their education to rebuild their lives and ensure their children had every opportunity in school and in life, irrespective of gender.

Today, this experience imbues Smits's understanding of the importance of education – at all ages and for both genders – which, in turn, is a central theme for Newton. Newton was a founding member of KickStart Money, a project that aims to take financial education to over 20,000 primary school children in three years.

Working through MyBnk, KickStart Money delivers in-school financial literacy workshops, complemented by teacher resources and homework challenges. "Your attitude towards savings and spending is formed by the age of seven," says Smits. "You need to talk to children and help them understand how to generate an income, how to save and how to spend responsibly."

Newton also works with older students. For 10 years it has sponsored the Royal Academy schools, which select 17 people a year on merit, irrespective of their ability to pay, for a three-year postgraduate course to help them develop as professional artists. For Smits, the attitudes of artists are shared by many successful investment managers. "You will see the ability to challenge the norm and to continuously improve oneself in good fund managers as well as good artists," she says. "Both are able to think outside the box and not follow the herd."

Newton contributes to academic research through its support of the Newton Centre for Endowment Asset Management at Cambridge Judge Business School, which is dedicated to furthering research in long-horizon investing. It runs programmes that strengthen research and facilitate engagement with people working in

long-horizon investing, such as sovereign wealth funds, charities and endowments. "We take that research into practitioners' circles to help them think about innovative methods of investment management," says Smits.

She adds that investment in education is important for ensuring long-term gender balance. "Ensuring women have a good understanding of the importance of finance through education creates a positive feedback loop," she emphasises. "Without education, we would never see diversity in the workplace or equal rights in society."

At a global level, BNY Mellon puts this philosophy into practice with its focus on harnessing the talents of the millennial generation, which will account for 75 per cent of the global workforce by 2025. Shifting demographics and advances in digital technology are changing the way people work. "The key for BNY Mellon is to turn change into opportunity, and open new paths for growth," says Jonathon Stubbs, Global Senior Director of HR – Asset Servicing and EMEA (Europe, Middle East & Africa) HR Director. "That means investing in talent." BNY Mellon's workforce is made up of three or four generations, each with differences that pose challenges and opportunities. BNY Mellon has introduced formal and informal programmes to position it as an employer of choice – irrespective of when or where someone was born.

The Emerging Leaders Programme (ELP) attracts, develops and trains high-quality, entry-level talent. Half of the London intake in the last two years were women. The 12-month programme includes three 12 to 14 week rotations across selected lines of business that combine learning with skills development through practical work. Female managers are heavily involved in ELP, acting as strong role models to encourage emerging talent.

BNY Mellon's commitment to diversity goes beyond gender balance to focus on the interconnected nature of different categories of workers, a shift from "Diversity & Inclusion 1.0" to "Diversity & Inclusion 2.0", which recognises the complexity and intersectionality

of employees' multiple identities and diverse attributes. A crowdsourcing pilot initiative in EMEA embraces this idea of diversity of thought and perspective. Using BNY Mellon's internal digital platform to share details on projects, the initiative invites individuals to make unique contributions outside of their functional roles. It facilitates enhanced levels of collaboration by bringing together people from divergent backgrounds across the world who wouldn't otherwise have an opportunity to connect and work with each other.

BNY Mellon's philanthropy strategy rests on two pillars of economic empowerment and building technological and digital capacity. Investing in education, and especially in STEM (science, technology, engineering and maths) skills, is a strategic imperative. BNY Mellon puts this into action through volunteering and grants. In 2017, employees around the world volunteered nearly 143,000 hours of their time, of which 47 per cent were skills-based hours.

The bank recently provided grant funding to the Carnegie Science Center (CSC) in Pittsburgh to co-develop a comprehensive STEM curriculum in partnership with Girl Up, an education and civic leadership organisation led by the UN Foundation. CSC is co-developing a 15-module curriculum to enable 1,900 girls in 98 countries to learn subjects such as design thinking, problem solving and engineering design. "The role of technology has created a breadth of opportunities for everyone in several ways," says Bridget Engle, BNY Mellon's Chief Information Officer. "Technology has enabled efficient access to information for anyone who seeks to learn more, which in turn has contributed to knowledge growth."

Engaging future female talent in technology is also a key driver for the company. BNY Mellon partnered with the Women in Technology and Entrepreneurship in New York initiative (WiTNY) to offer internships to five aspiring young women from local colleges. This programme is crucial for providing young women a first foot in the door and the opportunity to broaden their on-the-job experience through exposure to BNY Mellon's technological business.

One key area where BNY Mellon has maximised the benefits of technology is enabling automation and robotics to handle repetitive digital tasks, freeing up people to focus on providing greater client service. When used appropriately, robotics and automation can enhance the client experience, improve operating efficiency, increase accuracy and consistency, and improve compliance management.

Technology has also helped BNY Mellon meet its challenge of increasing gender balance. Engle says the flexibility offered by technology is challenging gendered roles. "By affording both women and men the possibility to work in agile ways, technology tackles the stigma around men taking time off for care-giving by creating dynamic and flexible ways to stay connected," she says.

Overarching the agenda of education, talent and technology is the need to ensure the organisation is diverse and inclusive, because these are levers for driving performance, differentiation and innovation. BNY Mellon has created an enterprise-wide strategy and set measurable goals that drive accountability.

These goals apply not just to senior leaders, but to everyone within the organisation. "It is incumbent on each of us to own that strategy, because we want to have a voice in the company we work for, play a role in building a culture and a company we can be proud of, and chart our course to rewarding and fulfilling careers," says Yau Ching Cheng, Global Head of Diversity & Inclusion. "When we make our differences work for us – when we value and leverage them as strengths – both, organisation and individual thrive."

Looking back over the 234 years that BNY Mellon has worked with clients, served complex markets and supported local communities, one thing has remained constant, says Hani Kablawi, Chairman, EMEA, BNY Mellon. "We believe our longstanding history and continued success would not be possible without our firm commitment to a diverse workforce and developing an inclusive culture. As we come together to mark this significant occasion in the gender-equality movement, it is important to reflect on the past and build upon it to shape a better future. The message is consistent. Gender equality and financial inclusion are not somebody else's issues; the responsibility lies with all of us to support the empowerment of women – in our workplaces, the markets and the world. It's time to take collective responsibility for a shared challenge and push ahead in working on a unified solution."

# CULTURE AND MEDIA

| | |
|---|---|
| Department for Digital, Culture, Media & Sport | 142 |
| Pinch Point Communications | 145 |
| The British Fashion Council | 146 |
| WPP | 147 |
| City Football Group | 148 |
| brookscomm | 149 |
| All3Media | 150 |
| Oystercatchers | 152 |
| Propellernet | 153 |
| The Institute of Practitioners in Advertising | 154 |
| Arts Council of Wales | 155 |
| Image Source | 156 |
| Zaboura Communications | 157 |

# DEPARTMENT FOR DIGITAL, CULTURE, MEDIA & SPORT

The fortunes of the DCMS have been radically transformed by the National Lottery

The Department for Digital, Culture, Media and Sport (DCMS) is one of the youngest departments in government. Created in 1992 as the Department for Culture, Media and Sport, it added the word "digital" in July 2017 to reflect the department's increased activity in the digital sector. It brought together those policy responsibilities most associated with leisure and quality of life from six different Whitehall ministries.

Its introduction was not universally welcomed. The author Robert Harris likened it to "a magpie's nest of glittering trinkets stolen from other departments: prizes that will one day have to be returned to their rightful owners". A leader in *The Times* warned that the sectors represented by it "may be cheering the new citadel, but they will soon turn to assault". For most observers, however, the Department of National Heritage, as it was originally named, was simply known as the "Ministry of Fun".

However, the first Secretary of State, David Mellor, saw it as an opportunity to give "culture" in all its forms – the arts, sport, broadcasting and the tourism industry – more of a voice in government. He knew the key factor in the department's success would be the creation of a National Lottery, with the explicit aim of using it to raise money for the

arts, heritage, sport and charities, as well as funding projects to mark the fast-approaching new millennium.

Pundits predicted that the lottery might even raise as much as £1 billion to that end. They were mistaken. By the time it celebrated its 20th birthday, the lottery had raised more than £32 billion.

More broadly, the DCMS has also grown in terms of the policy areas it covers. As well as the National Lottery, and the original subject areas from 1992, the department has taken on responsibility in government for gambling, the horse-racing industry, entertainment licensing and the four-year programme to mark the centenary of the First World War. It oversees Ofcom and the BBC. It stretches from luvvies to navvies – commissioning the rollout of broadband infrastructure to rural areas that the commercial world won't stretch to. It took the lead role in government for delivering the 2012 Olympic and Paralympic Games, the Queen's Golden and Diamond Jubilees and numerous other high-profile ceremonial events. And, as a sponsor of the Equality and Human Rights Commission, it led on the groundbreaking legislation to introduce same-sex marriage through Parliament.

The department's Permanent Secretary Sue Owen believes that DCMS priorities are very much in line with broader government objectives these days. "The DCMS focus since 2010 has been on big campaigns that contribute to government-wide strategy for long-term economic growth," she says. "Our sectors comprise 22 per cent of the economy. So promoting the creative industries, the fastest growing sector, worth £77 billion to the UK economy, is a priority. British films, musicians, computer-game designers, and artists in all fields are making a huge contribution to the economy, and providing a brilliant showcase for the country at the same time."

But it's not just the economy, stupid. Cultural sectors make a massive social contribution, with participation in sport and the arts having significant potential in achieving beneficial health and educational outcomes. Increasingly, research shows concretely what everyone knows – the positive impact that art and sport and culture and heritage have on personal well-being and happiness.

From the mysteries of our prehistoric past to the challenges of our digital future, the DCMS has earned its place at the cabinet table.

# "British films, musicians computer-game designers and artists in all fields are making a huge contribution to the economy"

# THE HONEST APPROACH

Pinch Point Communications is more than a PR firm – it's a consultancy that enhances and manages reputation

WWW.PINCHPOINTCOMMUNICATIONS.CO.UK

"There's no such thing as a public relations disaster," says Sarah Pinch, MD of Bristol-based Pinch Point Communications (PPC). "There may be operational disasters or management issues, but when it gets in the press it's because something has gone wrong."

Accountability, transparency and honesty may be seen as buzz words in the world of PR, but for PPC they are unmovable foundations that make up the company's core principles. "If clients aren't willing to put issues right then we wouldn't work with them," says Pinch. "We work in reputation management, so it's about helping companies own up and be honest, not cover stuff up."

It is this honesty and integrity that has seen PPC build up a national reputation and work on major campaigns for the NHS, schools, charities, social enterprises, public transport and public services. The firm also provides media training and mentoring to give clients the confidence and authority to engage effectively in broadcast interviews, presentations and meetings.

PPC is focused on providing an excellent service for its clients and is driven to do so by a commitment to ethical practice and a passion for equality and diversity. Pinch has been an advocate for equality throughout her career, even speaking in the House of Commons as president of the Chartered Institute of Public Relations, challenging the gender pay gap. Such work led to her recently being included in the *Financial Times* and HERoes Champions of Women in Business Top 50 list, and she is also chair of the Taylor Bennett Foundation, which mentors black, Asian and ethnic minority graduates pursuing a career in communications. "I won't stop talking about the issues that affect women, ever," Pinch says of her lifelong commitment to the cause.

This approach is shared by the highly experienced PPC team and one of the company's primary objectives, says Pinch, is to set up a mentoring scheme to help young women who "are ready to run the show".

For Pinch, PPC's principles have always guided its business and will point the way to the future. "We just want to continue to do what we're doing," she says, "and be known for the values that we bring and the positive changes to the cultures of organisations that our work leaves as its legacy."

# FLYING THE FASHION FLAG

The British Fashion Council supports new talent and promotes best practice across the UK fashion industry

WWW.BRITISHFASHIONCOUNCIL.COM

"There is no other country in the world that is recognised for producing creative talent in quite the way that the UK is," says Caroline Rush CBE, the CEO of the British Fashion Council (BFC). Since 1983, the BFC, a not-for-profit organisation, has been flying the impeccably tailored flag of British fashion excellence on the world stage with headline events like London Fashion Week, which in 2018 welcomed Her Majesty the Queen for the first time.

However, the core of the BFC's work happens away from the catwalk, with scholarships and bursaries targeted at Britain's brightest fashion students. Adding the cost of materials and tuition fees, studying fashion is hugely expensive, yet many successful designers come from disadvantaged backgrounds. "The fashion industry is inclusive," says Rush, "and we feel strongly about promoting that."

Talent is not enough to ensure future success in the fashion industry, which is why the BFC offers practical support for emerging designers, in creating business plans, using digital innovation to increase audience reach and interaction, and protecting their intellectual property. Newgen is one of BFC's most prominent initiatives, established in 1993 to identify and provide support for promising graduates. One of the first Newgen designers was Alexander McQueen; the BFC promoted his first professional show after graduation and gave him the resources to export his collections to the US. The scheme continues to support new graduates each year, now including accessories and jewellery under the guidance of milliner Stephen Jones and jeweller Stephen Webster.

More widely, the BFC campaigns to improve best practice across the industry. "Positive Fashion exists to shout about the fantastic things that are happening in fashion," says Rush. "It promotes local manufacture and craft, sustainability, gender equality, model health and diversity. We need to ensure that everyone is treated well in the industry."

The BFC's agenda not only furthers British fashion and the umbrella of creative industries it supports, but campaigns for an ethical, sustainable environment in which the UK's best designers can flourish. "People need to understand that fashion is an incredibly complex and exciting business full of hard-working individuals who are contributing to our worldwide reputation."

# STEPPING AHEAD

WPP's Lindsay Pattison has been a trailblazer for equality and diversity throughout her career

WWW.GROUPM.COM | WWW.WPP.COM

With more than 20 years of media experience to her name, Lindsay Pattison is now Chief Transformation Officer of both GroupM, the world's leading global media investment company, and GroupM's parent company, WPP. She is one of the most senior women within WPP and is responsible for getting its agencies to work more closely together for its top clients.

Pattison is passionate about gender equality. In 2016, as global CEO of WPP-owned media agency Maxus, she launched Walk the Talk, a global mentoring programme for the group's senior female leaders. The initiative aims to break down barriers so women c an achieve their potential, and progress to the highest levels possible. Investing in women's career development is a cause that has always been close to her heart.

"The Walk the Talk programme addresses some of the internal barriers that women face, helps develop goals and creates a support network to enable female leaders to get where they want to be," says Pattison, who is based in London. "I was hugely proud when we agreed to roll out Walk the Talk across GroupM and WPP, so that it reached hundreds of women around the world."

One of the most important lessons Pattison has learned during her career is to appreciate what she describes as "the power of the individual" and the value that each person brings to their role. "When you're more junior you don't realise the power of you, the individual, in terms of what both clients and your team buy into," she explains. "It is the confidence and energy of the individual and the passion and commitment to clients to create meaningful work that makes the difference."

Pattison is full of inspiring advice for the next generation of women who want to work in her industry. "To me, the key to success in marketing communications – and in most industries – is ensuring that you are always stepping in front of the work," she says. "You're saying 'yes' to every opportunity, having a voice, pushing yourself out of your comfort zone, building confidence and making yourself visible. Ultimately, your reputation is the thing that drives you through your career, and this comes hand in hand with building a network of allies – both female and male – to support you, champion you and help you succeed."

# CITY'S LEVEL PLAYING FIELD

City Football Group is committed to raising the game of women's football in Manchester and beyond

WWW.CITYFOOTBALLGROUP.COM

"There is a passion at Manchester City for both the men's and the women's teams," says defender Steph Houghton, Manchester City and England's team captain. "It's a real feeling of togetherness." Houghton, who signed for the club in 2014, is approaching the 100-cap mark for the national team and has made more than 100 appearances for City.

For the skipper, being a successful figure in the fast-rising world of women's football means more than just trophies: she and her teammates are an integral part of the Manchester City community. "From the moment I signed for the club I knew I was joining something special," she says. "We are really paving the way for women's football in this country and that's something I'm very proud to be a part of."

The women's team mirrors its male equivalent and maintains the same structure in all aspects of its operations, from community programmes to youth development, scouting, coaching, sports science and digital coverage. They made history when they clinched their first ever trophy, the FA Women's Super League (WSL) Continental Tyres Cup, in their inaugural season.

In 2016, Manchester City Women's Football Club won the FA WSL Continental Tyres Cup for a second time, the FA WSL league title and played in the UEFA Women's Champions League having qualified in the previous season.

Having received status as a Tier 1 Regional Talent Club from the FA in 2016, the club opened their girls' academy. Today the team, which includes nine England internationals, play their home games in the 7,000-capacity Academy Stadium at City Football Academy, Manchester City's training ground.

The togetherness at Manchester City was exemplified through the launch, in January 2018, of the club's *Same City, Same Passion* campaign to promote women's football. Based on the principle that the foundations of football are unchanging, *Same City, Same Passion* demonstrates that the same skills, the same excitement and the same passion exist wherever a ball is kicked. As part of the campaign, Manchester City merged their men's and women's social media channels, to ensure that supporters can experience all City's exclusive news in one place.

# INDIVIDUALITY AND DIVERSITY

Comms agency brookscomm offers flexibility to both clients and staff

WWW.BROOKSCOMM.COM

"Everybody's equal and everybody's equally welcome," says Mandy Brooks, Managing Director of brookscomm, a communications agency that she co-founded in the 1990s dotcom boom, specialising in technology and innovation. "I want to understand from each individual what will optimise their experience of being here and what will enable them to give the best of themselves. Understanding individuals' needs – that's key to diversity."

brookscomm offers a range of PR, marketing and social media services to its clients, who include the Surrey Research Park and tech firms Blink and previously Belkin. "We've been in business for 23 years, which we're very proud of," says Brooks. "We have changed and evolved as our clients have and as our industry has. We're a very different business from when we started – but our values are the same."

Brooks believes that her company's longstanding commitment to equality and diversity has been key to its success. "For me, the best way that we can support equality and diversity is by offering practical steps," she says. "There are often small, often hidden barriers

to workplaces offering equality and flexibility for all and diversity across the board. I've always been committed to trying to find those barriers, and a wish list of different types of people."

Brooks says there is a strong commercial imperative in offering flexibility, as evidenced by the high levels of motivation among brookscomm's 10-strong team. "There's a huge business benefit in making the conditons as favourable as possible to get the best out of everybody," she says. "To me, it's obvious. And I can absolutely say it's worked so well for us over the years. We've been able to get great people who just need a little bit of flexibility in their working lives. By giving them elements of flexibility, they deliver really well. We end up with a large-company skill set, but still with the flexibility and the agility of a small agency."

brookscomm is currently hatching plans to mark the 2018 centenary of the Representation of the People Act. "We're delighted to be celebrating that and be part of it," says Brooks. "We're really keen to encourage and support the next generation to offer even more diverse and inclusive workplaces."

# CLEAR VISION

Trailblazing television production company
All3Media sets out its blueprint for a diverse,
flourishing future

WWW.ALL3MEDIA.COM

"Women are brilliant at innovation. They're very creative right across the board, and our business model really enables talent to rise to the top," says Sara Geater, Chief Operating Officer (COO) at All3Media, where the three most senior executives are all women.

Headed up by Chief Executive Officer (CEO) Jane Turton, Chief Financial Officer (CFO) Angela McMullen and Geater, All3Media is one of the UK's largest independent television production companies, and it is honoured to be involved with media production for the Vote 100 celebrations.

All3Media is responsible for some huge TV favourites, including Liar, The Only Way Is Essex, Gogglebox, Call The Midwife (pictured, opposite), Hollyoaks, The Undateables, and Midsomer Murders. Since launching in 2003, the company has made and distributed programmes for Britain's biggest broadcasters, including the BBC, ITV, Channel 4, Sky, Netflix and Amazon, as well as selling its shows around the world. For the executive team, the role of women has proved key to that success.

"We have a portfolio of 27 production companies within the group, and many of those are run by women," says Turton. "At HQ level, in the more senior roles, we skew towards women. We haven't set out specifically to champion the cause of women, but we have absolutely created an environment where they can flourish. At All3Media, people are appointed on merit, and there are no barriers to success."

"I think that's quite common in television in the UK; although less so when you get to the top boards of the big players, and certainly less so in the US," says Turton. "The bosses of Channel 4, ITV, and the Director of Content at the BBC are all women; the bosses of the three biggest independents in this country – that's us, Endemol, and FremantleMedia – are all women."

Part of this, she adds, is down to the flexible working environments that many creative sector jobs offer. "We're very modern in the way we look at people's employment and careers," says Turton. "Having a good gender mix matters because it reflects society. It seems logical, given we're making something for the whole population, that the balance should be broadly 50:50."

While Vote 100 is all about celebrating how far we've come in the fight for equality and diversity, Turton firmly believes it's an ongoing job. "We've still got a class issue in television," she says, "which we're trying to do something about by making sure we pay interns and bring people in who have come from a variety of different backgrounds. We're always keen to ensure that we're as ethnically balanced as we can be, and I'm sure there's more we could do on disability and LGBT representation."

For them, the equality and diversity agenda is all about nurturing fresh talent – far more than just box-ticking. "We keep an eye on our overall stats, but we don't do any positive discrimination because we always want to have the best talent in the business," explains Geater. "However, we're very mindful of the diversity issues when we're assisting in training, and growing the next group of people who are coming through. Our business enables teams to have control and build their own cultures, which is why you get more innovation. We're a better example of that than any other UK production company."

# "We have created an environment where women can flourish"

———

Jane Turton, Chief Executive Officer, All3Media

# WOMEN OF INFLUENCE

Women are ringing the changes at
Oystercatchers and parent company Centaur

THEOYSTERCATCHERS.COM · CENTAURMEDIA.COM

"A lot of what we are doing with clients is quite radical," says Suki Thompson,
CEO of Oystercatchers marketing management consultancy. "It needs
to be, because the dynamics of business are changing radically. Customer
behaviour and expectation are fast-changing and we're leading transformation
in a complex world."

Since Thompson founded Oystercatchers in 2009, it has expanded
into the US, Europe and Asia, working with 80 per cent of the FTSE
250 as well as global communications leaders. In 2016, Thompson sold
Oystercatchers to leading media and marketing group Centaur Media.
She is now an ExCo member at Centaur, with responsibility for growth
and innovation across all Centaur brands. "Selling Oystercatchers is a
very important part of the journey," she says. "We've joined a like-minded
entrepreneurial management team, also led by a female CEO."

Oystercatchers was founded with the intention of reframing the
marketing industry by enhancing trust and collaboration between clients
and agencies, creating modern marketing models and empowering staff
through training. It works with leading companies including Sainsbury's,
McDonald's and Bwin.

In January 2017, Oystercatchers was engaged to design a simple,
focused and cost-effective marketing structure to help the Post Office
transform its marketing and digital engagement with multichannel
customers. The consultancy team, embedded in the Post Office, worked
on ways to unlock value from existing customers and their data, accelerate
sales and create an overarching modern marketing strategy for the
company. "We believe that successful strategies always put the customer
at the centre," says Thompson.

As an influential mentor (she lectures at the government forum 'Making
People Brilliant in the Digital Age'), Thompson is actively involved in working
with growing businesses, particularly those run by female entrepreneurs.
"I firmly believe entrepreneurialism and transformation are keys to modern
business success. The future of individual businesses and our economy depends
not on tokenism or special favours, but on true equality of opportunity. It's an
inspiring and dynamic time to be working in the business."

# THE DREAM FACTORY

Digital marketing agency Propellernet helps make dreams come true, for clients and employees alike

WWW.PROPELLERNET.CO.UK

Employee job satisfaction is a top priority for the management team at Propellernet, a digital marketing agency based in Brighton, and it shows. For the sixth year running, it has been voted one of the UK's top 15 best workplaces by the Great Place To Work Institute.

As Nikki Gatenby, Managing Director, explains, investing in its workforce is crucial to the firm's success. "For us, profit and people are equally important," she says. "We really want to get to know our team as people, not just as a skill set, because what propels them forward propels the business forward." Equality for its staff is also key. The gender ratio sits at 50 per cent male, 50 per cent female, and each employee is treated the same, regardless of role, with equal bonuses, pension contributions, benefits and opportunities for flexible working.

A pioneer in its field, Propellernet was the first company to combine technical search engine optimisation (SEO) with PR to help businesses be seen online. It has been instrumental in designing new technology products for the PR industry. Its web-based press coverage reporting tool, coveragebook.com, effortlessly shows clients the effectiveness of their campaigns, while answerthepublic.com is a free app used by thousands of content marketers around the world. Propellernet's ideas are explored in its upcoming book, *Superengaged*, and the accompanying website, www.superengaged.co.uk.

This innovative spirit is also evident in how it operates. The company implements unique polices that have seen its employee engagement levels soar to over 90 per cent – well above the national average. One such policy, "Propel Days", is a day a month when employees take time out to do something that inspires them. They also have a "Dream Ball" machine – a giant sweet dispenser that contains capsules with the name of each employee. When a target is reached, a capsule is dispensed, and the employee is given the help they need to realise their dream.

"Employee engagement and equality is at the forefront of our business plan," says Gatenby. "We want to take equality to the next level by setting a platform where we balance people, purpose and profit, and see each employee as an equal human being. Our mission is to be one of the best places to work in the world."

# ADVERTISING FOR ALL

The Institute of Practitioners in Advertising has been setting industry standards for the past century

WWW.IPA.CO.UK

"I want current and future generations to be proud to work in our industry," says Sarah Golding, President of the Institute of Practitioners in Advertising (IPA). Her ambition is built on strong foundations. Established around the time that the Representation of the People Act gave women the vote, the IPA recently celebrated its centenary and was awarded Chartered status.

While the industry's landscape has changed beyond recognition over the past hundred years, its commercial success continues to soar. The UK is one of the top-performing advertising economies, with gross value added (GVA) in the UK advertising and marketing sector measured at £10.7 bn in 2015.

Ensuring diversity is at the heart of the industry, at all levels, is vital to this continued success, explains the IPA's Head of Diversity Leila Siddiqi. "Not only does diversity of thought lead to creative advantage, it makes business sense to attract and retain the best talent and drive this approach top down." To achieve this, the IPA's training programmes and qualifications are exported to more than 60 different markets internationally, and its Creative Pioneers apprenticeship programme has

attracted more than 700 young people into the industry over the past five years. "Around 35 per cent of those apprentices come from BAME backgrounds and the gender balance is about 50/50," says Siddiqi.

Further, the IPA's biennial Women of Tomorrow awards scheme celebrates and champions women in mid-level roles, and Golding actively supports the UN's Unstereotype Alliance. For the future, the IPA has set ambitious targets. By 2020, it aims to see 40 per cent of leadership roles in advertising held by women and 15 per cent by BAME individuals, with 25 per cent of new starters hailing from BAME backgrounds. "We offer the industry a range of advice on our diversity hub," says Siddiqi, "while round-table events bring the creative industries together to share best practice."

"Having an impartial IPA that represents the needs of all those working in advertising and provides thought leadership, advisory services, training and professional development is as vital today as ever," says Golding. "We want to be somewhere people come to be inspired, learn, and meet their peers and heroes. That's how we will continue to work for the good of the public, and the good of the industry."

# ART OF A NATION

The Arts Council of Wales is challenging itself to become a beacon of diversity and a model for community interaction

WWW.ARTS.WALES

"The arts in Wales are all about developing a voice for communities that don't have one," says Diane Hebb, Director of Engagement and Participation at Arts Council of Wales. Together, the council's 67 arts organisations attract an audience of more than four million a year, with another million attending participatory projects of all kinds.

Gender leadership in Welsh arts is already diverse. "Of our eight national arts companies, four are led by women," says Hebb. "Tamara Harvey, at Theatr Clwyd and Rachel O'Riordan at the Sherman are running important venues. But there remains an issue about the female voice." To address this, the council will continue its public debate about diversity and leadership in Welsh arts. This will take place alongside projects designed to raise the profile of these issues, including "Processions", a UK-wide commemorative event led by Artichoke to celebrate the achievement of the vote for women.

In addition to gender issues, the council is especially keen to improve the representation of disabled and BAME women, and is working to ensure the arts workforce reflects that of Wales overall. "Look at Wales-based playwright Kaite O'Reilly," says Hebb,

"who has received an Unlimited Commission to visit Singapore to develop her 'D' monologues about difference and disability."

Since her first role coordinating public dance projects for Rhondda Community Arts in the 1980s, Diane Hebb has pioneered the inclusivity agenda, writing the council's first ever equalities policy. She is now the first person at board level with an equalities portfolio. She is passionate about Creative Learning Through the Arts, a project that she persuaded the Welsh government to support with £10 million of funding. It is transforming learning in Welsh schools, giving young people a stronger voice in their own learning. She also draws attention to community schemes like Valley and Vale's Through the Woods, which uses creative arts to raise awareness of the impact of trauma and sexual exploitation.

"My belief in the power of grassroots arts was shaped by working in the Rhondda during the Miners' Strike," says Hebb. "These projects help to build confidence, self-expression, improve personal and family relationships and increase emotional and physical wellbeing."

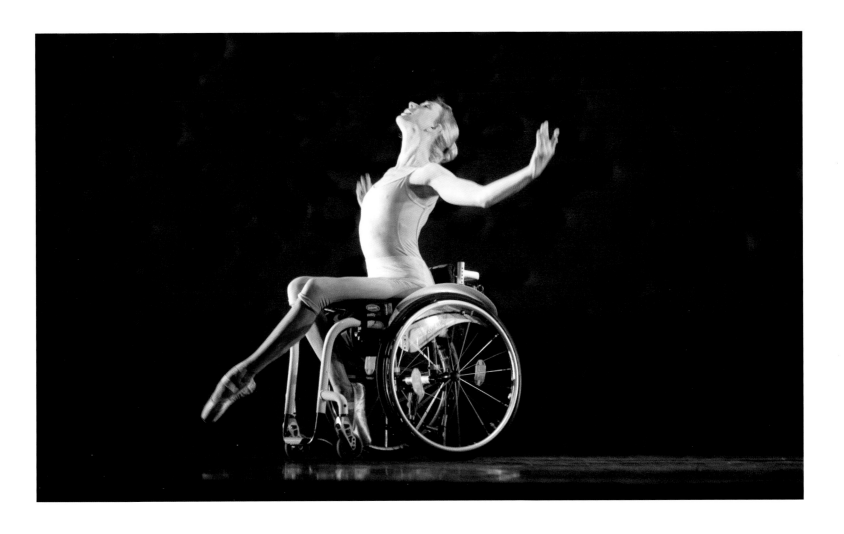

# PICTURE PERFECT

Based in London and New York, Image Source produces high-quality, modern imagery for its clients worldwide

WWW.IMAGESOURCE.COM

A picture, it is often said, is worth a thousand words. It's why the job of finding the right one for use in advertising and publishing is of crucial importance. The image is often one that reflects society, and usually it comes from a photography agency. Christina Vaughan, the Founder and CEO of creative agency Image Source, has built her company's reputation on the authenticity of its photography and its high production values. "We have always been premium," says Vaughan, "in terms of the work that goes into casting the models and sourcing locations. For examples, families need to look authentic and business models realistic. It's really important to deliver emotional connectivity because images impact on culture."

When Vaughan founded Image Source in 1998, families were typically represented as being white and blonde, with mum, dad, boy and girl. These days Image Source's galleries represent the diversity of our age with same-sex, mixed-race and single-parent families. The way Image Source creates beauty shots also sets it apart. "We often shoot with the female market in mind," says Vaughan. "Women respond to the fact that these are pictures of women for women. They aren't about trying to make them look sexy in a way a man might shoot them."

Vaughan runs offices in London and New York and works with around 150 distribution partners in 80 countries. With many freelancers, she embraces flexible and distance working. "Working remotely can make people more focused," she says. "They manage their time well. Flexible working makes good business sense."

Image Source is increasingly working with female photographers; and not simply for the children and baby shots that were once their standard brief. "I want them to be able to work outside their comfort zone," says Vaughan. "Otherwise we'd be missing out on some great talent." Image Source's "emotionally intelligent images" are only part of what her company offers. Its photographs are all technically and legally "hygienic", so that world-renowned distribution partners such as Getty Images can rest assured that model and property releases are secure.

Vaughan is building the future health of her business on progressive work practices and on creating images that reflect modern life. "Our expectations are higher than they ever were," she says. "So we are always thinking about what more we can do to reflect a fair picture of society through our images."

# PROMOTION OPPORTUNITY

Zaboura Communications is a media and PR specialist that has taken on a male-dominated industry and won

WWW.ZABOURA.COM

When Maggie Zaboura started out in the technology industry, it was a totally male-dominated working environment. She also had to learn on the job. "I had no relevant qualifications – I had to learn IT and computer programming as I went along," she explains. "There were constant barriers to be broken down back then. Men didn't expect women to be technical or to hold their own." However, as the daughter of immigrants, this successful businesswoman knew "how to graft", as she puts it. "This country gave me a great opportunity," she observes.

That was more than 20 years ago. Today, Zaboura's communications and media relations company counts multi-billion-pound IT leaders such as Kingston Technology and product-recall management business Stericycle among its global clients.

The challenges she has faced have influenced and informed her approach to recruitment. Key to her values is the mentoring of staff – just as her boss did when she started out. "He was very supportive and allowed me to mess up," says Zaboura. "One time, this £3,000 machine stopped working while I was showing it to clients. But I carried on and made the sale. My team said that I was the only person who was capable of demonstrating a product that didn't work! You develop an ability to roll with the punches, have no fear and be tenacious."

Actively hiring part-time mothers and women seeking flexible working hours is also important to Zaboura. "Women with children are often very organised and diligent," she says; attributes that make them a real asset to her eight-strong team. Zaboura Communications also has a strong track record of employing staff who came to the UK from other countries, such as Germany, Romania and Italy.

Zaboura's enlightened approach has earned the company several awards. In 2017, the Women in IT Awards made her a Business Leader of the Year finalist. Her firm has also twice won the award for Best PR and Marketing Agency for Channel Services from *PCR* magazine. For Zaboura, success also means providing her staff with opportunities. That includes actively encouraging them to leave her for the next career challenge: to become pioneers like her.

# SOCIETY

| | |
|---|---|
| The Home Office | 160 |
| Ministry of Defence | 162 |
| Ministry of Justice | 164 |
| Equalities Office | 166 |
| Ministry of Housing, Communities and Local Government | 168 |
| Department for Transport | 170 |
| Foreign and Commonwealth Office | 172 |
| Switchboard | 175 |
| Royal Navy | 176 |
| CMS | 180 |
| The Nutrition Society | 182 |
| Karma Nirvana | 184 |
| Francis House Family Trust | 185 |
| Hodge Jones & Allen | 186 |
| Cambridgeshire Constabulary | 188 |
| The Inner City Trust | 189 |
| Essex Police | 190 |
| Zoological Society of London | 191 |
| Kent Police | 192 |
| Durham Constabulary | 194 |
| Duchenne UK | 195 |
| Sussex Police | 196 |
| The Royal Association for Deaf people | 198 |
| Devon and Cornwall Police | 199 |
| Strength With in Me (SWIM) Foundation | 200 |
| Stirling Council | 201 |
| British Sociological Association | 202 |
| The GEO Group | 203 |
| ELM Group | 204 |
| Police Service of Northern Ireland | 205 |
| Anglican Mainstream | 206 |
| Laurence Simons | 207 |

# THE HOME OFFICE

The fortress-like institution that's been keeping
the Queen's peace for more than two centuries

The Home Office started as an offshoot of the
Southern Division of the Foreign Office, and – although
technically the senior of the two departments – it has
always remained the Foreign Office's shabbier, less
glamorous sibling. Where the FCO is based in palatial
buildings, designed in the late 19th century by George
Gilbert Scott, the Home Office spent much of the past
40 years stuck in a gloomy concrete brutalist block on
Queen Anne's Gate, variously described by assorted
Home Secretaries as a "fortress" or a "mausoleum",
or – according to Ken Clarke – "like the KGB prison
Lubianka". Few were disappointed when the Home
Office moved to its shiny modernist home at
2 Marsham Street in 2005.

    "This is the job in which you get to know your
country most closely," says former Home Secretary
Douglas Hurd. "Run-down housing estates, riots,
drabness and wickedness of all kinds, these come
your way more than any other department."

    The Home Office was originally formed in 1782
and originally focused on the internal government
of the UK, especially "maintaining the King's Peace".
By the 1830s, its employees numbered only 13 men
and "a necessary woman", and it still shared many
staff with the neighbouring Foreign Office, including
a "Decipherer of Letters" and a "Secretary of the
Latin Language". As Britain became a more complex,
industrialised society in the 19th century, its remit
expanded. Other departments were spun from it,
including responsibilities for the control of transport,
health, mining, broadcasting, military forces and
colonial business, while, in recent decades, many of
its responsibilities have been devolved to Scotland,
Wales and Northern Ireland.

    Despite this, the Home Office was still mammoth.
By the end of the twentieth century it was the UK
government's biggest department, with tens of

thousands of employees and a responsibility for the
police, prison, probation and fire services, immigration
and asylum, sentencing and criminal justice policy.

    The biggest change in the Home Office in
more than a century came in 2007, when the newly
appointed Home Secretary John Reid famously – and
controversially – declared the Home Office as "not fit
for purpose" and set about a radical reorganisation.
Chief among these was transferring huge chunk of
the Home Office's responsibilities – criminal justice,
prisons and probation – to the newly created Ministry
Of Justice. Having lost the "law" component of its "law
and order" remit, the Home Office would concentrate
its efforts and resources on crime, immigration and
counter-terrorism.

    However, as former Home Secretary Jack Straw
observes, the Home Office has always prided itself on
not being a Ministry of the Interior on the Continental
model. "It had duties on the other side of the equation,"
he says, "of balancing power with freedom, order with
liberty, of having consciously to limit the power of the
state which it had to enforce. It has thus also taken
responsibility for issues such as human rights, race
and community relations and data protection."

    For the latest Permanent Secretary, Philip
Rutnam, the goals of the Home Office are "to cut
crime, prevent terrorism, control immigration, protect
the vulnerable and respond effectively to crises. We
are at the heart of an operational community of over
300,000 public servants in over 100 organisations
in which the country invests around 1 per cent of
our national income. The role combines intellectual
challenge, a leading-edge transformation agenda, the
opportunity to work with some of the most talented
communications professionals across government,
and the chance to impact issues that directly affect
millions of people's lives."

# MINISTRY OF DEFENCE

Despite facing budgetary cuts in recent years,
the MOD is still tasked with defence of the realm

The Ministry of Defence (MOD) developed from the need for greater co-operation between the three services – the Royal Navy, the British Army, and Royal Air Force – that form the UK's Armed Forces. The modern MOD was formed in 1964, combining the roles of five departments – the Admiralty, the War Office, the Air Ministry, the Ministry of Aviation, and a previous iteration of the MOD.

"You've got to be able to live in a world of mixed cultures and inherent tensions; in a large and complicated organisation," says Stephen Lovegrove, the MOD's Permanent Secretary since March 2016. "And it's not civil servants; we work with military colleagues. It's a fusion of different cultures, because all three services have different cultures, too. You've got to be able to work in quite a complicated cultural landscape."

The MOD has been in the frontline of equality initiatives in recent years. The British Army has been opening most of its roles to women since 1992 and, in 2016, it was announced that women would be allowed to engage in frontline combat operations. The Royal Air Force recently opened up all roles to men and women, allowing women to join its ground-fighting force, the RAF Regiment. The Royal Navy has been integrating Wrens, or the Women's Royal Navy Service, into the service since 1992, and recently announced that, from 2019, women will be allowed to train as Royal Marine Commandos, removing the last gender distinction in the service.

Defence of the realm is, of course, the MOD's key responsibility. The MOD also needs to provide strategic intelligence: be it an aircraft scanning the ground for movements, or a soldier studying terrorist groups, the MOD needs to provide an understanding of what is going on in the world in order that the government to react appropriately. Providing nuclear deterrence is also a key function: it is regarded as the nation's ultimate response and final guarantee that Britain will never be an easy target.

There are also responsibilities that go beyond immediate military functions, such as supporting civil emergency organisations in times of crisis – be it floods or terrorist attacks. The MOD also works to support British influence around the world, not just by fighting wars, but by sending defence attachés around the world, or demonstrating British military skills with groups like the Red Arrows, or providing expeditionary capability to partners in the United Nations, NATO or other like-minded countries. And finally, the MOD provides security for stabilisation. This involves working very closely with other parts of government, none more so than with the Foreign and Commonwealth Office and the Department for International Development. Often this might be to help rebuild countries after wars or disasters.

After some quite substantial cuts since 2010 and an overhaul of its IT systems, the ministry is now on a strong and sustainable footing and is investing in the people equipment needed to keep Britain safe. "Our agile armed forces, which hundreds of men and women are joining every month, have the best people and kit to take on threats we face now and in the future," says Lovegrove. Investing in the best of British capabilities underlines that a strong defence requires a strong economy.

# MINISTRY OF JUSTICE

Formed in 2007, the Ministry of Justice
has become the fifth "great office of state"

A hugely significant decision was taken eight years ago to create a new government department – one which, for the first time, brought responsibility for all justice issues under one roof.

Previously these issues – including prisons, probation, sentencing laws and oversight of the independent judiciary – fell to different departments, primarily the Home Office and the Department for Constitutional Affairs.

But in May 2007 that all changed. John Reid, the Home Secretary under Tony Blair's third administration, famously declared that the Home Office "was not fit for purpose" and decided to divide up the department's two key functions – law and order – with the Home Office taking care of the order, and a new Ministry of Justice taking care of law.

The Ministry of Justice (MOJ) was tasked with delivering a wide range of public services. Its first annual report laid out its aims – supporting a vigorous democracy, ensuring the efficient and effective delivery of justice, guaranteeing rights, helping protect the public and reducing reoffending.

It was a wide-reaching remit, which explains why the Ministry of Justice quickly became one of the biggest government departments, employing around 70,000 people (including those in the probation service), with responsibility for 133 prisons in England and Wales and more than 500 courts. Not for nothing did Jack Straw, who took over as Justice Secretary shortly after the Ministry of Justice was formed, announce that his position was now "the fifth great office of state", alongside the "big four" of Prime Minister, Chancellor, Home Secretary and Foreign Secretary. They have all seen major changes

in their time at the department – with huge efforts being made to create a justice system fit for the 21st century.

The Ministry of Justice is a department which has to balance its drive to create a modern justice system with traditions which date back hundreds of years. Each Justice Secretary simultaneously holds the position of Lord Chancellor, with responsibility for the functioning and independence of the courts and judiciary.

That Lord Chancellor is custodian of the Great Seal, which dates from the times of Edward the Confessor in the 11th century, and is still used to symbolise the sovereign's approval of important state documents.

The department marked the 800th anniversary of the sealing of Magna Carta by working with the legal sector and other organisations to host an international event celebrating the document's principles of freedom and justice and our proud legal history. The Global Law Summit brought together leaders from governments, the legal professions and business from across the world to promote the international rule of law and showcase the UK's expertise in legal services.

The MoJ's current Permanent Secretary, Richard Heaton, has set out objectives to increase both diversity and inclusion in the ministry, and to embed that in all that the ministry does. "We want to ensure that we nurture a diverse pool of talented staff able to sustain and strengthen this over the long term," he says, "to build an ethos and culture that values difference and drives improved diversity throughout the organisation to increase representation, performance and organisational effectiveness."

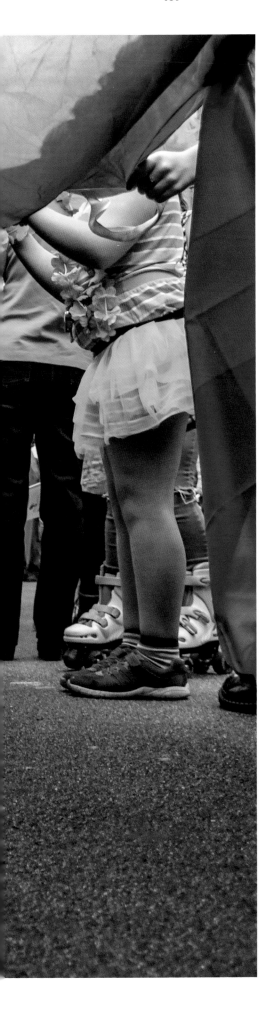

# GOVERNMENT EQUALITIES OFFICE

Dealing with equality in the fields of race, gender, sexuality, age and disability

In the history of British parliamentary democracy, laws against discrimination are a relatively recent development. The vast bulk of legislation referring to race, gender and sexuality has come into force only since the 1960s, while age and disability discrimination barely gets a mention until the 1990s.

For instance, it wasn't until the Race Relations Act of 1965 – later strengthened in 1968 and then 1976 – that discrimination on the grounds of "colour, race or ethnic or national origins" was outlawed in the fields of employment, the provision of goods and services, education and public functions. Homosexual acts were punishable by execution until 1861 and by imprisonment until the Sexual Offences Act was passed in 1967; they were still criminalised in Scotland and Northern Ireland until the early 1980s, while the gay age of consent was only equalised in 2004. And it wasn't until the Disability Discrimination Act of 1995 that the first attempts were made to outlaw discrimination against people with disabilities.

Laws against religious discrimination, however, go back much further. One of the first forms of prejudice addressed by Parliament was the 1778 Papists Act, aimed at prejudice against Roman Catholics, laws that were strengthened by the Roman Catholic Relief Act of 1829. MPs then started debating similar provisions for Jews, resulting in the Religious Opinions Act of 1846, although Jews were still prevented from taking up elected or legal positions unless they took a mandatory "oath of abjuration" (which asked them to renounce their Judaism). It took the Jews Relief Act of 1858 to remove this barrier.

Women's emancipation came later. Following the efforts of Suffragists such as Emmeline Pankhurst, the Fourth Reform Act of 1918 granted the vote to certain women over 30, something extended to all women with the 1928 Representation of the People Act. In terms of employment, the 1919 Sex Disqualification (Removal) Act had admitted women into areas of civil service, courts and universities, but it wasn't until Harold Wilson's administrations of the '60s and '70s that further progressive legislation was passed, in the form of the Abortion Act (1967), the Equal Pay Act (1970) and the Sex Discrimination Act (1975).

In 1972, Britain entered the European Economic Community (EEC). When the EEC was renamed the European Union 20 years later, the Maastricht Treaty included a Social Charter that dealt with anti-discrimination law, although the Conservative government opted out of this. The Labour government, elected in 1997, was more enthusiastic about these social provisions, and in 2000 it took on board the new directives explicitly protecting people from discrimination on the grounds of sexuality, religion, belief and age, as well as updating legislation on disability, race and gender discrimination. The last act passed by the Labour government before the 2010 election was the far-reaching Equality Act, which codified huge chunks of anti-discrimination legislation.

The Government Equalities Office (GEO) was established in October 2007. Initially known as the Women and Equalities Unit, it was based within the Department for Communities and Local Government, merged into the Home Office and then transferred to the Department of Culture, Media and Sport in September 2012, before moving in with the Department for Education in July 2014.

The GEO takes responsibility for equality strategy and legislation across government, and currently provides advice to many other departments. For instance, it advises the Department for Work and Pensions on disability discrimination and general age policy; liaises with the Department for Transport on provisions for disability and transport; and works closely with the Ministry of Justice on human rights policy. It aims to improve equality and reduce discrimination and disadvantage for all – at work, in public and political life, and in people's life chances.

# MINISTRY OF HOUSING, COMMUNITIES AND LOCAL GOVERNMENT

A small department with some big responsibilities
for decentralisation and community cohesion

# "I see great people from different departments who want to work more closely together"

The Ministry of Housing, Communities and Local Government (MHCLG) is one of Whitehall's smaller ministries, but it covers a wide range of high-profile policy areas for England, including local government, housing, planning, the fire service, integration and faith. It also shares responsibility for local economic growth with the Department for Business, Energy and Industrial Strategy, and is accountable for the Homes and Communities Agency and Planning Inspectorate.

The MHCLG can trace its lineage back to 1950 when Hugh Dalton became Minister for Local Government and Planning. The current department was established in 2006 as the successor to the Office of the Deputy Prime Minister, which was created in 2001, and absorbed the Department for Transport, Local Government and the Regions in 2002. The word "housing" was added to the title in January 2016, when it changed from a department to a ministry.

Since 2010 the office has been at the centre of major decentralising reforms. Arms-length regional development agencies were ended, along with a network of regional government offices. The Localism Act in 2011 transferred significant powers from Whitehall to local government. Local authorities now control more decisions about local services, housing, planning and economic growth, which are made in consultation with local communities and businesses. The Localism Act also introduced a series of new community rights that give people direct decision-making powers for their area, and are designed to encourage a cultural shift towards local action by citizens instead of the state.

They cover a wide range of issues, from running local services and proposing new housing developments, to enabling the protection of community buildings and land that are due to be sold, but are valuable to local people.

It was followed by the Cities and Local Government Devolution Act 2016, which aimed to introduce directly elected mayors to combined local authorities around England and Wales, with those areas having similar control over transport, housing, policing and strategic planning as the Greater London Authority and the Mayor of London. The Greater Manchester Combined Authority was the first to adopt this "metro-mayor" status, with Andy Burnham being elected mayor in May 2017. Sheffield, West Yorkshire, Cornwall, Liverpool, are set to follow suit, to be followed by combined authorities for the North East (comprising Newcastle, North and South Tyneside, Gateshead, Durham, Northumberland and Sunderland), Tees Valley (Darlington, Hartlepool, Middlesbrough, Redcar, Cleveland and Stockton-on-Tees) and the West Midlands (Birmingham, Coventry, Dudley, Sandwell, Solihull, Walsall and Wolverhampton).

The ministry has also been involved in agreements to devolve some health and social-care services in London boroughs, while there are 39 local growth deals which provide funds to local enterprise partnerships (LEPs) for projects to drive economic growth. "I see great people from different departments who want to work more closely together," says the ministry's Permanent Secretary, Melanie Dawes, "and sometimes it's about enabling that and supporting people who want to work differently."

While the ministry has transferred significant powers to local areas, it also maintains large capital investment programmes for house building, and administers high-profile homeownership schemes such as Help to Buy and Right to Buy. "Moving into delivery on housing is critical for us," says Dawes. "We are investing in professional programme oversight and stronger commercial experience in our main delivery agency, the Homes and Communities Agency. We also have to keep working closely with local government to understand their financial context, as we bring in new legislation to reform the system of business rates."

# DEPARTMENT FOR TRANSPORT

The body with duties for policies and legislation regarding road, rail, air or sea transport

Transport has been shaping the growth of Britain since the first Roman roads were built almost 2,000 years ago. For centuries, Britain's dominance of global shipping routes brought prosperity to the country, while its pioneering role in developing the world's first railways helped transform its economy during the Victorian era.

It wasn't until 1919 that David Lloyd George's coalition government created the Ministry of Transport – the first centralised body to oversee transport policy in Britain. The government body with responsibility for transport has changed its name and had various duties added or subtracted over the past century – for a while it was the Ministry of War Transport, or the Ministry of Transport and Civil Aviation, while between 1997 and 2002 it had local government, environment and the regions added to its remit.

Since 2002 it has been the Department for Transport (DfT), and currently employs more than 18,000 staff across the country, with headquarters at Great Minister House on Horseferry Road in Whitehall. The only surviving reminder of its original name today is the annual safety check for the roadworthiness of vehicles, which is still called the MOT test. Nowadays, of course, the modern Department for Transport is responsible for a lot more than simply road safety. DfT ministers are accountable for policy, legislation and public spending across all aspects of transport, whether by road, rail, sea or air.

Whether it's regulating one-man minicab firms or the global shipping companies that move 95 per cent of our food and consumer goods, it is the job of the DfT to make sure people and freight can get to their destination safely and reliably. That's no small responsibility in an island nation with some of the busiest ports, airports, roads and railways in the world.

Even though Britain has an impressive transport heritage, a modern economy relies on efficient transportation. So today the DfT is overseeing the most ambitious transport infrastructure programme for generations, with more than £70 billion of capital investment in transport.

Across Greater London, Crossrail's army of engineers are working on the biggest construction project in Europe – a 73-mile east-west route running through the centre of the capital, linking Reading in Berkshire with Shenfield in Essex. The DfT will soon start building HS2 – a new national high-speed rail network which plans to link London Euston with the Midlands, the north west and Yorkshire – and possibly the north east of England and central Scotland. British roads are also benefiting from a £15 billion investment that has been scheduled for the 2015 to 2020 period.

The DfT has also invested heavily in low-carbon transport, including cycling and walking, green buses, and electric cars. And, for the first time, it is trialling driverless cars on public roads in Greenwich, Milton Keynes, Coventry and Bristol.

All this activity means that the profile of the DfT, and public interest in transport, will continue to rise. Investing in transport is not just essential to keep Britain moving – it's also one of the best ways that any government can use to increase the GDP, rebalance the economy, and create new jobs. Nearly a century after the launch of the original Ministry of Transport, the work of the department has never been more important.

# FOREIGN & COMMONWEALTH OFFICE

Britain's most glamorous government department has been bedazzling foreign dignitaries since 1792

For the former Foreign Secretary, R A "Rab" Butler, the Foreign Office was rather like a Rolls-Royce – "you know it's the best machine in the world, but you're not quite sure what to do with it". Mrs Thatcher was also rather baffled by its function. "We have a Department of Agriculture to look after the farmers," she once said, "the Ministry of Defence to look after the soldiers – and we've got the Foreign Office to look after the foreigners."

The Foreign and Commonwealth Office (FCO), however, actually has a number of crucial functions. Britain no longer has an empire spanning a third of the planet, but it is still a permanent member of the UN Security Council, with seats at the top table of the G8 and NATO. And the FCO employs around 14,000 staff around the world. A third are UK-based, and two thirds are based overseas in the FCO's network of 270 diplomatic posts in 160 countries. One of the great offices of state, the FCO was originally known as the Foreign Office (FO) until it was united with the Commonwealth Relations Office and the Colonial Office in 1968. It was founded in March 1782, when Lord Rockingham's government merged two departments that had been active since 1660: the Northern Department (which dealt with the largely Protestant countries of northern Europe) and the Southern Department (the more senior wing, which dealt with the largely Catholic and Muslim countries of southern Europe and the Middle East, the Americas and the British Isles).

As the British Empire expanded throughout the 19th century, the FO became an increasingly influential component of government. Its headquarters in Whitehall, London, built at the height of Victorian imperial power, were specifically designed to impress and bedazzle foreign diplomats, with grand halls such as the Locarno Suite, the India Office Council Chamber and Durbar Court.

Commissioned in 1861 by Prime Minister Lord Palmerston – who spent 15 years as Foreign Minister – the building was completed in 1868 by George Gilbert Scott as "a kind of national palace or drawing room for the nation". This Palladian temple, hewn from Portland stone and richly decorated, works hard to establish parallels between the British and Roman empires. Its 22ft high corridors are even lined with statues of Victorian luminaries, bedecked in togas to resemble Romans.

"You get a strong sense that this is a building that has shaped the world," says former Foreign Secretary David Miliband. "It's where the Liberal Foreign Secretary Edward Gray looked out his window on the eve of World War I and made his famous speech about 'the lights going off all over Europe'. Many of the problems in this world have been started in this building, or have had very real links to it – from failed treaties or British-enforced borders that went wrong. So there is a sense of humility in this building, as well as a sense of grandeur."

Its current priorities are threefold. First, to safeguard the UK's national security by countering terrorism and weapons proliferation, and working to reduce conflict (the FCO is ultimately in charge of the Secret Intelligence Services, also known as MI6). Second, to build the UK's prosperity by increasing exports and investment, opening markets, ensuring access to resources and promoting sustainable global growth. And third, to support British nationals the world over through modern and efficient consular services (each year it deals with more than 1.7 million requests from UK citizens around the world).

For centuries, the FCO has had a reputation as being "full of toffs". In his history of Foreign Secretaries, Algernon Cecil wrote that it was "the last choice preserve of administration practised as a sport". Recent Foreign Secretaries have worked hard to open up the department to a more diverse and representative intake. But the FCO's mandarins still have to work in a very different way to other departments, as the former Foreign and Home Secretary Jack Straw observed. "Where the Home Office works by diktat," says Straw, "the FCO has to work by persuasion."

# BETTER CONNECTED

The charity Switchboard provides LGBT+ people with a vital source of support and sense of community

WWW.SWITCHBOARD.LGBT

"Switchboard's phones started ringing in 1974 and they are still ringing today," says Natasha Walker, a Trustee of Switchboard. "As one of the oldest LGBT+ charities in the UK, we have been at the forefront of supporting our communities for decades."

Switchboard is a confidential, non-directive service for members of LGBT+ communities and anyone who needs to consider issues around sexuality and gender identity. "We're here to listen," says Walker, "supporting people by giving them the information they need to make informed decisions. We never tell someone what to do." Since the service began, more than three million people have benefited from Switchboard's support and information on a wide range of issues.

There are 160 volunteers at Switchboard, who can be contacted via telephone, email or instant messaging. They undergo comprehensive training to handle a range of inquiries, often supporting people in sensitive and vulnerable situations. "One thing that many people call about, which they might not mention initially, is loneliness," says Walker. "LGBT+ people living in smaller communities around Britain can sometimes feel very

isolated. First and foremost, we try to make the caller feel comfortable and safe. In practical terms, it might be a case of finding out what LGBT+ groups or spaces are in their area, putting them in contact with others, or introducing them to the enormous online community."

A lot has certainly changed for the LGBT+ community since the turn of the millennium with the creation of the 2004 Gender Recognition Act, the 2010 Equality Act and the 2013 Marriage (Same Sex Couples) Act. But many people continue to face discrimination based on their sexuality or gender identity, while others lack the much-needed support that a charity such as Switchboard can provide.

Providing support for those in difficult situations isn't always easy, but the charity's volunteers also experience a sense of fulfillment that they are making a difference to people's lives. Walker recalls one occasion when she was on duty at a Pride festival stall. A man came up to her and said: "Thank you so much, you saved my life," before walking away. "It was so powerful," she says, "to realise that one phone call can make all the difference."

# A TRUE SEA CHANGE

A century after the formation of the Wrens, women
are playing a bigger part than ever in the Royal Navy

WWW.ROYALNAVY.MOD.UK/CAREERS

In 2017, the Royal Navy celebrated the centenary of the Women's Royal Navy Service (WRNS, but better known as the Wrens). The establishment of the Wrens allowed women to serve in the Royal Navy for the first time – something that was achieved before women were even entitled to vote.

One hundred years on, and the Royal Navy is preparing what Captain Ellie Ablett describes as the "final frontier": from 2019, women will become Royal Marine Commandos. "After that, all roles in the Royal Navy will be open to women," says Captain Ablett, who runs the HMS *Raleigh* training facility. "That's the last employment area previously closed to women."

When Captain Ablett joined in 1993, Wrens had just been amalgamated into the Royal Navy proper, allowing women to serve on the same terms as their male counterparts, having served at sea since 1990. Since then, progress has been steady. Women now serve on submarines and occupy senior positions, even if they still constitute only 9 per cent of the workforce.

"Every time there's been a change, we've used the experiences to learn," explains Captain Ablett. "There is always a certain amount of reticence even though people want to do the right thing and there can be a nervousness about the impact."

The improvements are vast. In maternity and childcare, the Navy has adapted to modern needs by providing a combination of flexibility and support. Women can transfer to the reserves after motherhood and then back to full service once they are ready, and a growing number of bases have creches. Support also comes from within: Captain Ablett formed a women's network that allows women in the Navy to connect both in person and virtually, sharing experiences and supporting each other.

"The aim is to share, inspire and empower," says Captain Ablett. "There was this idea that women working in a very male-dominated environment might have kept their heads down and I certainly didn't instinctively help women at first as I didn't want to be seen as different – I was sold on a certain vision of equality. But it dawned on me that I had missed a trick. Women have missed out on informal networking opportunities – playing golf or going to the pub. The other aim is to help the Navy. We are trying to harness these views and experiences to feed back to the Navy." Events are open to everybody, and some men have been so impressed that they are discussing creating networks of their own.

The Royal Navy offers tremendous opportunities for women seeking a challenge. Commander Felicity Campbell trained as a nurse and joined the reserves in 1992 before transferring her commission to the regular corps in 2000. She then served across the globe, and was deployed in Afghanistan seven months after returning to work from maternity leave.

"My husband got a lot of positive support to ensure he could manage the challenge of sole childcare," she says. "It was a very difficult tour and there wasn't a lot of contact with home. I had to trust my husband was managing the childcare just as any male who was overseas would. This is a difficult time in any women's life, whether she is working for the Royal Navy or a bank. We have a maternity buddy scheme and there is also flexible working where it is operationally appropriate. There's also a trial of part-time working.

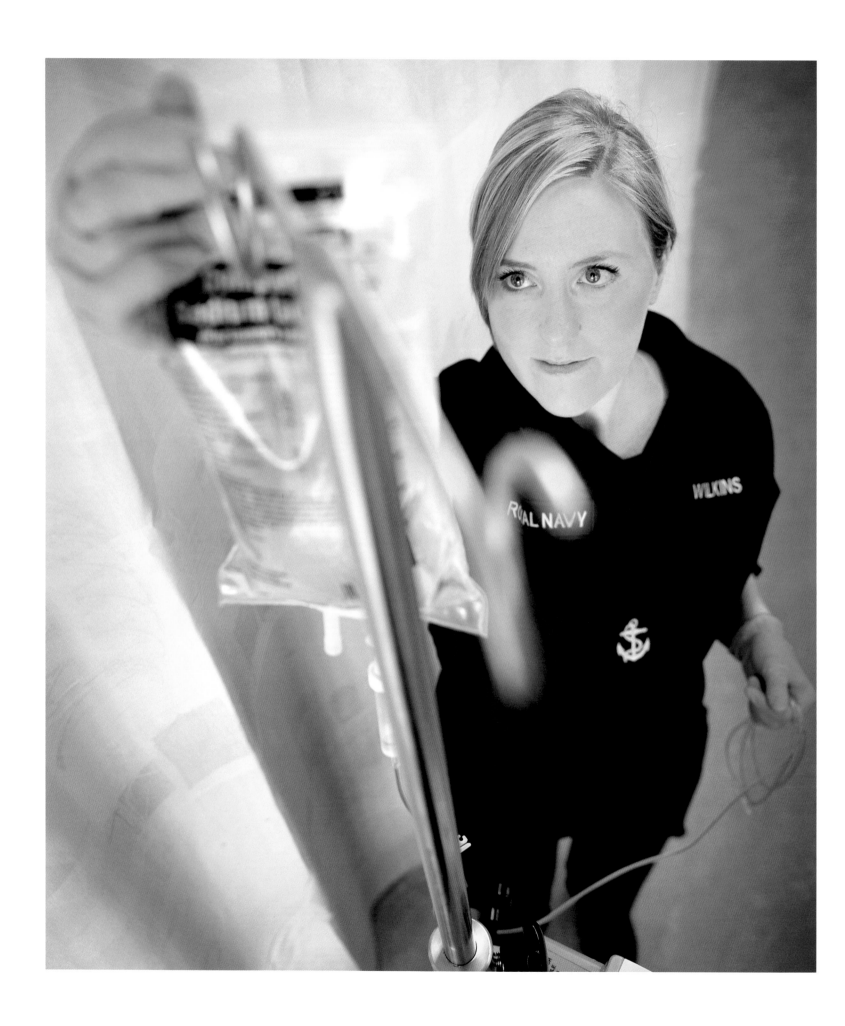

These are huge advances because it's important we have a diverse workforce and it's important that we reflect society. To do that, we need to retain female talent in service."

Commander Campbell enthuses about her experiences, explaining what women have to gain from joining the Navy. "I have worked in the best field trauma hospital in the world doing my job at the highest level and supporting soldiers, sailors and airman on the ground. It's a fantastic organisation that allows you to reach the pinnacle of your own abilities and will support you all the way." That is echoed by Commander Vicki Manders-Trett, who joined the Navy at the relatively late age of 24 following a period backpacking round the world. She enlisted as a steward and then worked her way up through the ranks, something that requires formidable fortitude as very few stewards – male or female – become officers. She mainly served at sea, at times as the only women aboard a ship, but now works at a base in Portsmouth.

Her father was also in the Navy and feared the rigorous structure and authority would damage her sense of individuality. "But I thrived and had so many opportunities I couldn't have found in another organisation," she says. "The Navy my father joined was very different. It was not diverse at all. What appealed instantly was the friendship. I wouldn't get that from other organisations, including the other two services. There were times when I was the only female out of 280 on a ship and you might think that was intimidating but I had 279 brothers, some who were younger and annoying and others who were caring and protective. It creates bonds that are hard to break."

There are still considerable challenges to recruiting and retaining women. Trying to attract women to serve as engineers is a particular problem due to the small numbers in the employment pool. "The challenge is sustainability," says Captain Ablett, explaining that not everybody would ever consider a job in the armed services so it's important to keep the ones who do. "We'd love to be 50/50 but our target instead is 20 per cent by 2020."

Many women are now engaged in outreach work, talking to students about the Navy's potential. "That can be an amazingly positive experience for those women who quietly go about their job and don't think about how incredible it is – whether that's mine clearing or flying helicopters," says Captain Ablett. "These are roles that people might not be aware women are doing and which some modest women might not talk about much."

Commander Manders-Trett is among those who spends time encouraging young men and women to join the service. "We show them what we do, and what the working and living conditions are like" she says. "We inform them that they can be anything from a chef to an engineer. You can be a medic or drive a warship; you can fix a Merlin helicopter engine or work in a nuclear submarine – and that most of the formal skills that you learn can be transferred to another employer. As the Royal Navy operates away from the UK, we have found it beneficial to give people an understanding of what life is like serving in the Senior Service, to make them aware of the opportunities available to them. We also highlight that there are more and more women in senior ranks – there is no glass ceiling now. When I see the prospects now available for younger female members of the Royal Navy, I've noticed a massive positive step change."

# A NEW PICTURE

CMS is a top-10 global law company with
a firm commitment to diversity and equality

WWW.CMS.LAW

> "A gender-inclusive culture, with a diverse, supportive and engaged workforce, is key to the success of our business"

Penelope Warne, CMS

"We live and breathe diversity each and every day," says Penelope Warne. "It's central to our strategy and having a successful business." As the Senior Partner at the prominent international law firm CMS, Warne has been instrumental in helping seek out diverse talent in what is often perceived as a male-dominated industry. Since becoming the Senior Partner in 2014, she has made it her mission to ensure that women's careers thrive at CMS.

This top-10 global law firm – whose name is derived from its two founding firms, Cameron McKenna and Sigle – provides legal and tax advice to clients including many FTSE 250 firms. With 450 partners and more than 4,500 lawyers, it is the UK's sixth-largest law firm, having combined with Nabarro and Olswang in May 2017. And, with more than 7,500 staff worldwide, it has a global reach that competitors can only envy.

The firm's brand ethos is "Your World First", a personal promise to understand the client's business as a priority. As one example, CMS set up The Women's Network to help identify and showcase female role models, and to encourage inclusive practices such as flexible working. Open to everyone, the network is rapidly growing across the globe, from the UK, to Dubai and Oman.

Success in attracting and supporting female talent is also achieved through CMS hosting, sponsoring and attending events for partner groups such as Women in Technology and the Association of Women Solicitors. "A gender-inclusive culture, with a diverse, supportive and engaged workforce, is key to the success of our business," says Warne. "We're really proud of our achievements, particularly of the role that we play in sharing our values, ideas, experiences and learning with our clients, partners and peers. This creates a

supportive and high-performing culture in which everyone's careers can flourish."

Photography can be a powerful way to raise awareness, so CMS has partnered with London photographer Leonora Saunders to create The Athena Project – a photography exhibition to highlight the importance of female role models, mentors and leaders. Portraits of women including Fiona Woolf (the former Lord Mayor of London) and Baroness Patricia Scotland (the first black female government minister), as well as women connected with the firm, have featured in a photographic exhibition that has toured the UK. "We have many amazing women leaders in our firm and among our clients," says Warne. "But this doesn't always mean they're visible to the wider business world. This project is our way of showcasing their amazing achievements and sharing their inspiring stories with a larger audience."

The commitment made by CMS to promoting and embracing diversity, both internally and externally, has been widely recognised. Accolades include *The Times* newspaper rating the company a Top 50 Employer for Women, and a ranking (number 31) in Stonewall's Work Equality Index of the Top 100 Employers for LGBT inclusiveness. The Innovative European Lawyers Awards has also listed Warne in its top 10, and she was one of *City AM*'s Power 100 Women in 2015 as well as receiving recognition in *The Sunday Times*.

As for future ambitions, in the past year alone, CMS has opened offices in Iran, Hong Kong, Peru, Chile and Colombia, with a focus on prioritising international economies that support the growing businesses of its clients. At CMS, success is measured in results for the sector, clients and people. And, as the firm well knows, it's achieved by letting talent thrive, regardless of gender or background.

# ADVANCING NUTRITION SINCE 1941

The Nutrition Society disseminates evidence-based studies of nutrition to academic, scientific and government institutions

WWW.NUTRITIONSOCIETY.ORG

In 1941, Sir John Boyd Orr, who later won the Nobel Peace Prize for his hunger relief work with the United Nations, invited a group of eminent nutrition experts in the world of nutrition to the Royal Institution in London, to discuss wartime agriculture and rationing and to "advance the scientific study of nutrition and its application to the maintenance of human and animal health." All 28 attendees were men.

The meeting marked the founding of The Nutrition Society, an international learned society which has now grown to more than 2,700 members worldwide. "I'm pleased to acknowledge that now, in 2018, at least 75 per cent of the society's members are women," says Mark Hollingsworth, the society's CEO.

Since the inception of The Nutrition Society, seven significant women in the field are celebrated among their peers for promoting the importance of nutritional science. Dr Isabella Leitch, a nutritional physiologist who worked in Aberdeen with Sir John Boyd Orr in 1942, was a founder member of the society's Scottish Section. A former suffragette, she is remembered for establishing high standards in scientific quality, and for founding and editing the renowned journal *Nutrition Abstracts and Reviews*.

Dame Harriette Chick, the society's President from 1956 to 1959, was celebrated for her research on vitamins, and for her Vienna rickets studies during the first half of the 20th century.

A decade later, after working at the Ministry of Food alongside Sir Jack Drummond in the 1940s, Dorothy Hollingsworth became the society's Honorary Secretary in 1962. She helped establish the National Food Survey, and in 1970 became the first female Director General of the British Nutrition Foundation.

Dr Elsie Widdowson, CH CBE FRS, President of the society from 1977 to 1980, carried out significant work in testing food rations during the Second World War and later studying children's diets in postwar Germany. *The Composition of Foods*, written with Dr Robert McCance and first published in 1940, continues to be the basis of most nutritional databases globally.

Christine Williams, Professor of Human Nutrition and Pro Vice Chancellor (Research and Innovation) at the University of Reading, served as President of the society between 1998 and 2001 and is now an Honorary Fellow. Williams was awarded the OBE in 2013 for services to higher education and nutritional sciences.

Head of the Medical Research Council Elsie Widdowson Laboratory, Dr Ann Prentice, OBE, was President from 2004 to 2007, and now chairs the Scientific Advisory Committee on Nutrition, providing advice on diet and health to the government. She is Honorary Professor of Global Nutrition and Health at Cambridge University and an Honorary Fellow of The Nutrition Society.

As Secretary General of the International Union of Nutritional Sciences, and Co-chair of its Capacity Building Task Force, The Nutrition Society's past President, Professor Catherine Geissler, continues to raise the global profile and professionalism of nutritional science.

In science, technology, engineering, and maths (STEM) education, the society looks forward to encouraging the development of others who strive to follow these outstanding examples.

"One of The Nutrition Society's important modern-day functions is to present strong evidence to government and policy makers on the importance and longevity of nutritional science," says Hollingsworth. "Some of the journal articles published in the 1940s are still being cited today."

## "The Nutrition Society presents strong evidence to policy makers on the importance of nutritional science"

Mark Hollingsworth, The Nutrition Society

# OUT OF ABUSE

Karma Nirvana is raising awareness of the issues around forced marriage and so-called "honour"

WWW.KARMANIRVANA.ORG.UK

Jasvinder Sanghera was awarded a CBE in 2013 for her outstanding contribution to supporting the victims of forced marriage and honour-based abuse. Her first campaigning step, 24 years ago, was to set up the charity Karma Nirvana. Since then, this national helpline has received more than 60,000 calls for service.

British-born Jasvinder recalls watching her older sisters being removed from school at the age of 15 and taken to India to be married without their consent. One day, it was Jasvinder's turn. "When I was 14," she says, "my mother sat me down and showed me a picture of a man I'd been promised to from the age of eight." When Jasvinder refused, her parents held her prisoner until she agreed to the marriage. She escaped when she was 16.

"My family took the view that either I went back, conformed and married," she says, "or be disowned, deemed dead in their eyes. So I chose a path that allowed me to have the freedom to embrace all that Britain stands for, facing many losses and struggles. I've been disowned for 35 years and if I were 16 today I would make the same decision. It means my own children will never inherit a legacy of abuse."

Jasvinder's sister Robina, however, did not escape. Deterred by her family from leaving an abusive marriage because it would bring "shame" on them, she committed suicide, setting herself alight. Robina's tragic death was the catalyst for Karma Nirvana, which was founded in her memory to give voice to other victims. Jasvinder broke her own silence and, gradually, thousands have followed by sharing their stories of abuse.

"Honour-based abuse has multiple perpetrators," she explains, "often immediate family members that include women. Normal adolescent life can be seen as a threat to the family and the victim is made to feel that they are going against the family."

Karma Nirvana has done much to raise awareness of the issues surrounding forced marriage, and has made a real impact to policy, practice and attitudes. "There's a lack of professional confidence," says Jasvinder, "and a fear of appearing 'racist' or treading on cultural toes."

Jasvinder herself was instrumental in the criminalisation of forced marriage in 2014. "We have moved an issue of abuse that was not recognised in the UK to one that now sits at the forefront," she says.

# PRECIOUS MOMENTS

Francis House Family Trust provides support for children with a short life expectancy and their families

WWW.FRANCISHOUSE.ORG.UK

"Families forget that we're a hospice," says David Ireland, Chief Executive of Francis House Children's Hospice. "They see us as a holiday home." Francis House plays a crucial role in the lives of the children and young people benefit from its support, going far beyond day-to-day medical care to offer emotional and practical backing to the whole family.

Francis House opened in Manchester in 1991. It was only the fifth children's hospice in the world – a pioneer in providing child-centred end-of-life care. It is a place of rest and recuperation but also fun and laughter, and there is a focus on supporting all members of the family. Siblings can use all of the hospice's facilities, such as the Jacuzzi pool and soft play, and are invited to take part in adventure activities.

As well as bereavement support for parents, there are sessions for bereaved siblings to help them work through their grief. By creating a place where the whole family can enjoy spending time together, Francis House enables people to find happiness and comfort in difficult times. "We help create good memories," says Ireland, "because good memories last longer than bad memories."

In the past few years, Francis House has also led the way in support for teenagers and young adults.

In 2014, it opened Francis Lodge, a parent-free space for older users. With music, gaming and movies, and trips to the cinema and shopping malls, it gives some much-needed independence to young adults with complex conditions. Emotional support services help children to talk through concerns and fears, and deal with their feelings of grief.

While Francis House receives some grants, it has to raise more than £3 million through charitable donations every year, so a great deal of work goes into fundraising. Volunteers are also essential to the running of the hospice and around 80 work in-house. Francis House is a big part of the local community, both for those who use it and those who support it. Although it grew out of a Christian background it has a completely inclusive philosophy: people of all faiths, or none, are welcome, and currently about 38 per cent of users are Asian Muslims.

Whatever their background or needs, every family is welcomed, respected and valued. The lives of those who go there may be short but, by focusing on the dignity of the individual, Francis House ensures these lives are fulfilled, dignified and full of happy memories.

# IN GOOD COMPANY

Law firm Hodge Jones & Allen upholds
a culture of fairness and inclusivity
that benefits clients and staff alike

WWW.HJA.NET

Shortly after qualifying as solicitors, three university friends – Henry Hodge, Peter Jones and Patrick Allen – set up a law firm together in Camden, north London. From the outset, the practice has had a radical edge and, 40 years on, continues to fight for justice, to right wrongs, and to make the law accessible to all people – irrespective of their means.

"We use the power of the law to help individuals," says Patrick Allen. "While acting on behalf of our clients, we also actively fight against reforms that we believe are not beneficial to the general public."

The firm's chief areas of personal legal services are personal injury, civil liberties, criminal defence, family law, clinical negligence, housing, wills and probate, employment and dispute resolution. The firm's reputation has been enhanced by a number of high-profile engagements in the fields of civil liberties and personal injury. It continues to act for Neville Lawrence – whose son Stephen was murdered in 1993 – in relation to ongoing investigations into police corruption. It also successfully represented claimants from the King's Cross fire in 1987 and the Marchioness ferry disaster in 1989.

Allen recently stood aside as managing partner, but retains the role of senior partner. "The law is complicated," he says. "The courts are scary places, and our clients are usually facing powerful, well-resourced opponents. So to help the ordinary person defend or assert their rights can be a potent thing – and winning a case often makes a massive difference to someone's life."

The firm believes resolutely in the civil and criminal justice system, and in its importance to the proper functioning of a modern democracy. "There used to be a comprehensive legal aid scheme," says Allen, "which has been gradually whittled away. The

civil justice system scarcely exists now, and the criminal justice system has also been deprived of funds."

Allen's place as managing partner has been filled by Vidisha Joshi who, at 39, is one of the youngest managing partners of a law firm of this size. The fact that she happens also to be a woman and of Asian heritage has effortlessly fulfilled the firm's commitment to diversity and gender equality.

Hodge Jones & Allen has a staff of more than 220, and turns over around £16 million per year. Its employees come from a range of cultural backgrounds, and 69 per cent of them are women – who also comprise 64 per cent of its partners and 50 per cent of the management board. Supporting local communities, initiatives and charitable organisations is part of the life-blood of the firm. An annual programme of fundraising events is interwoven into the work of the law firm each year, along with a season of evening concerts held within Club Inegales – the firm's resident jazz club.

"We like to do things differently at HJA," says Joshi "The firm has always been an enthusiastic supporter of the community. Most recently, we have proudly backed the founding of the Bonavero Institute of Human Rights at Oxford University."

HJA's website includes information detailing ongoing projects aimed at improving outcomes for clients. The HJA Innovation in Law initiative, for example, was established to help the firm to refine its internal processes and safeguard legal representation for all members of the public.

"We have always worked hard to help individuals fight their corner in terms of rights and access to justice," says Allen. "I know Vidisha and our other partners will continue to represent and assist others for many years to come."

# POSITIVE FORCE

Cambridgeshire Constabulary knows that a diverse and inclusive force is crucial to effective policing

WWW.CAMBS.POLICE.UK

Policing one of the UK's fastest-growing counties brings its own challenges, and for Cambridgeshire Constabulary these include keeping pace with the increasing diversity of rural and urban communities.

Chief Constable Alec Wood is proud of the force's investment in a diverse workforce – both for the strength it brings to the organisation, and the ability to represent and reflect those it serves. "We've come a long way since the Representation of the People Act," he says, "but, as a force, we still strive to be inclusive and embrace diversity."

The force currently employs around 1,300 officers, and a further 1,200 staff, Specials and volunteers, to police a resident population of around 800,000. That population is forecast to increase by 25 per cent between 2010 and 2031, while Peterborough, one of three urban areas policed by the force, was the UK's fastest-growing city between 2002 and 2012. Diversity is a key issue: more than 100 languages are spoken, there is a large eastern European community in the rural Fenlands, and a significant BME population in Peterborough, where more than 45 per cent of the community identify themselves as belonging to Asian, black, mixed or other ethnic groups.

It's why the force is committed to inclusivity across the organisation, with well-established support groups. The women's Fusion network aims to support gender equality and improve female representation across the force, while NEXUS assists the force's LGBT staff, and improves relations with LGBT communities. The BME Support Group is committed to improving the working environment for BME staff and establish good working relations with local communities, and the force's Gypsy, Roma, Traveller Police Association (GRTPA) supports GRT officers and staff, while improving relationships between GRT communities and the police.

Meeting the challenges of such diversity comes at a time when the constabulary is among the lowest funded in the country, and with competing demands on resources – including investigating child and domestic abuse, safeguarding victims, public protection work and tackling human trafficking.

"We are committed to making Cambridgeshire a safer place to live in, work and visit," says Wood. "Cambridgeshire has a diverse community, and we are dedicated to developing a representative workforce."

# PUTTING TRUST IN THE CITY

The Inner City Trust is breathing new life into Derry through physical, economic and social regeneration

WWW.INNERCITYTRUST.COM

Effective urban regeneration is a complex and longterm undertaking. A city such as Derry, recovering from years of underinvestment after emerging from the Troubles, requires strategies that impact on physical, social and economic renewal. Established in 1976, the Inner City Trust is continuing its positive and systematic contribution to this process. The main thrust of its strategy is the development and refurbishment of buildings around the city to generate income for further re-investment.

"We have the flexibility and vision to pursue our objectives and respond to the needs of the city," says the trust's CEO Helen Quigley. "Each year we invest and re-invest our income in pursuit of the charitable objectives of urban regeneration, skills development and the relief of poverty."

The newly opened Bishop's Gate Hotel is a prime example of the trust's heritage restoration programme. Once on the "at risk" register, the building is now a thriving boutique hotel. "Unlike the private sector, which relies on quick returns, we take the long view," says Quigley. "We had the foresight to invest in a

scheme that would provide jobs and a newfound confidence in the city centre, improve the streetscape, encourage footfall and enhance the tourism offer."

In Shipquay Street, the second-oldest building in Derry has been restored and now houses the Fashion and Textile Design Centre, supporting small business start-ups. "It is also a legacy project," says Quigley. "Derry was once famous for its shirt-making industry, and we are working to revitalise that tradition."

In job creation – whether in the hotel, the design centre or in the form of building apprenticeships on restoration developments – the trust is playing its part in tackling poverty and engaging a younger generation.

Since its foundation, the Inner City Trust has been involved in significant capital programmes in the city, as well as distributing substantial donations each year to other local charities. "We will help to meet the challenges of improving prosperity and helping to underpin the city's social fabric," says Quigley. "As our latest phase of investment draws to a close, the next phase is in the planning process. While we are content with what has been achieved, we'll never become complacent."

# THE FAIRER ESSEX

Essex Police is determined to continue the career progression of its women members

WWW.ESSEX.POLICE.UK

Until women were included as professional members of the British police force a century ago, the only women actively involved in policing were police matrons. These women were typically employed supervising female and child offenders in custody. "There has been huge progress since then," says Superintendent Cat Barrie, West Local Policing Area Command Team, and chair of Essex Police Women's Leadership and Development Forum (WLDF).

"Today, there's no job in the police force that a woman would be excluded from on grounds of gender," she says. "Skill and credibility are what count." There is, however, still room for improvement; and scope for further encouraging women to apply for high-ranking positions.

The WLDF is one of several existing networks aiming to achieve these goals. "The forum addresses professional issues," says Superintendent Barrie, "such as motivation and employment opportunities; as well as personal concerns to do with uniforms, flexible working patterns, menopause and so on." At a national level, the British Association of Women in Policing (BAWP) represents women from all 43 forces across England and Wales.

At the head of Essex's Operational Policing Command is Chief Superintendent Rachel Nolan. Her department deals with equipment from helicopters to firearms and dogs; and Superintendent Barrie describes it as "a fast-moving and hands-on policing environment which was previously heavily male dominated".

It's no longer so male dominated. Chief Superintendent Nolan's example is attracting more female officers into her department; and the WLDF is involved in consultation with a view to addressing their specific requirements. These include designing stab vests to suit female body shapes and commissioning weapons that fit comfortably in women's hands. Superintendent Barrie stresses that there are no compromises on fitness standards or pass rates.

Although frontline policing is the most visible sector of the service, Superintendent Barrie and the WLDF give equal attention to women staff working behind the scenes in professional and support roles. In collaboration with Kent Police, Essex has set up the Police Staff Leadership Pathway (PSLP) with a view to promoting talent.

Superintendent Barrie is optimistic about the future. "When I see confident young women in the Volunteer Police Cadets," she says, "I like to believe that in 20 years' time – when they are the backbone of the organisation – the things we're striving for won't be a huge issue any more."

# AN INSTINCT FOR EQUALITY

Zoological Society of London maintains an enlightened attitude to women

WWW.ZSL.ORG

International science and conservation charity ZSL (Zoological Society of London) has always had a different attitude to gender equality from most scientific bodies in Britain. Founded in 1826 by Sir Stamford Raffles, the charity now operates ZSL London Zoo and ZSL Whipsnade Zoo while undertaking science, conservation and education work in more than 50 countries.

From its inception ZSL was an important cornerstone for female zoologists in a climate that often excluded women from the sciences. A key instigator in this was Sophia Raffles, Sir Stamford's wife and the ZSL's first female fellow. "She was involved in the establishment of the organisation so it seemed appropriate to have this determined woman there," says Ann Sylph, ZSL's Librarian. "ZSL had women fellows and corresponding members, and there were women publishing in the *Proceedings and Transactions* journal, now called the *Journal of Zoology*, from almost the beginning."

Once Sophia Raffles had set a precedent, numerous prominent women became associated with the ZSL. For instance, illustrator Elizabeth Gould collaborated with her husband John on nature books, and illustrated birds for publications by Charles Darwin. Another was the entomologist Evelyn Cheesman, who was blocked from becoming a veterinary surgeon because at the time the Royal Veterinary Society excluded women. Undeterred, she forged a career at ZSL, joining the curatorial team in 1917 and becoming curator of its insect house in 1920.

This focus on achieving women continues today in the organisation, whose workforce is 52 per cent female. Inside the organisation, mothers are supported with generous paid maternity leave and flexible work options. There is also a fellowship scheme for women scientists returning to work. ZSL also aims to engage more female students with its educational work. Recent initiatives such as "Soapbox Science" (which has seen hundreds of female scientists give public talks) have helped stimulate interest in zoology among girls.

These measures add up to something strong and vital in the sciences. Dominic Jermey, ZSL's Director General, says: "By supporting women across the business and in zoology, we will be able to improve the outlook for gender equality within our organisation, and also share our experiences to benefit zoology more broadly."

# CHANGING FACE OF THE LAW

Kent Police prides itself on being representative of the community it serves

WWW.KENT.POLICE.UK

Back in 1941, Home Secretary Herbert Morrison said, "Police duty is, for the most part, a man's job. But such work as driving cars, typewriting and attending the telephone can be done by carefully selected women."

How times have changed. Kent Police has done much to progress equality – from pioneering the recruitment of women in the service in the early 20th century, to employing a raft of diverse senior female officers today.

"Four years ago we had one female chief superintendent in Kent; now we have five out of nine," says Chief Constable Alan Pughsley. "Our officers are appointed on merit and proven ability; and we're unusual in that we have more senior female officers in what is still often perceived to be a 'man's world'."

Despite the echo of Herbert Morrison, the presence of women in Kent police force can be traced back long before his time to 1916. Then, policewomen were deployed on Kent beaches to deal with prostitutes who were drawn to the concentration of men preparing for combat in Europe.

It took another war, though, to bring further advances. This time, conscription was the driver of progress. In 1939, the Kent constabulary took on more than 70 women to form the Women's Auxiliary Police Corps (WAPC). The recruits had no formal powers, but took on clerical, driving and catering duties.

The momentum continued when hostilities ceased. In 1951, the first woman detective was appointed. Further progress came with the Sex Discrimination Act in 1975, which made all roles within the force available to women, in theory at least.

"The case for diversity in the police is as strong as it was years ago," says Chief Superintendent Julia Chapman. "It is so important that the force represents your community. That's what we aim for: a service that respects and reflects all communities, whether that's in relation to gender, ethnicity or sexual orientation."

Today, a number of force support networks help create an environment where all staff feel supported and valued. Chapman is the current chair of a support group for women and has built on the success of her predecessors, Chief Superintendent Ali Roden and Chief Superintendent Andrea Bishop. Chapman thinks the network's strength lies in inclusion.

"We cater for needs across the force at all levels," she says. "We help with things like career progression, health and well-being or building confidence. When I joined the force in 1992, things were starting to improve. There had been a women's unit that dealt with child-related issues and was a separate entity. At that time women were only allowed to wear trousers at night. I heard stories of female officers chasing suspects over fences in skirts!"

Today, under Chief Constable Pughsley's leadership, Kent Police has equality at its core. "I am very proud of the fact that this force is continually rated as Outstanding for Legitimacy by Her Majesty's Inspectorate of Policing," he says. "This is a unique accolade. This achievement is due in no small part to my Chief Officer team and many others driving forward significant culture change, taking the force – and policing nationally – away from chasing targets to being victim focused. It is equally about empowering staff to do the right thing and recognises that integrity and equality are a golden thread."

One thing's for certain; when looking back over the last hundred years, Kent Police truly has developed a model fit for the modern age.

# MAKING A DIFFERENCE

Durham Constabulary's emphasis on community engagement and the victims of crime is a winning formula

WWW.DURHAM.POLICE.UK
WWW.DURHAM-PCC.GOV.UK

"I have never been stuck with conformity or a slavish regard for history," says Mike Barton, Chief Constable of Durham Constabulary. "If we as a force are not light on our feet, we cannot adapt to meet the needs of our community." Barton presides over the top-performing force in the country as rated by Her Majesty's Inspectorate of Constabulary (HMIC). Durham's innovative approach to early intervention, victim support and community engagement have curbed re-offending rates and bolstered public confidence, for which Durham is ranked one of the highest across UK forces.

Durham Constabulary's core remit is safeguarding the population. This includes intervening when people's lives become precarious through joblessness or addiction, and finding solutions that keep them out of the courts. The highly successful Checkpoint programme, developed with the University of Cambridge, offers minor offenders a four-month contract that includes community service and restorative approaches for victims. "Society would be poorer if we lacked the awareness and sensitivity to ask why an offender offends and to turn around the way they think," says Barton.

Working with Barton to develop Durham's strategic objectives is Ron Hogg, Police Crime and Victims' Commissioner. Engaging the public is central to Hogg's remit. "It's about giving the community a voice," he says, "and the voice here is very loud. We link community feedback with the force's objectives, and work very hard to ensure that community liaison is deeply embedded across the force." Hogg introduced "Victims" into his title to highlight the importance of taking better care of the needs of victims. "The change to my job title is vital," says Hogg. "Our Victim Care and Advice Service offers a thorough assessment of a victim's needs and points victims towards support that is relevant to those needs."

Collaboration between regional forces on operational and strategic levels is an increasingly significant part of Hogg and Barton's work, particularly around how the force uses technology. "We are accelerating the digital space because that is where new crimes are being committed," says Barton.

The "Durham Difference", comprising the values of positivity, fairness, courageousness and integrity, runs through everything the force does. According to HMIC, it's a winning formula.

# FIGHTING SPIRIT

Duchenne UK is raising money to overcome the most common genetic killer of boys

WWW.DUCHENNEUK.ORG

"We can either be defined by the disease, or by the attitude we have to it," says Emily Crossley, co-founder of the charity Duchenne UK. "The attitude we have is that we are going to fight this." When Emily's son was diagnosed with Duchenne Muscular Dystrophy (DMD), she became determined to accelerate the search for a treatment for the disease. She soon joined forces with another mother, Alex Johnson, and together they have raised millions of pounds to fund groundbreaking research.

DMD is a rare genetic disease that causes the gradual wasting of the muscles. It almost always affects boys, and those diagnosed with it are in wheelchairs by their early teens and rarely survive beyond their twenties.

Crossley, who previously worked as a television news anchor and reporter, had never heard of the disease when her son was diagnosed with it in 2012. "I couldn't believe how horribly cruel it was," she says. She discovered that research into treatments for DMD was at an exciting stage, but that it lacked funding. So Crossley founded the Duchenne Children's Trust and

set about attempting to raise £1 million a year to fund clinical trials. Her work brought her into contact with Alex Johnson, whose son had also been diagnosed with DMD and who had founded the charity Joining Jack. The pair decided to merge their two charities to create Duchenne UK.

Together, Crossley and Johnson make for a dynamic and ambitious team, and their charities have successfully raised more than £8 million over the past three years. Duchenne UK is now running its own clinical trials and has facilitated huge advances in the treatment of DMD: 90p in every £1 it raises is spent directly on research.

"When we set up five years ago, our mission was to put an end to Duchenne in 10 years," says Crossley. "We're not there yet but we're making incredibly promising progress. What makes our charity so powerful is that it's two mums who don't ever stop trying to fund research." Both women acknowledge that it can be challenging running a charity while caring for their own sons. But looking at all they have achieved so far they are enormously grateful they chose to fight, not just for their boys, but for every patient with DMD.

# FORCE FOR CHANGE

Sussex Police leads the way in
embracing diversity at work

WWW.SUSSEX.POLICE.UK

When Giles York, Chief Constable of Sussex Police, worked in his previous job in South Wales Police, his senior team of seven included two women and two black people. "It was vibrant and challenging because people thought in different ways," he says. He was surprised by the stark difference when he joined a team in Sussex of all white men. "It was like hitting a sandtrap," he says. "Everybody just had the same perspective."

York set about bringing out the difference in Sussex with a commitment that has seen him described as a "diversity extremist". He believes diversity is essential if policing is to represent and understand the society it serves. In his career as a senior policeman, some of the greatest changes he's seen have been in attitudes towards gender-based violence: crimes like sexual assault and domestic abuse, where the victims are overwhelmingly women.

"The way that Sussex Police supports female victims of crime has changed immeasurably in the last 100 years," says York, "and even in the last five. As a result, the number of people I have working as specialists in those areas has quadrupled in the last five years alone. There are also new crimes emerging that will disproportionately affect women, such as exploitation of the elderly and modern slavery. That's why it's important to understand what gender means."

Sussex became one of the first police forces to achieve "white ribbon" status (joining a campaign to promote male response to domestic violence). Under York's leadership, Sussex Police, along with Surrey, was the first global police force to join the United Nations HeForShe campaign, launched by UN ambassador Emma Watson. "It's about men speaking up for women's rights," says York. "We've pledged

to achieve parity for senior representation in Sussex Police and tackle gender-based violence."

As Sussex strives to become more representative, recruiting and retaining female police officers becomes increasingly important. This is not just to ensure that the force resembles the community it serves. A diverse range of voices brings greater knowledge and understanding of the issues facing different sections of society, making the force more effective. The success of senior women elsewhere – the leaders of the Metropolitan Police, the National Crime Agency and the National Police Chiefs' Council are all women – demonstrates that policing is changing. "These are real beacons of hope at the highest level," says York.

He praises the work of Evolve, the Gender Equality Network offering professional support and guidance primarily to the women of Sussex Police. York believes that there is a need for flexible working, but also a necessity to remove other impediments to women joining the workforce. "For instance," he says, "years ago, you couldn't ride a police motorbike if you couldn't lift a bike, so there were no women on the team. That may seem a relatively innocuous rule, but it serves no real purpose and merely acts as a barrier to joining. Just as other innocuous barrierst exist today."

Recognising and overcoming such obstacles is essential if policing is to have a successful future. "Policing is unique, because it is a service delivered with the consent of the public," says York, "so it's vital that we represent the society we serve. That's why it's so important to recruit difference, including women and black and minority ethnic officers and staff. That will only make us better performing, and understanding our communities better."

# WORK IN PROGRESS

The Royal Association for Deaf people is committed to improving the Deaf community's employment prospects

WWW.ROYALDEAF.ORG.UK

In 1841, a London bookseller called George Crouch, the father of five Deaf children, set up a society to improve their employment prospects. One hundred and seventy-seven years later, his society has royal patronage and today the Royal Association for Deaf people (RAD) remains committed to helping Deaf people find meaningful work.

Committed to working with those who are born Deaf, it campaigns for equality while celebrating Deaf culture. "Deaf people view themselves as a linguistic and cultural minority, rather than disabled," says Dr Jan Sheldon, CEO. "Which is why we spell 'Deaf' with a capital 'D'. British Sign Language (BSL) is a recognised language, not a signed English equivalent. English is a second or third language for most Deaf people."

Sadly, this puts the 77 per cent of Deaf children in mainstream education at a disadvantage. "They don't tend to have a good experience at school," says Dr Sheldon. "They're often forced to lip-read and leave with an average reading age of nine. This makes it hard for them to find work, and what work they do find is often manual."

RAD supports young job seekers by helping them create a CV, find work experience and prepare for interviews. "We do pre-employment training," says Dr Sheldon, "to help make them a better prospect for employers and increase their confidence."

RAD also provides Deaf Awareness training. "Employers might think they're taking on a disabled person, but they're not," says Amanda Casson-Webb, Director of Communication Services and Community Development. "They're taking on someone who communicates differently. Employers are entitled to Access to Work funding: this can pay for a BSL/English interpreter or other forms of support to level the employment playing field."

In the past three years, RAD has helped more than 700 people into work. Clients include Nayden, a 22-year-old Bulgarian who arrived in the UK unable to speak English or use BSL. He now works in KFC. "KFC could see his passion for cooking," says Dr Sheldon. "We worked with the branch manager and Nayden, guiding him through the process of setting up Access to Work support. He's now an active member of the team."

There are still barriers to break down. "But we're committed to working with Deaf people," says Casson-Webb, "to create a better, more accessible future."

# A FORCE TO RECKON WITH

Devon and Cornwall Police is
on a crusade to better represent
the community it serves

WWW.DEVON-CORNWALL.POLICE.UK

There's a theory that Britain's "policing by consent" model will only be really effective if police forces are more representative of the communities they serve. It has gained considerable traction in recent years among politicians, the public and the police themselves. And few forces are as committed to increasing the participation of under-represented groups as Devon and Cornwall Police.

"We're striving for a much more proportionate representation of the community within the force," says Superintendent Nikki Leaper. "We're not just talking about it, we're actively pursuing it." Leaper is a senior officer in the Operations Department and a former chair of the Women's Network, which offers support, mentoring and coaching across the force. "We want to inspire women to reach their full potential," she says.

In 2017, Superintendent Leaper received a Special Recognition Award from the British Association for Women in Policing. This was partly in response to her active role in connecting women staff with commercial and community organisations outside the force.

Leaper is quick to highlight the work of other staff-support networks, and she regards the senior management team as crucial in the force's move towards becoming a more inclusive organisation. Chief Constable Shaun Sawyer backed the recent introduction of Positive Action teams and ambassadors to increase job applications from under-represented groups. He also accepted the Women's Network challenge of a live Twitter Q&A on gender issues within the force.

Sawyer believes the Network's drive to increase the participation and development of women within the force also reflects the traditionally diverse nature of women's roles within the Devon and Cornwall communities. "In this largely rural area," he says, "men have historically worked long hours on the land or away at sea, so the work of women has always been vital."

The Positive Action ambassadors are about more than gender, though. They are working with all support networks, including the BAME, LGBT, disability and mental-health sectors. "There's been a step change in relation to inclusivity and diversity over the last five years," says Sawyer, "By encouraging applications from under-represented groups, we can work towards building a force which truly represents the community."

# SINK OR SWIM

One survivor is helping
to arm the next generation
against domestic abuse

WWW.SWIM-DV.ORG

Dr Diahanne Rhiney founded the Strength With In Me (SWIM) Foundation after surviving a murder attempt by a former partner. Drawing on her own experiences, she is determined to educate young people about what a healthy relationship looks like; and when to walk away.

As a former model, successful businesswoman and PR expert, Dr Rhiney is something of a professional superwoman. Yet she found herself falling victim to domestic violence, with almost fatal consequences. Her experience shows that this is an issue that can affect anyone, regardless of their background, and she believes that education is key to confronting it.

"If children cannot identify a healthy relationship," Dr Rhiney says, "then the chances are they can't identify a toxic one either. Toxic relationships are destroying the lives of our young generation." Statistics show that 75 per cent of teenage girls have experienced domestic abuse in a relationship.

Dr Rhiney set up SWIM, a non-profit organisation, to tackle this issue head-on, and it has already helped bring about some major changes. Throughout 2016 SWIM campaigned to make teaching healthy relationships compulsory in all schools. It successfully gained the support of MPs to form an all-party parliamentary group and, in February 2017, the government announced that, from September 2019, all schoolchildren will be taught about safe and healthy relationships.

SWIM also launched a global Twitter campaign, #CanYouHearUsNow, bringing together the voices of domestic abuse survivors from around the world. The aim was to give domestic abuse a "face" and create a grass roots movement pushing for change. On its first day the campaign achieved a social reach of more than 800,000 people. It was supported by high-profile campaigners such as the author Stella Eden, and actress Celia Peachey, whose mother Maria Stubbings was murdered by her ex-boyfriend.

SWIM is now working on delivering workshops in schools around the country. Using age-appropriate role-play and discussions, the Healthy Relationships workshops aim to raise awareness, and encourage young girls in particular to make positive relationship choices. "It's about empowering them to say, 'Actually, that's not okay, and I know my worth,'" says Dr Rhiney.

# STIRLING WORK

The "Gateway to the Highlands" is opening up to a fairer future for its staff

WWW.STIRLING.GOV.UK

Stirling Council oversees a population of around 93,000. It serves not only the people of the Scottish city of Stirling itself but also its extensive countryside, which stretches out to the mountains and Loch Lomond & The Trossachs National Park. These communities have a very varied demographic with many different needs, from business to transport – as well as the need to roll broadband out to more remote parts of the region.

Kristine Johnson has worked at Stirling Council since 2000, and is currently Chief Officer of Human Resources and Organisational Development. "One thing that links the whole diversity issue with the promotion of women is opportunity," she says. She explains that in local government, pay structures were previously devised so that some male staff – say, road and waste workers – got bonus payments. This benefit did not extend to female workers in the administrative, cleaning or catering sectors.

"Even though there was the Equality Act of 1970," says Johnson, "it's taken a lot of time for employers to sort that out. In 2009 we implemented single-status terms and a consistent job evaluation system, to measure and evaluate jobs according to a fair pay structure."

Development courses have been introduced for women to increase and enhance their opportunities in the workplace, while further improvements came with the living wage, introduced in 2012 and, three years later, the Living Wage Foundation accreditation. "It is having a positive benefit on our lowest-paid staff, who are predominantly women," says Johnson. "The difference from lowest to highest paid is just over seven times, low in comparison to other sectors. Over half of our managers are women and that is real progress, achieved through opportunities being available to learn and develop and the breakdown of occupational segregation."

Johnson believes that a blend of diverse views is essential for democracy to prosper. "The political parties benefit from having a mix of genders," she says. "Women sit alongside men and explore issues, develop priorities and plan around them. But diversity isn't just about men and women. We've got the nine protected characteristics under the Equality Act 2010: race, religion, sexual orientation, age and so on. A broad representation made up of all of those elements makes a powerful contribution to developing an area and looking to the future."

# A SOCIAL CONTRACT

The British Sociological Association not only studies gender equality, it puts it into practice

WWW.BRITSOC.CO.UK

Never underestimate the value of positive role models. "When you see women in leadership and hear their inspiring stories, it has an impact," says Judith Mudd, CEO of the British Sociological Association (BSA). "I've been influenced by women in my family, women who taught me, women I met through work and on my travels, women I've read about. They have given me the confidence to believe in myself."

It's no surprise, then , that Mudd is proud of the BSA's record in this area. The charity has over 2,700 members – most of whom are sociologists in British universities and schools – and 60 per cent are women. "All of the BSA's senior employees have been women," says Mudd. "Today, 46 per cent of our trustees are women, and we've got a female president." Indeed, women have played key roles at the BSA ever since it was founded in 1951.

With its remit to promote sociology, the BSA publishes four academic journals and organises more than 50 events every year. "These all touch on equality, to some extent, because sociology is the scientific study of the structure and function of society," says Mudd, "so academics in the field are interested in diversity issues."

The BSA celebrated its 60th anniversary in 2011 by establishing an annual Equality Lecture, in partnership with the British Library. High-profile speakers have included the politician and human rights campaigner Baroness Shami Chakrabarti, the sociologist, broadcaster and disability rights spokesman Sir Tom Shakespeare, and, most recently, the feminist writer and academic Professor Mary Evans. "I love those lectures!" enthuses Mudd. "They're open to the public, and they're really popular – which shows how relevant debates around equality still are."

Indeed, while women's lives have changed immeasurably over the past 100 years, Mudd highlights a recent survey of 13,000 senior female employees in the UK. "It found that women are still poorer paid than men, with less flexible terms and fewer promotional opportunities," she says. "They are also perceived as less competent managers than men." Mudd is, consequently, acutely aware of her responsibility as a positive role model. "We must jettison any notion that women are lesser than men," she says. "For the BSA, it takes research and analysis to show that there is still inequality – and we know that there is work to be done."

# JUSTICE FOR ALL

The GEO Group is transforming attitudes towards women in the British judicial system

WWW.GEOGROUP.CO.UK

According to government figures, women have always been substantially underrepresented among staff in the criminal justice system. A 2015 report by the Ministry of Justice found that just over a quarter of police and the judiciary are female – a statistic that makes the GEO Group, a provider of custodial services worldwide, truly exceptional.

The Florida-based company, which has been operating in the UK since 2006, has an affirmative action programme to employ and advance women, minorities, protected veterans and people with disabilities. As a result, 57 per cent of its UK workforce is female and, remarkably, all four of its UK executives are women. "The executive bias wasn't intentional," says Joanne Henney, Chief Operating Officer. "Each person was hired because they were right for the job and deserved to be rewarded."

GEO runs the Dungavel Immigration Removal Centre in South Lanarkshire and also transports offenders between police custody, courts and prisons. In these environments, the advantage of having a gender mix is clear. "I'm not saying women are more caring than men, but having a greater balance of men *and* women on a

team helps when working with offenders," says Henney. "And women in senior positions can help men see things from a different point of view."

GEO's focus on women also extends to those in its care. Female detainees are assigned a Women's Liaison Officer and are afforded the same opportunities for education, activities and work as men. "As true as the cliché is, we don't just believe everyone should be treated with dignity and respect," says Henney. "Rather we proactively challenge ourselves to really create equality of opportunity. That's why we have won awards for our approach to equality, diversity and inclusion." GEO has also been accredited as a Stonewall Diversity Champion

In order to attract talent, GEO offers competitive salaries, family-friendly shift patterns, holiday entitlement and childcare vouchers. The result is a company that is revolutionising the justice system.

"You wouldn't have thought it was possible to have a female prison governor until a few years ago," says Henney. "But things are changing – women are bringing more to the table than people have ever recognised before. I'm proud that we are part of that."

# WITH ALL DUE RESPECT

In the retirement home sector, the ELM group's ethical standards are a cut above the rest

WWW.ELMGROUP.ORG.UK

"Our philosophy is about treating our staff and customers as equals," says Lorraine Collis, Chief Executive of Ethical Leasehold Management (ELM). "That means responding to their needs, doing what we say we will do and, above all, being ethical." To this end, the ELM group has its own manifesto, "The ELM Way". It sets out guidelines that guarantee equality and fairness – not only within the organisation itself, but also in its dealings with customers.

The ELM group, which largely owns and manages properties in the retirement housing sector, operates with a clear-cut fee policy and no commission-based services: something Collis thinks sets them apart from other housing management groups. Transparency is paramount. For example, when the company upgraded the phone lines in each of the 50 properties they own, the £60 thank you they received from the phone company for each line installed was passed directly onto the leaseholders.

Collis believes that this kind of attention to detail helps inspire confidence and trust. "We want each of our leaseholders to feel like they matter," she says,

"and we put them first because fairness is important to us." Indeed, equality is at the heart of how the company shapes its future. The directors have an open-door policy when it comes to hearing the opinions and ideas of all employees, so they can actively contribute to decision-making.

"We're like a family," says Collis, "and promoting equality is absolutely key so that everyone feels they can make a difference." The results of a recent employee engagement survey demonstrate the success of this policy, with 94 per cent of employees confirming that they enjoyed working for the company. "Everyone bounces through the door," says Collis, "whether it's the office door or the estate where they're working, because they feel connected and an important part of the team."

"The ELM Way" is printed out and clearly visible to all leaseholders and staff. It reminds everyone of the core beliefs of the company and helps fuel its continued success: "The ELM Way helps us to continually deliver," says Collis, "and by sharing it with our customers, we help them feel like they are part of something important, too."

# POLICING IN AN AGE OF PEACE

Part of the country's peacetime transformation, the Police Service of Northern Ireland serves all the community

WWW.PSNI.POLICE.UK

Dealing with the everyday challenges of modern policing – from drugs and domestic abuse to sexual assault and violence – is tough enough. But add long-term community tensions and outbreaks of sectarian violence to that mix, and you get a better understanding of the task facing the Police Service of Northern Ireland.

Yet, against this backdrop, policing in Northern Ireland has undergone an incredible transformation. In 2001 the Royal Ulster Constabulary (RUC) ceased and the Police Service of Northern Ireland (PSNI) was established as an organisation much more representative of the community it serves. "I joined in 1989, and at that time less than 10 per cent of police officers were women," says Assistant Chief Constable Barbara Gray, the highest-ranking female among its 7,000 officers.

As the RUC, the police service in the province had dealt with horrific attacks and terrorist atrocities for several decades. But, as the peace process finally took hold after the Good Friday Agreement of 1998, the Patten Report – an independent commission and review of policing in Northern Ireland – led to the transition from the RUC to the PSNI.

"The introduction of the PSNI in 2001 was supported by specific legislation which stated that 50 per cent of the applicants for PSNI officer posts would come from a Roman Catholic background," says Gray. "Until that point, 87 per cent of the RUC was Protestant. The aim was to ensure that the police service became much more reflective of the society that it served. The legislation was in place for 10 years, and the additional unforeseen impact was that the number of female applicants to join the PSNI increased dramatically. It changed the face of frontline policing."

Although that affirmative action has now ended, the PSNI is still evolving. "That improvement has continued, and we're sitting at just under 29 per cent female representation in the service now," says Gray. "More diverse teams makes us more effective, supporting our community outreach efforts, and we're working hard to increase representation among both officers and staff.

"Ultimately," concludes Gray, "the transition to the PSNI has brought with it a focus on policing with the community – one of the key elements of the 'golden thread' of human rights-based policing."

# A BROADER CHURCH

Anglican Mainstream lobbies not just for Christian values but, above all, for reasoned debate and mutual respect

ANGLICANMAINSTREAM.ORGW

"We're not just a single-issue organisation," says Canon Dr Chris Sugden, who chairs the evangelical campaign group Anglican Mainstream. "In terms of mainstream Christian belief, we're concerned about a lot of things – poverty, injustice, famine, religious freedom – right across the board. There's a wide array of issues at stake."

Anglican Mainstream is part of an international collaboration to reassert and support traditional Christian understandings of marriage, the family and sexuality. The organisation expresses its values in diverse ways: it supports famine relief and charity projects across Africa, for example, and has also acted as a resource to the Grassroots Conservative movement at home.

Dr Sugden is unequivocal in his support for the British approach to political debate. "There's a view in this country," he says, "that while people may disagree with you quite significantly on some important and fundamental issues, it doesn't mean we can't work together for the common good. We can treat each other with the proper respect and proper engagement."

One matter Anglican Mainstream is keen to back is the importance of open discussion. However, Dr Sugden recognises that not everyone perceives traditional Christian organisations as diverse and inclusive. "There is a sense that the liberal elite believes it has the franchise on equality and diversity," he says, "and that everyone else is a bigot or a dinosaur. There is a very important point to be made here: that equality and diversity include, rather than exclude, those who don't agree."

Dr Sugden takes pride in the role he feels Christianity has played in spreading democracy. He points to findings by Dr Robert Woodberry that Christian missions helped sow the seeds of democracy throughout the world. Woodberry observes that, as "conversionary Protestants" taught people to read to enable them to access the Bible, they helped politicise them. Those in positions of power locally began printing their own information, leading eventually to wider knowledge, greater awareness of political ideas and, ultimately, democratic expression.

"Properly understood, mainstream Anglican Christian thinking has historically always levered participation, debate and engagement," says Dr Sugden, "for the benefit of the whole community. The key issue for us now is truth in public debate."

# SISTERS IN LAW

Legal and compliance search firm Laurence Simons takes an active role in diversity and talent retention

WWW.LAURENCESIMONS.COM

"When women sit in power, we have a particular responsibility to make our voices heard," says Clare Butler, CEO of legal and compliance search firm Laurence Simons. Since 1988, Laurence Simons has specialised in placing top level general counsel, partners and chief compliance officers within multinational companies and leading international firms. Through its understanding of the legal landscape, the firm is taking an active role in reappraising workplace diversity and talent retention.

"We as a business have to have the confidence to start the conversations about the gender agenda and diversity," says Butler. While leading law firms, including the top five so-called "Magic Circle", tend only to look at Oxbridge graduates, they risk overlooking what Butler calls the "hidden gems" from diverse backgrounds who can offer new, problem-solving perspectives.

"Lawyers have to be able to do the law," she says, "but if we are looking at intelligence, it is also about emotional intelligence and resilience." Butler advocates starting early, talking to primary school children, especially girls around 10 years old or younger, to open their eyes to the possibility of a career in law.

Improving diversity and gender balance in senior positions is one thing; retaining that talent is another. "The parenting issue is not a female/male issue, it is a people issue," says Butler. "In the legal profession, either women don't come back to work, or if they do, they are not on the same track."

Butler sees highly qualified female lawyers taking on unchallenging and less well-paid roles after returning to work, which in itself perpetuates the gender-pay gap. She and her team help firms embrace part time and compressed-hours solutions to allow couples to share parenting while keeping both their careers on track.

Laurence Simons uses its expertise to promote the conversations around diversity and equality that help companies re-think their employment strategies. Butler sees these conversations as vital starting blocks towards longterm policy shifts. "In short order, I would like to present my clients with shortlists of talent bursting with candidates of every ethnicity and background and an equal gender split."

# EDUCATION

Department for Education     210
The Brier School     213
Swansea University     214
Thornton College     216
Tormead School     217
Mount House School     218
The University of Sunderland     220
Merton Court Preparatory School     221
Royal Veterinary College     222
Devonport High School for Girls     224
King's High Warwick     225
York St John University     226
Altrincham Grammar School for Girls     228
The Centre of Excellence     229
The University of Central Lancashire     230
London College of Fashion     232
NASUWT     233
The University of York's Department of Chemistry     234
West Thames College     236
At St James Senior Girls' School     237
University of Exeter     238
Pearson     239
TeachBeyond     240
VTCT     241

# DEPARTMENT FOR EDUCATION

The department may have changed name, form and remit over the years, but education remains a crucial and contentious area of government

Policies and practices around education can always be relied upon to spark debate. It's a subject most people have an opinion about, and the reason for this is simple: it's something we have all experienced – both in having gone to school ourselves, and, usually, in seeing children we know attend. This means that issues around how children and teenagers are taught and assessed, and the opportunities for learning available to them, are hotly debated. "It's an inevitable consequence of the fact that education is an issue that people care about passionately," says the Department for Education's Permanent Secretary Jonathan Slater.

That is a long and rich history of UK government departments devoted to education issues. In its first incarnation, established in 1839, this was called the Committee of the Privy Council on Education. Since then, name, form and remit has shifted from time to time, taking in Education and Science, for example, from 1964 to 1992; adding employment to its portfolio to become the Department for Education and Employment (DfEE) between 1995 and 2001; and then rebranded as the Department for Education and Skills (2001–07) and the Department for Children, Schools and Families (2007–10).

The Department for Education (DfE), in its current form, has existed since 12 May 2010. It is responsible for education and children's services for those aged three to 19 in England, while also supporting professionals working with these young

people. Education in Scotland, Northern Ireland and Wales is delivered by different bodies in each respective region. Since July 2014 its offices in London and Manchester have also housed the Government Equalities Office, which responsible for equality strategy and legislation across government, taking action to remove barriers to equality and leading on issues relating to women, sexual orientation and transgender equality.

For all the debate surrounding education, most people today would agree that it plays a crucial role in extending social equality, and that we should strive towards children meeting high standards of numeracy, literacy, scientific and creative ability regardless of their background or circumstances. Cementing this idea in 2010, the then Education Secretary, Michael Gove, said: "It is only through reforming education that we can allow every child the chance to take their full and equal share in citizenship, shaping their own destiny, and becoming masters of their own fate. Education allows individuals to choose a fulfilling job, to shape the society around them, to enrich their inner life. It allows us all to become authors of our own life stories."

Although not without controversy, the English National Curriculum is usually presented as a tool for achieving such parity of opportunity. First introduced in 1987 by another former Education Secretary, Kenneth Baker, the National Curriculum is a guideline outlining teaching requirements, set by government. Most state schools are currently required to follow every area of this, although greater flexibility is extended to state-funded schools that exist outside local authority control, such as academies and the "free schools" introduced by the coalition government from 2010.

As for its content, a new "slimmed down" version of the National Curriculum was introduced in England in 2014, promoting traditional, knowledge-based teaching, such as spelling in English, times tables in maths, and a chronological study of history. Emerging subject areas were also introduced, including computer coding.

The overall aim of England's Department of Education can therefore be defined as equipping young people of all backgrounds with the skills they need to succeed in the 21st century. Whether it succeeds in that ambition will continue to ignite debate due to the relevance of education to all – and many would argue that it's precisely this national passion and interest that helps England achieve world-class education for all.

# "Education allows individuals to choose a fulfilling job, to shape the society around them, to enrich their inner life"

# OPPORTUNITY FOR ALL

The Brier School in Dudley provides pupils with an inclusive education and helps other schools do the same

WWW.BRIER.DUDLEY.SCH.UK

The Brier School is a beacon for educational excellence. Specialising in learning and complex communication difficulties for pupils aged 4 to 16, it became the first school in the borough of Dudley in the West Midlands to achieve the inclusion quality mark for inclusive education opportunities. It now acts as a role model for others in the area. "Schools send staff to see our work in practice and we offer advice freely," says Headmaster Russell Hinton, who was named a National Leader in Education in 2009.

With neighbouring mainstream primary and secondary schools, the Brier caters for a broad spectrum of learning capabilities. "We aim to educate pupils to bring out whatever skills or attributes they have," says Hinton. "All go on to further education, with some attending mainstream colleges and others joining a more supported sixth form. We make sure that all achievements are given equal recognition. We are just as proud of someone leaving the school with a Life and Living Skills diploma as someone who leaves with GCSEs."

The Brier was designated a National Support School in 2009 and has received a rating of "Outstanding" from Ofsted in its last three inspections. Emphasis is placed on providing a personalised learning environment that responds to the requirements of each pupil. The school motto, "Preparing for life – building on our strengths", acts as a benchmark. "Everybody has something to offer," says Hinton.

Equal weight is given to supporting pupil participation in a diverse extracurricular programme. Class trips to galleries, museums, cinemas, theatres and activity centres are a regular feature on the school timetable, along with seasonal visits at Christmas and in the summer. Pupils can also take part in the Duke of Edinburgh bronze award and attend a summer prom at the end of Key Stage 4.

"We want our pupils to enjoy coming to school and feel they are valued," says Hinton. The community spirit continues after hours and in the holidays through a home-school association called Friends of The Brier School, which runs film nights, family discos, coffee mornings, summer sessions and an advice network for parents. "Education doesn't just take place in the classroom," says Hinton, "but throughout the day and beyond the school gates."

# ENHANCING DIVERSITY

Swansea University's long-standing approach to inclusion has taken it from strength to strength

WWW.SWANSEA.AC.UK

Swansea University has a proud history of providing opportunities for women. Soon after it was founded in 1921, Swansea was the first UK university to appoint a woman to an established chair when it appointed Dr Mary Williams as Professor of French Language and Literature (as cited in her obituary). There were just 89 students at the university then – only eight of them women. Today the student body tops 20,000, with an even male/female split.

In 2014, Senior Pro Vice Chancellor Professor Hilary Lappin-Scott embarked on a major equality and diversity drive, resulting in the "Utilising all our talent" initiative, which is now bearing fruit. "I'm delighted to see an increase in women in leadership roles," she says. "They are providing wonderful role models, to whom women across the university can aspire."

Swansea has seen a spike in promotion applications from women academics, thanks to its introduction of an Academic Career Pathways scheme. In 2015/16, there was a 133 per cent increase in the number of successful female applicants for professorships; more than double the number appointed in 2014. For the first time, more female than male professors were appointed. This progress has continued. Last year there was a 78 per cent increase in female applicants, with seven of the 17 successful candidates being women.

Swansea is also determined to improve the number of women on key decision-making committees. By actively looking internally and externally for candidates with the right skill set, the university has succeeded in increasing the female composition of its council, from 21 per cent in 2012 to 52 per cent in 2018. Vice Chancellor Professor Richard Davies has pledged to achieve a 50/50 gender balance across all senior decision-making levels by 2020.

Swansea's efforts in supporting equality, diversity and intersectionality hasve not been in vain. In the last four years, the university has jumped 106 places to 29 in the Stonewall Workplace Equality Index and it received the Stonewall Cymru's LBGT+ Network award for 2017, becoming one of only 11 Stonewall top trans-inclusive employers in 2018.

Swansea University is the first Welsh university to win a Silver Athena SWAN Charter award from the Equality Challenge Unit (ECU) for its commitment to promoting gender equality. The university received bronze awards in 2009 and 2013, and is now the 16th higher education institute (HEI) to gain a silver charter award, out of 143 HEIs with charter membership. In addition, 100 per cent of its STEMM (science, technology, engineering, maths and medicine) departments hold awards ; and 100 per cent of its AHSSBL (arts, humanities, social sciences, business and law) departments will submit applications by 2020.

The Athena SWAN (Scientific Women's Academic Network) Charter was established in 2005 to encourage and recognise commitment to advancing the careers of women in STEMM employment in higher education and research. Ten years later, it was expanded to recognise work undertaken in the AHSSBL fields, as well as in professional and support roles, and for trans staff and students. The Charter broadly acknowledges efforts to address gender equality, not just the barriers to progression that affect women.

For Professor Hillary Lappin-Scott, this is fantastic news. "We have worked extremely hard to greatly increase diversity and inclusivity at every level," she says. "Our efforts moving forward will be directed towards ensuring continued progress. I'm very proud of the achievements made here. However, we are not complacent, and we continually seek to implement further initiatives to progress the equality and diversity agenda."

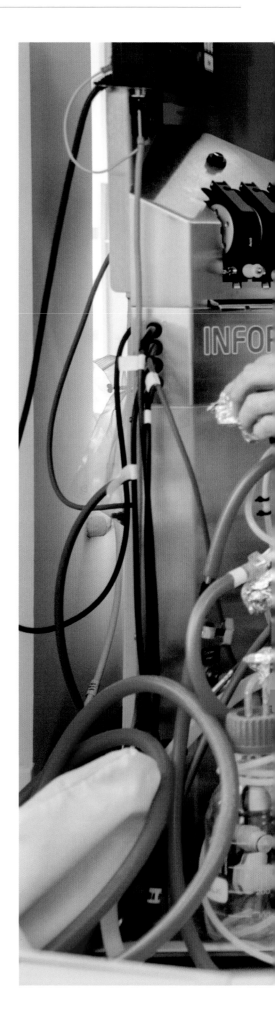

# STRENGTH IN DEPTH

Thornton College in Buckinghamshire is an independent Catholic school that embraces a diversity of learning experiences

WWW.THORNTONCOLLEGE.COM

When Thornton College was founded, its mission was to provide young women with an education akin to that of their male counterparts – a progressive aim in the early 1920s. The nuns who set up the school were dedicated to preparing their students for life, and their forward-thinking principles endure to this day.

"Students are encouraged to embrace the unexpected," says Jo Storey, who was appointed Head of Thornton College in 2015. "They are encouraged to become resilient, self-reliant young people, determined to excel in whatever they do, and destined to make a positive contribution to the society in which they live."

The independent day and boarding girls' school is set in 25 acres of parkland outside Buckingham and has 440 students, aged three to 18. Thornton College is a Catholic school, and the founding order of the Sisters of Jesus and Mary still live within its grounds and are represented among the school's trustees and governing body. Although the school has a strong Christian ethos, Storey says people of all faiths – and none – are a welcome and valued part of its community. Students come from a range of cultural and ethnic backgrounds, and an ethos of self-respect and tolerance of difference mean that all are equal. "We encourage all to live their lives by showing compassion, patience, understanding, forgiveness, humility and kindness," says Storey. "This makes us a very happy school to belong to."

Thornton College is non-selective, and every child receives an individually tailored education to ensure they achieve their best. "Our intake has talents in every area of life and we have teachers who will challenge and excite every ability level," says Storey. "Being a non-selective school does not mean that the students here are average – far from it!" The school has ranked as the top non-selective school in the UK in the *Times* Top Schools tables and ranked sixth overall for small schools (with a cohort of less than 60 in sixth form).

Storey has opened a brand new sixth form since she became head, as well as introducing six new GCSE subject options and enhancing the co-curricular programme. Future plans include an extension to the sporting provision and a dedicated music auditorium. "I am committed to offering academic and co-curricular programmes that are diverse and have real depth," she says. "We need to continue to offer an education that prepares students to excel in the world in which we now live. We are preparing them for the next 70 years, not the next seven!"

# TAKING CENTRE STAGE

Tormead School is an independent girls' school in Surrey that applauds achievement in all its forms

WWW.TORMEADSCHOOL.ORG.UK

A key approach of Tormead School is to stress that "girls are the players, not the audience". It is an ethos that has prepared this girls' school to play its part in more than a century of remarkable achievements for women. Founded in 1905 in Guildford, Surrey, this independent day school has evolved into a 21st-century institution for female students aged four to 18.

"Our history is important to us, but we are also very forward-looking," says Headmistress Christina Foord. "We're passionate about embracing new technologies, and we have just been made an Apple Distinguished School, thanks to our successful 1:1 iPad programme, which ensures that girls are adept in the use of new tech."

Environment is also key to Tormead's success: "We've invested a huge amount in trying to give the girls innovative, creative and light-filled spaces in which to work," says Foord. "We've always had a very impressive library, because that is a focal point of the school."

A partnership with Surrey Sports Park provides students with access to impressive facilities, such as an Olympic-sized swimming pool, and Tormead has achieved national and local success in gymnastics, netball and hockey. The school has also earned a reputation for public speaking, drama and music.

"Our fundamental aim is to ensure that the girls are happy, but we're also very ambitious for them going forward – in university, as professionals and in family life," says Foord. "We are passionate about preparing them for the world, from speaking a modern language to doing charity work or travelling the world. You can make a difference on every level, and that's what we encourage every girl to do."

While the school heralds its academic strengths, including a forte for A-level science and maths, there is also an emphasis on students applying what they learn to everyday life in the 21st century. "We are academically selective, but our first value is that we treat everybody with respect and dignity," says Foord. "We celebrate effort and achievement, outside school as well as in the classroom – being well-rounded is recognised as a strength. Whether it's getting further high grades, auditioning for a play or participating in The Duke of Edinburgh's Award, we encourage our girls to embrace the opportunities that life presents."

# A SENSE OF BELONGING

Mount House School in North London is a Christian
girls' school that nurtures individual growth

WWW.MOUNTHOUSE.ORG.UK

On a wall plaque at Mount House is written the quote:
"This is where I belong". It comes from a sixth-form student
and sums up the inclusive nature of this independent
Christian girls' school. "There's no such thing as a Mount
House girl," says Headmaster Matthew Burke. "We were
founded to treat everyone as an individual, whether
they're into science, sports or the arts. Like an extended
family, we all pull together for the public good through
good times and not so good times."

Unlike its competitors, this North London institution,
founded in 1903 and housed in Grade II-listed buildings,
is not academically selective. There's a maths, English
and non-verbal reasoning test at entrance, but it's not
a pass/fail exam. Instead, the focus is on recognising the
potential of each of the 250 girls educated at the school
and ensuring they make a positive contribution to society.

"When they come to us at 11 they may not know
what they're going to do, but they are encouraged to
nurture their passion," says Burke. "I tell pupils they
can be whatever they want to be and do whatever they
want to do. We have sportswomen representing at
international level, talented actors and bright girls
academically. We want them to take advantage of all
Mount House has to offer and of their talents, and to
contribute to life."

In return for believing in all its pupils, Mount House
expects parents to contribute to the school's success and
support its aims. When prospective pupils come for their
entrance test, the school insists on interviewing their
family, to find out whether they are totally committed
to the values and ethos of the school. "We select the
families, as well as the pupils," says Burke.

The school, based in the borough of Barnet,
was until recently known as St Martha's. It welcomes
students from all over North London and Hertfordshire,
and strives to provide both female and male positive
role models. Mount House pupils get to network with
UK business leaders through Women of the Future,
a programme to build professional relationships among
influential women. Dads also regularly come in and
talk about their careers and how they support gender
equality in the workplace.

"The focus is not on warning about glass ceilings but
instead encouraging the girls to dream that anything is
possible," says Burke. "It's important we strike a balance
between positive female and male role models."

At Mount House girls are encouraged to take
sensible risks and grow as individuals. This could mean
volunteering for the school talent show, where they
are cheered on even if they forget their lines, or taking
part in the Duke of Edinburgh's award, which is open
to all Year 9 pupils. As well as exploring beyond their
comfort zones, and studying Religious Education as a
core sixth-form subject, pupils are encouraged to give
back. They raise more than £10,000 for charity every
year by organising their own charitable events, which
includes selling poppies locally on Remembrance Day.

Looking to the future, the school plans to develop
its sporting facilities and has recently added new science
labs. The aim is to remain small enough to care – Burke
still knows every student by name – but big enough to
make a difference. With its dedication to bringing out
the best in each and every pupil, Mount House is one
"family" that has many more good years ahead.

# "The focus is not on warning about glass ceilings but instead encouraging the girls to dream that anything is possible"

Matthew Burke, Mount House School

# CAREER-READY LEARNING

The University of Sunderland is leading the way in providing students and industry with the skills to succeed

WWW.SUNDERLAND.AC.UK

Raising the aspirations and life chances of people with talent, regardless of their background, is crucial at the University of Sunderland. The UK's leader in widening participation, the university is building confidence in students by offering career-ready programmes, strong links with business and personal support, as well as international partnerships and student exchanges.

"A perfect example is our Living Lab," says Vice-Chancellor Shirley Atkinson. "It's a pioneering new facility designed to support the teaching of nurses, pharmacists and paramedics, and, ultimately, to improve patient care. It boasts the most advanced healthcare simulation equipment and interactive spaces." The university is also in discussions with the General Medical Council about opening a medical school to combat the region's shortage of doctors, and build on its exceptional reputation in biomedical science and applied research.

Elsewhere, the university is developing a growing programme of apprenticeships with various businesses that will provide employers with the high-level skills they need from their workforce. It has also pledged to supply the International Advanced Manufacturing Park – an

ambitious scheme that aims to create up to 5,200 new jobs and attract over £300 million of private-sector investment into the region – with the huge range of skilled employees needed to support such a large-scale operation. To do so, the university has opened a centre for enterprise and innovation on campus to back student and graduate enterprise, inspire regional business start-ups and drive innovation.

The university has been pivotal in Sunderland's growing cultural development, taking over the running of National Glass Centre and creating a Culture Company to establish the governance needed to attract national funding and nurture the creative sector. All this is set alongside an innovative curriculum that is informed by industry, sector partners and applied research.

The University of Sunderland has 20,000 students based in campuses in the north-east of England, London, Hong Kong and partner institutions in 15 countries. "Our strategic plan for up to 2021 sets out how we will cultivate sectors, develop our teaching and adapt to the requirements of modern learners and employers," says Atkinson. "This will ensure that students gain the skills and leadership qualities to succeed in their chosen career."

# SPRINGBOARD TO SUCCESS

Merton Court Preparatory School in Kent combines academic excellence with a healthy holistic approach

WWW.MERTONCOURTPREP.CO.UK

"We're an academic school, but we don't cut out anyone with potential," says Dominic Price, Headmaster of Merton Court Preparatory School in Sidcup, Kent. "We encourage pupils to achieve their best and learn the key skills that will help them through life. It takes hard graft and effort, but we shouldn't be afraid of that."

The co-educational, privately owned school was founded in 1899 and teaches 320 pupils from the ages of three to 11. Price, headmaster for 30 years, took over in 2016 from his late mother, Elizabeth, who bought the school in 1979.

"She was an educational trailblazer," he says, "a principled, focused Yorkshire lass who was already a headmistress at 24. She felt strongly about education and opportunities for girls when they weren't yet taken for granted. And, while schools can easily be turned into exam factories, she always pushed for a holistic environment that allows a child to discover what they are good at."

Guided by her legacy, Merton Court's academic success sees pupils gain places at well-regarded local grammar and independent schools. Smooth transition to senior school is helped by pupils moving classes for different subjects, taught by teachers with specialist knowledge rather than staying with just one teacher. Indeed children receive an inspiring introduction to learning from the very start, in their Early Years Foundation stage, which is rated Outstanding by Ofsted/ISI.

Merton Court boasts sports pitches, a sports hall, a swimming pool and dedicated science, music, art and IT rooms, but what sets it apart is its 17-acre grounds including a Forest School. "It is part nature reserve, part outdoor activity area," says Price. "Children can explore, follow trails, build camps and enjoy mud kitchens."

Languages are a strong subject at Merton Court. "Our Year 5 pupils visit France's battlefields," says Price, "and our Year 6 pupils spend a week in and around Barcelona honing their Spanish."

Merton Court, says Price, is a school that stresses the need to balance scholastic rigour with the space to flourish as individuals. "You should always aim high," he says, "and our role is to help pupils do as well as they can. We aren't pushy, but we are aspirational."

# A HEALTHY REPUTATION

The Royal Veterinary College lives up to its global reputation as an exemplary centre for veterinary and biological sciences

WWW.RVC.AC.UK

"We have a saying that if it can be done, we're doing it," says Professor Stuart Reid, Principal of the Royal Veterinary College (RVC). When the college was founded in 1791 it marked the establishment of the veterinary profession in Britain. Since then it has been at the forefront of the sector, recognised around the world for its pioneering work in teaching, research and the practice of veterinary medicine.

The RVC's long history makes it the largest and oldest veterinary college in the English-speaking world, and one of only three stand-alone veterinary colleges worldwide. It offers undergraduate, postgraduate and continuing professional development (CPD) programmes in veterinary medicine, veterinary nursing and biological sciences, and is regarded as a global centre of excellence. In 2016 and 2017, it was placed in the top three veterinary schools in the world in the QS World University Rankings.

The college's reputation attracts talent from around the world: approximately 25 per cent of its 2,300 students are international. The RVC's flagship hospital, the Queen Mother Hospital for Animals, boasts Europe's greatest concentration of veterinary specialists, who come from more than 20 countries. As a globally minded organisation, the RVC is proud of its cultural and ethnic diversity, and following the EU referendum it has joined the #LondonIsOpen campaign to show that it continues to welcome staff and students from around the world.

"Disease does not recognise political or geographical borders," says Professor Reid. "Education is an international business."

The college also boasts a history of championing women. "With women now comprising the majority of the veterinary profession – in Britain over three quarters of new veterinary graduates and 95 per cent

of veterinary nursing graduates are female – the role of women at the RVC has been pivotal," says Professor Reid. For decades female RVC graduates have held significant positions in the profession. In 1967, alumna Mary Brancker became the first female president of the British Veterinary Association, while in 1976 fellow graduate Dame Olga Uvarov became the first female president of the Royal College of Veterinary Surgeons. In 2012, the RVC appointed Elaine Acaster as its first female Vice Principal, and in 2016, Becca Bowes became the first veterinary nurse to be President of the RVC Students' Union.

With a focus on promoting equality and diversity in all areas, the RVC launched Gateway in 2005, a programme that encourages students from non-traditional backgrounds to apply for places on veterinary degree courses. The widening-participation programme offers a foundation year to students who, if successful, are guaranteed a place on the Bachelor of Veterinary Medicine course.

RVC graduates go on to lead the way in veterinary medicine around the world. Besides those in senior roles in clinical practice and research leaders, RVC graduates are employed in all of Britain's zoos and zoo parks. Others have taken on senior government appointments in places such as Botswana, Ethiopia and Zimbabwe, making a significant contribution to the conservation of wild animals in these countries. From 2008 to 2014, the positions of Chief Veterinary Officer for the UK, Scotland and Wales were all held simultaneously by RVC graduates.

Ever since its very foundation, the RVC has been a pioneer in veterinary medicine. For more than two centuries it has built on its reputation while moving with the times, to sustain its leading position in the global veterinary profession.

# WORLD CLASS

Plymouth's Devonport High School for Girls prepares its students to step up to roles on the global stage

WWW.DHSG.CO.UK

"An important part of our mission is to create successful, happy young women who have the skills to carry out leading roles in the world," says Anita Hemsi, Head Teacher at Devonport High School for Girls (DHSG) in Plymouth, Devon. One of the UK's 216 Specialist Language Colleges, DHSG has gained a reputation for its strong international links, as well as academic excellence, which help launch its students on their chosen career paths.

As a state grammar school, DHSG dates back to 1908. In 2005, it was accorded its language college status, and has since won the British Council's International School Award four times. It has forged links with 17 countries around the world, and in 2011 it acquired Academy Trust status.

The school has developed its curriculum around a global outlook and students and teachers participate in a number of projects that encourage transnational discussion and collaboration. These include the Comenius and Erasmus+ projects, part of the European Union Educational Programme. Through this scheme, DHSG students have worked with teenagers from Finland, Denmark and Spain, discussing such current issues as social mobility, the environment and conflict resolution. Beyond the EU, the school maintains links with countries from other continents, such as South Africa and Nepal.

Alongside its language specialism, DHSG has a reputation for all-round academic excellence and has been recognised by *The Telegraph*'s school league tables and *The Good Schools Guide* as one of the best performing schools in the country. There is an emphasis on providing strong female role models in the form of teachers and guest speakers, particularly in STEM (science, technology, engineering and mathematics) subjects. "We recognise that future success and empowerment, especially in traditionally male-dominated professions, requires us to provide those examples at school," says Anita.

The school also has thriving art, drama and PE departments, giving students the opportunity to explore a wide range of interests during their time at DHSG. The active student executive committee organises charity events throughout the year, raising thousands of pounds for good causes.

With its global outlook and excellence in languages, DHSG encourages strong communication skills, the celebration of diversity and an international perspective. Together with a first-rate all-round education, it provides students with the skills and motivation to excel in whatever field they choose.

# HIGH ACHIEVERS

King's High Warwick, one of the UK's leading girls' schools, is raising the bar in education

WWW.KINGSHIGHWARWICK.CO.UK

Fundraising by the parents' associationat King's High Warwick has an added impetus when there are exciting rewards such as new lab coats to wear in chemistry competitions and team hoodies for those playing in the under-14s national hockey finals. Recently ranked 26th nationally among girls' independent schools in GCSE results, King's High will be further enhanced by its new purpose-built campus, which will be completed in 2020.

"It's about opportunity and expectation," says Head Master Richard Nicholson. "We need to keep as many doors open for as long as possible." King's High sees 43 per cent of its girls opt for STEM (science, technology, engineering and mathematics) subjects at A level; and runs at least two physics sets in each year to meet demand. "The girls visited one of our alumni who is studying physics at Oxford," says Nicholson. "They came back buzzing after a tour of the labs." The school also has a METEOR (Modern Era Technology Entertaining Obedient Robot), one of only four in British schools.

The arts and humanities are valued equally highly, says Nicholson, and projects such as drama productions allow the girls the space to work creatively. "The girls do everything themselves: sets, lighting, costumes and direction, all the time learning about leadership and how to work together." Inspirational guests have included Dame Judi Dench, Professor Germaine Greer and Dame Lynne Brindley, Master of Pembroke College, Oxford. "It's important to get people at the top of their profession to talk to the girls," says Nicholson.

The first male head teacher at King's High since it opened in 1879, Nicholson is spearheading the move from the school's current site to a spacious campus that is already home to Warwick School for boys and Warwick Preparatory School. The pupils will benefit from new classrooms, science labs and sports fields. "The spirit of the new school will still be King's," says Nicholson. "We will, however, have world-class facilities and the site will allow for a more meaningful collaboration with the prep school and Warwick boys."

With diverse co-curricular classes and a broad academic programme taught by specialists, King's High Warwick prepares its girls for a future of opportunities taken and potential fulfilled. "Creating opportunities and working hard is the start," says Nicholson. "Our girls also have the interpersonal skills and leadership qualities to succeed in life and make a real difference in the world."

# A PIONEERING SPIRIT

York St John University has welcomed female students since 1846, and continues to champion inclusion to this day

WWW.YORKSJ.AC.UK

Picture a graduate. What do you imagine? Today's graduates come from multiple backgrounds, creating diverse, welcoming campuses. Yet this hasn't always been the case. Only in the late 19th century did women begin to apply to study for a university education and only much more recently has the number of female students begun to match or exceed their male peers in many institutions.

That's why York St John University (YSJ), founded in 1841, has always been a pioneer of women's equality and opportunity. As early as 1839, the original college's founders expressed an interest in training schoolmistresses. They opened the doors to women trainee teachers in 1846; and when that branch of the college relocated in 1862 it became Ripon College for Young Women's Teachers.

This history is a source of pride at the university today. "In those days one of the key ways in which women had a voice was through the teaching profession, and we were at the forefront of delivering that," says YSJ's Secretary Alison Kennell. "A commitment to women's achievements and a pioneering spirit are among our positive legacies; and we have some lovely stories to demonstrate that in our archive."

The 1916 alumni magazine, for example, reported Ripon's female students debating whether they were doing enough to support the war effort, given the impact of their role as educators. "Some of those young women achieved amazing things," says Kennell. "In the early 1900s, one set up a school in Japan. We really celebrate the impact our female students have on the world."

This spirit is still evident today. York St John is one of a minority of UK universities with both a female Vice Chancellor, Professor Karen Stanton, and a female Chair of the Governing Body, Ann Green CBE. Professor Stanton feels this reflects the university's ethos.

"Inclusive values are important here." she says. "We have always celebrated diversity and given a voice to women: in fact, more than 4,000 of our 6,000 students are female."

So it's fitting that International Women's Week is given prominence in YSJ's calendar, inspiring a whole programme of events. These include a Women's History in York map, through which English literature Director Dr Anne-Marie Evans and her colleagues traced the lives of prominent women – from pirates to politicians – who have helped shape the city. Lecturer in creative writing Dr Kimberley Campanello staged her own multimedia play based on the true story of two suffragettes in Ireland. And senior drama lecturer Rachel Conlon showed her short film of interviews with imprisoned mothers about the impact of their jail sentences on their children. The university also plays an important role in sharing this commitment with the wider community. For example, psychology lecturer Dr Beth Bell has worked with over 500 teenage girls in schools across the region to promote positive body image and challenge social media stereotypes.

The focus on equality has set the tone for the wider celebration of diversity and difference in everything YSJ does. "When it comes to giving women a voice, we are at the forefront," says Equality and Diversity Adviser, Marije Davidson. "We're currently developing policies to help staff understand the issues transgender students might face. We are progressively inclusive, allowing people to express themselves and hear different voices."

From its positive past, York St John is looking forward to an exciting future. "Equality, diversity and inclusion are living issues," says Professor Stanton. "These are our founding principles, and we ensure they are as influential today as they have ever been."

# "Equality, diversity and inclusion are our living issues, and are as influential today as ever"

Professor Karen Stanton, York St John University

# IN OUR NURTURE

Boasting excellent academic and extracurricular programmes, Altrincham Grammar School for Girls helps every pupil discover and fulfil her potential

WWW.AGGS.TRAFFORD.SCH.UK

"Every individual matters at Altrincham Grammar School for Girls," says Principal, Stephanie Gill. "Although a big school, we are concerned about each student and provide strong pastoral care to nurture them so that they can find their niche and do as well as they possibly can."

Founded in 1910, Altrincham Grammar is a selective state school with more than 1,300 students from a wide variety of backgrounds, including 46 per cent from minority ethnic groups. Situated in Bowdon in Trafford, Greater Manchester, it selects students who pass its entrance exam based on the proximity of their homes to the school, giving priority to those attracting pupil premium.

Rated Outstanding by Ofsted, Altrincham Grammar is consistently one of the highest performing schools in the country. Last year's students achieved 91 per cent A* to B grades at A level, while 21 students won places at Oxbridge. Alumni, who include BBC science presenter Helen Czerski, excel across many different disciplines. But academic success is only part of the picture. The school also values sporting and cultural achievements, and service to the community. Students are encouraged to get involved in a wide range of extracurricular activities, such as music, sport, politics and drama. On offer are, for example, an Indian dance society and a badminton club.

One pupil went to Latvia as part of the Erasmus+ scheme, where she met students from other European countries. "I made many friends and I have learnt a lot about different cultures and languages," she says. "By the end I was speaking to the Spanish girls in Spanish. The project inspired me to increase my worldwide understanding and become fluent in another language."

Politically minded students can take part in the Executive School Council. "It unites every year group and ensures that every pupil is represented," says one member. The school also holds mock elections. Some students are inspired to get involved in politics outside school by, for instance, joining the local youth council the Trafford Youth Cabinet.

"Enjoyment of learning, self-discipline, concern for others and opportunities for leadership lie at the heart of the school's ethos," says Gill. "Our outstanding and inspiring teachers aim to provide an education that opens all sorts of doors and avenues for our students, so they make an impact in society. We want all our students to build their confidence and do something that inspires them."

# COURSE AND EFFECT

The Centre of Excellence specialises in a wide variety of transformative online training

WWW.CENTREOFEXCELLENCE.COM

"Sometimes, the most difficult of times can turn out to be not only our biggest lessons in life," says Sara Lou-Ann Jones, the founder and Managing Director of the Centre of Excellence, "but also, ultimately, our biggest blessings in disguise."

It's a positive point of view that explains both the philosophy of the Centre of Excellence and the circumstances under which Jones established the centre in February 2012. "I came out of a long-term relationship and found out I was pregnant," she says. "But my partner at the time didn't want to be involved. It was a really difficult time for me, deciding what I was going to do, because I obviously wanted to create a fantastic life for my child."

From modest beginnings, the Centre of Excellence has grown into a worldwide organisation, selling over 1,000 different online training courses in more than 30 countries. It also has 20 members of staff, split evenly between men and women. Jones's background is in neuro-linguistic programming, but courses at the Centre of Excellence range from aromatherapy to creative writing, blogging to cake-making, NLP to life coaching. Many of these include an optional component designed to transform an individual's hobby into a business.

"All of the courses are online, so you can study anywhere at any time," says Jones. "They're accessible to everybody, no matter what age you are, and we try to make them as affordable as possible." To date, the Centre of Excellence has sold more than half a million courses worldwide, and has received numerous awards, including Best Online Education and Training Provider at the Online Business Awards 2016.

Despite having enjoyed her own success, Jones is most satisfied seeing the success of those who have taken a Centre of Excellence course, such as the woman who had three books published and set up her very own publishing company after taking the centre's creative writing course.

"It's fantastic to be able to inspire as many people as possible to create a life that they love," says Jones. "I had a baby girl last year, and I want to inspire her to think outside the box. You can do anything and our courses really try to reflect that."

# AN OPEN-DOOR POLICY

The University of Central Lancashire has been making quality education accessible to all for the past 190 years

WWW.UCLAN.AC.UK

There has been a centre of learning on the site of the University of Central Lancashire (UCLan) for the past 190 years. When the university was founded in 1828, its focus was on helping talented people from all walks of life to make the most of their potential through access to education. Back then this involved improving the literacy skills of maids and servants, alongside the provision of technical education. Nowadays, it involves offering a huge variety of courses to some 38,000 students from 120 nations.

From the outset, women have played a leading role in the educational provision at the university, and today that's still very much the case. For instance, UCLan professor Caroline Watkins received a damehood from Prince Charles last year for her services to stroke and nursing care. And Nicola Lowe, a professor of nutritional sciences, is leading a two-year study to examine the effectiveness of biofortified wheat to overcome a global zinc deficiency.

"That kind of trailblazing is what we do well," says Dr Joanna Heaton-Marriott, Head of Communications and Engagement. "When we talk about research it's not predominantly 'blue skies' academic work, it's working in collaboration with industry and with professions, focusing on things that make an immediate difference."

Indeed, a tagline for the university might be "having a genuine impact on people's lives", including in the local community. UCLan spends a lot of time inspiring the next generation to go into education. "Not necessarily to come here," clarifies Dr Heaton-Marriott, "although that's obviously a great outcome. But to open their eyes to the possibilities that education can offer."

UCLan's annual science festival, which receives 15,000 visitors a year, is a case in point. "The attendees are mainly young children and families who come completely free of charge," says Dr Heaton-Marriott. "We're showing them that there is a science resource right on their doorstep and inspiring them to see science as a career option." The university also has a science centre that is open to local schools: "Kids come in and do proper hands-on scientific experimentation that they wouldn't get to do at school," she says. "Above all, they learn that it's fun." Alongside this inclusiveness is academic rigour. UCLan is estimated to be among the top 3.7 per cent of universities worldwide according to The Centre for World University Rankings (CWUR) and is in the top 800 universities globally according to the *Times Higher Education* World University Rankings.

Since 2015, a £200 million "Campus Masterplan" has been in place to truly bring UCLan into the 21st century. The first phase, now in development, includes new buildings, green spaces, class-leading technologies and infrastructure. This includes the opening of a £30 million-plus Engineering Innovation Centre alongside two new social spaces designed to improve the campus experience by providing a place for staff and students to come together in a relaxed environment. The university is also working with the students' union to create a new £1 million bespoke multi-faith and spirituality centre, which will create the perfect environment for prayer, contemplation and reflection for all.

"Our intention is to host more events so we can engage with more people," says Dr Heaton-Marriott. "We want to be seen as an institution that has open doors. Many of our spaces are about linking the campus and the city and eradicating that false divide. Our university has a strong mission about social engagement, and our Vice-Chancellor is driving this. Universities are not there to be closed centres of excellence, they're about making a difference to the people around it."

# "When we talk about research it's focusing on things that make an immediate difference"

—

Dr Joanna Heaton-Marriott, University of Central Lancashire

# SHAPING LIVES THROUGH FASHION

London College of Fashion prepares students
for the business and ethics of a global industry

WWW.ARTS.AC.UK/FASHION

"Fashion is more than just frocks," says Professor Frances Corner OBE,
head of London College of Fashion (LCF), part of University of the Arts
London. "Clothes have a significant impact on the environment and on people's
lives, especially on women," she says. "More than three-quarters of garment
workers are female, and their exploitation remains one of the industry's most
significant challenges. It's issues like these that we encourage our students to
address. Our students are protagonists in their own future, which means taking
responsibility for their own decisions."

Using fashion to drive change has dominated the college's focus for more
than a century. Founded in 1906 in the East End, LCF's mission was to provide
education and training for women. In those days, girls as young as 12 were
taught skills including dressmaking alongside subjects like maths.

Today the college, with campuses around London, offers courses on every
aspect of fashion, from costume design to business management, to students
from more than 110 countries. "We've been providing education from before
women won the right to vote," says Professor Corner. "Our courses are developed
with fashion industry input. We set the agenda and teach our students to innovate
their chosen fields from the inside out. And, with roots in the East End, we've
always had a commitment to diversity and the importance of different cultures."

Building for the future has inspired many LCF programmes aimed at
social action. The college's Making for Change initiative with the Ministry of
Justice provides a fashion training unit in a women's prison, aiming to increase
wellbeing and reduce reoffending rates among participants by equipping them
with professional skills and qualifications. London College of Fashion also works
with the United Nations to raise awareness of the global initiative to end
violence against women and girls. As part of this, LCF students were briefed
to produce an image or film incorporating the colour orange, the UN's chosen
colour for the campaign.

"I believe our graduates can turn a lens on their own industry and challenge
it in areas where it falls short," says Professor Corner, "such as the conditions of
garment workers." As she says, fashion is about so much more than just dresses.

# TEACHING & EQUALITY

The NASUWT, the teachers' union, is tackling gender inequality

WWW.NASUWT.ORG.UK

A century ago, the Suffragettes sought to exercise their civil rights to give women a voice. "Then as now, trade unions exist to give voice to working people," says Chris Keates, General Secretary of the NASUWT. "We champion the rights of women and minorities both within and beyond the workplace, empowering them to campaign for social justice, equality and dignity at work through actions including lobbying, demonstration and withdrawing their labour."

Equality is at the heart of the work of the NASUWT, which represents teachers and headteachers throughout the UK. Three quarters of its members are women but, despite legislation and years of campaigning for equality, women teachers increasingly face discrimination in pay, promotion and working conditions.

"In a traditionally feminised profession, women still face huge barriers in terms of professional respect, recognition and reward," says Keates, the first woman General Secretary of the NASUWT and the first woman to lead one of the ten largest unions in the TUC. "Despite women's abilities and ambition too many face barriers to career progression and leadership positions.

Unless women teachers are treated fairly and equally the consequences for young women and girls are dire and all of society suffers."

In 2016, the NASUWT launched a Gender Equality Challenge to secure equal rights for women and girls nationally and internationally. "Schools should be places where the talent of all pupils should be nurtured," says Keates. "Education has a critical role to play in gender equality, empowering girls and women, encouraging them to challenge the future. The NASUWT supports teachers to make sure that children's life chances are not limited by gender inequality and prejudice.

"With over 60 million children across the world denied the right to education, the overwhelming majority girls, gender equality should be a key priority for us all. As long as women continue to be under-represented in power and decision-making structures; continue to suffer violence and objectification and exploitation; suffer job loss or demotion for taking maternity leave or requesting flexible working and are denied equal pay, feminism is as relevant today as it was when our sister Suffragettes fought to give women a voice."

# A WINNING FORMULA

The University of York's Department of Chemistry has been recognised for advancing women's careers in science

WWW.YORK.AC.UK/CHEMISTRY

"We want this department to be somewhere that's fair to everyone," says Dr Caroline Dessent of the Department of Chemistry at the University of York. "That's why we have equal and transparent policies. If you don't, it is known to affect women more than men. But when you adopt good practice, it's there for all."

With an enviable reputation for teaching and research, York's Department of Chemistry has 235 staff members including 59 academic staff, with more than 750 undergraduates and 150 postgraduates. Roughly 47 per cent of York's chemistry undergraduates are female, as are about 40 per cent of postgraduates and researchers. Around 25 per cent of the academic staff are female.

"We continually monitor these statistics and work over time to improve female representation," says Dr Dessent, a Reader in Physical Chemistry who chairs the department's Equality and Diversity Group. "Chemistry is traditionally a male-dominated academic discipline, particularly at the senior levels, and it's typical for over 90 per cent of staff to be male. So to have over 40 per cent of our junior lecturers as female is really excellent. We are still a male-dominated discipline – but we have seen considerable progress in female representation across our department over the last 20 years."

The department has won a record three Athena SWAN Gold awards, recognising a commitment to advancing the careers of women in science, technology, engineering, maths and medicine in higher education and research. To qualify for the award, the department had to submit data on its female/ male ratios, working practices, identify possible issues and draw up an action plan to tackle them.

"A lot of this information is sensitive," says Dr Dessent. "For example, which people are being promoted, what grades they're on, who's being recruited and length of contract. All of this work demands the time of dedicated professional and support staff in our department. Dr Helen Coombs, our Departmental Manager deserves special mention for her dedicated, behind the scenes work on gathering this information. Although this is hard work, it has made a considerable difference to us as a department. If you look at our senior female academic staff, they've gone up remarkably from 7 to 22 per cent in 10 years."

The Department of Chemistry has achieved this in part by retaining and promoting female staff, and by creating a flexible, family-friendly working environment. But the challenges are substantial. "We can only accept people into the department who apply to work or study here," says Dr Dessent. "We spend much time working on our recruitment literature and processes, aiming to attract as many females as possible."

Dr Dessent is keen to acknowledge the importance of leadership involvement to achieve progress. All the recent heads of the chemistry department have been members of the Departmental Equality and Diversity Group, including Professor Robin Perutz who began the Athena SWAN work when he became Head of Department in 2000 as well as the current Head, Professor Duncan Bruce. Their direct involvement has been crucial for enabling change.

"One of the most rewarding things is the way things have changed in the department over ten years," she says. "We have male staff who work part-time to share childcare responsibilities. That is something unique in academic departments. It shows that our male staff recognise that our female staff are able to be highly successful scientists while working part-time. And men are doing it as well now."

# INCLUSIVE EDUCATION

West Thames College is a lively, vibrant and dynamic college

WWW.WEST-THAMES.AC.UK

"Our college belongs to its students as much as the staff," says Tracy Aust, Principal of West Thames College in Isleworth. "Their voices genuinely bring about change. It's why I always welcome feedback."

The institution she leads is a lively, vibrant and dynamic college, and one with a diverse and sometimes challenging intake. With 4,500 adult students and 2,000 under-19s, many come to the college having struggled in mainstream education. Delivering vocational programmes at its main Isleworth site and its Skills and Logistics Centre in Feltham, there's dedicated provision for students with additional physical, emotional and educational needs.

Supported by a strong inclusion team and excellent facilities, West Thames provides opportunities such as Project Search internships, designed for those with learning difficulties or disabilities. Success stories include Roberto De Abreu, who recently graduated directly into paid employment at GlaxoSmithKlein. As for the high proportion of students who speak English as a second language, many enrol on an ESOL course; Navjit Kaur did just that in 2008, but fell in love with the progressive, productive environment and worked through the ranks, earning her HND in Applied Biology in 2017.

Environment is crucial in enabling such successes. Just six years old, the redeveloped Isleworth campus was designed with students' needs in mind, offering, for example, a specialised learning area with a sensory room and garden. More broadly, there are state-of-the-art salons, dance, music and TV studios, engineering workshops and an onsite nursery.

The staff are as diverse as the student body. More than 60 per cent of the 2016 cohort was female, with 52 per cent from black and minority ethnic backgrounds. "We're values-driven," says Aust. "Our staff and students agreed on principles of openness, integrity and respect." Staff regularly discuss the application of these values to make sure they lead the college culture.

"Our goal is about more than education," says Aust. "We deliver the skills and environment every individual needs to progress. Equality is embedded in everything we do, and when we bring back past students to share their experiences, I'm always bowled over by the fantastic things they've achieved. They're genuinely inspirational."

# A BEAUTIFUL MIND

At St James Senior Girls' School in London, mindfulness provides the basis for a well-considered education

WWW.STJAMESGIRLS.CO.UK

In 2015, a cross-party group of MPs recommended to Parliament that all schools teach mindfulness, a brain-training technique that uses awareness of breathing to achieve mental clarity. The benefits of the practice are apparent at St James Senior Girls' School, an independent day school in Kensington, London, where meditation and mindfulness have been a key part of the curriculum for more than 40 years.

Each lesson begins and ends with a short period of mindful reflection. "It's a wonderful way to let go of anxieties," says Headmistress Sarah Labram. "Those few minutes enable the girls to connect with themselves and really be present. We all benefit enormously from moments of calm."

Studies have shown that mindfulness can reduce stress, sharpen the memory and improve concentration. Unsurprisingly, pupils at St James excel academically: in 2016, 79 per cent of GCSE grades were A or A*, as were 51 per cent of A-level grades.

Another great benefit is less measurable but no less crucial: the pupils are happy. *The Good Schools Guide* has praised St James's "down-to-earth, happy and supportive" atmosphere. "There is a very warm, welcoming feel here," says Labram. "We really value the girls' emotional and spiritual well-being."

The school was founded in 1975 by a group of parents who wanted to combine a traditional "best of British" education with a practical spiritual philosophy. "We have children from every religious, ethnic and cultural background," says Labram. "We really celebrate difference. The level of respect the girls have for each other is unusual."

Labram was one of the school's first pupils in the mid-1970s and became Headmistress in 2014. "We still do many of the things I enjoyed as a child," she says. "We put on fantastic concerts, play lacrosse and teach the classics." Curriculum options include classical Greek and Sanskrit. "Universities are always thrilled to have Sanskrit students as candidates. It's a very well-respected subject."

Former pupils include actress Emily Watson OBE and Google Fellow Emma Mulqueeny OBE. "Our spirit of generosity and service is something that doesn't leave you," says Labram. "Most pupils go on to do something they believe in, in industries that make a difference."

# LEADING BY EXAMPLE

At the University of Exeter, equality and diversity are embedded in its culture and values

WWW.EXETER.AC.UK

The University of Exeter had a permanent impact on HR Director Jacqui Marshall when she was headhunted from the Ministry of Defence in 2013. 'The Vice-Chancellor had vision and charisma," she says. "He'd taken Exeter from a middle-ranking university to one of the top ten in the country. What chimed most, however, was that he genuinely and authentically believes in equality."

Since her appointment, Marshall has proactively promoted equality and monitored progress towards that goal. Salaries are analysed every year to ensure everyone is paid fairly, and her team assesses staff members' career and performance profiles, identifying any development opportunities. Several departments have been awarded Athena SWAN Charter status for their commitment to advancing women's careers, including the historically male-dominated STEM disciplines (science, technology, engineering, maths), and the university's Women of Influence network unites women from academia, professional services and local businesses with alumnae to offer mentoring and support. A groundbreaking new parental leave policy offers women 26 weeks full pay from day one and partners six weeks paid leave too.

"We need role models," says Marshall, "both women and men who acknowledge women's contribution in the workplace and don't present it in stereotypical terms." Exeter now has a female Provost, and an executive board with equal gender representation.

"Changing our approach has brought a big increase in the number of women going for promotion," says Professor Barbara Borg, Head of Classics and Ancient History. "I joined my department as its first woman professor. We now have five. Female postgrad students have said that having a female head of department helped their own progress." Prioritising equality has also brought a shift in teaching style. "Female students and those from minorities are often less vocal in class than some of their male fellow students," says Borg, "so we look for ways to encourage them to join the debate."

"In my previous career, it was a very male-dominated environment," says Marshall. "It was hard to speak out and there weren't strong role models. In contrast, at Exeter, equality and diversity are part of our everyday agenda; it's not just about saying we need to do something, it's about *doing* it, with authenticity."

# A FRESH OUTLOOK

Diversity and inclusion are at the heart of Pearson, the world's learning company

WWW.PEARSON.COM

For Pearson, the multinational learning and education company, a Diversity & Inclusion (D&I) strategy is absolutely central. "We live in an increasingly diverse society, meaning that the markets we serve and the society from which we draw our employees is diverse," says Kevin Lyons, Senior HR Manager for the Schools Division. "If we, as an organisation, do not have that same diversity, then how can we possibly connect with the people we're hoping to reach?"

Pearson – the world's largest provider of educational products and services – aims to create an environment in which all of its employees feel that they are truly accepted for what and who they are. Key to this policy is a network of local D&I advocates and, in the UK, Employee Resource Groups (ERGs). These initiate the conversation around diversity, exchange ideas and steer change throughout the many regions within which Pearson operates.

Gender equality is a significant focus, and a team is currently investigating how to encourage more female progression to the boardroom. "Sharon Hague, one of our Executive Directors, and somebody who rose through the ranks, is a great role model and an inspiration to women, but we need more females at that level," says Lyons. "We want other women to see her and think: 'if she can do it, so can I'."

The Women in Learning & Leadership ERG champions opportunities for women, and various policies – such as generous maternity provisions, phased returns and flexible working – guarantee that there are fewer barriers for women wanting to take their career forward. Other ERGs include Spectrum, which encourages opportunities for LGBT employees, and Pearson Able, which works for those with a disability. The creation of a new ERG for black, Asian and other ethnic minorities is also well underway.

With dedicated employees who rise to the challenge of making the company a more inclusive employer, Pearson has access to the widest talent pool possible, and, as Lyons explains, it all begins with a conversation. "We make a difference because we are prepared to talk about diversity," he observes. "It can be challenging, but we welcome that, because it is the way we become change agents."

# BEYOND BELIEF

TeachBeyond works with schools across the globe, combining quality education with Christian values

WWW.TEACHBEYOND.ORG.UK

"Education is about more than imparting knowledge," says David Midwinter. As UK director of the international organisation TeachBeyond, he is equally interested in students' personal growth and in the positive impact of religion in their community.

"As a Christian organisation, we have a holistic approach, delivering education to impact hearts as well as minds," says Midwinter. "The schools we work with teach children of several different religions and children of no religion. We believe that if they are exposed to values of truth, honesty, love and compassion, then all of those children, their families and societies will see a positive impact."

Based in Lancaster, TeachBeyond collaborates with more than 60 schools in 49 countries, from Germany to Mexico, the Philippines, the Democratic Republic of Congo and beyond. In international Christian schools, which follow a British or US curriculum and cater for expatriates and missionaries, Teach Beyond can help with teacher recruitment and professional development.

The organisation's work with national schools is slightly different. "We offer education to all classes of society, including orphaned children and rescued girls," says Midwinter. "Because the schools may not teach in English, local teachers are usually best suited to the job. We can help with professional development but we have to be culturally sensitive, giving teachers the tools to bring into their own setting by sharing principles and practices. English is often taught as a foreign language."

One key difference can be found in education for girls. "There might be cultural differences in the way some societies treat women," says Midwinter, "and the roles they view women as assuming. You have to understand the world as others inhabit it and hope that lives are transformed through learning tolerance and respect."

He believes that Britain can also benefit from these lessons. "Unfortunately, you don't have to look very far to find examples of a corrupt or damaged society," says Midwinter. "We want our students to become responsible citizens with a servant heart. We're reaching out to hearts and minds. We show people that they can become leaders, that they can be honest and trustworthy. Those things can have huge enduring benefits to any society."

# A QUALIFIED SUCCESS

VTCT oversees a range of high-quality vocational and technical qualifications for a variety of professions

WWW.VTCT.ORG.UK

"We play a critical role in helping people from all areas of society to develop the skills that give them a clear line of sight to a fulfilling career," says Alan Woods OBE. Woods is CEO of the Vocational Training Charitable Trust (VTCT), a specialist awarding organisation for internationally respected vocational and technical qualifications. VTCT is setting the standard for high-quality, well-structured courses at its 1,300 centres worldwide.

VTCT, as an Ofqual-regulated organisation, designs and assesses the qualifications it offers, working with further-education colleges and private training providers to offer students courses and apprenticeship assessments. Students work towards a range of qualifications across all educational levels, from entry level to GCSE and A level equivalents right through to the equivalent of second-year-degree level qualifications, principally in key sectors such as the creative industries, hair and beauty therapy, complementary therapy, sports and fitness, hospitality, business and retail.

"Learners are working towards either a job or better pay for a higher level of skill," says Woods. "A lot of people in hairdressing want to be technical specialists. Others are want their own business, which is why our qualifications include business management in running salons."

VTCT challenges the divide between what is considered academic and technical study with the quality, relevance and inclusivity of its qualifications. "Inclusion is a pretty fundamental value," says Woods. "If you study hairdressing, cutting Afro-Caribbean hair is different to cutting European hair. If you are into laser tattoo removal, you want your technician to be educated to a high level."

Course content and assessment is developed with industry and employers so that VTCT's qualifications are tailored to future employment. "Our qualifications offer an independent assessment of an individual's competencies and make sure they are well grounded in their subject."

VTCT is expanding globally, with around 300 learning centres overseas. It is also enhancing its support for colleges with digital assessment tools that chart student progress and streamline end-of-appraisal assessments. "Our work maintains the quality of the student experience and the integrity of the qualification," says Woods. "You have to ensure fairness across all assessments and give everyone the best chance of a good career."

# BANKING AND FINANCE

| | |
|---|---|
| HM Treasury | 244 |
| Queen's Award For Enterprise | 246 |
| Women in Banking and Finance | 249 |
| Schroders | 250 |
| KPMG | 252 |
| Prudential plc | 254 |
| Goldman Sachs | 256 |
| Invesco Perpetual | 258 |
| M&G Investments | 260 |
| Thomson Reuters | 262 |
| TSB | 264 |
| MV Credit | 266 |
| Kite Lake Capital Management | 267 |
| Western Union | 268 |
| PIMFA | 270 |
| Hannay Investments | 271 |
| Addidi | 272 |
| Development Partners International | 274 |
| Allied Irish Bank | 275 |

# HM TREASURY

The nation's bank manager, and quite possibly
the most important government department

The nation's tax collector and bank manager, Her Majesty's Treasury (HMT) is the longest established government department. It's the government's economic and finance ministry, maintaining control over public spending, setting the direction of the UK's economic policy and working to achieve strong and sustainable economic growth.

It's certainly the oldest of the three great offices of state, and one that actually predates Parliament – the term "exchequer" comes from the chequered cloth used by the king's treasurer nearly a millennium ago to count taxes. The position of collecting taxes and revenue has always been one of the state's most important jobs, and countless Chancellors of the Exchequer have often gone on to become Prime Ministers. In the last century alone it's happened to everyone from Baldwin to Brown, Macmillan to Major, Churchill to Callaghan; Chamberlain, Lloyd George and Asquith.

The Treasury had many different headquarters until 1940, when it moved into the Edwardian offices in Whitehall, at 1 Horse Guards Road, which is still its home today. It employs around 1,460 staff directly, most of them in Whitehall, but also at its offices in Norwich and Edinburgh. However, some of the departments that report to the Treasury employ many more: HM Revenue & Customs (HMRC) alone has 67,000 staff around the UK, while HMT also oversees National Savings and Investments (NS&I, based in Pimlico but with operational sites in Blackpool, Glasgow and Durham), the Royal Mint (based in Llantrissant, South Wales), UK Financial Investments (which manages the Treasury's shareholdings in RBS and Bradford & Bingley), the UK Debt Management Office, the Office For Budget Responsibility, and the Office of Tax Simplification.

Treasury staff have long had a reputation as rather dour maths obsessives. "It was a department that traditionally prized intellectual ability above anything else," said John Gieve, Treasury Official until 2001. "It had great brains who didn't have many social skills." And the former Chancellor Ken Clarke agrees. "It's the best department I ever served in," he says. "It's like an Oxbridge college, with brilliant minds engaged in open debate – and completely detached from the real world." Other chancellors have seen it as a dour institution. For Alistair Darling it was "a rather gloomy cathedral"; while Norman Lamont described it as "a dreary building, with red linoleum floors that resembled a Soviet psychiatric hospital". It's why the building was substantially refurbished in 2002 by Norman Foster's architectural practice.

Her Majesty's Treasury has long had a reputation as Whitehall's perennial killjoy – a constant brake on finances, designed to prevent ambitious governments from carrying out their mandates. "Whichever party is in office," said Harold Wilson, "the Treasury is in power." "At the core of the Treasury is its hostility to public spending," says Sir Nick Macpherson, who served as Permanent Secretary to the Treasury between 2005 and 2016. "It's probably why it has a reputation as a staid and slightly cynical institution."

The financial meltdown of 2008 led to the criticism of many financial institutions, HMT included. "One salutary lesson I drew from the banking crisis of 2007-09 is that one thing that professionals in the private sector and officials in the public sector have in common is that at times they can get risk management very wrong indeed," says Macpherson. "It is no wonder that the Treasury and Bank of England have reappraised their approach to risk management since the financial crisis. And boards across Whitehall have been doing the same."

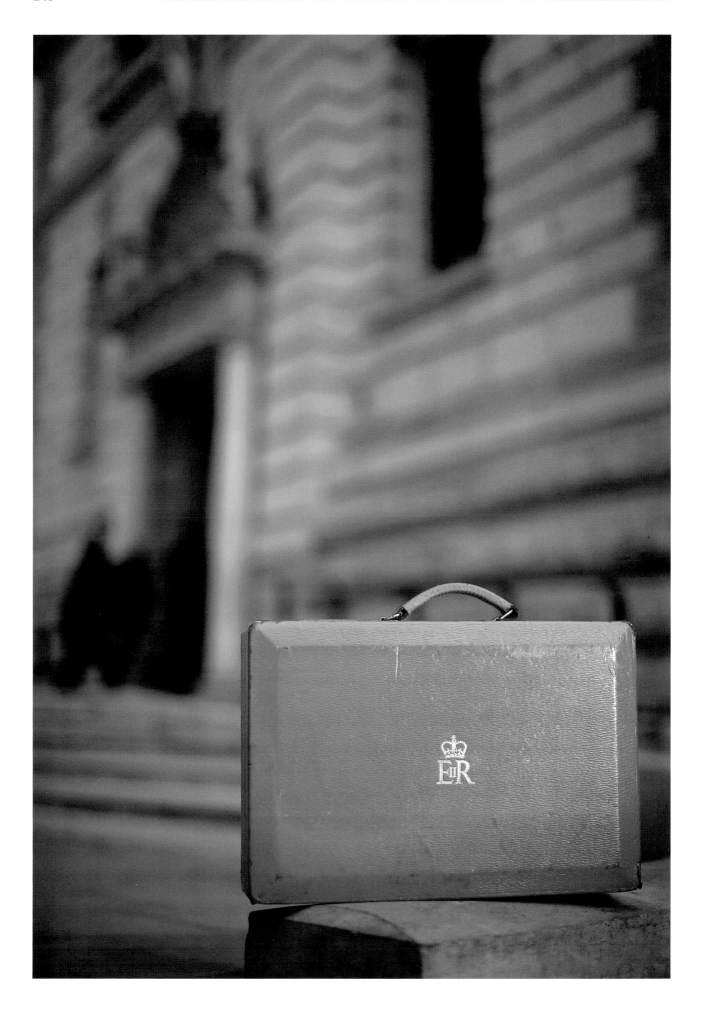

# THE QUEEN'S AWARD FOR ENTERPRISE

Half a century of rewarding innovation, sustainability, exports and excellence in British business

From language schools to arms manufacturers, from speciality cheesemakers to car makers, the Queen's Awards for Enterprise celebrate British business success in all its forms. The most prestigious accolade for British firms celebrates its 50th anniversary this year, but it's original aims – of promoting exports and driving economic growth – seem more relevant than ever.

Originally known as the Queen's Award to Industry, it was established by a Royal Warrant in 1965 and awarded to 115 organisations at the first ceremony in 1966 (winners were announced, as has now become customary, on the Queen's birthday, April 21). In 1975 it was renamed the Queen's Awards for Export and Technology, with separate awards in each category; by 1992 it had added a Queen's Award for Environmental Achievement. Following a 1999 review, chaired by Prince Charles, it was renamed the Queen's Awards for Enterprise, with awards under three categories: International Trade, Innovation and Sustainable Development. A fourth category, Promoting Opportunity Through Social Mobility, is a new award recognising companies with a social-mobility programme that has had a positive effect on commercial success.

In 2005, the Queen's Award for Enterprise Promotion (QAEP) was added, honouring individuals who make outstanding contributions to enterprise culture in the UK. The QAEP is equivalent to an MBE and is made by the Queen on the advice of the prime minister; they, in turn, are advised by an Enterprise Promotion Assessment Committee (EPAC), which includes representatives of government departments as well as entrepreneurs and business leaders. A maximum of ten QAEPs are awarded each year.

The awards are administered by the Department of Business, Energy, Innovation and Skills, and awarded on behalf of the Queen and the prime minister. They are supported by an Advisory Committee which is chaired by the head of the civil service and which comprises representatives of government, the private sector and the trade unions.

The awards process is rigorous and competitive, with somewhere between 100 and 200 businesses reaching the tough criteria each year – only 20 per cent or so of those that enter. The International Trade award, for instance, requires a company to show a substantial and sustained increase in export earnings over three consecutive 12-month periods, to a level that is outstanding for size of the organisation and the products and services concerned. For sustainable development a company needs to make detailed submissions addressing the "pillars of sustainable development", including environmental issues, management approaches and contributions to the local community.

The awards are open any UK-based business with a minimum of two full-time employees and a track record of outstanding commercial success. Some Queen's Award winners employ thousands, like Jaguar Land Rover and Anglian Water (both winners of Sustainable Development awards in 2015). Others might have just a handful of staff: 116 of the 2015 winners had fewer than 250 full-time employees; 17 of them employed fewer than 10.

Winners receive a workplace presentation from a Royal representative and an invitation to a reception at Buckingham Palace hosted by the Queen. They receive an engraved crystal bowl and a hand-signed scroll, but – beyond these physical awards – the actual benefits are often far-reaching: usually resulting in a boost in sales, an increase in publicity, and improved staff morale. They can also use the prestigious "award emblem" on company stationery, websites, on goods and in advertising, granting them an edge over competitors. For any firm, a Queen's Award is a real feather in the cap – the most prestigious accolade for any business in the UK, and something with a huge overseas clout and a high degree of credibility in the business community.

# "Some Queen's Award winners employ thousands; others might have just a handful of staff"

# BANKING ON PROGRESS

Women in Banking and Finance is a non-profit that encourages females in finance to shatter the glass ceiling

WWW.WIBF.ORG.UK

Tracy Jordan, who just happens to be a director at Credit Suisse, personifies the values promoted by the not-for-profit organisation Women in Banking and Finance (WIBF). She's also a philanthropist, mentor and the 2017 winner of the WIBF's Champion for Women award. She won it for striving to encourage women to "Be The Best You Can Be".

Championing women has been a primary goal for WIBF and its 1,000 plus members since it was formed in 1980. Run by volunteers, this UK-wide organisation is described by president Vivienne Artz as "one of a kind" in its drive to create more inclusive workplaces; and for providing support at all stages of women's careers. At once open and exclusive, WIBF aims to foster ambition, with networking events, development programmes and leadership opportunities.

"We were started by women with tremendous vision," says Artz, "and our goal is to be the voice of the industry. We tackle the relevant topics of the day including maternity and paternity parity, and get issues addressed, especially at government level."

WIBF helps to bolster the contribution of women in the sector through its advisory board, executive board, and a range of committees. These have helped identify problems affecting women's employment, such as a lack of focus on retaining female professionals during the earlier stages of their careers. As a result, WIBF has set up an initiative dedicated to helping millennials achieve their full potential.

"We've established that a diverse workplace appeals to them," says Artz, "and they want more varied careers. It's issues like these – how to support the next generation of leaders – that WIBF was set up to solve."

As well as individual members, WIBF attracts corporates such as Barclays, Lloyds Banking Group, KPMG and Sky. They are invited to take part in discussions where issues and challenges of the day such as the gender pay gap are debated. Men who contribute to women's career progress are also celebrated at WIBF; indeed, BP Treasurer Alan Haywood was the first ever male winner of its Champion for Women award. So when it comes to the advancement of women, even men can be the best they can be with the help of WIBF.

# CITY MISSION

In the male-dominated environment of
the City, Schroders is counting on women
to take on more top jobs

WWW.SCHRODERS.COM

"Schroders has made excellent progress but there is still more to do," says Emma Holden, who joined the company as Head of Corporate Communication in 2007 and is now Global Head of Human Resources and also a member of the firm's Corporate Responsibility Committee. "Only 20 per cent of our applications today come from women. The entire asset management industry needs to do more to attract women applicants." It's just the kind of frank, enlightened attitude that has earned the international asset management company a reputation for being ahead of the City game in the employment of women.

The first female secretary to a senior partner walked through its doors in 1906. Social and cultural forces have not, however, always made it easy for the 200-year-old company – which is responsible for helping institutions, intermediaries and individuals across the world manage their assets and build sustainable prosperity – to hang on to promising female staff. In 1973 its first woman graduate trainee, Tessa Nash, left after six years, telling the in-house magazine *Wagtail* that she could not, "with the best will in the world, be a banker and a devoted wife."

Clearly, a lot has changed since the 1970s in women's employment, both at the company and in society as a whole. However, it was also in that decade that Schroders recruited its first two female investment managers. One, Josiane Paine, went on to become the first female assistant director in 1980. She continued to break through glass ceilings to become the first female board member of Schroders' London operating company in 1985. Madeleine Hall was another of the company's female recruits of the 1970s. She wrote about the period's employment culture in *Wagtail*: "When applying for jobs in my final year at university in 1974, my ignorance prevented me from knowing that the City was a male bastion nearly as well protected as a chap's club. No doubt through some administrative oversight, I found myself being interviewed." She was offered a post as the first female graduate management trainee in the Banking division, "and duly purchased a briefcase and boarded a train with a lot of male persons in pinstripes. To everyone's amazement few earthquakes occurred."

By the 1990s Schroders was widely recognised in the City for being ahead of its time in promoting women. According to the *Financial Times*, "A number [of its female employees] have gone on to be the City's highest flyers." Among these is Karen Cook, who left the company not to concentrate on being "a devoted wife" nor to spend more time with her six children. Instead, she moved to Goldman Sachs' investment banking division where, as Chairman, she is known as the Queen of Mergers and Acquisitions. Then there's Dame Alison Carnwath, now the Non-executive Chairman of Land Securities; and Tessa Bamford, a top executive at influential headhunters Spencer Stuart.

Still at Schroders, Sheila Nicoll, Head of Public Policy, received an OBE this year. And Johanna Kyrklund, Global Head of Multi-Asset Investments, has ranked in London's Financial News among the top 100 most influential women in finance for six consecutive years. Indeed, Nicoll and Kyrklund are part of a formidable female force that makes up 31 per cent of those in senior management at Schroders.

Under the leadership of new Group Chief Executive Peter Harrison, the company signed up to the Women in Finance Charter in 2016. Harrison has pledged to increase the company's percentage of women in senior management roles to 33 by the end of 2019. There's still "more to do", but as he rightly points out: "Diversity of thought is critical to success in modern business."

# LEVELLING
# THE BOARD

Professional services firm KPMG is leading the
way in gender equality across all areas of business

JOBS.KPMGCAREERS.CO.UK

"We've come a long way since women got the vote," says Melanie Richards, "but it's interesting to look at what has – or perhaps what hasn't – actually changed over the past 100 years ."

Deputy Chair of the audit, tax and advisory giant KPMG UK, Richards makes a salient point. Although the vote was first extended to British women in 1918, workplace legislation has lagged behind. The Equal Pay Act was only introduced in 1970 and, Richards feels, "it wasn't until the late 1980s and 1990s that women's roles really started to develop."

Today, businesses are upping their game. Shining a light on high achievers is *The Times*'s annual ranking of the Top 50 Employers for Women – within which KPMG has earned a place every year since it began in 2010. KPMG was also one of *Working Mother* magazine's 10 best companies in both 2011 and 2016. "Diversity, inclusion and equality are integral to our business."

Collaboration is key, and campaigns such as the 30 Per Cent Club – which was established to achieve a minimum of 30 per cent women on FTSE-100 boards – are crucial. Embracing the challenge, KPMG's board is now 43 per cent female and its executive 31 per cent, but representation at partner level trails at 18 per cent. Richards hopes that by sponsoring the government's Hampton-Alexander Review of women in senior roles, activity can be further targeted towards redressing this imbalance.

At the wider end of the corporate pyramid are forums such as KPMG's Women's Network and its GROW development programme, which nurture employees' leadership skills. KPMG also published detailed targets around staff gender, sexual orientation, ethnicity and disability in 2014. This helps ensure transparency and has made the organisation more

mindful of its activities. Its graduate recruitment process, for example, now involves group assessments and networking with KPMG staff and partners. "It used to result in more job acceptances from male candidates than female," says Richards. "We're now seeing almost parity."

Research that was undertaken in 2014 on women below board level – compiled by KPMG, the business psychologist firm YSC and the 30 Per Cent Club – proposes a more seismic shift. Rather than "fixing" women to adapt to traditional structures or "beating men up" for their dominance, it seeks practical solutions. "There's a trap of thinking that just women need to support women," says Rachel Hopcroft, Head of Corporate Affairs. "With men still taking the majority of senior positions, male feminists are incredibly important."

But, in reality, to what extent can businesses take the lead? "Although we do a lot around gender equality, so much is influenced by society," observes Richards. She recalls her experiences of new legislation on parental leave. Introduced in 2015, the change allows mothers and fathers to share early childcare – yet Richards recently heard from a young man whose wife had come under such pressure from her parents that she ended up taking all of the leave. "These personal choices don't abdicate the responsibility of businesses, but we must accept that some developments rely on what society deems acceptable."

Perhaps this explains our slow evolution since the Suffragettes. "More people thought that women shouldn't be fighting for the right to vote than the few that did," says Richards. "But, while parts of society might not fully appreciate or embrace the contribution of women, business has a responsibility to bring this contribution to the fore."

## "With men still taking the majority of senior positions, male feminists are incredibly important"

———

Rachel Hopcroft, KPMG

£1,000    THIS ISSUE OF THE "DAILY GRAPHIC" CARRIES A FREE INSURANCE OF £1,000 UNDERTAKEN BY THE OCEAN ACCIDENT & GUARANTEE CORPORATION, Ltd.   (See p. 12)    LONDON EDITION

# The DAILY GRAPHIC

## ONE PENNY

### LONDON: SATURDAY, MAY 6, 1916

No. 8241.—Vol. CVI.     Registered as a Newspaper.

## THE WAR-TIME CITY "MAN" AND "HIS" LUNCH.

Wherever possible the City man, and in particular the clerk, has now been replaced by the City girl. A typical instance of the change is to be found in the Prudential Assurance Company, which now employs 2,000 women war workers. As an economy for them, and to give them greater efficiency, special luncheon rooms have been provided, where they receive an excellent hot meal for a few pence. They have also a pleasant roof garden and library for recreation. 1. A few of the 2,000 girls who lunch-in every day. 2. A corner of the kitchen. 3. At lunch.     ("Daily Graphic" photographs.)

# WOMEN OF PRUDENCE

Prudential plc has long been committed
to diversity and inclusivity

WWW.PRUDENTIAL.CO.UK/RESPONSIBILITY

## "Diverse and inclusive companies attract the best talent and make better decisions"

Tim Rolfe, Prudential plc

"We believe that diverse and inclusive companies attract the best talent, make better decisions, have better financial performance, and innovate more effectively," says Tim Rolfe, Group HR Director, Prudential plc. "This goes beyond gender and includes all our affinity groups and employees."

Prudential plc was founded in Hatton Garden, London in 1848 and soon started to make its mark with its distinctive army of door-to-door salespeople selling insurance policies. It first employed women in the 1850s as canvassers, and in 1871 was the first company in the City of London to introduce "lady clerks". By 1879, the company employed around 170 women, each of whom had to pass an exam in arithmetic, spelling and handwriting.

The two world wars expanded the remit of female employees considerably. By the start of the First World War, Prudential had introduced Red Cross Voluntary Aid Detachments into office life, providing classes in first aid and home nursing. During the war itself, 100 women were released to do part-time work in hospitals. Twenty-one more were released for full-time war duties, four of them overseas.

By the Second World War, nearly 10,000 women worked among the company's agency staff, collecting premiums door-to-door. "We were more than just collectors of money," recalled one wartime female agent. "We became good friends."

In 1938, just before the start of the Second World War, a young woman called Monica Allanach entered the actuary's office as an actuarial trainee. She would go on to be a trailblazer for women at the company, qualifying as a Fellow of the Institute of Actuaries in 1951, and working as Assistant Actuary in the Actuary Office Overseas in 1967. In 1970, she became the first woman to join Prudential's management when she was appointed as Deputy Actuary. The first woman appointed to the board was Mary Baker, who joined Prudential as a non-executive director in 1988.

Today, Prudential has a strategic, long-term approach to diversity and inclusion (D&I) across the group. The company invests in targeted activity across ten priority areas, which range from tackling unconscious bias to supporting various affinity groups and formal mentoring programmes. Sitting alongside Prudential's affinity group networks for mental health and the firm's LGBTQ community is the volunteer-based Prudential Women's Network (PWN), which aims to inspire, support and develop women to achieve their potential and fulfil career aspirations at Prudential.

Other initiatives that form part of the group's broad D&I agenda include engaging with recruitment firms to diversify pools of potential candidates, awareness campaigns, apprenticeships, traineeships, graduate schemes and partnerships with organisations which support women returning to work after an extended career break.

Prudential has also publicly committed to having at least 30 per cent women in its senior management team by the end of 2021 and has signed the HM Treasury Women in Finance Charter. At the start of 2017, Prudential had four women on its board of directors, including Anne Richards, Deputy Chief Executive of M&G Prudential. Overall, 20 women are part of the firm's senior management, including fellow Deputy Chief Executive Clare Bousfield, and Lilian Ng and Marcia Wadsten, who hold senior roles in Asia and America, respectively. The company used to be famous for "the man from the Pru", but it's clear that "the woman from the Pru" is every bit as important, looking both to the past and to the future.

# LEADING WOMEN

Goldman Sachs has taken great strides in supporting and promoting the advancement of its diverse workforce, especially its women employees

WWW.GOLDMANSACHS.COM

When Goldman Sachs was founded in New York in 1869, no one could have foreseen the firm's colossal international growth. Although it was just over a century before the finance company opened its first overseas branch, in London, its subsequent expansion has been rapid. Today, it has 60 offices in 35 countries, and more than 35,000 employees – drawn from 155 nationalities and speaking more than 100 languages.

The company continues to venture into new markets and take on new staff, and great care is taken, where possible, to employ local talent. "Enshrined in the firm's business principles is a recognition that our people are a key asset that delivers direct competitive advantage," says Sally Boyle, International Head of Human Capital Management. "In our efforts to hire, retain and empower the best talent at Goldman Sachs, we have made it a key strategic priority to actively promote diversity of thought and experience."

Goldman Sachs' culture of diversity starts with a range of measures aimed at inspiring the next generation of professional young women in financial services. This includes reaching out to them from pre-university through to business-school levels.

The firm is also conscious that, for many women, maternity has the potential to be a break point in a career. To address this, there is a deliberate focus on ensuring a plan exists to support women throughout their maternity leave with a goal of a successful return to work.

"Many women wanted to return to work after maternity leave but found the transition challenging," says Boyle, "particularly from a childcare perspective." Uniquely among its City peers, Goldman Sachs offers an on-site childcare facility, which is designed to ease the transition back to work and provide emergency backup care to parents of children under 12.

"Offering on-site childcare gives mothers one less thing to worry about. Supporting their needs in the short term helps us retain these women for the long term," says Boyle. "We also offer four weeks' free full-time care at the on-site facility to all women returning after having a child. In addition, all parents are entitled to a further four weeks of free care per child per year." As a result of these initiatives, the firm is widely recognised as a leader in supporting women, particularly through the maternity experience.

Goldman Sachs is also committed to supporting its women employees as they progress into more senior roles at the company. For example, all of the women pictured (opposite) were promoted to partner in the company's Europe, Middle East and Africa region last year. In recognition of its efforts, the firm's sponsorship initiative – which engages senior leaders to support the advancement of high-performing women and other underrepresented groups in their careers – was given the Progression Award at the 2016 Business in the Community (BITC) Workplace Gender Equality Awards.

"Research tells us that women are less likely to organically develop sponsor relationships in the organisation, some of which are acknowledged to be vital to career progression," says Boyle. "So we have put our efforts into addressing this sponsorship gap."

Although Goldman Sachs is pleased with its progress to date, the firm recognises that – in common with many others in the financial services sector, it has yet to achieve its gender diversity goals. "We continue in our commitment to increasing the representation of women overall – especially in senior management roles," says Boyle. "Goldman Sachs will never stop trying to maximise the potential of all our people – especially women. It is fundamental to the firm for the long term."

# "We have made it a key strategic priority to promote diversity of thought and experience"

Sally Boyle, International Head of Human Capital Management

# PERPETUAL MOTION

Too few women consider asset management a viable career option, but Invesco Perpetual is aiming to change that

WWW.INVESCOPERPETUAL.CO.UK

As one of the country's largest asset management companies, Invesco Perpetual believes its commitment to a long-term strategy is crucial to securing successful outcomes for its clients. The company applies this to the way it manages funds for a variety of private and commercial clients, but Caroline Atkinson, the company's Head of Human Resources, believes it is equally applicable to the way Invesco invests in employees, particularly in the area of improving diversity. "For a few years we have been looking at how we can recruit in a more creative and diverse way," she says. "As well as the business benefits of doing this it's also the right thing to do, which is important to our organisation."

Atkinson acknowledges that trying to improve gender diversity in the financial services sector is a challenge, particularly since the 2008 crisis. Because of its greater focus on long-term returns, the prevailing culture in asset management is very different to that of other areas of the finance industry; but this might not be obvious to potential employees. This is just one of many obstacles Invesco is determined to overcome. "The process began with an employee survey," says Atkinson. "Reviewing and discussing the output and people's experiences was the starting point for an ongoing conversation with our employees. We wanted to understand what the key issues were, where we should focus our efforts for maximum effect as well as raising awareness of the value of diversity for the future success of the company."

Since then, a number of avenues have been explored. A women's network and a mentoring scheme have been introduced. "We have been thinking about recruitment and what we can do better," says Atkinson. "We are challenging ourselves to be more creative about where we source and find people. We also strive to have senior women on interview panels, and to be thoughtful about the language we use when listing the attributes we are looking for." In 2017, Invesco plans to join the financial services voluntary charter, which will require the company to disclose publicly its diversity-related targets.

Part of the challenge is the lack of women who consider finance as a career option: a limitation that goes right back to schooling. To redress this, Invesco employees such as Stephanie Butcher, a fund manager on the European equities team, volunteer to talk to schoolchildren and undergraduates. She and her colleagues are motivated in part by the belief that the company's profile – long-term thinking about risk, acting with integrity, working collaboratively with clients – suits women. Women who have flourished at Invesco are also involved in the company's efforts. Take Mandeep Jhuti, who works in the Treasury department and is actively involved in the women's network, organising networking events with a personal-development focus; and Kerry Bulgin, who was hired through Investment 2020, an entry-level programme that aims to improve diversity within asset management. "Kerry now works permanently within the HR team," says Atkinson.

The diversity programme has the full support of Invesco executives, who recognise that, like asset management, it involves acting with focus and integrity over a sustained period. "Our CEO and senior team are very supportive of this," says Atkinson. "They understand the need for greater diversity from both a moral and business perspective, and are driving the agenda hard. We know that it's a long-term project with no single silver bullet."

# A LONG-TERM INVESTMENT

M&G Investments is forward-thinking in its pursuit of inclusivity, gender balance and employee engagement

WWW.MANDG.COM

M&G believes that diversity of thought is driven by diversity of talent and an inclusive culture. Improving gender diversity is a long-standing issue in banking and finance, but this City-based investment management firm, which employs more than 2,000 people worldwide, is determined to overcome the imbalance in some parts of its workforce. "Graduate recruitment especially affects the long-term employment of women in critical roles," says Anne Richards, Chief Executive. "It's an issue we take very seriously."

The company's customers include individual savers and investors, and some of Britain's largest pension funds. Since it was founded in 1931, M&G has built a reputation for its progressive approach towards recruitment, and has taken steps to attract more female talent into its graduate and apprenticeship programmes. M&G's Career Returners hiring initiative is designed to attract returning professionals, while it has also strengthened relationships with job-search firms and other suppliers to identify suitable recruits.

A key reform has been the introduction of student insight events to educate young people about the investment management industry, and to open up positions to graduates with any degree discipline, including the humanities or the sciences. The positive outcome is that men and women are now represented equally on M&G graduate schemes.

The company's reputation for being forward-looking is borne out by its championing of inclusion in the workplace. Since 2012, all new and existing employees have gone through an extensive induction process involving face-to-face inclusive behaviour training. From managers to trainees, these sessions are aimed at schooling employees in M&G's core beliefs around inclusivity. The session challenges "unconscious bias": unwitting prejudice triggered by an individual's background, environment or upbringing. "What we do is try to help people understand what our beliefs are and then challenge their own," says Richards. "It's about treating everyone equally."

M&G has been instrumental in encouraging and enabling employees to set up their own affinity networks. Supported by a member of the M&G board as a sponsor, network groups now include M&G Pride (which provides support to lesbian, gay, bisexual and transgender staff), M&G Mind Matters (focusing on mental health) and M&G CAN (on cultural awareness). "These groups have grown organically around the field of inclusion," says Richards. As a result of such measures, a recent employee survey shows that 92 per cent of staff agree with the statement: "M&G respects the individual differences (e.g. cultures, backgrounds, disabilities, sexual orientation) of its employees."

Like any employer, M&G has people on its staff at very different stages of their careers: from millennials to those near pension age. "As our workforce becomes more diverse, multi-generational and digitally enabled, the expectations of our employees upon us as a company, as well as our needs of them, are evolving quickly," says Richards. "We need to become more flexible, adapt our ways of working managing and leading. In response, we have created a 'Future of Work Community' to consider how we should adapt working practices to meet the future needs of our employees."

In championing fairness and equal opportunities, as well as treating people as individuals, M&G strives to ensure that all of its staff have happy and rewarding careers. It is a shrewd investment that is clearly already paying dividends.

## "Graduate recruitment especially affects the long-term employment of women. It's an issue we take very seriously"

Anne Richards, Chief Executive, M&G Investments

# DIVERSE AND PROFITABLE

Thomson Reuters' D&I Index proves that diversity equals profit – and investors are beginning to listen

WWW.THOMSONREUTERS.COM

Does diversity work? It's a question increasingly asked in boardrooms, and one that Geoffrey Williams, Head of Diversity and Inclusion at Thomson Reuters, seeks to answer with a blend of persuasion and cold, hard facts.

A company with a long history in news media, and now in finance, tech, accounting and more, Thomson Reuters has long been a leader in workplace equality. To that end, the company conceived the Diversity and Inclusion (D&I) Index, a comparison tool to convince the hardest-boiled CEO that diversity equals profit. The index uses publicly available data on a company's environmental and social governance (ESG) to rank it on 30 different principles, and identifies companies that perform well financially and are also strong on diversity and inclusion.

Comparing D&I-listed companies' performance against the benchmark of the Thomson Reuters Global Equity Index of 10,000 worldwide stocks, the divergence is stark. Since the D&I Index's inception in 2009, listed companies have seen equity growth of 123.6 per cent, against 86.4 per cent for the Global Equity Index. "People assume diversity is about social justice and not financial return," says Williams. "They think it's a nice thing to do, to have more senior women or more people from ethnic minority backgrounds. But our index proves there is financial value."

Nor should it be assumed that these D&I-indexed companies are growing from a small base or working in a narrow sector, with names such as The Gap, Johnson & Johnson, Diageo and Cisco Systems all in the D&I top ten. Thomson Reuters appears at number 40, and it's part of Williams's role to ensure the firm doesn't just preach diversity but walks the walk. "I look at what diversity means for us," he says. "Can we attract and retain the right talent? It's my job to develop a strategy that supports our long-term goals and drives the agenda forward."

Williams balances this internal role with efforts to promote the diversity agenda globally, a task requiring keen attention to cultural difference. "We take the lead from our on-the-ground stakeholders and must be respectful of all cultures and current regulations and at times adjust our strategy appropriately," says Williams. "But globally, as a firm, we believe that the most diverse workforce is the most innovative and the most productive."

Another way in which Williams seeks to advance these principles is in working with young people. He runs a conference called Rocking Ur Teens which offers teenagers an understanding of the world of work, diversity and inclusion. "We want to galvanise the next generation into seeing gender equality in the right way," he says. "Prince's Trust research has found that across all social classes young people don't understand the world of work, so we try to bring that to life in a fun and engaging way."

Enlightening the next generation is one way forward, but perhaps a bigger challenge is to tackle already-entrenched views. "A lot of barriers are societal," says Williams. "There's a perception that, say, if you're a man and want paternity leave, you're stepping back from your career. Until we are able to challenge society's perceptions, we can't move the dial as much as we'd like because the conversations are too disparate. There's definitely still work to be done."

Diversity and gender equality have always been a tough sell in business, but the rigorous analysis offered by the Thomson Reuters D&I Index is a powerful tool to keep that dial moving in the right direction.

# BANKING THE DIFFERENCE

TSB uses diversity as a way of challenging group think and increasing financial returns

WWW.TSB.CO.UK

"Banks have lost their way and some of them have lost the trust of the consumer," says Helen Rose, Chief Operating Officer for TSB. "One of the ways to earn that trust back is to just do a really good job. Great customer service really motivates us."

Born out of the financial crisis when it separated from Lloyds, TSB is not only interested in changing the way banking is perceived but also the way that banking operates, thinks and looks. "We're about embracing technology and moving forward," says Rose. "So it's about meeting customers' needs as a bank and not having people worried about whether we're investing money behind the scenes or doing anything that led to the financial crash. We are very much a retail bank focused on the retail banking needs of our customers, as opposed to what might be called 'funny stuff'."

With more than 550 branches and in excess of 5 million customers, it's clear that TSB is bringing people on board with its new, progressive ways. In order to better reflect the diverse needs of its increasing and varied customer base, TSB is also focusing on diversity within the organisation, too. Not only because it's the right thing to do and aligns with the company's ethos, but also because it's good for business.

"We very much see diversity as a business issue," says Rose. "The reason we care about it is because we believe diversity stops you having group think, so if you don't have people from different backgrounds, races and genders, you run the risk of people all thinking the same and not having diversity of thought and not reflecting your customer base. If you have a more diverse workforce, you'll have better financial returns."

Rose is also TSB's Executive Sponsor for Gender and the organisation is fully behind the current surge in support for gender equality. "We are very focused on female talent," she says. "We want 45 to 55 per cent of the top 500 roles in our company to be filled by women." This is something that will be achieved through the organisation's talent pipeline, which helps push along promotion-ready staff members to find more senior roles, coupled with its offering of schemes such as shared parental leave.

"What's great about the gender pay initiative is that it's caught the imagination of the media in a way that other gender work hasn't," says Rose. "I think it's really powerful. It creates a momentum and a push. Companies are doing good work in this area but that doesn't always translate into actual gender equality. Gender pay has helped push this, and other areas, and helped progress."

All of this ultimately leads to a working environment that can help drive both the company, and the individuals who work within it, forward together into a brighter and more representative future. "We want everyone to fulfil his or her potential," says Rose. "We want people to be themselves in the workplace and to not feel they have to hide who they are. It's about encouraging people and making sure that there are no barriers to what you can achieve. If you're passionate about something then in today's workplace you can make that happen. Passion and fulfilment matter – we want to inspire people."

# CREDIT WHERE IT'S DUE

Boutique private credit firm MV Credit prides itself on its ethical and diverse ethos

WWW.MVCREDIT.COM

The private credit firm MV Credit believes a policy of equality and diversity is fundamental to its success. "Without diversity we simply wouldn't be as successful as we are," says Managing Partner Nicole Downer. "We absolutely celebrate cultural and professional difference because, when making a loan, having people with different mindsets and backgrounds coming at the issue is key to making good decisions."

Based in London, MV Credit specialises in lending money to mid-cap companies (businesses with an enterprise value of between €250 million to €1.5 billion) across Europe. With a ratio of 11 women to 13 men, it is at the forefront of promoting gender equality in the financial sector, and continues to actively encourage women to join the firm.

"It can be a challenge to attract women in such a male-dominated sector," says Downer. "But having a healthy culture of a flexible work and personal life balance helps to make us an attractive prospect. We have created a family feel within the firm, and it's important to us that everyone has an equal chance to express their voice and opinion as to how we are run.

This creates a high level of respect and trust that makes us the most stable team in the industry."

For Downer, this stability, coupled with 130 years of combined experience in investment across all credit cycles, is what makes MV Credit attractive to investors and clients. The firm's commitment to equality and diversity stretches across all aspects of its business. A strong belief in fairness underpins its philosophy when it comes to where it will invest and, as a signatory to UNPRI (UN Principles for Responsible Investing), it adheres to a robust policy of ethical and responsible investment. Alongside standard due diligence, the firm looks carefully at the environmental, social and governance aspects of a company before committing to any loans.

This ensures that its investors' money does not flow to unethical companies. "We ask specific questions and see whether we are comfortable with the responses," says Downer. "From the very beginning we've had industries we will not lend to, and these checks and balances continue to be crucial to all of our decision making."

# HAPPY RETURNS

Kite Lake Capital Management is forging a new future for women in financial management

WWW.KITELAKE.COM

As a female Chief Investment Officer at the helm of a flourishing UK-based hedge fund, Massi Khadjenouri is a symbol of gender equality in what continues to be a male-dominated industry. For Khadjenouri, who established the event driven fund Kite Lake Capital Management (UK) LLP in 2011, this has less to do with discrimination and more to do with a shortage of women pursuing a career in hedge funds. "The talent pool in our industry is still dominated by men," she says. "We still receive far fewer applications from women."

Kite Lake has taken positive steps towards addressing gender imbalance in the industry by welcoming a female partner in the most senior role and championing an inclusive approach towards business. "We believe that diversity of gender, religion and nationalities is an asset to our company," says Khadjenouri. "It contributes to our culture and our success. Having female professionals in management positions, and involved in decision-making processes, brings a different perspective, which can only be beneficial to a community and a business."

After six years of hard work, the London-based fund has established a solid reputation in the industry and is entering a growth phase with an increasing number of clients on board. "Years of sticking to our mandate and delivering what we preach have built our credibility and respect in the investment community," says Khadjenouri. "Seven nationalities are represented in our small firm and there's an inclusive culture in which we celebrate our differences and learn from them."

Recently, the firm has attracted the attention of a number of US investment organisations seeking out high-performing female-led funds. It's a trend that Khadjenouri believes will grow as the industry accommodates a more gender-equal and diversity-conscious perspective. "We've had corporate approaches from outfits in the US with specific minority mandates, such as state pension funds," she says. "Our industry is not witnessing this kind of development in the UK and I think it would be a positive step to encourage in this country."

While Kite Lake scores points with equality-conscious investors, the company's history of excellent returns with minimal volatility are what continue to attract increasingly high-profile investors. "Our industry is incredibly competitive," says Khadjenouri, "and you have to generate consistently good returns if you're going to be successful. That is always true, regardless of gender."

# POWER IN A UNION

Women make up most of Western Union's
customers and a growing number of its employees

WWW.WESTERNUNION.COM

Ever since Western Union was founded in 1851, women have played an essential role. At first, these were mainly limited to telegraph operators transferring messages. Today, the company is charting a powerful story and more opportunities have opened for women within Western Union and for the customers they serve.

As a leader in cross-border, cross-currency money movement, Western Union says that women are proving themselves as today's prominent drivers of growth with education and empowerment.For Pia De Lima, Western Union's Global Head of Communications for Global Money Transfer, women serve an important role when it comes to moving places and moving money. "Western Union's own customer base today mirrors the change in women's roles across the globe," she says. "Of the 150 million people who send or receive money each year through Western Union, a majority are women."

More than a quarter of billion people are living in a country where they weren't born, and more than half of them are women. Some $537 billion in money transfers link people who have left their country and those who stay home, and around 75 per cent of that money goes from people working and living in developed nations, back to developing nations to pay for living, education, medical expenses, and micro-investments into businesses.

"Money movement between our customers has layers of emotional and economic benefits," says De Lima. "While sending money demonstrates a powerful emotional connection, functionally, it leads to significant change. Paying for education drives empowerment and economic opportunity. It means our customers are people with ambitions for the younger generations back home. They are educating their children as never before. We are proud of our role of financial inclusion by connecting people through money movement."

Women are playing a significant role empowering potential of education. In developing nations, for the five out of ten people receiving a university education, three of the five are women – proof of a growing qualified base. Women are also steadily increasing their presence in the world of small business.

Across Western Union's global workforce, more than 50 per cent of employees are women, and two of the company's nine board members are women, attracting recent recognition by the US organisation, 2020 Women on Boards. At the leadership level at Western Union, women head significant roles of Legal, Technology and Compliance and the company is seeking to drive further balance.

"Under the direct stewardship of Western Union Global CEO Hikmet Ersek," says De Lima, "the company has created an all-female senior advisory group called Women@WU (pictured, opposite). Its mandate is to create an action plan to promote women's success through recruiting, mentoring, promoting, and measuring progress, while fostering a culture of greater inclusiveness for our customers as well as our employees."

Since 2001, the Western Union Foundation has given more than US$113 million to fund projects that have reached more than 800,000 people in 137 countries. The foundation's primary focus is on education as the basis for employment.

# A NATIONAL WEALTH SERVICE

PIMFA is the trade association for financial advice and wealth management firms across the UK

WWW.PIMFA.CO.UK

In an uncertain world, providing sound financial advice and wealth management is an important responsibility for members of the Personal Investment Management and Financial Advice Association (PIMFA). "It's about looking after the money that you've already got," says Chief Executive Liz Field. "But, as well as wealth preservation, it's about growing the wealth you have, whether that's a pension pot, larger sums of money for the future, or stewarding money for future generations." It is an essential component for everyone in planning their financial future.

PIMFA is a relatively young organisation, which is addressing an age-old challenge. "We represent firms who help individuals and families plan for their financial journeys," says Field. The association was launched in June 2017 following the merger of two industry bodies which had existed for more than 20 years: the Wealth Management Association and the Association of Professional Financial Advisers, and which represents over 2,000 firms who look after £1.5 trillion of private individuals' assets.

PIMFA's objective is to create the optimal operating environment for its member firms to deliver their services and meet clients' needs and leads the debate on policy and regulation for its members. As part of this strategy, PIMFA launched a Millennial Forum, consisting of millennials working in the sector, to examine the needs of future clients. This generation faces challenges such as high housing prices, student debt and the end of defined benefit pensions. The clear message from the forum was the need to educate young people as to the benefits of putting some money aside in their youth because of the advantages this will deliver when they are older. Other work highlights the value of advice as an essential part of an individual's planning toolkit.

A proud signatory of HM Treasury's Women in Finance Charter, PIMFA also runs Women in Wealth forums to promote diversity in the workforce. "The benefits of a diverse workforce are clear from a business point of view," says Field. "Our long-term vision is to raise the profile of the industry as a great place to work and a force for good, empowering individuals to plan for their financial future with confidence. In 10 years' time, I hope we will have helped create an environment in which our firms can do what they do really well for a client base that is much bigger."

# INVEST IN YOUR LIFE

Hannay Investments offers bespoke, long-term financial advice that is female-friendly and holistic

WWW.HANNAYINVESTMENTS.CO.UK

"We are proud to be a three-woman firm," says chartered financial planner Vanessa Barnes, who established Hannay Investments in 1996. "It is probably unique to our industry." Together with her colleagues, Kelly Warden and Anne Ratnam, Barnes dispenses bespoke financial advice – on everything from pensions to investments, inheritance to school fees – from the company's offices in Ealing Broadway, west London, and meeting rooms in Hanover Square.

She set up Hannay after 10 years with Chase de Vere. "I felt there was a heavily male bias in financial services, and a general miasma of misogyny," Barnes says. "I wanted to create a company with a more relaxed, female-friendly, flexible working environment and a different approach from the rest of the industry.

"I hate to use gender stereotypes but I do think that, as women, we can often have a more empathetic way of working – better listening skills. We understand that, for clients, financial planning is not always about how your portfolio performs, but about how you sleep at night, about family dynamics, or worrying about your children and grandchildren. We've all had life

stuff to deal with, such as coping with children and elderly parents, and that informs our ethics."

It's what Barnes calls holistic financial planning. At Hannay, which now has around 300 clients, both male and female, the focus is on building lasting relationships. The firm doesn't advertise, relying on word-of-mouth recommendations. "I have clients who have been with me for 30 years," says Barnes. "We provide a genuine long-term service, which makes a lot of commercial sense, too. It's so important that you're comfortable with your financial adviser, so we offer an initial free consultation to see if the fit is right."

Helping clients to enjoy their lives, as well as to plan for the future, is important to Hannay Investments. "Research shows that, after the age of 75, people stop spending on themselves. We take a lot of time talking to people about enjoying their retirement, as well as providing for others."

There is a token male in the office, though. "We keep some gender balance with Billy, the office cocker spaniel," says Barnes. "Although he keeps falling asleep during Budget statements."

# BEAUTIFULLY DIFFERENT

Addidi is a wealth boutique for women with
a progressive approach to delivering value

WWW.ADDIDI.COM

"Nurture" and "me time" are words not usually associated with wealth management or independent financial advisors. However, Anna Sofat is on a mission to change the male-dominated and transacional world of finance. Her female-focused company Addidi Wealth aims not just to improve monetary returns for clients, but also to make their lives "richer" in personal and social terms.

"It's the ultimate irony of the modern existence that the more success and wealth we accrue, the less time we seem to have to revel in its promises," says Sofat, founder and Managing Director of the London-based "finance boutique". "Money can be a cold bedfellow, and if you're already at your comfort point financially then talking about financial returns all the time doesn't mean much."

It's why Addidi Wealth doesn't simply concentrate on maximising returns for clients. "We focus on so much more than making their money work for them – it's also about adding value in other ways," explains Sofat. "We look at what their wealth enables them to do, like helping their family and friends, a charity, or mentoring, or maybe just buying a great pair of shoes."

The company's Pioneers club benefits local projects that are attempting to solve social issues. Along with funding from Addidi, clients invest a proportion of their wealth in not-for-profit schemes such as working with supermarkets to recycle discarded food. "Just writing out a cheque isn't always good value," says Sofat. "This approach tries to solve problems in a way that's sustainable and provides social and personal returns. We have met some of the most inspiring and passionate people working in this space."

Born in India, Sofat comes from a background where equality was not guaranteed. It means she never takes equality for granted and strives to uphold the values of fairness, transparency and honesty.

"I was fortunate because, educationally, my dad always told me 'you can be whoever you want to be'," she says. "But, in many families, there was always an assumption that the boy was going to university and the girl was going into, say, nursing. That's not just the case in India, but all over the world. Even in some of the most seemingly progressive countries, girls are still seen in very different ways to boys and are not afforded equal opportunity or treatment."

Sofat's message to women is not to take anything for granted. "Women have to be clear about what they want," she says. "I think women have the leadership skills to bring better outcomes for families, businesses and humanity in general." To this end, Addidi launched its Inspiration Awards in 2009 to celebrate women in history known for wealth creation and making a difference. Alongside this initiative, Addidi set up its Enterprise Club to provide a collaborative approach to angel investing and a pool of female talent to help businesses scale up.

"There are plenty of examples of some great women doing amazing things throughout history," says Sofat. "But, in general, we need more accessible role models for women – not just those who are exceptional."

Although Addidi was set up to help women manage their money, it is inclusive. "We work with single men, families, older and younger ones, as well as those who are well-off and others moderately so," says Sofat. That inclusivity applies to the staff who work for the company. One advisor recently retired from the firm at the age of 70, while Sofat makes a point of mentoring young staff starting out in the industry.

Through Sofat's inspired approach to finance, Addidi is on course to make the lives of everyday women exceptional – and that is an aim worth championing.

# "We need more accessible role models for women, not just those who are exceptional"

Anna Sofat, Addidi Wealth

# VISIONARY INVESTOR

The success of DPI is as remarkable as the
company's talented and diverse senior staff

WWW.DPI-LLP.COM

"We built a leading pan-African private equity firm," says Runa Alam,
co-Founding Partner and CEO of private equity firm Development Partners
International (DPI). "While we always promote and hire on merit, we pride
ourselves on the level of diversity within DPI, ranging from gender, age,
ethnic, cultural, and sexual orientation. I believe that's one reason for our
success as a company and the position of our first fund, which has been
benchmarked by Cambridge Associates as a top quartile fund."

In an industry where only 7 per cent of senior staff are female, three
of DPI's six partners are women – including, even more unusually, its CEO –
and more than 40 per cent of its staff are women. Born in Bangladesh
and raised in both the US and Europe, Alam studied development
economics at Princeton and holds an MBA from Harvard Business
School. She worked in Wall Street before setting up the first international
investment bank in Bangladesh, and began investing in private equity
in Africa in the late 1990s, co-founding DPI more than ten years ago with
Miles Morland. Today, the firm employs 34 staff in its London-based head
office, and manages $1.1 billion in assets across two funds.

Previously chair of the African Private Equity and Venture Capital
Association, Alam still sits on the board. She is also the chair of the
Sustainability Committee, which ensures private equity companies
consider their environmental and social impact to the extent DPI does.
"This company focuses on many different constituencies," she says.
"We care equally about our investors and our employees. We care about
our companies in Africa, the management teams, and also Africa as a
whole – the community. Development economics has been my lifelong
passion, and I'd like to think that we have a transformative effect on
Africa's development."

DPI is growing rapidly, both in terms of people and funds under
management. "What's important to us is how we get the highest returns
to our investors while making sure all the constituencies I mentioned are
taken care of," says Alam. "We're not passive investors, we work closely
with the management teams. Within our portfolios, even in challenging
macro environments, our companies are growing at 20 to 30 per cent a year.
That's what leads to a profitable and high-growth company."

# CLOSING THE PAY GAP

Allied Irish Bank is a beacon of diversity in the financial sector

WWW.AIBGB.CO.UK

With the current focus on employment equality and the gender pay gap, few businesses can claim to have resolved the many significant challenges. But Steven Cochran, Head of Products and Growth Platforms at Allied Irish Bank (AIB), believes things are moving in the right direction: "There's a lot of work still to do," he says, "and it's an industrywide issue, not unique to AIB. But we are making real progress."

AIB has been addressing the issue of gender equality for several years, and was among the first companies to sign up to the Treasury's Women in Finance Charter, targeting a 50–50 gender balance across its managerial level by the end of 2020. A year on from making that commitment, the proportion of female managers has already increased from 39 to 42 per cent.

But gender is not AIB's only diversity focus; feedback from staff raised other areas of concern, such as ethnic diversity, sexual orientation and family life. In response, the company set up six employee resource groups, centred on families, roots (background and ethnicity), ability (disability, wellness and mental health) and LGBT issues, as well as women's and men's groups.

"All our employees now have the ability to find a voice," says Cochran. "By joining up to any of the groups, they have a vehicle to raise the profile of the issues concerning them, and make changes to our policies. All of which contributes to making AIB a more diverse and inclusive place to work, which is our overall aim."

As well as increasing employee engagement with diversity issues, the company continues to expand opportunities for flexible working, enabling more staff to balance work and family life. It holds regular diversity and inclusion events – including its own centenary celebrations of women gaining the right to vote – and around a quarter of the bank's 1,000 UK staff have also completed unconscious bias training, designed to ensure all employees and job applicants have equal opportunities to succeed.

"The training has quite an impact, and really helps to raise the profile of diversity," adds Cochran. "I don't think anybody would be calling the sector an example of best practice just yet, but there has been a noticeable change."

# HEALTH

Department of Health and Social Care — 278
Children's Heart Surgery Fund — 280
Rethink Mental Illness — 281
RB (Reckitt Benckiser) — 282
Home Instead Senior Care — 284
NHS Slough Clinical Commissioning Group — 286
Bradford District Care NHS Foundation Trust — 288
Bury Hospice — 289
NHS Eastern Cheshire Clinical Commissioning Group — 290
Richmond Fellowship — 292
St Margaret of Scotland Hospice — 293
PJ Care — 294
Camden & Islington NHS Foundation Trust — 295

# DEPARTMENT OF HEALTH AND SOCIAL CARE

The department that's working to increase the integration of health and social care, with long-term sustainability in mind

In a phrase, the purpose of the Department of Health and Social Care's (DHSC) is to help people live better for longer. Its responsibility is to lead, shape and fund health and care services across England, so as to ensure that every person has the support and treatment they need, when they need it, and with the dignity and compassion they deserve. This is done through assuring the delivery of health services, and the creation of relevant legislation and policies – always in the best interest of the individual patient, as well as the general public and the taxpayer. The department additionally oversees the work of the NHS, which is the largest and oldest single-payer healthcare system in the world, and one that celebrates its 70th anniversary this year.

As with most other departments, the DH has had several names and roles over its long history. These have included the Ministry of Health (formed in 1919) and the Department of Health and Social Security (formed in 1968), the latter of which was divided into two in 1988. In the January 2018 cabinet reshuffle, "social care" was added to its title. Today, the department employs 2,160 staff across the country and is supported by 25 agencies and public bodies.

When the Health and Social Care Act 2012 became fully operational on 1 April 2013, it highlighted one of the department's major policies: to increase the integration between health care and social care. This joining up of services is fundamental in view of the UK's ageing population. Indeed, the percentage of people over the age of 85 is set to double in the next two decades, which will mean an increase in "complex health issues" that encompass both areas of need.

As such the DHSC's aim is to create and improve an integrated care system, which works collaboratively to address accurately a person's individual health requirements. Initiatives include the allocation of a named professional to oversee each individual's case across all services, the creation of a shared electronic database, and improving the support for those moving between services, such as from children's to adult's services or from hospital to home.

On a local level, achieving a greater level of integration has meant the introduction of clinical commissioning groups (CCGs) across the country. CCGs are groups of general practices in the same region that work together to plan and design local health services for that area, via the devolution of decision-making. To ensure that services meet the individual needs of each area, the CCGs work alongside patients and care partners. As Andrew Lansley, Secretary of State for Health between 2010 and 2012, said: "Clinical commissioning groups put healthcare professionals in the driving seat so that they have the freedom and responsibility to design services on behalf of their patients – delivering better quality and integrated care."

The department's core principles can be condensed into three statements: living and ageing well (helping people to live healthier lives); caring better (raising standards in health and care, and improving the quality of care); and preparing for the future (by maintaining and improving on quality and financial performance, and investing in innovation and research).

Other current priorities are improving out-of-hospital care, building and developing the workforce, and improving services through the use of digital technology, information and transparency.

"We champion innovation and improvement by supporting research and technology, promoting honesty, openness and transparency, and instilling a culture that values compassion, dignity and the highest quality of care above everything," says the department's Permanent Secretary, Sir Chris Wormald.

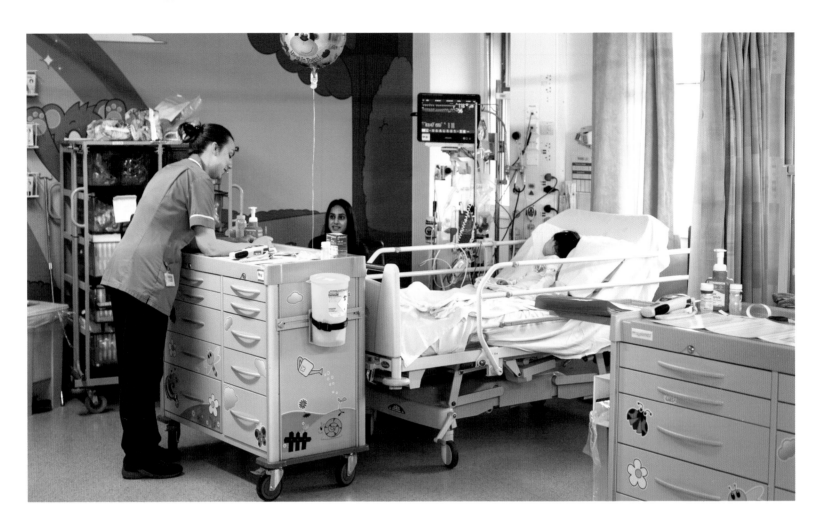

# FOR THE YOUNG AT HEART

Children's Heart Surgery Fund is helping to ease the experience of congenital heart disease

WWW.CHSF.ORG.UK

For children and adults diagnosed with congenital heart disease – and even more so for their families – hospital can be a forbidding experience. It's something Children's Heart Surgery Fund (CHSF) makes more comfortable.

"One of the many ways we do this is to work with play specialists, to engage kids with activities to keep them distracted when they enter hospital," says Andy McNally, CHSF's Communications and Marketing Manager. "We have a mascot called Katie Bear, and we've recently created a children's book aimed at young patients called *Katie Bear Goes To Hospital*. It explains the patient pathway to children, their parents and their siblings."

These are just some of the many approaches adopted by CHSF. "Our four priorities are to look after the heart, the mind, the family and the future of congenital heart patients," says McNally. "For the heart, we are funding innovative equipment to save and improve lives, as well as keeping up with every improvement in the congenital cardiac field. For the mind, we support a restful ward experience for patients, which includes playrooms, communal areas, TVs, toys and resident goldfish, and we have in the past funded a psychologist.

"In terms of the family: anyone with congenital heart disease in Yorkshire and North Lincolnshire will be treated at the Congenital Heart Unit at Leeds General Infirmary. It's a vast area, and family members might have a three-hour journey to get here. We provide parental accommodation and award living-cost grants. We also have community groups on social media for the families of patients to chat to each other, compare notes and allay their fears."

For the future, CHSF funds research into congenital heart disease and supports ongoing projects. "We're currently raising money for a unique heart theatre," says McNally, "bespoke to Leeds General Infirmary, for treating babies and children with congenital heart disease."

CHSF was formed in 1988 by Duncan Walker, a Leeds surgeon who saw a shortfall in the NHS's cardiac provision. "He was a rather flamboyant figure who left an amazing legacy," says McNally. "The NHS is never going to have enough money, but it provides the infrastructure to keep people alive. We work alongside them to make the patient's life more comfortable and encourage innovation. People living with congenital heart disease can go about their daily lives knowing they have this extra support."

# A PATIENT APPROACH

The charity Rethink Mental Illness aims to improve awareness of mental illness and to boost patient support

WWW.RETHINK.ORG

Marilyn Monroe, Nina Simone, JK Rowling — three powerful women, celebrated worldwide. Yet all three featured five years ago in a list published by the mental health charity Rethink Mental Illness to commemorate International Women's Day. "None of them let what they lived with or what people thought get in the way of influencing the world," Rethink announced at the time.

Rethink Mental Illness started life in 1972 as the National Schizophrenia Fellowship. It was renamed in 2002 to reflect its work in a broad range of mental health issues. Recently the charity reports a dramatically positive shift in attitudes to mental health. According to Brian Dow, Director of External Affairs, "The public conversation has changed in the last five, or even three, years. It's fascinating that Theresa May, a prime minister dealing with something as immense as the consequences of the Brexit vote, used one of her first big domestic speeches to pledge a commitment to mental health."

The charity provides support to both men and women. Its current campaign in association with MIND, "Be In Your Mate's Corner", shows three tough guys marching down the street to help out a friend dealing with mental illness. When they reach the garage where he works, they act like they're readying him for a boxing bout. Though most mental issues affect both sexes, the charity also addresses some gender-specific issues: in this case men's reluctance to open up about their problems.

"While men generally find it harder to talk about mental illness," says Dow, "women have often been more ostracised and stigmatised. There are certain times in life when mental illness can have a particularly devastating impact. Post-natal depression affects a lot of women, and in some cases women can be affected by psychosis after pregnancy. In the past, women's health issues have been very unfairly politicised – just think about the word 'hysteria', from the Greek word 'hystera', for 'womb'."

At a time when major public commitments are being made to the improving of mental health support, Dow says it's up to charities such as Rethink to ensure there's sufficient investment and dedication to make that a reality. Whatever Theresa May's political motivation, he says, her promise to put mental health at the heart of her government was "a genuinely extraordinary moment. It is hard to imagine that would have happened five years ago."

# DARE TO BE DIFFERENT

RB is the global leader in health, hygiene and home consumer goods that is driving diversity and inclusion

"I've had to call out all sorts of myths about what women can and can't do," says Gurveen Singh, Chief Human Resources Officer for the British consumer goods firm Reckitt Benckiser (RB). "When I started work 37 years ago, there was hardly anyone supporting a woman's voice in the workplace."

Today, her determination has created a professional culture designed to support a diverse workforce. RB is a FTSE Top 20 business that produces dozens of household products that we use every day – including Nurofen, Durex, Dettol, Strepsils, Calgon, Clearasil and Cillit Bang. It is also committed to doubling the number of women in top management roles by 2020.

"The key principles for encouraging diversity are challenging bias and promoting inclusive leadership," says Singh (pictured opposite, centre, with RB colleagues). These principles are part of RB's global leadership-development programmes, which around 1,000 of the company's managers go through each year, and its talent-acquisition strategy. This enables Singh to instil uncompromising standards of inclusivity.

"I simply won't accept a shortlist from internal or external recruiters that does not reflect diversity, that isn't 50-50," says Singh. "At RB we value diverse backgrounds and experiences, which bring different perspectives and new ideas. Our Executive Committee is made up of seven nationalities and its members have had experience in multiple countries during their RB careers. International assignments are part of our way of life here and range from the most strategic to the most operational roles. Being immersed in different cultures helps our RB talent to challenge conventional thinking and appreciate diversity."

In 2015, RB introduced its DARE (Developing, Attracting, Retaining and Engaging talented women) programme. The initiative supports work/life balance, international mobility and dual careers, as well as actively challenging bias. In addition to a global maternity policy, DARE includes a female middle manager leadership programme and mentoring.

The latest addition to DARE involves further harnessing male colleagues' support at RB – via a "HE Dares SHE Dares" campaign. Singh believes that men are critically important in supporting women in the workplace. "We want even more men at RB to act as ambassadors for our DARE initiative," she says.

RB is the leading global health, hygiene and home goods company, whose brands also include Air Wick, Scholl, Gaviscon, Mucinex, Lysol, Veet, Harpic, Enfamil, Nutramigen, Mortein, Finish, Woolite and Vanish. From the foundations of wellness and infant nutrition, to the fundamentals of a hygienic home, its global brands help people live healthier, happier lives, and RB now has operations in over 60 countries.

Singh believes RB's unique culture is at the heart of its success. Its drive to achieve, passion to outperform, and commitment to quality and scientific excellence are manifested in the work of 40,000 employees worldwide. RB is signed up to key United Nations' Sustainable Development Goals (SDGs) including SDG 5 (Gender Equality), while RB CEO Rakesh Kapoor was recently ranked in the Top 10 Champions of Women in Business list, organised by the *Financial Times* and HERoes.

After 25 years at RB, Singh can only wonder at how much the profile of the workforce has changed. "When I joined RB in the early 1990s," she says, "I was the only woman in senior management. I started a management training programme to bring women into departments such as sales where there hadn't been any. It's a question of pushing boundaries relentlessly."

## "We value diverse backgrounds, which bring different perspectives"

———

Gurveen Singh, Reckitt Benckiser

# HOME FROM HOME

Since launching in America 22 years ago, Home Instead
Senior Care has become the world's biggest provider
of home care for the elderly

WWW.HOMEINSTEAD.CO.UK

When one Home Instead Senior Care caregiver learned that her client, a lady in her eighties, had loved horse riding as a young girl, she arranged for her to have a memorable day out at a local stables. "We are all about those little, extra-special moments," says Michelle Begley, Head of Marketing. "The client is at the heart of everything we do."

The company was founded in Omaha, Nebraska 22 years ago by Lori and Paul Hogan, who were looking for a care home for Paul's grandmother. "The 'Home Instead' name comes from her," explains Martin Jones, the firm's UK Managing Director. "When they went through the options, she told Paul that she wanted to stay home instead. Paul, struggling to find carers, had a light-bulb moment, and the rest is history."

Home Instead is now the largest provider of home care around the globe, with franchise operations in 15 countries and a revenue of $1.4 billion. The UK arm – a network of 190 franchise offices, 8,000 carers and 9,500 clients – was set up 11 years ago. Thirty of its offices have received an outstanding rating from the Care Quality Commission and, in 2016, the company received the Queen's Award for Innovation, the UK's highest accolade for business success.

"We are not task-focused, unlike most of our competitors," says Begley. "The care that we offer is relationship based. It's about choice and treating people with the dignity and respect that we would want for our own parents. Clients are matched with a caregiver who becomes their point of contact."

In order to provide this bespoke care, Home Instead needs to attract a particular type of caregiver. "We're not looking for people who just want a 40-hour a week job to pay the mortgage," says Jones. "We need people who

have tangible life skills, who can hold a conversation and build relationships with clients – people who want to make a difference. That's why our caregivers tend to be older – the average age is 49. The message we try to get across in our recruitment advertising is that caring is a meaningful job, not a menial one."

Jones says that Keith Aldritt, a retired police sergeant and former teacher, is a great example of the type of person the company employs. Named Caregiver of the Year 2015, he took a part-time job with Home Instead because he wanted to continue to stay active in his community and give something back.

"Using both his police investigative skills, and the patience and empathy he utilised working with children, he turned 'true-life detective' and helped clients build photographic memory books," says Jones. "One man had lost his confidence and become reclusive, but Keith persuaded him to go outside again, taking him back to revisit landmarks from his childhood photographs."

Home Instead works alongside GPs, district nurses and Macmillan nurses to support people in their home and community. Using a team of experts in ageing and dementia from around the world, a pioneering dementia training programme has been developed, which is City and Guilds accredited. It also provides free dementia-awareness community training and has trained over 40,000 people across the UK, including taxi drivers, retail workers, nurses, police officers, fire fighters and even MPs in the House of Commons.

"Our mission is to change the face of ageing," says Jones. "We aim to become the UK's most admired care company and to keep on expanding into more areas across the UK so that we can touch as many lives as we can."

# "We are all about those extra-special moments. The client is at the heart of everything we do"

Michelle Begley, Home Instead Senior Care

# BLAZING A NEW TRAIL

NHS Slough Clinical Commissioning Group has marshalled some of its top female GPs to improve health outcomes and inspire the next generation

WWW.SLOUGHCCG.NHS.UK

High rates of emergency hospital admissions for care-home residents was a major concern for Dr Jim O'Donnell and his colleagues. "Managing frail and elderly patients is extremely demanding," says Dr O'Donnell, Clinical Chair of NHS Slough Clinical Commissioning Group (CCG). "The care is underfunded, which is why many GP practices don't want to make it a key part of their work."

But within two years, this CCG, based 20 miles west of London, has reversed the trend. It's achieved this with the help of "supernovas", a group of female doctors dedicated to changing healthcare for the better. The team came about after Dr O'Donnell recognised what he saw as "an issue around gender".

"We don't have an issue with ethnic diversity because we deliberately recruited GPs that mirror the local population," he says. "But our doctor workforce is overwhelmingly male and that doesn't reflect our gender-equality values."

To address this, Dr O'Donnell identified a team of outstanding women GPs from local practices. The aim was to support and encourage them in leadership roles – and the outcomes for patients have already proved transformational.

Among this trailblazing team is Dr Siva Sithirapathy, who introduced a weekly review programme for Oak House, Slough's largest care home. This has led to a drop in the number of patients admitted to A&E from 38 per cent to 33 per cent, year-on-year. Getting staff to identify patients with deteriorating health earlier and ensuring pharmacists reduce unnecessary medication have been among the successful reforms introduced by Dr Sithirapathy. "It's demonstrated how attention to equality and diversity can address our CCG's deficits and in-patient care," explains Dr O'Donnell.

Asthma care is another health area that has been transformed. Slough did have one of the country's highest hospital admission rates for asthma and respiratory conditions, that was until Dr Sabina Shaik identified cigarette smoking and poor understanding about treatment as key contributing factors.

"Every day people die from preventable asthma," says Dr O'Donnell. "Yet some parents didn't want their children to use steroid inhalers because of their mistaken concern about side-effects." It's why Dr Shaik trained nurses to go into hospitals, establish a rapport with patients and families, and educate parents about the condition. The result has been a 45 per cent reduction in acute admissions for asthma year on year.

The success of the supernovas has already led to career promotion for one of the team, gynaecologist Dr Lalitha Iyer, who is now Medical Director for three CCGs: Slough, Maidenhead and Bracknell. With the help of her colleagues, she has improved support for women who have had adverse experiences during pregnancy and childbirth.

Spotting the next generation of female leaders is an ongoing mission for Dr O'Donnell, and the supernovas are already acting as role models and mentors for a new wave of future experts. "The programme is inspirational and encourages female trainees to realise they too can lead," he says. "This is instead of accepting a situation where most leadership is done by men. Our message to trainees is: 'you too can do this'."

By encouraging female GPs to step forward and take on leadership roles, Dr O'Donnell and NHS Slough CCG have allowed their true talent to shine. The stellar work of these supernovas has already proved instrumental in improving the lives of patients – and there's no doubt others will follow their bright example.

# CARE THROUGH DIVERSITY

Diversity is key for the Bradford District Care NHS Foundation Trust

WWW.BDCT.NHS.UK

"Like letters in a stick of rock, our values are represented throughout our organisation," explains Sandra Knight, Director of Human Resources and Organisational Development at Bradford District Care NHS Foundation Trust. "These aims include progressing diversity, both in our workforce and in how we reach out to different communities."

Bradford has an ethnically diverse population, and the NHS in this West Yorkshire city has gained a national reputation as a progressive employer. However, in 2013 the trust discovered that there was still much that could be improved when a study revealed that more than a third of black, Asian and minority ethnic (BAME) staff were not happy with their career progression. "BAME staff raised other concerns too, which we realised we needed to address," says Knight. "This was in order to recruit and retain an ethnically diverse workforce."

In response, the trust developed its BAME Diversity in Employment Strategy. Launched in 2014, it includes the Moving Forward programme, supporting staff who have the desire and potential to move into senior management. Emotional intelligence and positive thinking are among the techniques covered, and the approach is already paying dividends. More than half of those who have completed the Moving Forward scheme have been promoted or changed roles.

It is fulfilling, too, for those providing the support. Knight, along with other board members, provides coaching in professional skills including interview techniques. One colleague in community nursing sought advice from her on how to handle job interviews. With Knight's support, her colleague was offered not just one position but two. "She was going for her dream job, but was nervous because she'd not succeeded before in interviews," says Knight. "The staff member felt she couldn't be her real self. It was great to see her succeed, and now she wants to carry on with the coaching to boost her confidence further."

By building an inclusive workforce that reflects the population of Bradford, the trust can relate to the needs of the people it treats. "We'll continue to develop each individual's potential through and through," says Knight, "because that leads to great patient care."

# CARING TO THE END

Bury Hospice in Greater Manchester offers palliative care to help ease its patients' end-of-life journey

WWW.BURYHOSPICE.ORG.UK

"It's a myth that hospices are miserable places," says Eloise Burke, Acting General Manager of Bury Hospice. "A good sense of humour and great communication skills are key. Our staff recognise the needs of the patient and the needs of loved ones and that's just as important as anything. To work at a hospice you need to be passionate about palliative and end-of-life care as well as dedicated, empathic, conscientious and professional."

Burke joined Bury Hospice on the clinical side in 2004 and is now one of a number of females occupying senior roles. Ange Anderson is the Hospice Care Team Manager, Dr Heidi Donnelly is Senior Speciality Doctor, Sam Duncan is Retail and Volunteer Services Manager, while one of their top fundraisers is Lorraine Taylor, a mum who lost her daughter Sarah to ovarian cancer in 2016 aged just 28. Taylor has raised over £40,000 for Bury Hospice in just over a year.

Hospices are not just places where people come to die. Bury Hospice, which recently acquired a CQC rating of Good, offers a Hospice At Home service to help people with life-limiting illnesses as well as day-care services where pain is managed or a medication regime established. There is also pre- and post-bereavement support for families.

Those who do spend their final days at Bury Hospice receive care in large, private rooms, purpose built to allow space for family and friends to spend time with their loved ones. There is also an award-winning Japanese Garden on site, which is maintained by volunteers who support the hospice.

Burke can see the role of the hospice evolving as more people live to an older age. "Over the next 25 years, the number of people with a need for expert end-of-life care is likely to increase," she says. "Hospices will need to develop new models of care and adapt existing services to meet increasing demands for their services.

"They will need to work closely with other organisations, including the NHS, local authorities and care homes. Collaboration between hospices will also be important to maximise resources and increase efficiency. Hospices will not just be service providers, but they will need to be champions of change for care in their local communities."

# WELL THOUGHT OUT

NHS Eastern Cheshire Clinical Commissioning Group
is finding effective ways to serve the health needs of its
population of more than 200,000

WWW.EASTERNCHESHIRECCG.NHS.UK

When a school realised that an anxiety problem in an able boy was causing challenging behaviour and difficulty in his learning, it was able to do something about it. The school worked with NHS Eastern Cheshire Clinical Commissioning Group (CCG) to organise a multidisciplinary team – including mental health, social care and education professionals – to support the child to feel safe in school. He was thoroughly assessed and given an Education, Health and Care Plan (EHCP), which meant he could access one-to-one teaching assistant support. As a result, his attendance improved, he started going to lessons daily and his anxiety levels decreased.

This, says Penny Hughes, Designated Clinical Officer, is just one example of the group's new services for children with special educational needs and disabilities. "It shows how the CCG is now working as a team around the child," says Hughes, "with parents as a vital part of the jigsaw. By doing this, we were able to make a difference early on in a child's life. We hope this work will reduce the possibility of him developing any more significant mental health needs, ensure he has access to education and improve his overall life chances."

In another innovation to support young people, the CCG partnered with NHS South Cheshire CCG and Cheshire East Council to develop the initial pilot sites for Emotionally Healthy Schools, a national initiative to place emotional wellbeing at the centre of the school day. Following a successful first year involving 14 Cheshire high schools, the programme has now become a central part of the Children's and Young People's Mental Health Transformation Plan to support emotional wellbeing and ensure those experiencing mental health problems are quickly identified and given the right help.

At the other end of the age spectrum, the CCG is meeting the challenge of having the fastest ageing population in the North West. Every year, more than 4,200 patients over 75 are admitted to Macclesfield Hospital as an emergency, equating to nearly half of unplanned hospital admissions.

Delivering safe, effective and consistent care to older people with complex needs and frailty is therefore seen as one of the greatest challenges facing Eastern Cheshire. Accordingly, the CCG has invested £1 million in a new 'Frailty Approach' provided by East Cheshire NHS Trust.

This will support the integration of other key local services for older people with frailty. These include a GP-led multi-disciplinary team, working in accident-and-emergency wards and in the community to support people at home; and a GP-led Acute Visiting Service to complete urgent visits in a person's own home. The CCG also provides psychiatric liaison in A&E to support people with mental health problems, and a Community Falls Responder Service provided by the voluntary sector at all times, working with North West Ambulance Service.

Designing services around the needs of frail, older people has supported an overall reduction of 1,649 (3.8 per cent) in emergency hospital attendances while emergency admissions of older people have reduced at a higher rate than for the general population.

"In line with our Caring Together transformation programme to integrate health and social care," says CCG Clinical Chair Dr Paul Bowen, "the 'Frailty Approach' will shift the balance from hospital-based services to home-based health, social and community support to achieve improved quality of care and person-centred outcomes."

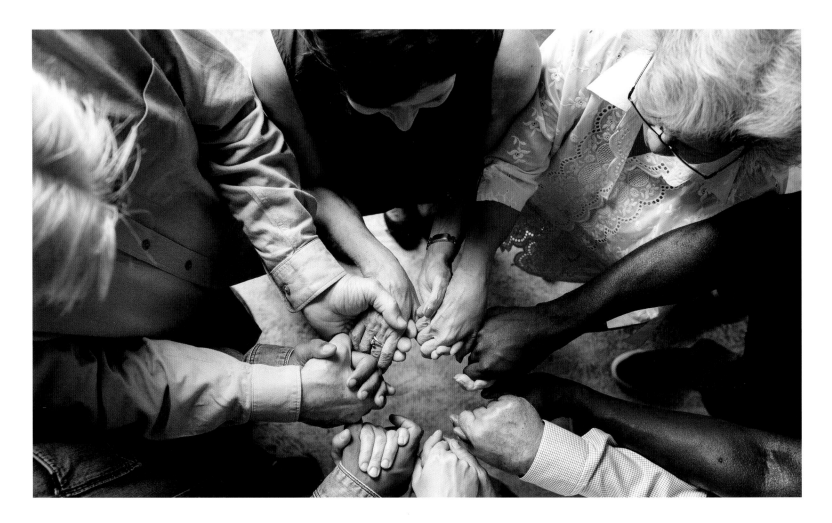

# HEALING CIRCLE

A pioneering charity encourages people living with mental ill health to help themselves and others

WWW.RICHMONDFELLOWSHIP.ORG.UK

One in four people will suffer from mental ill health in their lifetime. It's a stark fact; and one that is finally penetrating the public consciousness, to the relief of Richmond Fellowship. "It's been on our agenda for over 55 years," says Derek Caren, Chief Executive. "But the NHS Five Year Forward View shows that mental health is now very much on the government's agenda too."

Founded in 1959, the national mental-health charity is one of the biggest providers of its kind in the country, offering housing, employment, community support services, to name a few. But the world has changed. "We live in an increasingly demanding society," says Caren, "and that creates more stress, anxiety and depression."

Richmond Fellowship addresses this by working together with the people it supports to give them ownership of their own recovery. "We don't tell people what to do," says Michelle Snowden, Group Head of Communications and Marketing. "We work with individuals who live with mental ill health to help them understand their goals and aspirations in life, and we give them the support and confidence to achieve their

personal goals. The concept of working together is one that is very close to our hearts and we know it has a positive impact on the people we support. One of the lovely things about Richmond Fellowship is that the people who use our services often end up working with us to help others. They account for around 30 per cent of our workforce, and some sit on our board."

But the charity isn't complacent. Although it has achieved Investors in Diversity status and is ranked 75 in the top 100 organisations by the National Centre for Diversity, Richmond Fellowship is always looking to do more. Changes in society are influencing the partnerships it forms. "Integration is important," says Caren. "So we're working with Clinical Commissioning Groups, local trusts, local authorities and even the private sector. Employers are starting to realise they need to consider the mental well-being of their workforce and that's a really positive step forward."

This joined-up thinking typifies Richmond Fellowship's approach. "When companies look after their own people, everyone benefits," says Caren. "It's a circle of accepting help and offering it back."

# CARING TO THE END

St Margaret of Scotland Hospice offers first-class palliative care for Glasgow's terminally ill

WWW.SMH.ORG.UK

When you picture a hospice you probably don't imagine a swimming pool, Jacuzzi and gym but at St Margaret of Scotland Hospice these facilities are considered an essential part of end-of-life care. The Glasgow hospice was founded in 1950 and now has a staff of 150, beds for 58 patients and a day hospice for another 50, plus outpatients and community nurses. It was formed when an Irish Sister of Charity, newly arrived in Clydebank, was approached by a man with throat cancer who had nowhere to turn. A nursing sister was sent from Dublin to help, and the hospice had its first patient. It is open to anybody over 16 with a life-limiting illness.

"There is tremendous need for our services," says Sister Rita Dawson, the Chief Executive. "Not everybody can or wishes to die at home and it is very important that families are able to have the support of our Palliative and Community Care team. While many advances have been made in medicine which is helping people to live longer, we need more palliative care for people of all ages. Cancer and all life-limiting conditions have no respect for age."

Sister Rita presides over a team of doctors, nurses and allied health professionals, who ensure that a patient's final days are as comfortable and as life-giving as possible. That doesn't just mean alleviating physical pain but also the resulting emotional and mental strain for the patient and their family. "People are very vulnerable when they are ill, so we need to make sure they feel cherished, loved and supported," says Sister Rita. "We wish people to have an excellent quality of life and, to me, it's the most rewarding work, helping people at their most vulnerable. We need to look after people who are seriously ill, cherish them no matter what their age and always help them to feel they still can make a contribution to society."

St Margaret's receives NHS funding but relies heavily on donations, which are used to ensure that people at a difficult stage in their lives can be treated with dignity and respect. "We should cherish our health and look after it every day," says Sister Rita. "Being ill makes you feel very low, but here there are people who really care for those who need looking after and who are and always will be our priority."

# A HEALTHY ATTITUDE

PJ Care harnesses its predominantly female staff to provide first-class neurological care

WWW.PJCARE.CO.UK

"We wouldn't have a successful business without our staff," says Jan Flawn CBE, founder of PJ Care, a Milton Keynes-based leader in specialised neurological care. Since she set up the company in 2001, compassion, care and commitment have been this nurse's mantra, and these values inspire how she treats her workforce.

With several care centres, including a neuro-rehabilitation unit, PJ Care specialises in caring for people with acquired or degenerative neurological conditions, specifically early onset ones, including dementia, Huntingdon's disease, brain trauma and motor neurone disease. From soldiers injured in battle to those involved in an accident, or patients with a degenerative and sometimes hereditary condition, such residents require intensive and often long-term specialist care.

To ensure the best care, Flawn funds vocational and university training for the company's carers and nurses, as well as providing extensive onsite training in each of her specialist centres. She also pays for their time to attend beneficial conferences. With over 40 different nationalities represented at PJ Care, all foreign staff also receive training in English as a second language. "Paying

for our staff to gain experience shows that they're valued," says Flawn. "It also benefits our residents. The hope and motivation they provide is essential in helping people recover and receive the best quality of life."

As a working mother who has also been recognised with a National Women in Business Award, Flawn knows the challenge of combining a job with parenting. It's why she ensures shift patterns are organised to accommodate the needs of staff with children. Women on maternity leave are encouraged to stay in contact with the company after they have had their baby. "We want to keep our nursing staff," she says, "so we ensure they feel included and keen to return when ready."

Staff are welcomed from all backgrounds, and PJ Care recently embarked on an overseas recruitment programme. This commitment to diversity has earned the company numerous honours, including platinum accreditation from the Investors in People Awards.

However, the greatest reward for Flawn and her team is providing all residents with quality of life and helping them to retain independence. That's a testament to the empathy and dedication of this diverse team.

# BY WOMEN, FOR WOMEN

Camden & Islington NHS Foundation Trust is an innovator in mental health support for women in crisis

WWW.CANDI.NHS.UK

Camden & Islington NHS Foundation Trust provides mental health and substance abuse services to residents of the north London communities it serves. The trust has around 2,000 employees working across the boroughs of Camden and Islington, as well as facilities in Westminster and Kingston.

Among its services for people of all genders, Drayton Park Women's Crisis House has marked out Camden & Islington NHS Trust as a trailblazer in offering dedicated support to vulnerable women. Drayton Park was an innovation when it opened in 1995, entirely staffed by and designed for women. The trauma-informed residential service is a safe space for women in acute crisis, offering a range of interventions for 12 women who would otherwise be hospitalised.

Shirley McNicholas has managed Drayton Park for 22 years and has the role of women's lead across the trust. "We set the service up with feminist and empowerment principles," she says. These principles run through the management and practice of the service, and many of the founding team members are still there. "We recognise the impact of the world we live in,

and what happens to women in this world: the level of oppression against women, discrimination, trauma and abuse, impacting on your mental health and being a major contributor to women's mental health problems."

Drayton Park Women's Crisis House is run by a team of women, from a variety of therapeutic backgrounds including counselling and nursing. It's an environment that has yielded results through the years, both in lower hospitalisation rates and in positive outcomes reported by former residents.

"We're not perfect – there's no single approach that can work for everyone and we are also not the right service for every woman," says McNicholas. "But many women report that they feel very differently about themselves due to staying at Drayton Park. It's not just their symptoms – they feel more validated as women."

Not content with past successes, the trust has embarked on a five-year project to redevelop its entire estate, with exciting proposals including a new inpatient facility, brand new community centres housing more clinical outpatient services under one roof and an Institute of Mental Health Research on its St Pancras site.

# INDUSTRY AND COMMERCE

Department for Business, Energy
   and Industrial Strategy 298
William Hill 300
Cisco 302
Yoox Net-a-Porter Group 305
Royal Mail 304
Korn Ferry 308
Which? 310
Archco Developments 312
Lookers 314
Brightstar 316
Wates 318
Arm 320
Opus Energy 322
JK7 324
CGI 326
Ford 328
Procorre 330
Estelon 332
Carl Zeiss Vision UK 334
Kohinoor 336
ThoughtWorks 338
Elurra Gold 339
Crest Nicholson 340
UBM plc 342
Aster Group 343
Tesco 344
glh Hotels 346
Qudini 347
Cox Automotive 348
Ruby Cup 350
Ofgem 351
Edina 352
Worldwide Fruit 353
E.ON UK 354
Panalpina 355
NTT Data 356

# DEPARTMENT FOR BUSINESS, ENERGY AND INDUSTRIAL STRATEGY

The newest government department is working to aid economic growth through higher education, research and enterprise

The government department with a responsibility for business has been through more changes than any other area of cabinet since 1970, when it was first named the Department for Trade and Industry (DTI). Since then it has been through an alphabet soup of acronyms, gaining and losing policy areas and being recalibrated under successive governments.

Its current incarnation – the Department for Business, Energy and Industrial Strategy (BEIS) – was formed on 14 July 2016 by Theresa May shortly after she became prime minister. It merged together the Department of Energy and Climate Change (DECC, formed in 2008) with the Department for Business, Innovation and Skills (BIS, formed in June 2009) – the latter having been created from the merger of the Department for Innovation, Universities and Skills and the Department for Business, Enterprise and Regulatory Reform.

"For quite a number of people working both in DECC, as it was then, and BIS, there was a sense of a kind of almost a reunification," says Alex Chisholm, Permanent Secretary of the BEIS. "A lot of people, including myself many years ago, had worked in the DTI which included energy in its remit, so there was a sense in which there was a recombination or reunification."

It might only be two years old in its current incarnation, but BEIS's roots stretch back as far as 1621, when James I directed the Privy Council of England to establish The Board of Trade to investigate the causes of a decline in trade and consequent financial difficulties. Over the subsequent centuries the department has had a range of challenges, ranging from the care of the colonies in the 18th and 19th

centuries to clothes rationing in the Second World War; from dealing with insolvency to calibrating weights and measures. Today, the role of BEIS is to bring together responsibilities for business, industrial strategy, science, innovation, energy, and climate change, but its core purpose is still economic growth, with the Secretary of State carrying out the dual role of President of the Board of Trade.

This does not, however, mean that BEIS serves to fight only for big business. "One thing I keep firmly in my mind is that business is not only the FTSE100 companies or the big inward investors," says Chisholm. "It's the 5.5 million firms that operate right across the UK." To this end, the department invests in skills and education to promote trade, boost innovation and help people to start and grow a business. BEIS also protects consumers and reduces the impact of regulation.

The department has around 2,500 staff working for BEIS plus around 500 more working for UK Trade & Investment in the UK. The old Department of Energy and Climate Change is also in the process of moving its 1,600 staff to the BEIS headquarters at 1 Victoria Street, SW1. It also has 46 partner organisations and public bodies. As well as regional offices around the country, there are major offices in Sheffield and Aberdeen.

Along with Foreign & Commonwealth Office and the newly formed Department for Exiting the European Union, BEIS is also one of the main government ministries that will be dealing with the challenges of Brexit. "Brexit is going to be a central preoccupation for us," says Chisholm. "We need to strengthen resources to negotiate the new free trade agreements with countries outside of the EU."

# BETTING ON GENDER EQUALITY

Betting and gaming company William Hill works hard
to fight gender bias and promote female talent

WWW.WILLIAMHILLPLC.COM

## "We are ahead of most of our peers in the sector"

Karen Myers, William Hill

"William Hill is a traditional business with a presence in local communities, but also one that is at the forefront of technology," says Karen Myers, Group Human Resources Director at William Hill.

Founded 84 years ago as a postal and telephone betting service, William Hill plc now has 2,342 licensed betting offices on Britain's high streets, as well as online operations in the UK, US, Italy and Spain. Its latest innovations include installing self-service betting terminals in its branches and introducing #yourodds on Twitter, which allows you to request odds for your own unique bets on many sporting events, and Bet Boost, which enhances betters' odds.

This desire to be at the forefront of change has inspired William Hill's longstanding commitment to ensure that women play a vital role in all parts of the business. More than half (52 per cent) of the company's 14,147 UK employees are female, as are 49 per cent of its global workforce.

The company has introduced a range of initiatives, both large and small, to deliver improvements in gender balance and diversity. Job advertisements are now worded neutrally and do not use words and references that conjure up masculine images. The company trains its job interviewers to help them identify unconscious biases they may hold towards certain roles, and managers carry out checks to ensure there are no barriers to women making shortlists for vacancies.

The company was heavily engaged in International Women's Day this year, hosting inspirational external speakers and inviting female employees from all sectors and levels of the company to tell their stories and share their experiences. A recent internal staff survey (to which almost nine out of 10 responded) showed that 72 per cent of female staff agreed or strongly agreed that the company treated all employees fairly, irrespective of gender, age, disability, religion or sexual orientation.

William Hill is committed to reducing its mean gender pay gap of 17.2 per cent to 10 per cent by 2020. Since the gap can be explained by a gender imbalance at senior levels, it is tackling that issue by focusing on recruitment practices, family-friendly policies and access to female mentors and role models, to ensure women's pathways to senior management are not blocked. To attract more women into well-paid tech jobs, it recently launched a Technology Graduate Programme that had an 18 per cent female intake in its first year.

The company ensures that female shop workers who want to progress in their careers are encouraged and have the means to do so. It analyses performance ratings to ensure there is no underlying or unseen bias that could feed through to salary and bonus outcomes. "The theory and plan are very simple," says Myers, "we just need to put them into action."

William Hill is also working to deliver greater gender balance at the top of the company. It is a member of the 30% Club, which campaigns for greater representation of women on the boards of FTSE100 companies, and the three women on its 11-member board represent a 27 per cent share. "Although we are pleased that women make up 27 per cent of both our board and group executive – which we consider to be ahead of many of our peers both in and outside of the sector – we recognise there is further progress to be made and therefore further benefit to be had," says Myers.

# DIGITAL SKILLS FOR ALL

The future is digital – and female –at the international technology giant Cisco

WWW.CISCO.COM

Some industry forecasts predict that 90 per cent of future jobs will require digital skills, meaning that a wide cross-section of society will need to engage with technology. How to respond to this new demand for digital skills is part of the culture at Cisco, and means supporting a widely diverse workforce.

"We believe that having a diverse workforce will help us to understand the needs of our customers," says Angela Whitty, Managing Director, Partner, Cisco UK and Ireland. "Our organisation needs to reflect that of our customers and partners – if we understand their organisational and business challenges, we can continue to innovate and be creative with our solutions."

Cisco, with its Europe, Middle East, Africa and Russia headquarters in Bedfont Lakes, London, employs 70,000 staff around the world to help create secure and intelligent platforms for digital businesses. Eighty per cent of the world's internet traffic runs over Cisco equipment. "We stop more network threats each day than there are Google searches per day," says Whitty.

The firm prides itself on its progressive workplace culture. "There has always been an appetite at Cisco for supporting staff through their life changes," says Whitty. She joined Cisco in 1993, when it was still a relatively small company, and credits Cisco's working culture for enabling her to balance a busy home life with children and her career. The company has a flexible working policy, aimed in part at women coming back to work as well as supporting other challenging life events.

Staff are given their birthday as a holiday, plus five "giving back" days a year, which allow them to volunteer for their chosen charitable organisations. They can also take emergency leave when needed to cope with health or childcare issues, for example. That 46 per cent of Cisco's top management globally is female is testament

to the company's commitment to supporting its staff when and how they need it throughout their careers.

Cisco's connection with its employees extends well beyond an annual review. "We use interactive tools," says Whitty, "so, as a manager, you can react quickly if an employee needs help. These tools offer a week-by-week snapshot of the health of the company through its employees, and have helped connect people to their teams and their experience of working here."

Working with 4,000 partner organisations in the UK alone, Cisco's working practices have an impact on many smaller businesses. "Our internal work can positively influence the experience of other firms," says Whitty. "Whilst Cisco has made great progress in encouraging diversity in its own organisation, we know that there is still more to be done, so we are actively working to ensure diversity is a given in future."

Cisco staff and apprentices have access to online educational tutorials and are given regular training programmes to help them progress and develop new skills. Cisco Networking Academies – of which there are 330 in the UK in schools, colleges, prisons and libraries – extend that teaching into the wider community. These academies have trained almost 250,000 people, and aim to double that number in the next few years. "The digital skills that the country needs are being driven to the places where people can access them," says Whitty.

Cisco has led by example in promoting a diverse and nurturing work culture that has played a big part in its success. "Our inclusion and diversity journey is something that has been going on for a long time," says Whitty. "It's not gender-, race- or culture-specific. It's about including the entire workforce so that we can create a digitally enabled, fully diverse workforce to meet the needs of the future."

# CONSCIENTIOUS COUTURE

Internet retailer Yoox Net-a-Porter Group ensures that
it is female-friendly – both online and in the boardroom

WWW.YNAP.COM

As the world's leading online luxury retailer, selling labels such as Stella McCartney and Saint Laurent, Yoox Net-a-Porter Group (YNAP) is known for setting the trends that others follow. But directional fashion isn't the only way in which this fashion-tech firm is ahead of the curve. It is also pioneering a new business model that puts promoting women at the heart of everything it does.

From new hires – 63 per cent are women – to its majority-female management team, YNAP is unique in the way it empowers women to succeed at every level. In the UK, women still hold less than a quarter of all board positions, but at YNAP 50 per cent of executives are female. Most remarkably, the organisation does not have the pay gap challenges of others companies.

"We firmly believe talent should be remunerated in the right way, irrespective of gender," says Deborah Lee, the group's Chief People Officer. "It's about being a true meritocracy, so when someone contributes more, they should receive those rewards. And it just so happens that in our business, it's the women who tend to earn more."

YNAP's game-changing approach to attracting and retaining talent has earned it global recognition as a top recruiter and employer. The group was listed among the Top 300 Graduate Employers in the UK by *The Guardian* newspaper and was included in the Top Attractors in the UK rankings, compiled in June 2016 by professional network LinkedIn.

The company's message is that empowering women and closing the gender pay gap isn't just the right thing to do, but a key business priority. "Women form half the world's population," says Lee. "It's a travesty that this isn't represented in business or politics. We can't change the world, but we can make sure our company sets an example we'd like to see elsewhere."

YNAP was created in 2015 from the merger of the Italian fashion giant Yoox, founded by Federico Marchetti, and hugely influential luxury retailer the Net-a-Porter Group. Both organisations recognised the importance of supporting women and, in 2017, enshrined this belief in a public pledge.

"We're committed to empowering women, developing young talent and leading the drive towards sustainability in fashion," says Bruno-Roland Bernard, Communications Director. "Equality is a natural part of the culture of the group. It's not even a question for our millennial workforce."

YNAP's policies include offering flexible working, and supporting mothers with individual coaching before, during and after maternity leave. "Our CEO leads from the top," says Lee. "We seek out and destroy any reason for bias. There are no set rules about what you need to be like. We allow people to flourish in different ways and bring their whole selves to work."

Lee and Bernard believe it's the 21st century formula for success. "We are a growth business and we offer great service to our customers, but we can only do that by having the best talent," says Bernard. "That means engaging that talent differently."

The company's aim is for this enlightened attitude to create a ripple effect in the world of tech and beyond. "We hope that other companies will follow our lead and adopt similar fair-hiring, promotion and compensation practises," says Lee. "Equality isn't complicated. It's simply a matter of removing the excuses."

# DELIVERING CHANGE

The Royal Mail is one of Britain's oldest names,
but it boasts a thoroughly progressive approach
to the career advancement of women

WWW.ROYALMAILGROUP.COM

When Moya Greene was appointed CEO of Royal Mail in 2010, she became one of only three female CEOs of companies in the FTSE100. Seven years on, she is one of six, showing that while progress is being made it is still exceptionally difficult for women to rise to the top of the country's largest companies. At Royal Mail, Greene is doing her best to rectify this.

"Moya has already done so much to correct the imbalance of representation of women in our workforce," says David Gold, Director of Public Affairs at Royal Mail. "She set up a number of initiatives to facilitate women in the company getting on the management ladder. We are also getting more women into the frontline. But we recognise there's still some way to go."

Founded 500 years ago, Royal Mail is justifiably proud of its record of championing women workers. The company recognised women's employment rights before they were enforced by law and it recruited thousands of female workers during both world wars, when women played a vital role in keeping the service going. "It's no exaggeration to say that without its female employees, Royal Mail would not have coped," says Gold. "In the First World War, with so many men overseas for so long, this was especially true. During the Second World War, before Christmas 1940, a call was put out for women workers and women responded so swiftly they had half the 8,000 they required within hours."

In 2008, Royal Mail recognised the role of exceptional women in British history through a set of commemorative stamps. Among the six women of distinction was Dame Millicent Garrett Fawcett, the pioneering suffragette who campaigned for women's voting rights since her teens in the 1860s. Fawcett later led the National Union of Women's Suffrage Societies until 1919, the year after the right to vote was finally secured.

Royal Mail recognises that the battle for gender equality is not over. Greene has created a women's network in Royal Mail to free up the pathway into management for more women, as part of a general drive to address diversity throughout the company. "On the ground, we look like the communities we serve and we want this to be the case higher up the ranks," says Gold. "Like any employer, we are adapting to the needs of modern families and we offer part-time work, which can be advantageous for mothers and fathers. Delivering the mail is physically demanding and a lot of people can't handle it whatever their age or gender, but we have many women driving or sorting in our mail centres."

As well as the women's network and mentoring scheme, Royal Mail has introduced the Springboard Women's Development Programme, which offers non-management female employees a series of workshops aimed at boosting confidence; and an outreach programme designed to attract more females into the company from universities and colleges. As a result, Royal Mail has been named one of the UK's top 50 employers for women and has been commended for encouraging career progression for mothers.

There's a recognition that such measures need to be accompanied by a change of recruitment culture, with managers encouraged to think differently to avoid unconsciously recruiting in their own image. "It's about learning to think differently without doing things artificially," says Gold. "Moya will not look at a shortlist unless it is 50–50 men and women. If that isn't the case she will tell the recruitment agency that they have to look harder."

**VOTES FOR WOMEN**
SUFFRAGETTE LEADERS AT EARL'S COURT, 1908

**VOTES FOR WOMEN**
WOMEN'S FREEDOM LEAGUE POSTER PARADE, c.1907

**VOTES FOR WOMEN**
WELSH SUFFRAGETTES, CORONATION PROCESSION, 1911

**VOTES FOR WOMEN**
LEIGH AND NEW RELEASED FROM PRISON, 1908

**VOTES FOR WOMEN**
LONE SUFFRAGETTE IN WHITEHALL, c.1908

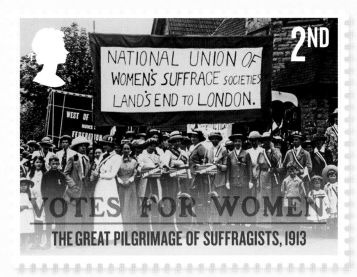

**VOTES FOR WOMEN**
THE GREAT PILGRIMAGE OF SUFFRAGISTS, 1913

# EXCEEDING POTENTIAL

Korn Ferry, the world's preeminent people and organisational consulting firm, understands that gender equality is crucial to success

WWW.KORNFERRY.COM

"Korn Ferry aligns an organisation's talent with its strategy to enable it to achieve exceptional performance through its people," says Karin Barnick, Senior Client Partner at Korn Ferry, the world's preeminent people and organisational consulting firm. Korn Ferry places a candidate every three minutes. It has a database of over 4.4 million professionals, and more than 100,000 people benefit from its leadership-development programmes each month.

The company was founded in Los Angeles in 1969 and was focused on placing executives in roles. However, since acquiring Hay Group in 2015, it now works with clients across all aspects of their talent strategies. While Korn Ferry remains the largest executive search firm globally, nowadays more than half its work is in advising companies on every element of their people and organisational strategy from pay and reward to organisational design.

"We help our clients design their organisation – the structure, roles and responsibilities," says Barnick. "We help them understand the talent they need to execute that strategy, the gaps they have and how to close that gap, be that through recruiting external talent or developing internal talent." Korn Ferry has tremendous reach through its 50 offices and 7,000 employees around the globe and an annual turnover of $2 billion. One of the company's flagship offices is in London, which is home to approximately 700 employees.

Nearly half a century of work in executive search and talent consulting has provided Korn Ferry with a deep understanding of the issues surrounding gender balance in the workplace. "Having a gender balance at the top of an organisation is critical to success," says Barnick. "A diversity of experience and opinions leads to better and more rounded business decisions."

Despite this, she feels, there are still too few women in senior positions within business, for many reasons. A male majority at senior levels can lead to unconscious bias which can impact many aspects of talent strategy from recruitment to career paths and compensation. Korn Ferry uses its unique combination of executive search and strategic consultancy to help clients create inclusive workplaces. They advocate a 'shared responsibility approach' where employees, managers, leaders and other stakeholders all have a role in tackling any systemic barriers impeding efforts to achieve diversity and inclusion.

This business model has earned Korn Ferry significant recognition. It won gold in the People and Performance category in the *FT* Management Consultants 2018 awards. Last year, it was recognised by Hunt Scanlon as the world's largest search firm. The firm supports its consulting capabilities through the Korn Ferry Institute, its research and analytics arm set up to share expert viewpoints on talent and leadership and to demonstrate how strategic talent decisions contribute to firms' competitive advantage, success and growth.

The company's September 2017 report, *Women CEOs Speak*, supported by the Rockefeller Foundation, sought to identify the common success factors among 59 US chief executives. It found that 60 per cent had a background in STEM (science, technology, engineering and maths) skills or had financial, business or economics experience.

"It shows that there needs to be a schoolroom-to-boardroom approach," says Barnick. "If you are going to change the world, you can't do so by intervening at a single point. You have to have a holistic approach."

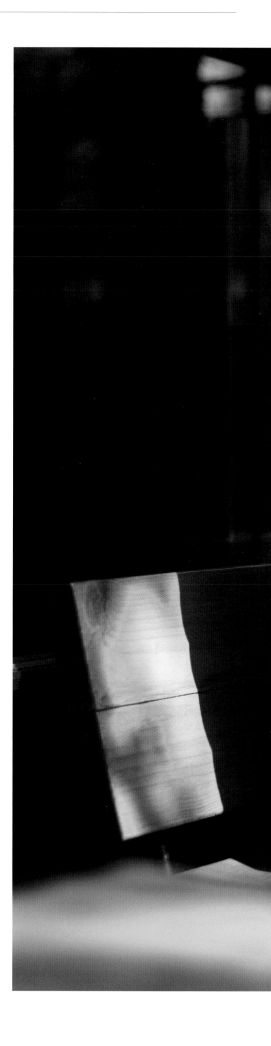

# KNOWLEDGE IS POWER

Which? has been championing the rights of consumers for 60 years

WWW.WHICH.CO.UK

Pity the shopper of 1956, for whom every purchase was something of a lottery. Would this washing machine prove to be good value? Was this toaster built to last? Consumers lacked independent advice – and so, in a London garage in 1957, *Which?* magazine began testing goods and services, and publishing the results. From this humble beginning, Which? has grown to become the UK's largest consumer organisation, with more than 1.7 million members and supporters.

The world may have changed, but Which? is still a voice for consumers, asking questions on their behalf and championing their rights. "We put power into the hands of the consumer," says Group People Director Angela Williams. "Our ambition is to tackle consumer detriment, as we give impartial, expert advice on important decisions that matter in people's daily lives – whether it be choosing a TV, buying a house or writing a will." The general public can also access free information online, from consumer rights advice to choosing a university: Which? aims to support consumers at every life moment.

Which? takes a campaigning role too, working with government, regulators and businesses to drive change. The "Safeguard us from Scams" campaign is a great example of how Which? harnessed legal powers, listened to consumers' experiences, and provided expert advice to deliver results that will make a difference. This super-complaint to the Payment Systems Regulator resulted in a series of actions for the banking industry to help protect consumers from scams and offer them redress in the future.

For Which? employees, internal practices reflect the company's external reputation of fairness and trust. "We project our values back on ourselves," says Williams, "ensuring that our people feel passionate about what we stand for." Which? recently reviewed the design of

its leadership team, creating a broader structure that has – for the first time – a female Chair of its commercial board, reflecting the equal role already played by women on the Executive Committee, the Council of Trustees and the employee population as a whole. As a consequence, Which? has seen a change of pace.

"We've seen a move towards up-skilling and recognition that we need more diverse skills," says Williams. "We're working more flexibly, enabling our people to take greater responsibility and have autonomy."

This involves nurturing new recruits, while developing the talents of existing employees. A change in environment has helped. "We have a lovely, listed building in central London, but it was quite dark, with people siloed into their area of activity," says Williams. "With the newly refurbished space we're more agile. We no longer have fixed desks; people come together to collaborate in cross-functional teams and our ambition is to become a 'digital-first' organisation."

Thanks to this new approach, employees can work together on projects to find solutions and deliver them in a creative and timely manner. On A-Level results day, a team from the press office and Which? University spent the day together responding to media enquiries and offering much-needed advice to students via online question and answer sessions.

At the heart of this revolution, Which? continues to tackle consumer detriment and make individuals as powerful as the organisation they deal with in their daily lives. One organisational value is the idea of action; of doing things today, not tomorrow. "The world may have changed, but our aims are still the same," says Williams. "We are a voice for the consumers, asking questions on their behalf, championing their rights, and giving impartial advice on important daily decisions. We'll do the same for the next 60 years too."

# ARTISTS IN RESIDENCE

Led by two dynamic women, Archco Developments
has taken the male-dominated world of property
development by storm

WWW.ARCHCO.CO.UK

"A home is the most expensive thing most people will ever buy," says Siobhan Cook, CEO of Essex-based Archco Developments. "We create developments that are personal because of the individual details we add. We offer something the customer wouldn't get from another developer, which is why 80 per cent of our developments sell off-plan."

In 2016, Archco Developments topped the Fortuna 50 index of fastest-growing, women-led small businesses, published in the *Sunday Times*. The company's position reflected a growth rate five times that of its nearest competitor. What was also striking was that Archco Developments was the only property developer on the list. "People tend to think of property development as a male industry," says Cook, "but I think that as women we bring a whole new level of organisation and scrutiny to it. We cut out all the building jargon for one thing. As long as you really know your industry, you get respect."

Cook and her business partner Gayle Horne, who has 25 years' experience as an estate agent, launched Archco Developments in 2007 – a less than auspicious time for the property sector. They quickly proved themselves adept at refurbishing neglected properties and spotting vacant plots of land with development potential. "You can't know everything at the start," says Cook, "so we built up a team of site managers, architects and building professionals, all at the top of their game, who we continue to work with today."

Building regulations and shifting environmental standards require constant vigilance but, as Cook says, "We like to go above and beyond the ordinary. Regulations can change during the lifespan of a property, so you need to be really mindful of that and use only the best quality materials. We're thorough in everything we do. For instance, we employ an acoustician on all

of our projects. There is nothing worse than moving in and finding you can hear the neighbours."

Cook's training and expertise as an interior designer have contributed greatly to Archco Developments' reputation for beautifully finished properties. "Buying a new-build can mean you still have work to do before you move, but we are design-driven," she says, "we make our apartments and houses look as nice as they can so our clients don't need to upgrade. You develop a rapport with the people you are selling to, so it's important that they get something unique for their money."

Building good relationships locally has resulted in Archco Developments taking on an expanding role in social housing work, for which it provides architectural and building services in return for the chance to develop, say, unused church land. "It is more than just building houses; it's about providing housing in mixed-use developments that benefits a community."

Cook, who is a Prince's Trust mentor with Lambeth Council, sees a future in which Archco Developments continues to build bright, contemporary and beautifully fitted homes, while bringing its high standards and expertise to a growing list of community-based projects. "I love the residential work," she says, "but with our experience we are in a position to give something back through mixed-use developments that are more than just commercial ventures."

Archco Developments' recent endorsement from the Fortuna 50 judges and its steadily growing residential and mixed-use portfolio are impressive enough. But the company's achievements are all the more remarkable given that it rose from the property crash into a flourishing, female-led company that is making its mark on homes and communities in a traditionally male-dominated industry.

# THE WHEELS ARE TURNING

The auto dealership Lookers is driving diversity in the traditionally male-dominated world of cars

WWW.LOOKERS.CO.UK

You might not expect a car dealership to be a rainbow flag-waving champion of diversity. But over the past year, the British motor retailer Lookers has become just that, with a series of initiatives that have marked it out as an impressive driver of change.

Aiming to be "meaningfully and noticeably different", the company has created a culture of equality by supporting women, families and LGBT people. "We live and work in around 160 communities across the country and employ more than 8,500 staff," says Ian Dinning, Head of Marketing Communications. "It just makes sense for our staff to be reflective of the people who come into our dealerships."

The UK car industry has always been a male-dominated one: the international body Catalyst, which aims to accelerate progress for women in work, estimates that only 16 per cent of the sector are female. For Andrew Stephenson, Group People Director at Lookers, the first challenge was how to progress brilliant women through the ranks.

"To be honest, we found that a lot of women were taking maternity leave and not coming back," he says. "So one of the first things we did was to introduce a maternity package of 12 months full pay, plus benefits. It's designed to give women the financial support to take the first year off, then hopefully return and build a career with us."

The company also aligned itself to the 30% Club, which aims to achieve 30 per cent representation for women on FTSE100 boards by 2020. "There has already been a massive change in mindset," explains Stephenson. "For example, women used to make up just 0.1 per cent of all our technical apprentices.

Now it's 5 per cent and we are confident we'll get that up to 30 per cent in two years' time."

Lookers has also been working hard to promote LGBT diversity. It joined forces with Stonewall to become a Diversity Champion, educating staff to ensure that lesbian, gay, bisexual and transgender people are accepted without exception. "We have hired a Group Diversity Manager and we're about to launch our first LGBT network," says Stephenson.

Other initiatives are aimed at promoting a healthy work–life balance. "Our sector is notorious for long hours," says Stephenson. "So last year we added 40,000 days of holiday into our business, which means the vast majority of people now have at least five weeks annual leave. Many have seven."

Ian describes the company's policies as "the first steps on a long journey", but the results are already impressive. As well as achieving a dramatic reduction in staff turnover, Lookers was recognised by the Top Employers Institute as one of the Top Employers in the UK in 2017. It was also rated the second highest in Glassdoor's 20 Companies for Work–Life Balance.

"The motor industry is very competitive," says Stephenson, "and being meaningfully and noticeably different will make us a more attractive place to work, which means we can recruit the best people and continue our success."

Stephenson hopes that the company's progressive policies will help accelerate change across all sectors. "There are lots of people talking about this kind of stuff, but we're not just talking about it," he says. "We are taking diversity incredibly seriously and hopefully our actions will have a big impact."

# UPWARDLY MOBILE

Multinational corporation Brightstar aims to lead the way
in opening up lines of communication – especially for women

WWW.BRIGHTSTAR.COM

## "The benefits of increasing online access in terms of education, health and prosperity will be enormous for everyone"

Emer Timmons, Brightstar

"A can-do attitude is what determines success in Brightstar," says Emer Timmons, the company's Chief Marketing Officer and President, Global Enterprise Channel. Brightstar's dynamic ethos and focus on talent has seen it carve out a special position in the mobile technology industry, while becoming a beacon of diversity. By actively promoting equal opportunities, the company demonstrates that a diverse workplace makes for a better work environment and a more successful business.

Brightstar looks after mobile phones for leading carriers, retailers, enterprises and public-sector organisations across six continents. Its services include supply-chain and retail solutions, financing, insurance, repair, accessories, trade-in and recycling. Headquartered in Miami, the company has more than 50,000 clients and handles in excess of 100 million devices every year. "What makes Brightstar unique is the combination of our scope and scale, and the people, platforms and intelligence that we bring together," says Timmons. "All businesses generate an ever-increasing amount of data, but we put it to work to drive the outcomes that our customers want."

The company maintains its competitive edge by constantly investing in innovation, including in people as well as systems and products. Timmons herself is a prime example of Brightstar's recruitment of talent. She joined the company from BT, where she was the first female president in the telecommunication giant's history. She has been a member of the Women's Business Council since 2013; and her work promoting gender equality saw her placed fourth on the *Financial Times* and HERoes Champions of Women In Business list.

Brightstar's commitment to equality was one of the things that most attracted Timmons to the company. She has become involved in its internal Women's Network, which regularly holds breakfast meetings; and in other initiatives to champion women both within and outside the company. This builds on Timmons's work in the public arena, where she gives speeches, including an address to the United Nations at the Annual Women's Commission on the Status of Women globally.

Brightstar is a founder member of Next 3B, an organisation that seeks to realise the global potential of the next 3 billion people joining the internet. Initial projects are now taking place in India and Rwanda, providing underprivileged women with access and training to network-connected smartphones. The aim is to improve their lives and create a ripple effect of economic and social activity with their families, friends and into their villages. Timmons is spearheading Brightstar's partnership with The Next 3B. "The benefits of increasing online access in terms of education, health and prosperity will be enormous," she says. "And while all genders will benefit, it will be of particular advantage to females."

Timmons is developing her work in the wider field of gender equality. This includes launching Men as Agents of Change, which aims to encourage male executives in the FTSE 350 to actively sponsor female talent. "It's 100 years since women won the vote in the UK," she says, "and we've travelled an immense way in that time. But women are still under-represented at board level in Britain, so there's still work to be done."

Passionate about gender equality, Timmons is proud to work for a company that shares her values. By taking steps to build a diverse workforce, Brightstar is proving that what's good for women is good for business, the economy, and society too.

# BUILDING FOR THE FUTURE

Family-owned construction firm Wates is expert at everything from high-density housing to high-profile heritage properties

WWW.WATES.CO.UK

There are very few British companies that can still describe themselves as family-owned more than a century after they were founded, but Wates is very proud to be a member of that elite band. "The vision and values that the family has had through the years forms the bedrock for how the company does business now," says James Wates CBE, Chairman of the Wates Group. "It ensures a long-term perspective that is integral to the whole way in which the company operates."

Edward Wates established the business as a housebuilder in 1897. Now, 121 years later, his great-grandson James is chairman of what is now a construction, development and property services group. In its most recent financial year, Wates enjoyed a pre-tax profit of £35.5 million (a 17.1 per cent annual increase) on a turnover of £1.53 billion (up by 20.4 per cent).

Wates is a UK-wide contractor engaged in a broad range of commercial and mixed-use developments. It is heavily involved in homebuilding with a focus on high-density housing, such as the development of Greenwich Peninsula that will provide homes for 23,000 residents within 48 acres of green, open space. It is also a specialist provider of senior living and student accommodation.

In addition, the group has a growing reputation for managing heritage projects. For instance, Wates Construction was behind Amanda Levette's stunning Exhibition Road Quarter extension for the V&A, is advancing building work on the major refurbishment programme at the House of Lords' Millbank House in Westminster, and is upgrading the Palace of Westminster's fire detection and alarm systems.

Wates also has a substantial mechanical and engineering (M&E) presence following the acquisition of Shepherd Engineering Services (SES) in 2015. SES specialises in the design and installation of building

services and infrastructure solutions covering all aspects of M&E. Last year, it successfully provided full design and build services to more than 250 apartments across 13 floors of the Plimsoll Building in King's Cross, London.

Wates is now one of the UK's leading providers of maintenance services for the social housing sector, looking after 500,000 properties for local authorities and housing associations. With around 4,000 staff and a supply chain that employs a further 10,000, Wates is very much a people business. A good example is the Zero Harm: We're Safer Together campaign, launched in 2016 as part of the group's commitment to creating a safe and secure environment wherever it operates. This has contributed to a marked reduction in safety incidents: in 2016 there was a 73 per cent reduction in dangerous occurrences, and a 28 per cent fall in the lost-time injury rate.

Wates's mission is to deliver outstanding buildings on time and on budget while collaborating with customers, consultants, supply-chain partners and the communities in which it works. Its Reshaping Tomorrow programme puts sustainability at the heart of the business with a specific focus on ensuring that all of its projects include at least one social enterprise. This helped Wates twice win the Queen's Award for Enterprise in the Sustainable Development category. In 2016/17, it swept the board at industry awards and was named Contractor of the Year by both *Construction News* and *Building* magazine, while Chief Exec Andrew Davies was named CEO of the year.

As Wates prepares for its 125th anniversary in 2022, it is focused on a strategy that is already well embedded in the company. "We go into the future with optimism without being over-confident," says James Wates. "We believe that we are following the right path, working within our core capabilities and ensuring we have a well-balanced portfolio."

# "The vision the family has had through the years forms the bedrock for how the company does business now"

—

James Wates CBE, Chairman of the Wates Group

# THE POWER OF DESIGN

Global tech company Arm designs the "brain" running the world's smartphones and connected devices

WWW.ARM.COM

"No one individual makes us successful," explains Kirsty Gill, Chief People Officer at Arm. "It's all about the collective, with people being able to share their views and ideas with anyone in the organisation. Everyone's perspective is listened to. I joke that I have 100 people in my team but in reality it's around six thousand – that's the total number of people the company employs."

This semiconductor intellectual property company doesn't make any products, but it designs the "brains" behind many of the processing units and chips that power everything from sensors to smartphones to supercomputers all over the world, working with partners such as Samsung, Google and Huawei.

Originally founded as Acorn in Cambridge in 1978, it made some of the first home computers, including the BBC Micro. In 1990 the company became Arm when it worked with Apple on its Newton device. This innovative handheld computer was a commercial flop, and Arm's growing expertise in designing processors for such devices was a skill without a market while PCs dominated the tech field. When the mobile revolution hit at the end of the decade the company's fortunes soared, and Arm now employs staff all over the world, with its UK headquarters still based in Cambridge.

Among Arm's "Core Beliefs" is allowing each staff member to "be your brilliant self". "There isn't an 'Arm person' as such," says Gill, "because people don't leave their individual personalities at the door when they come to work," she says. "They're required to be personally brilliant, but also in a collective way that reduces internal competition and benefits everyone around them."

With diversity and inclusion, the emphasis at Arm is to challenge people's belief in what they think they know. In the male-dominated tech field, that means changing mindsets about gender imbalance – such as assuming there are not enough women engineers, or that the market is too competitive. "It's easy to find barriers in the industry around gender," says Gill. "It's easy for people to get comfortable, to say: 'This doesn't apply to me or my team.' We focus on the success stories, on putting across the message that it's possible."

For women in the company, Gill and her team look at the way the company hires, develops and retains them. The same approach applies to people from different nationalities and backgrounds, or to non-English speakers. This inclusive approach to working has earned the company international recognition. *Forbes* named Arm the 12th most innovative company in the world, Arm won the OC Excellence Award for corporate social responsibility in 2016, and this year it was ranked by job website Glassdoor's anonymous employee ratings as one of the top five UK companies for work–life balance.

Arm's diversity strategy not only chimes with its corporate culture but is also crucial to its future success. With its sights set on continuing to grow beyond the present mobile and handheld devices, Arm needs to diversify and attract talented staff with a new way of thinking. "That's why it's important to bring people in from different aspects of life," says Gill. "We need engineers, for example, with a broad mindset who have experienced life in different ways." Arm's culture of inclusivity and innovation is at the heart of its success, and the key to its future as the power behind the connected world.

"We need engineers with a broad mindset – who have experienced life in different ways"

——

Kirsty Gill, Arm

# POTENTIAL ENERGY

Small-business specialist Opus Energy takes
pride in offering positive opportunities

WWW.OPUSENERGY.COM

Over the past 15 years, Opus Energy has enjoyed rapid expansion from its position as a fresh-faced start-up to become the sixth largest B2B energy provider in Britain. It works alongside hundreds of thousands of small- and medium-sized businesses, supplying on average 90 per cent renewable energy to its customers. It achieves this partially by working with, and buying from, independent generators such as farmers who specialise in solar, hydro, wind and anaerobic digestion power. For the company's customers, it prioritises certainty and simplicity, so customers can focus their energy on running their businesses.

Nikki Flanders, who became Opus Energy's Chief Operating Officer in February 2017, believes that it is vital for businesses of all sizes to work side by side, maintaining a network of support. "One opportunity we have as UK businesses is to actively collaborate with each other," she says. "We do this is by creating channels to share knowledge in a digestible way." Via an online platform called Brighter Business, Opus Energy provides leadership advice from experts who have successfully founded businesses and offers tips and guidance to people who are considering starting or expanding a small business.

Diversity is a hugely important part of Opus Energy's strategy. "It is about giving everybody a positive opportunity," says Flanders. Bringing employee voices to the forefront is one way in which Flanders strives to implement diversity of thought at Opus Energy. "Especially in an established company, mechanisms need to be created that give team members a platform to inform decision making," she says. "It is our job as leaders to ensure voices are heard, and then decide where change can be made. We have created 'mini boards' to cover all key areas of the

business so that subject matter experts at all levels can directly shape our business outcome. Employee forums and leadership roadshows give our teams a platform to ask questions and challenge."

A great deal of work has been done at Opus Energy to build early career opportunities and in ensuring their apprenticeship schemes represent as wide a range of people as possible. "The current programme has a nearly 50/50 split – 47 per cent female," says Flanders. "But as well as the gender split, we have a really diverse group of individuals in the apprenticeship team: different backgrounds, cultures, ways of looking at things. That is critical for any successful business."

It's clear that Flanders believes that the key to diversity lies in ensuring that there is diversity of thought and that it's the leader's responsibility to create the environment to tap into the intellectual property that each team member provides. "For me, it is too sweeping to say that we simply need to focus on any one demographic. As business leaders, we need to innately understand the value and richness that diversity brings, so it is not seen as a box-ticking exercise."

Opus Energy works hard to create a positive working environment. "Running a growing business requires a lot of hard work from a lot of people," says Flanders. "We try our best to balance the work with fun, by making a meaningful contribution to our local communities, as well as supporting individual growth through development opportunities." With support mechanisms in place, such openness can be reciprocated. "If people are respectfully saying what they think without being shut down," says Flanders, "everybody becomes a bit braver."

# CREAM RISES TO THE TOP

JK7 sees a role for women as the crème de la crème in the field of skincare treatments

WWW.JK7SKINCARE.COM

For Karin Klein, co-founder and CEO of the skincare specialist JK7, women are key to her business. "I would not work without women, as we together create a very harmonious environment and really make things happen in the now," she says. "Women can contribute to a huge change for the better of the planet, creating business that focus on the wellbeing of each individual, rather than power and destruction."

When her husband, Jurgen Klein, founder of skincare company Jurlique, sold his brand and moved to Hawaii, to set up a luxury spa retreat, Karin encouraged him to set up a company specialising in more advanced treatments. "He was sick and tired of the lies people tell in the industry," says Karin. "But then he started to make his own spa products in the commercial kitchen, and they were wonderful. I challenged him to stop complaining and instead to create something better than what was available commercially. I said: 'Can you bring a product to market that is truly natural, organic and high performing with no chemicals at any stage of production?' He was hesitant – he's a biochemist and knows the difficulties – but he rose to the challenge."

And so, in 2015, after seven years of research and testing, JK7 was born. It is a pure, organic and anti-ageing, high-end skincare brand, handmade in tiny batches, using only the best natural ingredients and the most precious and expensive essential oils (including rose, myrrh and jasmine), powerful JK7 Signature Extracts and healing herbs. They are designed to improve the health of the skin, as well as its appearance.

"The abundance of herbal and natural ingredients in our products creates a synergy to help the skin function exactly as it's supposed to," says Karin. "We

can't stop skin ageing – any cream that claims that is lying – but we can work against free radicals, preventing protein degeneration and accelerated ageing. We see skincare as one of the tools for a better, healthier holistic lifestyle. Our customers tend to be people who already have a high awareness of ecology and of their bodies, and who make conscious choices about the products they use. Kathy Freston, best-selling vegan author, is one of our fans."

The range is currently available for purchase in London, New York, Hawaii, Switzerland and Austria, from selected spas, hotels, high-end retail outlets and airport lounges, and is about to be launched in the Netherlands, Japan, Hong Kong, Taiwan and Russia. Products can also be bought online via JK7's website. Future plans include an all-natural skin-whitening cream that works against age spots and discoloration as well as expansion into the Far East and Australia.

There are now 22 different products in the range, including face washes, serums and lotions. "Our skincare is very exclusive and will never be for the mass market, or available everywhere," explains Karin. "That's because we took the decision not to compromise on quality or standards at any stage of the process. For example, each plant extraction takes about 50 hours with our spagyric extraction method that enhances the lifeforce of each healing plant, and every bottle is hand-sterilised, hand-filled and hand-packed. We have created something that is truthful, effective as well as luxurious. There is no comparison anywhere else on the market."

"I feel a strong call to clear the illusion of any quick fix and support women to find their inner beauty and themselves. Then they can radiate out and life in their full power."

# LAYING FOUNDATIONS FOR THE FUTURE

IT and business services specialist CGI is creating a high-tech culture that is truly inclusive

WWW.CGI-GROUP.CO.UK

From local and public government to defence, energy, utilities and financial services, the information technology services company CGI has been a pioneer in the IT industry since it was founded more than 40 years ago. CGI has laid the foundation for critical technology infrastructure across a diverse group of sectors. The company has also been hard at work laying foundations that will shape the future of the IT industry by fostering greater diversity in the workplace.

"The technology sector was born in the last 40 years, so in many ways it's still in its infancy," says Tara McGeehan, President, CGI in the UK. "It's very important that we set examples, focus on progress and create environments that present equal opportunity for all." She observes that IT-based degrees still attract more male than female applicants. "We tend to see more males coming into the sector so we have to work hard to increase gender diversity – not just for altruistic reasons, but because we want a better mix of ideas and opinions."

To this end, CGI has established schemes aimed at laying a foundation for the future. Female employees on maternity leave and planning a return to work are offered online training courses while still at home. CGI has also rolled out an ongoing series of unconscious-bias awareness sessions, and implemented a successful "Bring Your Daughter to Work" programme.

The company's search for talent begins when the employees of tomorrow are still at school. CGI is a patron of The Prince's Trust, and members regularly volunteer to visit pupils and promote career opportunities. In 2016, to coincide with CGI's 40th anniversary, the company introduced a new global programme called Dream Connectors, to help employees connect with the community around them.

In addition to seeking candidates with diverse skill-sets not specific to gender and increasing opportunities around STEM (science, technology, engineering, maths) at entry level, CGI established an apprenticeships scheme that provides women with a path into the IT industry.

"Apprenticeships are important to us and to the government," says McGeehan. "We're using our various apprenticeship schemes – including a Higher Apprenticeship Programme and a Service Desk Apprenticeship Programme – to encourage more young women to join IT in a way that doesn't disrupt their lifestyles. We are trying to be as creative as we can be to level out the playing field and ensure that the work environment presents opportunity for everyone entering the workforce who is interested in a position in IT."

In recent years, the company has also assisted a technological breakthrough in the voting process, thanks to an electronic vote-counting system called eCounting. After being awarded a £6.5 million contract, CGI introduced eCounting in the 2012 Scottish local government elections, using it again in 2017. It enabled voters to see the election results much sooner. Where manual counting of ballot papers can take up to four days to complete, digital scanning takes only a matter of hours and calculations are made in mere minutes. "We're actively involved in making the process of calculating votes easier," says McGeehan.

CGI has been widely recognised for these innovations, winning plaudits such as the Top Employers Institute's Top Employer in the UK Award, as well as Top Employer Europe certification for five years running. It supports a workplace environment that values a variety of opinions, perspectives and cultures, in order to maintain a working team that boasts not only breadth but the highest standard of performance.

# "We work hard to increase gender diversity because we want a better mix of ideas and opinions"

Tara McGeehan, CGI

# DRIVING DIVERSITY

Ford's female-friendly staff policies are breaking down barriers in the automotive world

WWW.FORD.CO.UK/EXPERIENCE-FORD/CAREERS

The car industry is usually reckoned to have something of a masculine image, making it a challenge to attract female talent. One company determined to overcome this is Ford, which is not only consistently the country's best-selling vehicle brand but also the market leader when it comes to maternity rights.

"We have a maternity policy that is probably best in class, not just in our industry but across the UK," says Lara Nicoll, Ford's Diversity and Inclusion Manager. "We are working with the government to tackle discrimination against women because we believe that we have really strong policies to share with other businesses."

Technology and electrification are driving a shift in the automotive industry not seen since Henry Ford first made the car accessible to the masses over 100 years ago. Traditions are being challenged and diversity embraced as the industry shifts into a new era.

Women have always made up an important part of the company's workforce and, despite the fact that historically it has been difficult to attract women into engineering and the STEM subjects, Ford works hard to promote equality. "We know that a gender-balanced workforce performs better than one that isn't balanced, and we also know that from a consumer perspective, women have a significant voice in purchase decisions," says Andy Barratt, Ford of Britain Chairman and Managing Director. "It's also important, outside of any other moral or social consideration, that you have a workforce that represents your customer base."

To challenge stereotypes, Ford sends female representatives to schools and universities, whilst also inviting students to the company's manufacturing plants. "We try and send women engineers to work with schools so that children's first impression of what an engineer looks like is a woman," says Nicoll. "That can make such a

difference." Because of the relatively limited number of women with engineering qualifications, it is even more important to retain female employees after pregnancy. That's why Ford has placed an emphasis on maternity care that offers more than just enhanced pay. This approach includes a personalised maternity calendar, subsidised NCT antenatal classes, dedicated maternity guidance and regular company workshops, enabling pregnant employees to share their thoughts about parenting in a work context. The latter has proved so successful that it has been extended to expectant fathers.

The firm also takes a positive approach to flexible working, and one of its larger sites has a crèche. "We have a wide ranging approach, but it's things like the workshop, which is so simple to do, that attract the most interest," says Nicoll. "We want to share this process with other companies and exchange ideas."

In addition to its policies on maternity and education outreach, Ford supports a number of other initiatives. It has a women's network, supports and promotes National Women In Engineering Day and hosts International Women of Excellence workshops that address the workplace needs of female employees. The company also co-sponsors *Autocar* magazine's awards for the top 100 British women working in the automotive sector – with Ford itself having more than 20 members of staff featured.

The company's proactive approach is geared towards another major target that Nicoll identifies – reducing the national gender pay gap. "Research suggests that if more women went into STEM-related occupations, then the pay gap would decrease," she says. "This is an evolving issue but now there is momentum from the government and a focus on gender pay. As engineering is a relatively well-paid industry, it's one that we need to encourage more women into."

# EMPOWERING FEMALE CONSULTANTS

Procorre is helping women to enjoy a
prosperous life in the world of consultancy

WWW.PROCORRE.COM

Despite the potential benefits of greater career flexibility, better work–life balance and higher hourly rates of pay, women remain significantly under-represented in contracting – the proportion of working women who are self-employed contractors is less than half that of men. Global professional services consultancy Procorre is determined to redress the balance, by encouraging and supporting more women to join its highly skilled, 1,500-strong contractor workforce.

"We advocate women in the workplace, we encourage women to join our consulting workforce, and we know that clients often consider women to be more diligent and versatile," says Procorre's Group Sales and Marketing Director Anne O'Donnell. The company began in Switzerland as a collaboration of professional services consultancies, and now has offices in London, Bristol, Dublin, Geneva, Singapore and Perth, with consultants across many sectors, including finance, medical devices, automated intelligence, energy and resources.

"While it's great to see almost a million women in the UK bringing their skills and expertise to bear on a consultancy basis, they are significantly in the minority compared to men," says O'Donnell. "Women can break through the glass ceiling as a contractor by collaborating together – we can empower one another and build stronger teams with equal vision, experiences and ability to deliver our projects. As the economic outlook improves and demand for contractors increases, we expect to see more women look again at how consultancy could work for them as a positive career move."

By offering support, generous financial benefits and global project opportunities, Procorre helps its female consultants strike the right work–life balance and enables them to have full control of their workload. It is also partnering with the Wise campaign, which inspires women and girls to study and build careers in STEM (science, technology, engineering and manufacturing) disciplines, where females have always been under-represented. As a trusted provider of advisory and implementation solutions to clients worldwide and operating across STEM sectors, the company is ideally placed to support the campaign's aim to "boost the talent pool from classroom to boardroom".

Procorre consultant Caroline Chenier, a long-standing IT training contractor and project manager, believes more women are benefiting from the freedom of choice that comes with being a contractor. "I think the reason more women don't take the plunge is because they like the security of employment and are often reluctant to sell themselves," she says. "But I can finish one contract on a Friday and, if I want, start another on the Monday. Most of my work is through word of mouth or being headhunted. I've not had to look for a single job, so I definitely don't regret becoming a consultant. I really enjoy the freedom – the fundamental aspect I love about working with Procorre is the amount of life I get back."

O'Donnell recognises that moving into contracting can be a daunting challenge for some women; but she believes Procorre has the structures in place to enable female contractors to build successful careers.

"Going self-employed is not always an easy decision," she says, "particularly for those with young families who may be concerned that there is less financial support for maternity breaks and childcare compared to their employed peers. However, the change to the childcare voucher regime should be significant in encouraging more women to consider making the switch, and we offer advice to help people get their consultancy careers off the ground, as well as ongoing support to ensure they get the most out of this rewarding career choice."

## "Women can break through the glass ceiling by collaborating together"

—

Anne O'Donnell, Procorre

# MOTIVATIONAL SPEAKER

A balance of creativity and technology, Estelon's speakers
stand head and shoulders above the competition

WWW.ESTELON.COM

A small collection of battered old radios and stereos lies in a cabinet at the head office of luxury speaker manufacturer Estelon in Tallinn, Estonia. "This is the root of Estelon's history," says Alissa Vassilkova. "These belonged to our grandparents – they're how my father Alfred learnt where sound comes from. He opened them up and made them better as his love of music evolved into a curiosity for physics." They signify the start of a lifetime devoted to the dream of delivering perfect sound – a dream that led Alfred Vassilkov to found Estelon in April 2010.

Alfred Vassilkov, now 60, was born in St Petersburg and grew up surrounded by music. His father played the accordion at dances, his aunt taught piano and Alfred himself would tune into Radio Luxembourg to hear tinny renditions of his favourite Western pop songs. Soon his love of music and his inquisitive nature combined to take things in a new direction. "I wanted to understand how you could create sound from electricity," he says. "I began to take radios apart and adjust them to make them better."

After studying acoustics in St Petersburg, Alfred began to build speakers from scratch for himself and his friends, even making the speakers for his own wedding, although Soviet-era restrictions meant that materials were limited. In the early 1980s, he moved from St Petersburg to Estonia, where his mother had been born, and began designing speakers for a company that made radios. Alfred started to develop and deploy innovative techniques, not only to secure the best sound but also to make skilful use of scarce resources.

Following the collapse of the Soviet Union, Estelon faced competition from western technology giants. Alfred continued to experiment, but also visited international shows to see the latest in speaker technology and discover what consumers wanted and needed. He travelled with his daughters, Alissa and Kristiina, schooling them between shows on the science of sound. Both daughters, as well as their partners, are involved with Estelon. "We can support his ideas and bring them to the world," says Alissa. "We are helping his dream come true every day."

Alfred continued to develop his own speakers, working on a prototype for five years until he was ready to reveal it to the family. Over breakfast, they agreed to start a company and within six months the first Estelon speaker system was showcased in Denver in the US. It immediately drew acclaim thanks not only to its incredible sound quality but also to its striking appearance. "The speakers look amazing but their sculptural quality is crucial to their engineering," he says. "They are built from the inside out and the appearance creates the best conditions for all the components inside."

Awards soon followed, with Estelon continuing to push the boundaries with each new model. "The Extreme, our largest speaker system to date, contains a lifetime of experience and knowledge and can be adusted in rooms of different sizes," says Alfred. "Our latest model is the Lynx, which is wireless and features modular hardware that can be upgraded to account for the latest technological developments."

With a presence in more than 25 countries and a reputation for cutting-edge engineering, Estelon is growing in size and prominence. Through it all, Alfred has remained the pioneering spirit at its heart, drawing on decades of experience and his fascination with the physics of sound in his determination to trailblaze new frontiers.

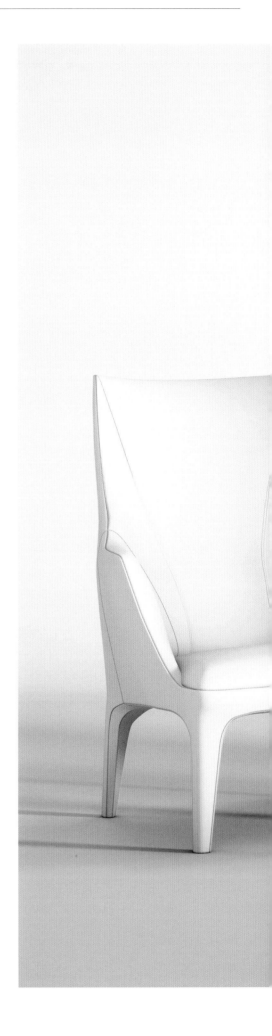

# A CLEARER VISION FOR EVERYONE

With an ethos rooted in social responsibility, Carl Zeiss Vision UK is focused on an inclusive and fulfilling workplace

WWW.ZEISS.CO.UK/VISION

Many companies talk about social responsibility but few have it as a founding principle. An optician called Carl Zeiss formed a company in Germany in 1846 to perfect the manufacture of lenses for scientific instruments, and the company that bears his name continues to perfect everything from medical instruments to spectacle lenses.

In 1889 the Carl Zeiss Foundation was founded. This set out to do three things: to safeguard technological progress in its field; to demonstrate awareness of its responsibility towards employees; and to support charities, especially those promoting science and engineering in education.

Ninety per cent of the company's business is now outside Germany, and Zeiss employs 27,000 people globally. Last year it had the best results in its 170-year history. This has allowed it to maintain its numerous worldwide initiatives. These range from granting €80m to universities pursuing excellence in science to saving the sight of over 100 million people through diagnostic techniques used in areas like the Amazonian basin.

For several years Zeiss has been a collaborator on the Mercy Ships, working alongside local communities to provide medical care for the most deprived regions in the world. In Britain, the company has donated equipment to the University of Cambridge, run clinical trials with Aston University and encouraged wider participation for children with fewer opportunities in the STEM (science, technology, engineering and maths) subjects.

"Another facet of the company's social responsibility relates to its own staff," says Andrew Leong-Son, UK & Ireland General Manager of Carl Zeiss Vision UK. "We've introduced programmes supporting a healthier lifestyle." He believes that employees today seek greater engagement with their workplace, wanting more from

work than just their salary. The company has provided its employees with Fitbits, free public transport, healthy cooking demonstrations and talks on improving sleep and managing mental health.

Carl Zeiss Vision UK has adopted policies to support a diverse, dynamic workplace. It actively looks to encourage an inclusive and supportive work environment. It also uses annual employee surveys to listen to staff feedback. "We are successful because of our employees, and we want to find and retain people who add quality and value," says Leong-Son. "If you are going to be an attractive employer for forward-thinking and diverse candidates, you need to consider the work culture and make people feel valued for their contribution. We have been restructuring competitive pay and policies including maternity benefits. From these changes we can create an exciting culture at work."

Central to this is the belief of a diverse organisation, where every employee can fulfil their potential and are part of Zeiss's founding fabric. "The focus here on employee and social responsibility as well as the financial future of the company, makes for a completely different atmosphere," says Leong-Son. "It's a different way of doing things and good people are increasingly attracted by companies that offer value in these ways."

The next challenge is to improve diversity at senior levels by attracting and nurturing top talent regardless of gender, colour, religion, age and sexual orientation. "The aim is to grow our talent from within," says Leong-Son, "so we are recruiting people who have the potential to lead the business in the future. We are investing in the necessary training on personal and technical skills to give them the opportunity to become the senior managers of the future."

# STONE ANGELS

Family-run jewellery firm Kohinoor is
inspired by Indian art and architecture

WWW.KOHINOORJEWELLERS.COM

Agra is a city steeped in history, famous for the iconic white marble Taj Mahal, built by Mughal emperor Shah Jahan. The former Mughal capital has for centuries also been home to jewellers, artisans and artists inspired by the rich heritage around them.

Family-owned and now in its fifth generation, the exclusive, appointment-only Kohinoor Jewellers creates distinctive pieces for a discerning global clientele. "Our business developed out of our heritage," says owner Ghanshyam Mathur. "Now we work with a contemporary fusion of art and jewellery based on Indian art, architecture and paintings."

The Mathur family's ancestors came to the old walled city of Agra in 1857 with the court of the last Mughal emperor Bahadur Shah Zafar. Since then, the family has collected fine gemstones, jewellery and art, becoming experts in the intricacies of Indian art over the generations. Ghanshyam, like his father before him, is a connoisseur of Indian art collected from diverse regions, periods and religions.

"We never run out of inspiration," he says. "There is so much variety in our past. And of course we have the Taj Mahal itself, which was the inspiration for the Taj Signature Collection. But we have also created a successful golf-themed collection, and a collection based on Bharatanatyam, a classical Indian dance, using the shapes and elegance of the dancers."

Ghanshyam's daughter Ruchira Mathur is Kohinoor's Executive Director. She works alongside her brother Milind Mathur, the company's Artistic Director and a graduate gemologist, certified by the Gemological Institute of America. "They both have a flair for working with gemstones," says Ghanshyam. "It's in their blood."

"My proudest work has been to help make Kohinoor an influential brand in the world of jewellery," says designer Ruchira. "The blessing of being born into an ancestral business family gave me the wings to fly with full support of the family. Women are now able to spread their talented knowledge in various spheres, be it designing or marketing. The sky is the limit."

The artistry and love of colour and pattern in Kohinoor's jewellery is expressed through gemstones of the highest quality. "Our jewellery is all about the stones, sapphires from Sri Lanka, for example, and rubies from Burma," says Ruchira. "We tend to buy stones in rough form and cut them to our specification." Often Kohinoor's jewellery begins not with a design but with the gemstones themselves, the design serving to enhance and display their particular qualities.

The brother-and-sister team bring a western sensibility to the jewellery collections, attuned to the tastes of the international visitors who come to Agra. "Ruchira and Milind have helped expose our jewellery to worldwide trends," says Ghanshyam. "Our customers demand the best quality and they know their jewellery. They immediately see that we offer very fine pieces."

The company also offers a bespoke jewellery service, which is particularly suited to overseas visitors staying in Agra. The combination of stones and choice of settings are discussed and detailed design options created. The finished pieces are then shipped on completion.

Kohinoor Jewellers exactly defines what Ghanshyam calls "contemporary fusion": the perfect setting of expertly cut gemstones, reflecting the cultural and artistic traditions of India, and a stylish ability to bring these strands together in refined contemporary jewellery. "This fusion of modern, bespoke and heritage comes through in all our work," says Ghanshyam. As in-the-know visitors to Kohinoor Jewellers have discovered, the Taj Mahal isn't the only thing of beauty worth seeing in Agra.

# THOUGHT LEADERSHIP

Positive social change is just one of the ways in which software consultancy ThoughtWorks is ahead of the curve

WWW.THOUGHTWORKS.COM

From its origins as a small management consultancy in a Chicago basement in the 1980s, ThoughtWorks has grown into a global software consultancy, which operates with a staff of more than 4,500 across 15 countries.

Its pioneering approach to software design and delivery has earned the company a reputation for independence of thought, and had a dynamic impact on the technology sector. The TechRadar section of the firm's website, for example, is considered vital reading across the industry for its unbiased assessment of new trends. And its revolutionary software developments continue to have a transformative effect on its clients.

ThoughtWorks energetically promotes positive social change, and has garnered widespread respect for its successful efforts towards equal gender distribution in its workforce. "In an industry with notoriously low female representation, half of all our graduates globally are female," says Chief Technology Officer Rebecca Parsons.

The company's structure is non-hierarchical, and every employee is encouraged to have an equal voice. "This also means that we are all equally accountable for our actions and success," says Parsons. In 2012, the company began to invest in global programmes such as the WiLD (women in leadership development) training programme for future female leaders. Its success can be measured by the number of senior roles that are now filled with alumni from these groups.

ThoughtWorks has also identified a productive benefit from diverse representation on its client projects. Women on software teams have remarked that having a healthy balance of women and men enables them to focus on their work, without the social pressures that can complicate a non-diverse environment.

In 2016, the company was named the winner of the Top Companies for Women Technologists programme by the Anita Borg Institute (ABI), a non-profit organisation focused on the advancement of women in computing. With the highest overall score, ThoughtWorks was recognised by the institute as "a true leader in recruiting, retaining and advancing more women in technical roles".

ThoughtWorks' mission for equal gender balance remains steadfast. But while it recognises the progress it has made, as Parsons said on accepting the award: "We're not done yet!"

# THE FABRIC OF LIFE

The silk scarves made by Elurra Gold are both a fashion statement and an assertion of self-worth

WWW.ELURRAGOLD.COM

Designers often talk about the power of their clothes. Few mean it quite as literally as Joyce Stockley, the designer behind the Elurra Gold label, whose luxury silk scarves are created to enlighten, empower and inspire women.

Made from silk crepe de Chine, they are both a fashion statement and an elegant, eloquent assertion of feminine potential. "I've called the collection B.E.E., which stands for 'believe, envisage, experience'," says Stockley. "The concept is that life offers unlimited opportunities for you to experience who you want to be, if you choose to believe and envisage yourself in that experience."

The collection features four different designs – Maidenhood, Motherhood, Womanhood and Sisterhood – intended to reflect the different stages of a woman's life. Each is a riot of creativity and colour, laced with motifs drawn from mythology, flora and fauna. "The scarves are designed to offer inspiration for each phase," explains Stockley. "For example, the Motherhood scarf features primroses, symbolising eternal love."

Elurra Gold isn't the first label to channel the transformative power of silk scarves: Hermès has built

a fashion empire on it. However, it is the first to style them as a self-help tool. "Our products are designed to build self-worth and help women feel amazing," says Stockley, who became a self-help convert after a near-fatal accident in 2011. "I was walking my dogs when I was hit by a car on a pedestrian crossing," she says. "I received major trauma injuries that confined me to a wheelchair for months. My convalescence gave me time to seek insight and purpose in life. I realised I wanted to create something that would offer that sort of inspiration in readily appreciable, portable form. That's when I thought of the scarves."

Her designs are inspired by art nouveau. "That was a period when women really broke the mould," says Stockley, "so it suits the idea of creating confidence." They are made at Beckford Silk in Tewkesbury and endorsed by the Made in Britain Campaign, which promotes British businesses.

As well as being beautiful, the scarves give a whole new meaning to the term "retail therapy". "I want to offer inspiration and comfort to women," says Stockley. "I believe it's important to help other people, if you can."

# CONSTRUCTING CONNECTIONS

For housebuilding expert Crest Nicholson, bringing
women onboard is crucial to the company's growing success

WWW.CRESTNICHOLSON.COM

The latest Office for National Statistics data reveals that, of the 2.3 million people working in the UK construction industry, only 12 per cent are women. This alarming statistic reveals the challenge the sector faces to increase diversity in a traditionally male-dominated field.

"At Crest Nicholson we recognise the importance of closing this gender gap and are taking proactive steps to encourage more women into the industry," says Jane Cookson, Group HR Director at the Chertsey-based housebuilder. "We have made significant changes to how we recruit new talent and are beginning to see positive results."

Crest Nicholson is making a name for its forward-thinking approach to recruitment. Established in 1963, the company builds nearly 3,000 new homes per year in the southern half of the UK, with an annual revenue of just over £1 billion. At 36 per cent, the proportion of women in the Crest Nicholson workforce may not sound immediately remarkable, but it's almost three times the construction industry average.

There are sound business reasons for this. "Our industry has a massive challenge ahead with a growing skills gap," explains Cookson. More than 800,000 new skilled workers are needed if housebuilding targets are to be met. "An important part of our strategy to fill this gap involves diversity and inclusion," says Cookson.

Over the past four years Crest Nicholson has invested significantly in its graduate recruitment programme to ensure it is reaching the right candidates to improve diversity and safeguard the future of the business. "We are working directly with universities that offer the right balance of talent," says Cookson, "as well as with the Royal Institution of Chartered Surveyors to

actively target female candidates and talk to them about the range of career opportunities at Crest Nicholson and across the construction industry. Our current graduate make-up is 34 per cent female, a significant increase from four years ago when we launched the programme." This shows the positive change that can be achieved when the business and education sectors work together to achieve a common goal.

One of the key challenges facing the construction industry is encouraging more women into apprenticeship roles, particularly on-site. "Currently only 13 per cent of our apprentices are women," says Cookson. "As an industry we must ensure the facilities and support systems are in place to encourage more women to enter traditionally male-dominated environments."

To encourage more women into the industry, Crest Nicholson hopes to capture the imaginations of potential workers early. "We get involved at the youngest possible age," says Cookson. "We engage with local schools, inviting pupils to site and showing them how you build a house and what it's like to be on a construction site. With older children, we've hosted workshops on STEM subjects [science, technology, engineering, mathematics] at our sites." Crest Nicholson hopes these young people will be inspired to apply for one of the 30 apprentice placements it offers every year or enrol on its award winning Site Management Academy.

Beyond the urgency of the skills gap, breaking down rigid gender roles in the industry improves performance all-round. "As a business we find that gender-balanced teams perform better," says Cookson. "The more balanced the workforce, the wider the range of characteristics and skill sets at our disposal."

# "As a business we find that gender-balanced teams perform better"

Jane Cookson, Group HR Director, Crest Nicholson

# EVENTS HORIZON

As UBM plc celebrates its centenary it remains as forward-looking as ever

WWW.UBM.COM

UBM plc reaches its centenary year as forward-looking as ever, bringing together and inspiring 3.4 million visitors a year at over 350 trade shows around the world. UBM was set up as United Newspapers in 1918 by the Liberal Prime Minister David Lloyd George. It has since had to adapt to change many times. From a newspaper publisher with interests in regional and later national editions, media, television and news distribution, UBM has emerged more recently as a focused business-to-business events organiser.

Connecting people at trade shows across 11 major business sectors (and many more sub-sectors) in more than 20 countries UBM events offer a unique opportunity to empower businesses and inspire the people that make up these professional communities. UBM events create tailored experiences that go beyond helping these companies simply showcase their work – they enable business people to achieve their ambitions, both professional and personal.

"UBM is in a unique position, given its ability to shape the content at these events, to ensure that the issues that business communities are grappling with, including diversity, can be addressed," says Tim Cobbold, UBM Chief Executive. "Whether it is discussions on the under-representation of women in the world of tech, networking events for women in the pharmaceutical industry, or free passes for underprivileged students studying advanced manufacturing, important topics like diversity and social inclusion can be brought to the fore."

UBM is committed to gender diversity, with more than 60 per cent of total employees female. It ranks 38th in board-level female representation among FTSE 250 companies in the Hampton-Alexander Review. With 33 per cent of its directors and 38 per cent of the Executive Committee represented by women, it has made good progress but is seeking to improve further. Empowering all employees through a variety of initiatives including women's leadership and cultural diversity forums, mental health awareness training, supporting volunteering and adopting a flexible working culture, UBM tries hard to live to its values in a diverse and inclusive culture.

# HOME ADVANTAGE

Diversity and a strong social focus are hugely important to the housing developer and landlord Aster Group

WWW.ASTER.CO.UK

"Equality and diversity are a key part of our strategy," says Rachel Credidio, Group People and Transformation Director at housing developer and landlord Aster Group. "It is not just about what is right and fair. We believe there is also business logic in having a diverse workforce."

Aster Group owns and maintains 29,000 homes across the south of England and serves 75,000 residents, offering homes for affordable rent and shared ownership, as well as some for sale on the open market. It's a not-for-dividend organisation – which means it's not bound by the need to provide returns to shareholders.

"We aim to increase our profits so that we can reinvest into delivering new homes and better services for those who need them," says Credidio. "We have a strong social purpose, encapsulated by our vision that everyone should have a home."

Diversity in the workplace is key to Aster Group's mission to provide social value. "We want to ensure that all of our colleagues have a great day at work," says Credidio, "and we develop our talented people

to ensure they are able to reach their potential, now and in the future. We're passionate about all kinds of diversity, including gender diversity. Women are well represented across all our boards and committees."

However, for Aster Group, diversity shouldn't just be limited just to gender, ethnicity or sexuality. "We also look at how people have grown up," says Credidio. "We're currently reviewing all of our job specifications to assess whether having a degree, for example, is necessary to do a job and how we could bring in people via alternative routes."

Aster Group plans to play an active role in its partnership with Vote 100 and in commemorating 100 years since the Representation of the People Act, a milestone in equality legislation.

"We'll be running sessions throughout the year to give our employees an opportunity to engage with the campaign and understand its objectives and significance," says Credidio. "Meanwhile, our involvement underlines our ongoing development as an outstanding employer committed to building a truly diverse and fair workplace."

# MARKET INTELLIGENCE

As the UK's largest retailer, Tesco's inclusive approach has long encouraged a diverse and ambitious workforce

WWW.TESCO.COM

Helping people to advance in their careers is what drives Alison Horner. "It's the reason I get up in the morning," she says. As Chief People Officer for Tesco, Alison has responsibility for shaping the futures of nearly 500,000 staff employed by the multinational retailer.

With a policy of "everyone is welcome", Britain's biggest supermarket chain is committed to inclusivity. Its Regeneration Partnership Programme, for example, provides opportunities to the unemployed, an initiative that began in 2000. Almost a third (30 per cent) of new store vacancies are ring-fenced for people who have been out of work for more than six months. Last year, a total of 14 stores were opened, offering this job guarantee, and more than half the applicants who took part in the three-week training programme became permanent staff members.

"This guarantees job placements for people of all ages," says Horner. "We work with Jobcentre Plus in the run up to a new store opening to get people skilled. Our aim is to convert as many vacancies as possible to permanent opportunities."

Since 2016, the retail chain has been partnering with Remploy, the organisation that provides job placement services for those with disabilities or health conditions. What Tesco does is guarantee an interview to people, including those with mental health problems. They include a young man called Lee who was so depressed he was unable to look anyone in the eye. Now working for Tesco, Lee is a valued member of the store team. The ambition, according to Horner, is for at least half of people on a work placement to secure a job at the end.

Tesco, which is headquartered in Welwyn Garden City, Hertforshire, already has a strong representation of women in certain jobs within the organisation. Indeed, 58 per cent of its customer assistants and two in five of its team managers are female. Yet, ever keen to improve its approach to inclusivity, the company is eager to ensure that women are not hampered in their career progression by restrictive policies towards working. "We are attempting to turn the dial," says Horner, "so that flexible working becomes commonplace and improves our female representation."

To help achieve this, the company has teamed up with Timewise, a specialist in flexible working in the retail sector, and with firms such as John Lewis to find ways of increasing staff progression to more senior roles. "We're identifying barriers and exploring how we can structure our jobs differently," says Horner. "Career progression can be more challenging especially for women unless employers compromise. It's about how we balance job roles and responsibilities with the individual life circumstances of our colleagues."

No employer can claim to be inclusive without meeting the needs of LGBT staff. Tesco boasts the largest LGBT network in Europe with 2,500 members, which was instrumental in the company becoming a gold sponsor of Pride. During the annual event, Tesco stores carry a chevron symbol to celebrate diversity. "The focus for Tesco via the network is on removing any barriers that exist for people," says Horner, "and providing support when needed."

Founded in 1919 as a group of market stalls, Tesco is now the third largest retailer in the world. With influence comes responsibility, and that includes giving people opportunities they would never have dreamed of before. That's an incentive for anyone to get out of bed.

# GREAT LONDON HOSPITALITY

glh Hotels operates a diverse and dynamic community of top-rated London hotels

WWW.GLHHOTELS.COM

"It's about delivering the best service we can, every time," says Jessica Collingwood, HR Director for glh Hotels. "As London's largest owner-operated hotel group, having end-to-end control, it allows us to operate like a community."

This community includes the prestigious brands of Amba, Guoman, Thistle, Thistle Express and Hard Rock London. These make up an eclectic bunch of 3 to 5 star hotels that represent the vibrant, dynamic and ever-changing city that they occupy and love: London. "The hotels aren't cookie-cutter," says Collingwood. "They are different shapes and sizes – a lot of them are historic and iconic."

Just like the hotels and people that occupy them, glh's team is equally assorted, understanding the importance of diversity and celebrating it within its workforce. "We are an open-minded organisation that just really likes people," says Collingwood. "I hesitate to call it a family because most families aren't that diverse. We are very multicultural and multigenerational – it's a community." This also extends to the organisation's approach to gender equality and it has a reputation to be proud of. "At every level, right up to the leadership team, there is gender equality and equality in pay," says Collingwood. "Part of my job is to bang the drum for diversity and inclusivity, and at glh Hotels I'm not having to do that, it genuinely already happens."

This natural process, Collingwood feels, comes down to welcoming employees in the same way it would welcome a paying guest. "You join this company and you have a voice. You're part of this journey with us. We don't expect to cut people open and find 'glh' stamped through them, we want employees to feel that it's an organisation that they can align themselves to and recognise the same values."

The clear vision of uniting passionate people to deliver unforgettable hospitality has seen glh win multiple awards, such as a prestigious Business Travel Award in 2016, and a 2017 Golden Keys Concierge Award for the Amba Hotel Charing Cross. Despite the organisation's successes, it is always keen to expand on them. "We're not sitting back and saying 'job done'," says Collingwood. "It's about constantly looking at transformation and improvement."

# WAITS AND MEASURES

Waiting in line could be a thing of the past with the new customer experience platform Qudini

WWW.QUDINI.COM

It is said that the British are good at queuing, but our patience appears to be waning. These days, a disinclination to stand in line is resulting in more commerce taking place online. Qudini is a cloud-based customer experience management platform that helps to reduce queues in shops, restaurants, museums and health clinics, through its Virtual Queue Management and Appointment Booking System.

An original idea for managing queues in theme parks won Qudini founders Imogen Wethered and Fraser Hardy a Telefónica-sponsored Hackathon in 2012, and a resulting place in Telefónica's Wayra start-up accelerator. "Now we improve customer experience for global brands across a variety of sectors, from retailers to museums to the NHS," says Wethered. For its international retail work, Qudini was endorsed as a "Cool Vendor" by the IT research firm Gartner and Wethered was cited as one to watch in *The Guardian*'s 2017 list of Women in Tech.

Clients who have benefited from Qudini's solutions include O2, which has seen a 62 per cent reduction in store walkouts. This is attributed to Qudini's ability to reduce customer frustrations while they wait by providing customers with estimated wait times and regular SMS communications. Using the same solution, an NHS health clinic has been able to reduce its total complaints by 95 per cent and has increased its appointment time efficiency by 17 per cent. Some of Qudini's restaurant clients are seating more than 120 additional customers per night! The system is also supporting businesses within the leisure industry, including the golf leisure venue TopGolf and the LA County Museum of Art.

Qudini's core mission is to transform the high street as the place to go for great experiences and building relationships. "Retail is becoming increasingly focused on service and experience, as opposed to pure transactions," says Wethered. "Retailers are transforming their stores accordingly, in order to convert more customers and build long-term loyalty."

Clearly not one to wait silently in line herself, Wethered started building the company at the age of 23 and is extremely grateful for the support she has received from her mentors and clients. "It is an amazing time to be building a business," she says. "I feel so grateful for all the support I have had as a woman in tech."

# A SHIFT IN MINDSET

Cox Automotive is championing diversity throughout its workforce to challenge the machismo of the car industry

WWW.COXAUTO.CO.UK

The automobile industry remains a largely male-dominated environment, so when Sarah Dawson, Senior Vice President of Global People Strategies at Cox Automotive, approached her boss to discuss improving the firm's people strategy and diversity in all areas, including gender, she wasn't sure how he would respond.

"I promised that I wouldn't add bureaucracy but would create multi-talented, highly engaged teams, and that he would see the effect on business results," she says. "He gave his complete support to the project. We've had the same level of support across all markets and that's allowed us to put the right people in place to provide thought leadership. This, in turn, ensures that people are treated fairly, whoever and wherever they may be across our international markets."

Cox Automotive is a division of Cox Enterprises, which was founded by former teacher, journalist and governor James M Cox in Ohio in 1898. He purchased a local newspaper from which a global giant has since grown with divisions in media, communications and the automotive sectors. Cox Automotive is a family of brands that provides a comprehensive set of services and solutions for the automotive market, whether running websites where cars can be sold, allowing dealers to acquire, finance and service their inventory, or providing car buyers with the tools they need to find a car.

"We provide the link between the consumer and the dealer, so a vehicle can be marketed across multiple channels to reach a potential customer much quicker," says Sarah (pictured, left). "We have over 30,000 team members across the organisation in around 25 markets." As she notes, you don't often see women selling cars or presenting *Top Gear*, but she has helped to devise a rapid transformation in the way Cox Automotive approaches diversity. Her motivation is to establish

a thriving culture of fairness and equality. "It's inspiring and empowering," she observes. "It promotes a can-do attitude so everybody has the same possibilities. It creates a different workplace: people can bring their true selves to work if they feel they will be recognised."

This has been achieved through various measures, such as bonuses that reward managers who pursue diversity, flexible working, mentoring and a "Women with Drive" initiative, which specifically empowers women across the wider industry. One project saw a Cox Automotive team (pictured, right) climbing Mount Kilimanjaro. "We have changed really rapidly and now have women in very senior positions, across a number of areas including finance and IT. We have transformed the way we recruit and it's now a more diverse workforce."

This level of change has been made possible through targeting senior roles, ensuring diverse representation on boards to provide positive thought leadership. Managers have had training in unconscious bias to allow them to make more informed recruitment decisions. "It's required some very tough decisions but we need people with the right mindset," says Sarah. "Sometimes the only way to change a manager is to change a manager."

As a result, Sarah believes that Cox Automotive is leading change in the industry. "We are trying to get ahead of the curve so we can position ourselves as a great employer," she says. "We have leading-edge practises and policies that are very exciting. It's not what you'd expect to walk into in this industry but we've shown people can flourish. We now have women running auction centres. The traditional mindset would have seen people afraid to employ a woman for such traditionally male jobs, but we want to challenge the status quo and simply employ the best people for the job. And guess what? Some of them are women."

# "We want to employ the best people for the job. And guess what? Some of them are women"

Sarah Dawson, Cox Automotive

# THE CUP
# THAT CHEERS

Ruby Cup is a menstrual care
solution that is giving comfort
to women around the world

WWW.RUBYCUP.COM

When Julie Weigaard Kjaer packed her bags for Kenya in 2011, she never dreamed her trip would last longer than a few months. In reality, the Ruby Cup founder stayed for three years. "When we saw what impact this tiny little menstrual cup could have on women's lives, I thought: we have to make this work," says Kjaer. "It really makes a difference."

Ruby Cup isn't just an eco-friendly alternative to pads and tampons – it's a social enterprise with a unique goal. The business model is simple: for every purchase of a medical-grade silicone menstrual cup, another is given to a girl or woman in need. It's called the Buy One, Give One programme and it's changing lives.

Ask Kjaer about Ruby Cup's work in East Africa, Nepal and Ghana, and you'll soon discover that the firm's social mission is, in her own words, its "reason for being". Since the company was launched at the Copenhagen Business School in 2011, Ruby Cup donations have helped more than 30,000 women and girls access this healthy, sustainable and cost-effective product – both in Europe and in developing countries such as Kenya, where Kjaer experienced her big wake-up call.

"I met a girl who said she bled for two years without knowing that it was her period," says Kjaer. "She thought she was sick and she was going to die." A menstrual cup may sound like a simple solution, but the impact can be profound. "If women can access it, and get information and support about how to use it, then at least they have one less thing to worry about."

As for customers here in the UK, it's been six years since Kjaer was, in her own words, "cupverted", and she's keen to challenge traditional mindsets when it comes to menstruation. This begs the question: is a cup really better than a tampon? Absolutely, she says. "It's more practical and comfortable than a tampon, with three times its capacity."

Ruby Cup is determined to dismantle the taboos surrounding menstruation, not just in the developing world but wherever they occur. "We call it 'period positivity'," Kjaer quips with a smile. "We're working towards that."

# THE BALANCE OF POWER

Energy regulator Ofgem believes that if you're in public service, you should reflect the public you're serving

WWW.OFGEM.GOV.UK

There is power in diversity. Ofgem – the Office of Gas and Electricity Markets – is the government body that regulates the gas and electricity industries in Britain. It is also committed to equality across its team. "At Ofgem, we embrace diversity in all of its senses," says Associate Director for People, Sue Allis. "We want to use different skills, and the range of experience and expertise that people bring."

In addition to its focus on professional development, Ofgem is also notable for its far-reaching range of employee groups, established and run by members. Its Women's Network has been active for more than two years and currently has more than 167 members. "We have events that focus on gender balance and equality strategies," says Anna O'Connor, Policy Manager for Energy Efficiency and Social Programmes, "in addition to what we're doing in flexible working, extracurricular activities and the overall working environment."

Ofgem has responded to the "Women On Boards" government-backed review, which was spearheaded by the former Minister of Trade Lord Mervyn Davies. In 2015, Lord Davies raised the voluntary target for women on the boards of FTSE 100 companies to 33 per cent by 2020. This also reflects Ofgem's broader approach to diversity, which has long included an LGBT group, a BAME group, a disability group called Enable, and further groups ranging from carers to young professionals. Obviously, many members overlap more than one of these groups.

"We are a civil service department," says Allis, "and the UK civil service has a long-standing and laudable approach to improving diversity. There is the belief that, if you're in the public service, you should reflect the public that you're serving."

"It is important that our workforce is as diverse as possible," adds O'Connor. "There is a sense that we should lead by example to major energy suppliers, and there are a number of good collaborative approaches, including joint events with external groups such as POWERful Women and Women In Energy."

All of these inclusive approaches are key to Ofgem's underlying approach. "We have an ethos here," says Allis, "where we learn from others, share experience and share best practice."

# THE BALANCE OF POWER

Edina is changing the way the energy sector thinks about gender and sustainability

WWW.EDINA.EU

A frisson of excitement runs through the offices of energy-supply company, Edina, as it is announced as winner of a prestigious Queen's Award for Enterprise, Innovation category, for a second time. The thrill is palpable. Since the Queen's Award was set up in 1965 as the highest official honour to British businesses, Edina is the only company within its industry sector to win the Innovation award twice.

Victoria Keys, Edina's Head of Human Resources, believes credit for such a feat is due to the company's unwavering commitment to its employees. "Our staff is our greatest asset," she says. "We are successful because our employees are all treated equally. We make sure that everyone feels that they can be the best that they can be, and has the opportunity to diversify and expand on their skills so that they can really progress. If we didn't invest in our staff, we simply wouldn't be winning these awards." Sitting happily next to the Queen's Awards is the company's "Investors in People" accreditation, further confirmation of its focus on employee wellbeing.

Edina is a leading supplier, installer and maintenance provider for combined heat and power (CHP), gas, and diesel power generation solutions. Edina is the official UK and Ireland distributor for MWM-manufactured gas engine technology and is the German engineering firm's biggest customer with over 500 megawatts of electrical installed generation across these territories.

A company that began modestly in Ireland 30 years ago, Edina now has offices in the UK, Ireland and Australia, and expansion continues. Clients include BAE Systems, NHS trusts, major food companies, commercial, public and industrial sectors, waste-management operators and universities, all of whom look to Edina's power-generation solutions to reduce energy costs, carbon emissions and maintain security of power supply.

The energy sector is traditionally a male-orientated one, and creating more equality for women is very much on the agenda for Edina. "We have our first female Director of Commercial and Business Development, but we hope she is the first of many," says Keys. "We want to reach out to other women and show them that gender is no barrier in our business. Each employee is judged solely on merit, and we really want every woman to feel that they can reach their full potential with us."

# THE FRUITS OF LABOUR

Lincolnshire's Worldwide Fruit is employing a range of initiatives to retain and inspire its workforce

WWW.WORLDWIDEFRUIT.CO.UK

When Tricia McCarron joined fruit marketing and distribution company Worldwide Fruit three years after its inception in 2003, labour turnover in its packhouse ran at an astonishing 33 per cent. Today, following a raft of initiatives aimed at inspiring, and thereby retaining, its workforce, this figure has dropped to just 5 per cent.

"We were constantly training new people who quickly left the job," says McCarron, Worldwide Fruit's HR Director. "Obviously, if you can keep your workers, you're not continually training people and they're not continually making mistakes. And it's just a better place to be because staff get to know what they need to do. They buy into the values; they buy into the ethos. They like coming to work."

Based in Spalding, Lincolnshire, Worldwide Fruit is a specialist in sourcing apples, pears, avocados and stone fruit, supplying 100 per cent of the apples and pears stocked by Waitrose and Marks & Spencer. And it appears that its staff really do enjoy coming to work: in a recent opinion survey, 71 per cent of respondents said that Worldwide Fruit was "a great place to work".

"In terms of the fresh-produce sector, we've a reputation as a forward-thinking business," says McCarron. "We've worked hard to promote diversity and encourage people to develop. There are many examples of people who've been promoted internally." In practical terms, Worldwide Fruit runs a scheme called Growing Our Own by which every one of the 360 staff has an opportunity to further his or her learning and training. This can mean English lessons for non-native speakers – of whom there are many – professional qualifications, apprenticeships or management training.

It's little wonder, then, that the company was recognised by the Investors in People Awards recently, and has received a host of other honours. While such plaudits provide timely justification for Worldwide Fruit's innovative approach to its workers, it is also felt that they have benefited the firm commercially.

"It certainly helps with the bottom line," says McCarron. "I think our approach also helps raise the bar and sets a precedent for the rest of the industry. Marks & Spencer and other organisations have asked if some of its other suppliers can visit us to see how we do things."

# THE POWER OF DIVERSITY

Energy company E.ON UK is focused on hiring, retaining and promoting women into senior management

WWW.EONENERGY.COM

"Our company mission is about improving people's lives," says Chris Norbury, E.ON UK's HR Director. "Our values are about putting our customer first, working together, improving and innovating, winning together and acting responsibly with an open mind."

Based in Coventry and with around 10,000 employees in this country, E.ON UK has become one of the UK's largest energy providers by focusing on each customer's specific needs – a task that Norbury says is made easier by the company's policy of diversity, equality and inclusion within its own workforce.

"Everybody's difference is valuable," he says. "To be able to relate to our customers we need to be reflective of that customer base, to ensure that we have a diverse colleague population that brings a difference of thought and enables us to pull on lots of different capabilities and talents."

E.ON UK's success in achieving those aims can be measured by its selection for the Inclusive Top 50 UK Employers list in 2017. The company's gender equality policy has been in place since 2010, with the aim of hiring and retaining female employees and promoting

more women to senior management. One current area of focus is on the effect of the menopause on women's careers. "Statistics say that one in four women consider leaving their job because of the experiences they have related to menopause," says Norbury. "So it's thinking about what we can do to make sure we don't lose that talent from the business due to experiences of the menopause. We're raising awareness of it and having a policy in place, so people realise it's okay to talk about it – it's not taboo."

E.ON UK believes that diversity is sound business sense, ensuring that the company is an attractive employer for its staff, now and into the future, and is in touch with the country's changing demographics. Diversity creates a virtuous circle that can help, educate and support staff and customers. "We're looking to personalise energy," says Norbury, "so that every single customer feels that the experience they have with us is individual, and that's what we're aiming to do with our colleagues, too. To make sure their opinions matter and that voices are heard; that they are trusted and empowered."

# BUSINESS LOGIC

Panalpina is helping to make the world of logistics a more inclusive and female-friendly environment

WWW.PANALPINA.COM

"We are like a travel agency for freight," says Katie Herdman. "We provide supply-chain solutions to companies across many industries." Herdman is Head of Human Resources for Panalpina, a global freight-forwarding and logistics company that employs 14,500 people worldwide, including 340 people in Britain.

Some 43 per cent of Panalpina's UK staff are women – but it recognises the need to do more to help female employees to reach the top echelons of management. "As with other organisations, unfortunately, women can face a glass ceiling," says Herdman. "Even more so in the logistics industry, which is historically male-dominated."

Panalpina is making headway in its efforts to address gender disparities in the supply chain. Women are being encouraged to return to work after maternity leave. Female employees are also being offered greater flexibility, such as job sharing, part-time work and working from home, when feasible. "The change is not happening as quickly as we would like," says Herdman, "but the senior management team is fully committed to achieving it."

The company is working in several other ways to improve equality within its business. Managers are required to undergo diversity training to address the unconscious biases that they may have, and Panalpina intends to participate in Vote 100 events to celebrate women's suffrage.

Panalpina also uses the international spread of its business to improve awareness of diversity and to celebrate difference. "We have a Chinese exchange programme where we have people from the UK going to China, and people from China coming here," says Herdman. "For three months they work in each other's shoes, so to speak. Just to pick up the culture, the environment, the market and the knowledge, and then bring it back to their respective country."

As well as the moral imperative, Panalpina recognises that there are sound commercial reasons for capitalising on diversity and the "richness of experience" in its business. "If you have a clone organisation you'll serve only a clone market," explains Herdman. "It simply makes business sense to embrace the diversity of the market you want to reach."

# INCLUSION PRINCIPLE

Inclusion, diversity and innovation are the priorities for consulting and IT provider NTT Data

WWW.NTTDATA.COM/INDEX.HTML

When Kim Gray began working nearly four years ago at NTT Data, the world's sixth-largest consulting and IT provider, she was pleased to see there were more women employees than at other companies she had worked for. But she still felt more could be done, so she set up a Women's Business Network to give women a forum to discuss their work. "We were originally focused on confidence building and getting voices heard," she recalls. "We then encouraged men to join, as women's networks are more effective when male colleagues take part."

The network remains at the heart of a thriving diversity and inclusion programme now ingrained in the company's practices, backed by its headquarters in Japan. "Inclusion, diversity and innovation are NTT Data's corporate priorities," says Gray. "Our President & CEO, Toshio Iwamoto, recently confirmed that our immediate focus is on recruiting, retaining and developing women across the global organisation." Initiatives include mentorship programmes for young women students, days of cultural celebration for foreign employees, sponsorship of the 2018 Pride in the City event and an annual diversity conference.

"Every member of the leadership team in Britain is involved in the scheme and they are not paying lip service," says Gray, who also runs NTT Data's insurance division. "They have a set of targets in their annual objectives that they are measured on, and that includes the number of women they bring into the organisation."

Recruiting and retention remain core challenges. "We get a fraction of women's CVs compared with men," says Gray, "but we make a lot of effort to address that. We reinforce the message that women can, and do, have a fantastic career in this business. Retention is also on the agenda and Sarah Wood, who now runs the Women's Business Network at NTT Data UK, is driving the conversations about flexible working, and looking at what we can offer to get people back into work."

Everything NTT Data does in this area shows a commitment to employees, and a belief that a contented workforce will ultimately benefit clients. "We are a people business," says Gray, "and we want our people to feel very supported in the workforce, whatever their background. This is a fundamental cornerstone to our growth and continued success."

# ILLUSTRATIONS

**CHAPTER ONE**

pp. 8–9: © Parliamentary Art Collection WOA 26

p. 10: City of Westminster Archives Centre E133.2(5)

p. 11: Shakespeare Birthplace Trust, DR759

p. 12: © Parliamentary Art Collection WOA 2359

p. 13: © Parliamentary Art Collection WOA 1618

p. 14: © Parliamentary Art Collection WOA 6594

p. 15: © Parliamentary Art Collection WOA 6799

p. 16: © Parliamentary Art Collection WOA 6795

p. 17: Valence House Museum

pp. 18–9: © National Portrait Gallery, London, NPG D19693

p. 20: Walker Art Gallery

p. 21: © National Portrait Gallery, London, NPG 412

pp. 22 & 23: Parliamentary Archives, HL/PO/JO/10/8/106

p. 24: © National Portrait Gallery, London, NPG 1085

p. 27: Parliamentary Archives, HL/PO/PB/1/1801/41G3n287

pp. 28–9: © National Portrait Gallery, London, NPG 3845

p. 29: © Parliamentary Art Collection WOA 744

p. 30 (top): ©Parliamentary Art Collection WOA M0633

p. 30: © Parliamentary Art Collection – Curator's Reference Collection

p. 31: © Parliamentary Art Collection WOA 2037

p. 33: © Parliamentary Art Collection WOA 589

---

**CHAPTER TWO**

pp. 34–5: © Parliamentary Art Collection WOA 6787

p. 37: Hulton Archive / Getty Images

p. 38: Parliamentary Art Collection WOA 372

p. 39: National Portrait Gallery, London, NPG 118

p. 40: Parliamentary Archives, HC/LB/1/112/248

p. 42: Hulton Archive / Getty Images

p. 43: © Parliamentary Art Collection WOA 7486

p. 44: London Stereoscopic Company/Getty Images

p. 45: The Women's Library Collection, LSE Library

p. 46: The Women's Library Collection, LSE Library

p. 47: © Parliamentary Art Collection WOA 1752

p. 48 (left): Photograph courtesy of Stephen Rabagliati

p. 48: Parliamentary Archives, PHO/11/1/46/4

p. 49: Photograph courtesy of Elizabeth Crawford

p. 51: Parliamentary Archives, HL/PO/6/11A

p. 52: © Parliamentary Art Collection WOA M0655

p. 53: Hulton Archive/Getty Images

pp. 54–5: © Parliamentary Art Collection WOA 7627

**CHAPTER THREE**

pp. 56–7: © Parliamentary Art Collection Curator's Reference Collection

p. 59: © Parliamentary Art Collection WOA 5438

p. 60 (top): LSE Library 2NWS/A/2/1/2

p. 60: © Parliamentary Art Collection WOA S750

p. 62: © Parliamentary Art Collection WOA 6971

p. 63: © Parliamentary Art Collection WOA 3645

p. 64: © Parliamentary Art Collection WOA M0564

p. 65: © Parliamentary Art Collection Curator's Reference Collection

p. 66: © UKParliament

p. 67: Parliamentary Archives, HC/SA/SJ/3/1 and HC/SA/SJ/10/12/6

p. 68 (top): ©UK Parliament

p. 68: © Museum of London

p. 69: Women's Library Collection, LSE Library

pp. 70–1: ©Parliamentary Art Collection

p. 72: Parliamentary Archives,

# ACKNOWLEDGEMENTS

This book is a collaboration between The History of Parliament Trust, the Parliamentary Archives, the Parliamentary Art Collection and St James's House. The editors are particularly grateful for the help of colleagues in the Parliamentary Archives and Parliamentary Art Collection, and staff of the LSE Library, in providing images for the book.

**The Parliamentary Art Collection** is owned jointly by the House of Commons and the House of Lords. It is the national collection illustrating the history of parliament and British politics over the centuries. The Speaker's Advisory Committee on Works of Art and House of Lords Works of Art Panel pursue active acquisition policies. Current priorities include the commissioning of portraits of current and recent eminent parliamentarians and reflecting women's contribution to parliament, both pre and post 1918. To find out more about the Collection, visit www.parliament.uk/art.

**The Parliamentary Archives** provides innovative and expert information management, preservation, access and outreach services enabling anyone in the world to use Parliament's records, both now and in the future. It holds over 8km of physical records dating back to 1497 and its digital repository is growing rapidly. These records include many of the most important constitutional records in the UK, as well as four million others which have touched the lives of everyone and every community in this country and many abroad. To find out more about the Archives, visit www.parliament.uk/archives.

**The History of Parliament** is a research project creating a comprehensive account of parliamentary politics in England, then Britain, from their origins in the 13th century. Unparalleled in the comprehensiveness of its treatment, the History of Parliament is generally regarded as one of the most ambitious, authoritative and well-researched projects in British history. It consists of detailed studies of elections and electoral politics in each constituency, and of closely researched accounts of the lives of everyone who was elected to parliament in the period, together with surveys drawing out the themes and discoveries of the research and adding information on the operation of parliament as an institution. For more information about the History of Parliament, and to access over 20,000 articles on parliamentarians and constituencies, visit www.historyofparliamentonline.org.

# CONTRIBUTORS

Paula Bartley has written historical biographies of Emmeline Pankhurst, Ellen Wilkinson and Queen Victoria and is presently writing a biography of women Labour Cabinet Ministers.

———————

Elaine Chalus is Professor of British History at the University of Liverpool. She is particularly interested in the operation of gender and political culture prior to 1832.

———————

Krista Cowman is Professor of History at the University of Lincoln. She has written widely on women's lives and women and politics in the late 19th and early 20th centuries.

———————

Emma Crewe is Professor of Social Anthropology at SOAS, University of London, and is author of *House of Commons: an Anthropology of MPs at Work* (Bloomsbury, 2015).

———————

Amy Galvin-Elliott is a PhD student jointly supervised by the History Department at the University of Warwick and the Parliamentary Archives. She is currently researching female experience of parliamentary spaces in the 19th century.

———————

Oonagh Gay was head of the Parliament and Constitution Centre at the House of Commons Library, and has written widely on constitutional matters. She is a volunteer for the UK Parliament Vote 100 project, producing blogs and papers on early women MPs.

———————

Elizabeth Hallam Smith, formerly Librarian at the House of Lords, is now a Leverhulme Trust Emeritus Research

Fellow based in Parliament, currently researching the history of St Stephen's Cloister and Undercroft.

———————

Helen McCarthy is Reader in Modern British History at Queen Mary University of London and author of *Women of the World: The Rise of the Female Diplomat* (Bloomsbury, 2014).

———————

Simon Morgan is Head of History at Leeds Beckett University, author of *A Victorian Woman's Place* (I.B. Tauris, 2007) and co-editor of *The Letters of Richard Cobden* (Oxford University Press, 2007–15).

———————

Louise Raw is an independent historian, speaker and journalist. She is author of *Striking a Light: the Bryant & May Matchwomen and their Place in History* (Bloomsbury, 2011)

———————

Sarah Richardson is Associate Professor of History at the University of Warwick and author of *The Political Worlds of Women: Gender, Politics and Culture in Nineteenth-Century Britain* (Palgrave, 2013).

———————

Kathryn Rix is Assistant Editor of the House of Commons 1832–1945 project at the History of Parliament Trust and has recently published *Parties, Agents and Electoral Culture in England, 1880–1910* (Boydell and Brewer/Royal Historical Society, 2016).

———————

Jane Robinson is author of *Hearts and Minds: Suffragists, Suffragettes and How Women Won the Vote* (Doubleday, 2018).

Paul Seaward is British Academy / Wolfson Research Professor at the History of Parliament Trust. He has written on the history of Parliament and on 17th-century politics and political thought.

———————

Anne Stott is an independent researcher who has written on William Wilberforce and Hannah More. She is currently writing the life of Princess Charlotte, the daughter of the Prince Regent.

———————

Duncan Sutherland came from Canada to study British parliamentary history at Cambridge University. He worked at the Centre for Advancement of Women in Politics at Queen's University Belfast and has also studied Singaporean and Jamaican history.

———————

Mari Takayanagi is Senior Archivist at the Parliamentary Archives, and a historian who works on Parliament and women in the early 20th century. She is the co-curator of "Voice and Vote: Women's Place in Parliament".

———————

Jacqui Turner is Lecturer in Modern History at the University of Reading. Her current research interests concern Nancy Astor and early female MPs. She has recently written on religion and the labour movement and Conservative women.

———————

Melanie Unwin is the Deputy Curator and Head of Interpretation for the Parliamentary Art Collection. She is the co-curator of "Voice and Vote: Women's Place in Parliament".

# CREDITS

St James's House
298 Regents Park Road
London N3 2SZ

+44 (0)020 8371 4000
publishing@stjamess.org
www.stjamess.org

Chief Executive
Richard Freed
richard.freed@stjamess.org

Managing Director
Stephen van der Merwe
stephen.vdm@stjamess.org

Sales Director
Richard Golbourne
r.golbourne@stjamess.org

Communications Director
Ben Duffy
ben.duffy@stjamess.org

Head of Editorial
Stephen Mitchell
stephen.mitchell@stjamess.org

Senior Designer
Aniela Gil
aniela.gil@stjamess.org

Deputy Editor
John Lewis
john.lewis@stjamess.org

*Photography*

New York Stock Exchange,
Getty Images, John Houlihan, iStock,
Tam Minchin, Richard Murgatroyd
Photography, Leonora Saunders,
Waltham Forest College.

London College of Fashion: Work
by Kelly Murray, MA Costume Design
for Performance. Photograph by
Emmi Hyyppa.

Royal Mail: Votes for Women stamp
designs, reproduced with kind
permission of Royal Mail Group Limited
© Royal Mail Group Limited 2018.

Other images are the copyright
of individual organisations.

# ABOUT THE PUBLISHER

St James's House is a London-based producer of high-quality publications. It is part of the SJH Group, a world-leading creative media group that delivers bespoke solutions for a global client base and has offices in London, Manchester, Los Angeles and New York City.

*Voice & Vote* is St James's House's second collaboration with the History Of Parliament Trust. In 2015, we published *The Story Of Parliament: Celebrating 750 Years of Parliament in Britain* – a lavish and fully illustrated history that drew from the Trust's extensive expertise.

The History of Parliament Trust is just one of the many prestigious organisations that St James's House has worked with in recent years. In 2016, we were the official publishing partner for Her Majesty's The Queen's 90th birthday celebrations at Windsor and, over the past decade, our publishing partners have included the Confederation of British Industry, the Royal Air Force, the National Health Service, the Institution of Civil Engineering, the UK-based Rolls-Royce Enthusiasts' Club and the US-based Rolls-Royce Owners' Club.

In 2015, we worked with the Confederation of British Industry to publish *CBI: 50 Years of Business Innovation*. This year we have worked closely with the RAF to publish two books celebrating the air force's 100th anniversary, and we are currently collaborating with the Institution of Civil Engineering to commemorate ICE's 200th anniversary later this year, celebrating 200 iconic international achievements in the world of civil engineering.

Today's high-end publishing companies frequently serve as strategic partners for organisations that understand the power of

well-connected publishers to communicate key messages for awareness, education and diversity. To this end, our world-class strategists provide companies, governments and campaigning bodies with publishing, business and marketing expertise for entertaining, informing and engaging some of their most important audiences. As a recognised global publisher with top-tier clients and relationships with major sales outlets, our publications provide our partners with a once-in-a-lifetime chance to create a tangible product that tells their story, defines their DNA and clearly differentiates them in the marketplace.

In a media landscape that is saturated with digital, broadcast and disposable print formats, our books command attention and respect from readers and provide a timeless resource for decades to come. SJH Group publications – as well as their associated promotional activities – also provide our partner organisations with a unique opportunity to strategically engage with journalists, clients, business partners, professionals, academics and industry bodies.

Our publishing imprints include Black Dog Press, which produces high-end arts books, and Artifice Press, which publishes volumes on architecture and design. SJH Group books are consistently well received by their intended readerships, and several of our books have appeared in the Amazon Top 100 book chart. On average, our publishing group prints more than 300,000 books each year. This places us on the UK's top-ten list for media distribution, and makes us one of the country's most influential distributors of published content across a broad range of specialist subjects.

# INDEX

**A**

Abbott, Diane   106
Abolitionism   23, 25
Abolitionist movement   39
Ackworth   42
Actresses' Franchise League   65, 74
Adams, Irene
   (Baroness Adams of Craiglea)   106
Adamson, Jennie   90, 95, 96
Addidi   272
Addison, Edward   26
*Address to the Opposers of the Repeal
   of the Corporation and Test Acts*
   (Anna Letitia Barbauld, 1790)   22
all-women shortlists   106
All3Media   150
Alliance Party of Northern Ireland   106
Allied Irish Bank   275
Altrincham Grammar School for Girls   228
Amos, Valerie (Baroness Amos)   123
Anderson, Betty Harvie   117
Anderson, Louisa Garrett   75
Andover, Mary Howard, Viscountess   16
Anglican Mainstream   206
Anti-Corn Law League   39, 42
Anti-Slavery Society   25
*Appeal against the Extension of
   the Parliamentary Franchise to Women*   55
Apsley, Lady Violet   90
Arbuthnot, Harriett   29
Archco Developments   312
Arm   320
Arthur, Jane   50
Arts Council of Wales   155
Ashworth & Co   55
Ashworth, May   55
Aster Group   343
Asquith, Herbert   62, 69, 72
Astor, Nancy (Viscountess Astor)   81, 82, 85,
   88, 90, 94, 95, 99, 100
Astor, Lord Waldorf (Viscount Astor)   82, 99, 100
Atholl, Duchess of   88
Attlee, Clement   95
Austin, Sarah   29
Ayrton-Gould, Barbara   96

**B**

Backbench Business Committee   118
Bacon, Alice (Baroness Bacon)   95, 96, 121

Baldwin, Stanley   86
Balfour, Clara Lucas   39
Banbury, Frederick   76
Barbauld, Anna Letitia   22, 23
Bax, Ernest Belfort   47
Beaumont, Baroness   100, 103
Becker, Lydia   48, 50, 54
Beckett, Margaret   116
Begg, Ferdinand Faithfull   55
Bell, Gertrude   72
Bellamy, John   32
Bellamy, Maria   32
Berkeley Square   28
Besant, Annie   53, 54
Beston, Jacqy (Jacqy Sharpe)   113
Bevin, Ernest   94
Billinghurst, Rosa May   69
Billington-Greig, Teresa   65
Birmingham Female Political Union   45
Black Friday (18 November 1910)   69, 74
Black Rod   31, 113
Black, Clementina   52
Blair, Tony   116, 117
"Blair's Babes"   117
BNY Mellon   126–39
Boards of Guardians   50
Bodichon, Barbara Leigh (Barbara Leigh Smith)
   42, 47
*Bolton Evening News*   98
Bondfield, Margaret   88
Bonham Carter, Violet (Baroness Asquith
   of Yarnbury)   121
Boothroyd, Betty (Baroness Boothroyd)   117
"boroughmongers"   16
Bottomley, Virginia (Baroness Bottomley)   106,
   116
Bow matchwomen strike   52–4
Boyle, Nina   78
Boz (Charles Dickens)   32
Braddock, Bessie   95, 96, 98, 103, 118
Bradford District Care NHS
   Foundation Trust   288
Brailsford, HN   69
Brandish, Frances   32
*Brief Summary of the Most Important Laws of
   England Concerning Women*
   (Barbara Leigh Smith, 1854)   42
Brier School, The   213
Bright, Jacob   48, 49, 50
Bright, Patricia McLaren   48

Bright, Ursula Mellor   48
Brightstar   316
British Sociological Association   202
British Expeditionary Force   75
British Fashion Council, the   146
Broadhurst, Henry   47
Brooke, Barbara (Baroness Brooke
   of Ystradfellte)   121
brookscomm   149
Brown, Anne   32
Bryant & May   52, 53
Buchan, Priscilla (Baroness Tweedsmuir)
   95, 96, 98, 103
Bulwer-Lytton, Lady Constance   70
burgages   16
Burke, Edmund   22, 23
Burney, Fanny   23
Bury Hospice   289
Butler, Josephine   44, 54
Butler, RA   94

**C**

Cambridge House   28
Cambridgeshire Constabulary   188
Camden & Islington NHS Foundation Trust   295
Cameron, David   116
Campbell-Bannerman, Henry   62
Campbell, Jane   26
Canning, George   28
Carlile, Anne   39
Carl Zeiss Vision UK   334
Carlton House Terrace   28
Caroline, Queen   12, 29
Carpenter, Mary   36
Carter, Elizabeth   26
Castle Riding   16
Castle, Barbara (Baroness Castle)   96, 109,
   113, 114
Castlereagh, Lord   29
"Cat and Mouse Act" 1913   70
Catholic emancipation   29
Cavendish, Georgiana,
   Duchess of Devonshire   14, 26, 27
Caxton Hall, Westminster   61, 65
Cazalet-Keir, Thelma   90, 94, 95
Centre of Excellence, the   229
CGI   326
Chamberlain, Neville   90
Chartist movement   45, 47

Chidley, Katherine 22
Children's Bill 1908 66
Children's Heart Surgery Fund 280
*Chorlton v Lings* 1868 48
Church League for Women's Suffrage 65
Churchill, Clementine
  (Baroness Spencer-Churchill) 121
Churchill, Winston 69, 85, 90, 94, 98
Cisco 302
City Football Group 148
Clark, Elsie 74
Clark, Mabel 74
Clarke, Sarah 113
Clwyd, Ann 112
CMS 180
Co-operative Movement 96
Coalition government
  (Second World War) 95
Coalition government 2010–15 117
Cobden, Jane 50
Coke, Elizabeth 17
Colman, Grace 96
Committee for the Abolition of the
  Slave Trade 23
*Common Cause, The* 58
Conciliation Bills 1910–12 69
Conservative Central Office 106
Conservative party 29, 48, 50, 62, 69, 70,
  82, 86, 90, 95, 98, 103, 106, 109, 112,
  116, 118, 123
Contagious Diseases Acts of 1864 and 1866
  42, 44, 54
Cook, Robin 118
Corbet, Freda 96
Corn Laws 21, 39, 42, 47
Corrupt Practices Act 1883 50
Court, May 75
Court, Robert 75
Courtney, Kathleen 76
Covent Garden Theatre 39
Cox Automotive 348
Coxon, Maureen 113
Crawshay, Rose 50
Crest Nicholson 340
Crewe, Frances Anne, Lady 28
Crimean War (1854–6) 36
Cripps, Stafford 96
Crosby by-election 1981 114
Curzon, George (Marquess Curzon
  of Kedleston) 72

Curzon, Irene (Baroness Ravensdale
  of Kedleston) 103

**D**

D'Souza, Frances
  (Baroness D'Souza) 123
Dáil Éireann 78
*Daily Mail* 58, 65, 85
*Daily Mirror* 65
*Daily News* 25
Darwin-Wedgwood clan 29
Davidson, Frances (Baroness Northchurch,
  Viscountess Davidson) 90, 95, 98, 121
Davies, Emily 47, 50
Davison, Emily Wilding 66, 69
*Declaration of the Rights of Man and
  of the Citizen* (1789) 22
Department for Business, Energy
  and Industrial Strategy 298
Department for Digital, Culture,
  Media & Sport 142
Department for Transport 170
Department for Education 210
Department of Health
  and Social Care 278
Derby, Lord 29
Derby, The (race) 69
Desaguliers, Dr Theophilius 32
Design Copyright Act 1968 113
Despard, Charlotte 65, 75
Devadason, Stella 113
Development Partners
  International 274
Devonport High School for Girls 224
Devlin, Bernadette 106
Devon and Cornwall Police 199
Dickens, Charles 32
Dickinson, Willoughby 76
Disraeli, Benjamin 7
Divorce Act 26
Domestic Violence and Matrimonial
  Proceedings Act 1976 112, 116
Doorkeepers 113
Downing, Lady 17
Drummond, Flora 65, 69, 70
Duchenne UK 195
Dunwoody, Gwyneth 106, 118
Durham Constabulary 194
Duval, Victor 74

**E**

E.ON UK 354
East London Federation of Suffragettes 74
Eden, Anthony 95
Edgeworth, Maria 29
Edina 352
Edinburgh National Society for
  Women's Suffrage 48
Education Bill 1944 94
Edward VII 69
Edwards, Thomas 22
Egremont, Lord 16
Election Fighting Fund (EFF) 70
Elizabeth II, Queen 100
Elliot, Katherine
  (Baroness Elliot of Harwood) 103
ELM group 204
Elurra Gold 339
Employment Act 2002 116
Endell Street Military Hospital 75
*Endymion* (Benjamin Disraeli, 1880) 27
Engel, Natascha 118
English Civil War 21, 23
*English Woman's Journal* 42
Equal Franchise Act 1928 86
Equal Opportunities Commission 121
Equal Pay Act 1975 116
Equal Pay Campaign Committee 94
Equality Act 2010 117
Essex Police 190
Estelon 332
Estimates Committee 96
Ewing, Annabel 106
Ewing, Margaret 106
Ewing, Winnie 106

**F**

Faithfull, Lucy (Baroness Faithfull) 121
Falkland, Viscount 66
Falklands War 116
Family Allowance 88
Family Allowance Act 1945 95
Family-friendly hours in the Commons 118
Fawcett, Henry 58
Fawcett, Millicent Garrett 36, 48, 54, 58, 61,
  70, 72, 74, 76, 82
Female Genital Mutilation Act 2003 112
*Fifteen Good Reasons Against the Grant of
  Female Suffrage* (Lord Curzon, c1910) 72

First World War (1914–8) 74, 95
Fookes, Janet (Baroness Fookes) 112
Ford 328
Ford, Patricia 105
Foreign Office 90, 172
Forsyth, William 50
Foster, Norman (Lord Foster) 123
Fox, Charles James 27
Fox, Helen 66
Franchise and Registration Bill 1912 69
Francis House Family Trust 185
Franco, General Francisco 88
*Fraud of Feminism, The*
  (Ernest Belfort Bax, 1913) 47
French Revolution 17, 22
French, Sir John 75
Fry, Elizabeth 36
Frye, Kate Parry 74
Furniss, Gill 106

**G**

Gaitskell, Anna (Baroness Gaitskell) 121
Gang of Four (the SDP founders) 114
Ganley, Caroline 96
Garrett Anderson, Dr Elizabeth
  47, 50, 58, 74
Gawthorpe, Mary 61
Geddes Axe 85
General Election 1918 78
General Election 1929
  (the "Flapper Election") 86
General Election 1931 88
General Election 1945 95
General Election 1979 114
General Election 1997 117
General Election 2015 118
GEO Group, the 203
Girl Porters at the Houses
  of Parliament 74
Gladstone, William 49, 52
glh Hotels 346
Goldman Sachs 256
Goldsmith, Vera 75
Gordon, Duchess of 27
Government Equalities Office 166
Grand National Consolidated
  Trades Union (1833) 45
Great Pilgrimage, The (1913) 70
Green Party 106

Greville, Lady Charlotte    28
Grey, Sir Edward    61, 69

**H**

Hale, Brenda (Baroness Hale)    122
Halifax, Lord    95
Hames, Andrew    121
Hamilton, Duke of    14
Hannay Investments    271
Hansard    66, 90, 113
Hardie, Agnes    90, 94
Hardie, James Keir    62, 66
Harley, Katherine    70
Harman, Harriet    106, 117
Harrison, Martha    31
Hart, Dorothy    75
Hayman, Helene (Baroness Hayman)    106, 112, 123
Heath, Edward    114
Herbison, Margaret    96, 118
Heyrick, Elizabeth    25
Hicks, William Joynson    86
History of Parliament Trust    109
Hodge Jones & Allen    186
Hodge, Margaret    118
Holingshead, Anne    32
Holland, Lady    27
Holloway Prison    78
Home Instead Senior Care    284
Home Office    94, 160
Horsbrugh, Florence    88, 90, 95, 98
House of Commons    10, 26, 32, 49, 55, 61
House of Commons Library    98
House of Commons Nursery    118
House of Commons, Smoking Room    109
House of Lords    21, 25, 26, 69, 98, 99, 113, 122, 123
House of Lords Act 1999    121
House of Lords Appointments Commission    122
House of Lords' Committee for Privileges    99
House of Lords, women in    98, 99, 103, 121
Houses of Parliament fire of 1834    12, 28, 35
How-Martyn, Edith    65
Howard, Charles, (Duke of Norfolk)    16
Hughes, Anne    32
Hughes, Thomas    32
Hume, Margery    66
Hunt, Henry    31
Hyde Park, London    70

Hylton-Foster, Audrey (Baroness Hylton-Foster)    123

**I**

*Illustrations of Political Economy* (Harriet Martineau, 1832)    25
Image Source    156
*Immediate, not Gradual Abolition* (Elizabeth Heyrick, 1824)    25
Incledon, John    32
Independent Labour Party    47, 52
Infant Custody Act 1839    42
Inglis, Elsie    75
Ingrams, Davina (Baroness Darcy de Knayth)    122
Inner City Trust, the    189
Institute of Practitioners in Advertising, the    154
Intoxicating Liquor (Sale to Persons under Eighteen) Bill    85
Invesco Perpetual    258
Irish Home Rule    62, 69
Irish Nationalist party    69
Irwin, Frances (Lady Irwin)    16
Isaacs, Stella (the Dowager Marchioness of Reading, Baroness Swanborough)    103
Iwi, Edward    100

**J**

Jarrow March 1936    89
Jersey, Lady    27, 28
JK7    324
Jowell, Tessa    116
*Justification of the Independent Churches of Christ, The* (Katherine Chidley, 1640)    22

**K**

*Karma Nirvana*    184
Keck, Lady Susan (Lady Susan Keck)    12, 14, 16
Kedleston, Marquess Curzon of    103
Kenney, Annie    61
Kensington Society    47
Kent Police    192
King's High Warwick    225
Kite Lake Capital Management    267
Kitchen and Refreshment Rooms Select Committee    118
Knight, Jill (Baroness Knight of

Collingtree)    113
Knokin, Baroness Strange    103
Kohinoor    336
Korn Ferry    308
KPMG    252

**L**

Labour party    47, 52, 61, 69, 70, 82, 86, 88, 90, 95, 98, 100, 103, 106, 109, 112, 116, 117, 118
Ladies' Anti-Slavery Society    25
Ladies' Gallery    36, 48, 66
Ladies' National Association for the Repeal of the Contagious Diseases Acts    54
Lady Members' Room    81, 82, 98
Lamb, Elizabeth    27
Lansbury, George    62
Laurence Simons    207
"Lavender list" 1976    121
Lee, Jennie (Baroness Lee of Asheridge)    86, 103, 121
Leeds Tailoresses Union    52
Lenton, Lilian    70
*Letter To William Wilberforce, A* (Anna Letitia Barbauld, 1791)    25
*Letters on the French Revolution* (Helen Maria Williams, 1790)    25
Levellers    22
Liberal Democrat party    106, 109, 114, 118, 121
Liberal party    29, 48, 49, 50, 52, 58, 61, 62, 69, 70, 74, 82, 90, 96, 98
Life Peerages Act 1958    103, 121
Lilburne, John    22
Llewellyn-Davies, Annie (Baroness Llewellyn-Davies of Hastoe)    123
Lloyd George, David    62, 69, 70, 96
Lloyd George, Megan    90, 95, 96, 98
Local Government Act 1894    50
Lockwood, Betty (Baroness Lockwood)    121
London College of Fashion    232
London County Council    50
London Female Democratic Association    47
London National Society for Women's Suffrage    54
Londonderry, Lady    26
Long Parliament, The 1640    22
Long, Naomi    106
Longford, Lord    123
Lookers    314

Lowther, James, Speaker of the House of Commons (Viscount Ullswater)    76, 82
Lowther, Sir James    16
Lucas, Caroline    106
*Lusitania*, SS    76
Lytton, Lord    69, 70

**M**

Mackworth, Margaret Haig (née Thomas), Viscountess Rhondda    76, 99, 100, 103
MacLeod, Fiona (Fiona Martin)    113
Macmillan, Chrystal    76
Magdalen Asylums    39
Major, John    116, 117
Malmesbury, Lady    28
Malthus, Thomas    25
Manchester Free Trade Hall    61
Manchester Independent Labour Party    61
Manchester National Society for Women's Suffrage    48
Manchester Police Court    61
Manchester Society for Women's Suffrage    55
Manhood Suffrage Bill    69
Mann, Jean    96, 98
Manning, Leah    96, 98, 100
Mar, Margaret (Countess of Mar)    122
Marcet, Jane    29
Markievicz, Constance (Countess Markievicz)    78
Marshall, Catherine    76
Martineau, Harriet    25, 26, 29, 36
Matiland, Lady Olga    112
Matrimonial Causes Act 1857    42
Matters, Muriel    66
Maxwell, Lily    48
May, Theresa    116
McKenna, Reginald    70
McLaren, Patricia Bright    48
Melbourne, Lady    28
Melbourne, Lord    27
Men's League for Women's Suffrage    74
Men's Political Union    74
Merrington, Martha    50
Merton Court Preparatory School    221
Metropolitan Police    85
Middleton, Lucy    96
Middleton, Margaret    25
Middleton, Sir Charles    25
Midwinter, Kay    90
Milk (Special Designation) Bill 1949    95

Mill, James   25
Mill, John Stuart   47, 48
Mills, Elizabeth   31
Milner-Barry, Alda   113
"Ministry of all the Talents Coalition" 1806   27
Ministry of Defence   162
Ministry of Education   95
Ministry of Health   90
Ministry of Housing, Communities
    and Local Government   166
Ministry of Justice   164
Ministry of Pensions   96
Ministry of Food   95
M&G Investments   260
Modernisation Committee   118
Molony, Dorothy   66
Montagu, Elizabeth   26
More, Hannah   23, 26
Mount House School   218
Municipal Franchise Act 1869   49–50
Murray, Flora   75
MV Credit   266

**N**

National Association for the Promotion
    of Social Science   39
National Expenditure Committee   90
National Government (1930s)   88
National Health Scheme   94
National League for Opposing Woman
    Suffrage (NLOWS)   72
National Service (No.2) Bill   94
National Society for Women's Suffrage
    (NSWS)   48, 54
National Union of Conservative and
    Constitutional Associations   50
National Union of Women's Suffrage Societies
    (NUWSS)   55, 58, 65, 70, 74, 76
NASUWT   233
NATO   112
Neesom, Elizabeth   47
New Constitutional Society
    for Women's Suffrage   74
NHS Eastern Cheshire Clinical
    Commissioning Group   290
NHS (National Health Service)   96
NHS Slough Clinical Commissioning Group   286
Nicholson, Emma
    (Baroness Nicholson)   106
Nightingale, Florence   36, 44

Northcote, Stafford (Earl of Iddesleigh)   61
Northern Counties Amalgamated
    Association of Cotton Weavers   52
Norton, Caroline   42, 44
NTT Data   356
Nutrition Society, the   182

**O**

O'Connell, Daniel   28
*Observer, The*   85
Office of Works   81
Ofgem   351
Old Palace Yard   62, 66
Open University   96
Opie, Amelia   29
Opus Energy   322
Overseas Aid Select Committee   118
Oystercatchers   152

**P**

Pacifists in First World War   75
Page Three (*The Sun*)   112
Palace of Westminster fire of 1834   31, 32
Palace of Westminster Home Guard   90
Palace Yard   65
Palmerston, Lady   27, 28, 29
Panalpina   355
Pankhurst, Adela   75
Pankhurst, Christabel   61, 65, 69, 76, 78
Pankhurst, Emmeline   48, 58, 61, 65, 69, 75
Pankhurst, Richard   48
Pankhurst, Sylvia   74, 75, 76
Parkes, Bessie Rayner   42, 47
Parliament (Qualification of Peeresses)
    Bills 1924–30   99, 100
Parliament (Qualification of Women)
    Act 1918   78, 99
Parliament Act 1949   100
Pass, Margaret   113
Paton, Florence   98
Pay, Jill   113
Payne, Lady   28
Pearson   239
Peel, Robert   27
Peerage Act 1963   103
Penalties for Drunkenness Act 1962   113
Peterloo massacre, Manchester   31
Pethick-Lawrence, Emmeline   76

Pethick-Lawrence, Frederick (Lord
    Pethick-Lawrence)   69, 100
Phillips, Mary   31
PIMFA   270
Pinch Point Communications   145
Piozzi, Hester   26
Pitt, Harriot   17
Pitt, William   25
PJ Care   294
Police Service of Northern Ireland   205
Ponsonby, Henrietta (Countess of
    Bessborough)   17
Poor Law (1834)   45, 50
Primrose Dames   50
Primrose League   50
Prisoners' Temporary Discharge for
    Ill-Health Act 1913   70
Procorre   330
Prohibition of Female Circumcision
    Act 1985   112
Propellernet   153
Prudential plc   254
Public Accounts Committee   118
Public Bodies (Admission
    to Meetings) Bill   113
Public Gallery of the
    House of Commons   10

**Q**

Queen's Award For Enterprise   246
Queensbury, Duchess of   10
Qudini   347

**R**

Rathbone, Beatrice (Beatrice Wright)   90
Rathbone, Eleanor   76, 86, 89, 90, 95
Ravensdale, Baroness   100
RB (Reckitt Benckiser)   282
Reading, Marquess of   100
Red Cross   75, 90
Reding, Deborah   32
*Reflections on the Revolution in France*
    (Edmund Burke, 1790)   22
Reform Act 1832   21, 31
Reform Act 1867   47, 48
Reform Act 1884   49, 54
Remond, Sarah Parker   39
Repeal of the Corn Laws 1846   47
Representation of the People Act 1918   76, 78

Rethink Mental Illness   281
Richard I, King   66
Richardson, Jo   112, 116
Richmond Fellowship   292
Rickman, Anne   31
Ridealgh, Mabel   96
Rights of Entry (Gas and Electricity Boards)
    Act 1964   113
Roe, Marion   112
Rollit, Sir Albert   50
Roper, Esther   55
Royal Association for Deaf people, the   198
Royal Mail   306
Royal Navy   176
Royal Veterinary College   222
Ruby Cup   350
Ryder, Sue
    (Baroness Ryder of Warsaw)   121

**S**

Salisbury, Lord   50
Samuel, Herbert   78
San Francisco Conference 1945   95
Sandhurst, Margaret   50
Sarah Matthews   31
School Boards   50
Scottish National Party (SNP)
    106, 109, 118
Second World War (1939–45)   90, 95
Serota, Beatrice (Baroness Serota)   121
Sex Discrimination Act 1975   106
Sex Disqualification (Removal)
    Act 1919   86, 99
Shephard, Gillian (Baroness Shephard of
    Northwold)   116
Short, Clare   112
Short, Renee   118
Schroders   250
Simon, Sir John   76
Singh, Princess Sophia Duleep   74, 75
Sinn Féin   78
Sismondi, Jessie   29
Six Point Group, The   99
Smith, Barbara Leigh   42
Smith, F.E. (Viscount Birkenhead)   99, 100
Smith, Jacqui   116
Smith, John   106, 116
Smith, Mary   31
Smith, Sarah   32
Social Democratic Federation   47, 52

Social Democratic Party (SDP) 114
Social Science Association 42
Society for Promoting the Employment
 of Women 42
*Society In America*
 (Harriet Martineau, 1837) 26
Speaker's Conference on Electoral Reform,
 1916/17 76
Spencer, Georgiana Countess Spencer 17
St James Senior Girls' School 237
St Margaret of Scotland Hospice 293
St Margaret's Westminster 32
St Stephen's Chapel 10
St Stephen's Hall 61, 66, 74
Stanley, Henrietta (Baroness Stanley of
 Alderley) 28
Stedman-Scott, Deborah (Baroness
 Stedman-Scott) 123
Stephens, Anne 32
Stirling Council 201
Strangers' Gallery 66
Strangeways Prison, Manchester 61
Strength With In Me (SWIM) Foundation 200
Suffragettes of the WPSU 76
Summerskill, Edith (Baroness Summerskill)
 89, 90, 94, 95, 121
*Sun, The* 112
Supreme Court 122
Sussex Police 196
Sutherland, Countess of 28
Sutherland, Duchess of 27
Swanborough, Baroness (Marchioness
 of Reading 121
Swansea University 214
Swinson, Jo 121
Switchboard 175
Symons, Margaret Travers 66

---

**T**

Tate, Mavis 90, 94, 95
Taylor, Ann (Baroness Taylor of Bolton) 118
Taylor, Harriet 47
Taylor, Helen 47
Taylor, Susannah 29

TeachBeyond 240
Tempest, Anna Maria 42
Tesco 344
Thatcher, Margaret (Baroness Thatcher) 82,
 106, 113, 114, 116
Thomson Reuters 262
Tormead School 217
Thorndike, Sybil 100
Thornton College 216
ThoughtWorks 338
Tillard, Violet 66
*Time and Tide* 99
*Times, The* 10, 85
Tory party 27
Townsend, Lucy 25
Treasury, HM 244
Trades Union Congress 47
Transport Bill guillotine debates 1947 98
Transport Committee 118
Treweek, Rachel, Bishop of Gloucester 122
Truss, Liz 116
TSB 264
Twining, Louisa 36

---

**U**

UBM plc 342
Unemployment Assistance Board 96
United Nations 90, 95, 103
University of Central Lancashire 230
University of Exeter 238
University of Sunderland, the 220
The University of York's Department
 of Chemistry 234

---

**V**

Vernatty, Peternelle 31–2
*Village Politics* (Hannah More, 1792) 23, 25
*Vindication of the Rights of Men* (Mary
 Wollstonecraft, 1790) 22
*Vindication of the Rights of Woman*
 (Mary Wollstonecraft, 1792) 22–3
*Vote, The* 86
VTCT 241

**W**

Waldegrave, Lady 27, 28
Wallace-Dunlop, Marion 74
Walpole, Horace 23
Walpole, Margaret, Countess of Orford 17
War Injuries Act 1939 94
Ward, Dame Irene (Baroness Ward
 of North Tyneside) 90, 98, 113, 121
Ward, Mary Augusta (Mrs Humphry
 Ward) 55, 72
Ward, Thomas 32
Waterman, Mabel 75
Wates 318
Wedgwood, Elizabeth 29
Wellington, Duke of 27, 29
West Indian sugar 25
West, Rebecca 100
West Thames College 236
Western Union 268
Westminster Hall 31, 32, 47, 55, 66
*What The Vote Has Done*
 (Millicent Fawcett 1926) 82
Which? 310
Whig party 28
widows of MPs 16–7
Wilberforce, William 25
Wilde, Samuel 31
Wilkinson, Ellen 81, 85, 86, 88, 89,
 90, 94, 95
William Hill 300
Williams, Helen Maria 25
Williams, Marcia
 (Baroness Falkender) 121
Williams, Shirley
 (Baroness Williams) 82, 113, 114
Wills, Edith 95
Wilson, Harold 114, 121
Winder, Jean 90
Wintringham, Margaret 81, 85, 95
Wollstonecraft, Mary 22, 23, 26
Wolstenholme Elmy, Elizabeth 48, 55
Woman Power Committee 94
Women and Equalities Select
 Committee 118
Women in Banking and Finance 249

Women for Westminster 90
Women's Auxiliary Army Corps 75
Women's Co-operative Guild 55
Women's Consultative
 Committee (WCC) 94
Women's Franchise League 55
Women's Freedom League 66, 74, 76, 78
Women's International Congress,
 The Hague, 1915 76
Women's International League for Peace
 and Freedom 76
Women's Liberal Federation 52
Women's National Liberal
 Association 52
Women's Parliament 62, 65
Women's Party 78
Women's Peace Army 75
Women's Royal Air Force 75
Women's Royal Navy 75
Women's Royal Voluntary Services 103
Women's Social and Political Union (WSPU)
 58, 61, 62, 65, 66, 69, 70, 74, 75
*Women's Suffrage Journal* 48
Women's Tax Resistance League 74
Women's Trade Union Association 52
Woodall, William 49
Wootton, Barbara (Baroness Wootton
 of Abinger) 103
Worldwide Fruit 353
WPP 147
Wright, Elizabeth 32
Wynyard, Anne 32
Wynyard, John 32

---

**Y**

Yates, Rose Lamartine 76
Yoox Net-a-Porter Group 304
Young, Janet (Baroness Young) 116, 123
York St John University 226

---

**Z**

Zaboura Communications 157
Zoological Society of London 191